BLACK POLITICAL ACTIVISM AND THE CUBAN REPUBLIC

ENVISIONING CUBA   Louis A. Pérez Jr., editor   • • • •

THE UNIVERSITY OF NORTH CAROLINA PRESS *Chapel Hill*

Melina Pappademos

BLACK POLITICAL
ACTIVISM AND THE
CUBAN REPUBLIC

© 2011
The University of
North Carolina Press
All rights reserved
Manufactured in the
United States of America

Designed by
Jacquline Johnson
Set in Monticello by
Tseng Information Systems Inc.

The paper in this book meets the guidelines for
permanence and durability of the Committee on
Production Guidelines for Book Longevity of the
Council on Library Resources.

The University of North Carolina Press has been a
member of the Green Press Initiative since 2003.

Library of Congress Cataloging-in-Publication Data
Pappademos, Melina.
Black political activism and the Cuban republic /
Melina Pappademos.
p. cm. — (Envisioning Cuba)
Includes bibliographical references and index.
ISBN 978-0-8078-3490-9 (cloth : alk. paper)
ISBN 978-1-4696-1888-3 (pbk. : alk. paper)
1. Blacks—Politics and government—Cuba—
History—20th century. 2. Blacks—Cuba—Social
conditions—20th century. 3. Cuba—Politics
and government—1909–1933. 4. Cuba—Social
conditions—20th century. 5. Cuba—Race relations—
Political aspects—History—20th century. I. Title.
F1789.N3P37 2011
323.11960729I—dc22   2011005518

cloth 15 14 13 12 11   5 4 3 2 1
paper 18 17 16 15 14   5 4 3 2 1

Parts of this book have been reprinted in revised
form with permission from the following works:
"From *Cabildos* to *Continuadora* Societies: Political
Community in the Black Cuban Imaginary," *Negri-
tud: Revista de Estudios Afrolatino-americanos*
2, no. 2 (Winter 2009); 152–77, and "'Political
Changüí': Race and Political Culture in the Early
Cuban Republic," *African and Black Diaspora:
An International Journal* (2011), reprinted by
permission of Taylor & Francis Ltd.,
http://www.informaworld.com.

For Amalia *and* Isabella
In loving memory of my father,
John, *and* brother, Nick

Contents

Illustrations

Acknowledgments

This project has united for me domains once neatly divided; their old, thick walls are now porous.

I would not have completed this project had I not first relied on the collegiality of Cuban scholars, acquaintances, and friends. As I navigated the complexity and joy of research in Cuba, their willingness to assist and discuss issues from several angles helped me to produce sharper, more historically grounded work. I want first to thank researchers and staff who were both knowledgeable and kind in my budding research years, when finding one's legs is so elusive. At the Archivo Nacional de Cuba, I thank Julio, Isabel, Olga, Martha, and Bárbara for their professionalism and expertise. Staff at the Archivo Histórico Provincial de Santiago de Cuba and the Archivo Municipal de Santiago de Cuba (Vivac) and Julia at the Elvira Cape Provincial Library's Rare and Valuable Collections department were accommodating beyond all reasonable expectation. I am indebted to Fernando Martínez, Marial Iglesias, Ricardo Guíza, Leyda Oquendo, Tomás Fernández Robaina, Bárbara Danzie, and Jorge Macle for their rigorous conversations. I gained a nuanced eye from the experiences and insights of former activists, including Daisy Heredia, Manolo Sánchez Casamayor, Enriquito Cordiés, Sabas Hechavarría, Magda Betancourt, Araminta Portuondo, Efraín Romero, Celso Joubert, Germán Joubert, Remember Maceo, and the great labor leader Juan Taquechel. Their collective knowledge of republican social and political life piqued my intellectual curiosity and flamed my commitment to the topic; they indelibly mark this book.

My scholarly pursuits were nourished, too, by ties of affection freely given. For that, I am exceedingly grateful to Yolanda and Mercedes; Caridad, Mercedes, and Migdalia Gómez; Griselda, Dianita, and Rosita; Mauro and Sonia Gómez and Zenaida Castañeda; Bárbara Danzie, the late Nilo Danzie, and Mercy, Aryelis, and Albertico; José Ramón, Teoby, and Reins Maceo;

Mirta Rodriguez; Darío Gómez and Juana Mengana; and Ana Sánchez. Here at home, Lisa, Carol, Amy, Lillien, and Ella have been courageous friends and a source of unflinching support. Lillien Waller's friendship, in particular, is a defibrillator. Her warmth, acumen, and sheer patience have anchored me on my best path, more than she knows. My mother, Ella, especially, has always served me from her better bowl. Moreover, she has been outspoken since before I was born and is forever my model of how one makes another's struggle one's own.

This book was brought to fruition by a number of institutional resources. My work at home and abroad was made possible by numerous fellowships and grants—from the Ford Foundation, the U.S. Department of Education Fulbright-Hays program, Harvard University's W. E. B. Du Bois Institute for African and African American Research, Wesleyan University's Center for the Humanities, New York University, and the University of Connecticut Research Foundation. New York University, too, was a watering hole for a number of very sharp minds and deeply amiable hearts. I owe a sizable debt to Ada Ferrer, who shaped my early arguments and, from graduate school to now, has been a model for both scholarly rigor and kindness. Robin Kelley has been an important intellectual influence. His energizing conversations and steady encouragement helped me to shed uncertainties and to progress, as did the skilled, obliging mentorship of Sinclair Thomson and Lisa Duggan. I very much appreciate critiques of my work and the analytical space opened for African Diaspora Studies by Michael Gómez; and I am grateful to the participants of New York University's African Diaspora Workshop, where several of my early ideas and arguments were proposed and refined. My graduate cohort stays with me still, in its fading yet rooted memories and lasting friendships. To varying degrees and for disparate reasons, I am indebted to Dayo Gore, Aisha K. Finch, Harvey Neptune, Fanon Ché Wilkins, Daniel Widenor, Natasha Lightfoot, Jerry Philogene, Zoya Kocur, Tanya Huelett, Edwina Ashie-Nikoi, Rachel Mattson, Kristen Bayer, Micki McElya, and Kim Gilmore. As a fellow struggling graduate student, Lillian Guerra offered dialogue and shelter toward completing this project.

I am fortunate to count among colleagues so many friends. Their collective support, humor, and scholarly insights are a wonderful trove from which to build community. For this I thank Evelyn Simien, Michelle Williams, Bede Agocha, Jeff Ogbar, Karen Spalding, Mark Overmyer Velázquez, Anne Lambright, Guillermo Irizarry, Samuel Martínez, Chris Clark, Roger Buckley, Eric Galm, Ami Omara-Otunnui, Marisol Asencio, Shayla Nunnally, Heather Turcotte, Kaaryn Gustafson, Micki McElya, Manisha Desai, and, especially, Blanca Silvestrini. Several people reviewed portions of the manuscript at different stages. Herman Bennett, Michelle Stephens, Erica Ball, Charles Venator, and Aisha Finch read my work with diligence, care, mutuality, and enthusiasm. I am grateful to Paula Wald and the two anonymous readers at the University of North Carolina Press, whose suggestions and critiques helped me to define and refine the manuscript and have made this book stronger. And I appreciate Louis A. Pérez and Elaine Maisner for their interest in the project. Elaine, in particular, provided energy and support throughout manuscript preparation.

For those with whom I live every day, gratitude only partially attests to the inseparability of our lives. I am grateful to my husband, Verónico, for his assistance with this project, for helping me to maintain the dignity of the story and its actors, and, most of all, for partnership, especially in raising our daughters. And last, to my daughters Amalia and Isabella, who oblige me to disorder and reorder life perpetually and who make me so happy. Thank you.

At the Crossroads of Republic

Hear this!: even when the most outstanding of our race struggles in organizations other than our party, though they are our friends we will not join their battle; nor will we grasp at American eagles.

　Black affiliates of the National Party of Oriente (1904)[1]

As one segment of the national whole, the class of color has only one task, that of working within the parties to fulfill, more than their considerable collective needs, the general needs of the entire country. Without believing that any of our political parties are evangelical apostles, we can draw from them abundant resources for an outcome of practical convenience and regeneration.

　Rafael Serra, "To the Class of Color," in *Para blancos y negros* (1907)

The Imprecision of Community

In July 1900, as European armies installed themselves on the African continent, taking lives and pillaging resources in places such as the Congo Free State, French West Africa, and Southern Rhodesia, thirty eminent black leaders, representing the United States, Africa, and the West Indies, met in London. There they formed a permanent committee of the Pan-African Association and convened a Pan-Africanist conference—arguably the first of several twentieth-century, international, Pan-African congresses meeting to establish Pan-African unity and challenge the horrors of colonialism in Africa and elsewhere—on behalf of the "natives in various parts of the world, viz. South Africa, West Africa, the West Indies, and the United States."[2] W. E. B. Du Bois delivered the event's culminating address, "To the Nations of the World." In the opening paragraph, he asked how long power would be used to deny the "darker races" opportunities and privileges in the modern world. He then pronounced the famous edict: "The problem of the twentieth century is the problem of the color line," thus identifying racial inequality as the most salient political issue of the new century and urging an international community to join Pan-Africanist leaders as they challenged colonial abuse of Africans and their descendants throughout the world.[3]

At about the same time, blacks on the island of Cuba found themselves at a crossroads. On the one hand, Cuba's new independence seemed to offer unprecedented equality for all. The thirty-year-old, anticolonial insurgency (1868–98), in which black and white Cubans together had fought for independence and won, defeated the 400-year-old Spanish empire. Their anticolonial movement engendered egalitarian beliefs and at least the ideal of a raceless national community. Moreover, the multiracial Cuban Liberation Army that conquered Spain's loyalist forces had in many theaters drawn particular strength from black sacrifice. Thus, on the question of an inclusive Cuban body politic, blacks were undeniably heirs apparent to the insurgency's social philosophies now crystallized in the independent republic. In the way that silences speak, they appeared to be fully represented by the national community and even safely cloaked by the philosophy of national racelessness (that is, race without political valence) upheld by nationalist philosophers such as poet José Martí: "Man is more than white, more than mulatto, more than Negro. On the battlefields of Cuba black and white together have died and their souls, risen together to heaven."[4] In fact, the same year that the Pan-Africanist Du Bois entreated the world's nations to reject the uses and abuses of race, Cuban constitutionalists (such as the white man of letters and law Manuel Sanguily and the black, polyglot, activist-intellectual Juan Gualberto Gómez) endeavored to do just that. As the shadow of their anticolonial victory grew inchoate and long, thirty-one Cuban men gathered in Havana from November 1900 to June 1901 to deliberate over the new constitution and slowly chisel the official face of the new Cuba. Though in practice the public writ was unable to undo ingrained social inequalities, nonetheless they meant to set the tone and trajectory of an inclusive new order.

Their constitutional assemblage was burdened by political compromise: the delegates themselves had been elected by only a fraction of the adult male population, due to suffrage restrictions,[5] and the Platt Amendment, imperiously hawked by U.S. officials, portended indefinite U.S. presence in Cuban affairs.[6] Already in 1898 North American hands were molding the new nation's infrastructure. Shortly after 1898, for example, U.S. officials in Havana, with the goal of sanitizing the local population, ordered house-to-house sweeps. Several months later, in 1899, Secretary of War Elihu Root proudly reported that his troops were "disinfecting" between 120 and 125 Cuban homes per day.[7] Public schools were also erected according to North American design and then stocked with books, desks, and supplies; prisons were reformed (a writ of habeas corpus was passed in 1900 to protect against unlawful detention); an electoral law was enacted on April 18, 1900, that allowed only select Cubans to vote; tobacco and cane fields were planted; and military personnel went to work busily remapping Cuban topography and "renovating, repairing, and reconstructing" public buildings, roads, sewers, waterworks, streets, and lighthouses.[8] North American involvement in Cuba was facilitated (and justified) by such whirlwind operations. In the same fashion that the constitutional convention's composition and its outcome were carefully scrutinized, North American muscle flexing in Cuba inevitably flavored constitutional debates then under way.[9]

In their deliberations, however, constitutional delegates were also persuaded by popular, Cuban, cross-racial demands for inclusion, as well as by the philosophical imperatives of a representative democracy that, seemingly, would distinguish the new Cuba from its colonial antecedents and remove the pall of old inequalities. In January 1901, delegates voted in favor of universal suffrage rights to all Cuban men irrespective of racial identity or economic status and in doing so, fired on two birds with a single shot. They addressed some of the most salient nationalist philosophical tenets honed during a protracted revolutionary process (for example, that in independent Cuba, social egalitarianism and race-transcendent relations would prevail); and they addressed postrevolutionary expectations for a redemptive body politic.

For blacks at this juncture of nation building, however, anxiously peering down a crossroads to locate the articulation, the joint, where social justice sentiments and political practice might meet, there was familiar foreboding. Indeed, far from ensuring full and equal political participation for the burgeoning multiracial citizenry, in fairly short order universal male suffrage became a mechanism of historic inequality. As it turned out, a critical new measure of power in Cuba was electoral outcome, and here discrepancies abounded. For one, in the early republic, access to government office overwhelmingly determined socioeconomic opportunity. Those who ran for office, and won, controlled the public treasury (and government jobs, contracts, and funds), a fact that gave votes, and electoral contests generally, considerable importance. Electoral (political) success often determined access to (economic) resources. Electoral processes also were burdened heavily by voter coercion and fraud, as well as by dense, and at times impenetrable, social networks based on nepotism and favoritism. This culture extended beyond the political sphere. Business owners, for example, preferred to employ friends, family, and followers, rather than tap into a more diverse applicant pool. Under these conditions of intense political competition and extralegal modus operandi, the egalitarian potential of Cuban universal suffrage ceded ground to Cubans' scramble for public office.

Early republican racial politics exacerbated these simmering inequalities. The island's budding political culture boded ill for most Cubans—and for the African-descended in particular. The segregationist propensity of the first U.S. occupation government (1899–1902) to appoint sympathetic white Cuban elites as the island's first civilian administrators (those believed most "prepared" for leadership and most fit to shepherd U.S. interests) and, shortly thereafter, of early republican political parties to slate white candidates eliminated the vast majority of black Cuban men from political competition. Further, many Cuban elites and a bevy of complicit newspapermen endorsed a particularly virulent racialist and culturalist national vision, which called into serious question blacks' capacity for civic and political life; those seen as capable of leading the nation were by definition almost always whites of one or another privilege. Despite being cast as members of a national community (and social equals, according to both the myth of Cuban racial democracy and article 11 of the new constitution), blacks were thoroughly marginalized by the early republic's economic and political systems.[10] Irrespective of their numeric presence in Cuba, few blacks ran for office and even fewer won.[11] Blacks' political authority, even their capacity to lead, was far more often challenged and undermined than legitimated. When mainstream parties did slate black candidates for office, it was generally on the basis of their value for attracting black voters.

Moreover, blacks' political authority and their opportunities for advancement nearly shriveled on the vine under the weight of widespread racial marginalization and disdain for race-conscious mobilization—buttressed by the idea of Cuban racelessness. In 1902, for example, when black veterans and civic activists approached the nation's first president, Tomás Estrada Palma, for access to government jobs, their request for equal employment offended the president, who purportedly called them "racists."[12] And by 1910, lawmakers promulgated the infamous Morúa Law, which prevented the formation of political parties based on racial identity.[13] In essence, lawmakers sought to prevent not black votes but black (and alternative) political mobilization. When, in 1912, in defiance of that law, a small group of men, overwhelmingly of color, affiliates of the outlawed Independent Party of Color, rose up anyway to protest their lack of access to lucrative civil service jobs, they met with unprecedented government-sponsored racial violence. The Independent Party of Color, concentrated in Oriente province, consisted of several hundred disaffected political activists who hoped to penetrate political networks within their party and wrestle a share of resources from the republic's dominant political parties. Their egregiously un-successful uprising ended in violence: thousands of black men, women, and children were slaughtered, mutilated, and hanged. Black efforts to mobilize along racial lines for equality, then, were made both illegal and untenable. In turn, this failure of early Cuban democracy reinforced the island's long-standing system of resource distribution, for which the principal avenue to socioeconomic resources was appeal to public officials and authority figures for patronage favors, rather than struggle for socially informed legislation.

Given the general climate against black mobilization, it is unsurprising that when faced with an ultimatum—of either principled death or partner-ship with the capricious game of patronage—black activists turned to the devil they knew. In October 1904, 106 black adherents of the newly formed Moderate Party stated that their interests were best protected by rejecting race-conscious activism. Their preference for upholding the party system of the new nation rather than mobilizing according to universal racial con-sciousness speaks to their pragmatism. It also reveals their identification with the national project and their simultaneous, deep ambivalence regard-ing the nation's captains. As Moderate Party affiliates, they placed their hope in their party to at least partially resolve persistent and growing socioeco-nomic disparities among the races. What is more, they entreated their black brethren to join them, urging militancy along party, not racial lines:

> In complete accordance with our party's principles, we (and this "we" is singular not plural) as Cubans are prepared to claim our rightful share within the party; that is, in a manner as appropriate as it is measured, we claim from our party all that, as [black] Cubans, we deserve yet which customarily has been denied us. Experience, that greatest of all counsels, has shown us that this manner of claims-making, which tempers hope and apportions the most positive results, is the best path. In this vein [of par-tisanship] we reject as insincere and of little importance those who offer us their assistance without supporting our party's credo as much as those who, due to self interest, praise or even censor us. Within our party we hope for and will demand all we deserve.[14]

They called for Moderate Party allegiance in a national political climate of intense electoral competition for voter support. It suggests that they entered into political negotiations with the Moderate Party leadership for black votes. It also reflects the men's investment in patronage politics (as they contemplated the most viable strategy to win resources in independent Cuba), but only in careful balance with their nationalist convictions and strivings, including confronting marginalization on their own soil. Arguably, given that patronage politics permeated the republic's political fabric and that electoral democracy was generally unable to guarantee equal access to resources, all Cubans competed fiercely for jobs, contracts, letters, and other political favors. Most often, patronage networks provided to Cubans of all colors access to socioeconomic benefits (such as education, professional employment, and freedom from incarceration). Yet blacks bore the brunt of unequal resource distribution. The 1907 census suggests that whites were more literate, possessed more professional and academic titles, and secured more lucrative employment than blacks. They were also much less likely to be incarcerated.[15]

Perhaps domestic pressure to support the new national government or the looming presence of the United States in Cuban affairs (facilitated by the Platt Amendment) deterred blacks from pursuing alternatives to the dominant party system. In fact, in those instances when black Cubans mobilized along racial lines in the early republic (such as the short-lived black political directorate formed in 1907 or the Independent Party of Color, founded in 1908), at the core of their disparate discourses and strategies for socioeconomic access was participation in localized politics.[16] Thus, as Pan-Africanists in London called for black world unity, black partisans in Cuba opted to attenuate racial mobilization. Their fidelity to mainstream political organizations continued well into the republican period, although by the 1930s their faith in national "racelessness," and in the black officialdom that spoke publicly of social justice, had clearly diminished. Their sentiments thus raise certain questions about early republican politics. What were viable political formations for black activists? How did they negotiate pressing racial concerns, given their practical strivings for resources? Finally, and more broadly, in what sort of political waters did they pull oar? In general, arriving at answers to these questions necessitates a clearer picture of formal and informal political structures and the workings—on all sides—of racial power. Until recently, however, the literature on blacks in the republic has not been in sustained dialogue with scholarship about political structure and culture. In fact, much of the early literature regarding black Cubans from colonial to early republican times has steadfastly depoliticized them.

Race in the Republic

Recent historical narratives about black Cubans are deeply concerned with defining the African-descended as political actor. This represents a break from early twentieth-century histories that cast the black population during and after colonial rule almost exclusively in relationship to African slavery—first as objects of the plantation system and as ongoing victims of their former "slave condition" and then as the practitioners of an inherently vulgar culture. Past trends, in fact, doubly bind black lives to quaint and atavistic folkloric traditions and labor regimes.[17] Where this template has best been challenged is in treatments of upward mobility and civil society, including histories of black colonial militias, civic organizations, journalism, and participation in Cuban national becoming.[18] These histories dispute the complete philosophical subordination of blacks to economic structure and Western civilization by examining the lives of the African-descended outside slave labor systems and folklore to include free black mobility and civic participation.[19] In particular, by interpreting blacks' cultural expression as dynamic political engagement, they have recovered a degree of black agency and refined significantly the "folklore" paradigm, which conceptualizes the African-descended (often termed "Afrocuban" or "Afro-Cuban") as cultural artifacts of the nation, visible primarily as the vectors of Cuba's Africanist past in a larger project of national self-discovery. Yet even this model naturalizes blacks' subordination to an enduring struggle for national advancement. According to this logic, nationalism is socially redemptive and the most salient organizing principle for both Cuban political history and the history of black activism. More recent studies show that although civic participation and mobility narratives have ongoing significance for Cuban race relations history and for the construction of an inclusive national identity, nationalism should be interrogated in its own right. By analyzing the relationship between nationalism and eugenicist theories and policies, as well as antiblack violence and blacks' strategic adoption of the racelessness ideal, students of race in the republic have brought into relief the implications and limitations of nationalism in historical narratives; they recover the history of black political discourses and their relations with dominant racialist ideals, thereby assigning the African-descended greater agency.[20]

Yet these revisions, though welcome, have drawn, perhaps too heavily, on a conceptualization of strict racial consciousness, which presumes an analytic continuum of state and elite racialist policies at one end and overt, racially conscious activism at the other. This more closely models the U.S. context, where, despite a history of socioeconomic complexity, the politics of integration and separation, marginality and domination—spatial relationships that emphasize an analytic of core-versus-peripheral identities—still dominate the lexicon of racial politics. Conceptions of racial sensibilities in these ways, as polarized, and as the overriding component of worldview, are influential in much of the recent literature on race in republican Cuba.

Many factors, however, such as black anticolonial insurgency against Spain, national racelessness, patronage, U.S. neocolonial domination, and a history of socioeconomic and ethnic differences among Cubans of African descent that predates the republic, bid us revisit the set of scholarly questions most often raised about black politics in republican Cuba and be amenable to its fundamental reconfiguration. This book offers a crucial reconfiguration of these questions and, therefore, of how black Cuban activism has been understood. It recovers blacks' political machinations (such as clubs' pledges of political support in exchange for favors) beyond ideological appeals to the apparatuses of representative democracy. And rather than presume that the experience of racial marginalization drew blacks together into a shared (universal, global) racial consciousness or that it engendered the rise of an unproblematized "black community," the book reconstructs blacks' social and political heterogeneity by showing that they were motivated by complex circumstances to negotiate political relationships with Cubans of all colors. This book examines how local social and political experiences and the republic's political matrix informed black activism, often inspiring blacks as much if not more than blind commitment to racial community. In fact, one implicit argument of this book is that the study of black activism should consider black political machinations, reject facile assignations of a universalist race consciousness, and abandon the presumption that blacks, alone, have a racial valence around which they mobilize. Part kaleidoscope, part monocle, this book recovers black life histories by revealing patterns of culture, sociability, and political engagement and brings clarity to the story of blacks' activism by examining the range and meaning of their formal and informal political participation. That is, this book narrates black experiences using a model that contextualizes their subjectivity within historical processes, not beyond their pale.

Further, because scholars have conflated studies of Cuban "race relations" (the interplay of racial discourses and actors) with the study of black politics and have confused blackness (identities and coalitions constituted by daily experience) with universal racial consciousness (an undifferentiated, unchanging response), this study historicizes the process by which black politicians and clubmen (blacks of relative socioeconomic privilege) built political authority and won resources in republican Cuba. It maps the experiences of black activists in the formal political arena and shows that their political behavior was shaped by pragmatics and by the struggle for social status within localized cultural and political coalitions, rather than a shared, universal racial consciousness.[21] In the public sphere, black activists did craft a unified, racially conscious "black community." Yet that community was largely symbolic. In fact, I use the terms "activist" and "black activist" in the utilitarian sense, and not to describe black Cubans' political mobilization based on racially informed philosophies, lofty ideals, or legislative change. Activists functioned often in formal politics as self-interested agents rather than as leaders politicized by derivative race consciousness on behalf of a universal and monolithic "black community." Black activists insisted that they advocated publicly for "the class of color"; yet other than a short-lived progressive manifesto on the state of black Cuba issued in 1936 and limited calls for antidiscrimination legislation after 1940, there were no mass black political actions or mobilizations on behalf of a "black community."

More often, black activists organized by building local organizations, such as a group of black women in Santiago de Cuba in the 1920s, who founded the Admiradoras de Moncada (Admirers of Moncada) organization to honor the fallen black general Guillermo Moncada and to celebrate their singular ties to national patriotism. Their goal, "to love the patria . . . and respect Cuban liberators," was met by commemorating several high-ranking black and mulatto officers of the Liberation Army, all veterans from the Santiago area: the patriot Agustín Cebreco, who, like Moncada, was raised in the black, Los Hoyos neighborhood; the Maceo family brothers, Antonio and José, both anticolonial generals, who were reared near Los Hoyos; and General Flor Crombet, who was born in the neighboring town of El Cobre.[22] The black organization Legión Maceista de Oriente (Maceo Legion of Oriente) worked similarly to disseminate to children biographies of black, homegrown heroes in the Santiago school district; both groups' activity suggests that their political identities were highly influenced by specific local black experiences.[23]

The recent spate of historical literature on race in the republic has not fully recovered blacks' participation in political structures or the heterogeneity of "blackness," even though both of these influenced republican politics. Two highly influential texts, Alejandro de la Fuente's *A Nation for All* and Aline Helg's *Our Rightful Share*, both on the topic of race in the republic, come to mind. Although de la Fuente's rich delineation of race and nation in the republic examines in great detail the way blacks pressed their claims using the ideal of national racelessness and Helg's exhaustive study of the 1912 Race War forces scholars to move beyond the nationalist myth of racial harmony to show how racial constructions were likely to spark political conflict, both studies focus primarily on race relations and deploy a nationalist frame for recovering black activism. This book owes a sizeable debt to their critical and important work; I build on it by decentering nationalism as the principal frame for understanding racial politics and black activism and by excavating the multiple social and political communities that blacks created within the larger system of republic. It examines how they participated in political structures and articulated ideologies on their own terms. Thus, the project moves beyond the conventions of nationalist and "race relations" histories: the black/white dichotomy; black social and ideological homogeneity; black politics as an extension of nationalist paradigms; blacks as objects, not subjects, of political structure; and the exteriority (rather than interiority) of a black experience for which state policies serve often as its principal muse.

This book also builds on existing historiography by expanding conceptions of African diaspora consciousness and activism, recovering complex articulations of community and understanding these as influenced centrally, yet only partially, by race. The Cuban case, for example, is useful for expanding scholars' theoretical grasp of racial politics in the Americas, especially the United States, by moving beyond racial binaries and explicating the historical dimensions of black experience and racial discourse. The book analyzes racial selfhood among the African-descended in Cuba, using constructions of gender as well as the critical role of class, ethnicity, and cultural practices (shows of social refinement and intellect, ethnic loyalties, and patriotic acts), all of which are factors that operated in conjunction with racial politics in the construction of what for Cubans of African descent were competing group loyalties and strategies. These intersections are undertheorized in the extant literature on race in the republic, which overwhelmingly assumes black political homogeneity. This book contributes to a more satisfying account of twentieth-century black activism and identities, as well as racial politics generally.

Chapter 1 examines republican political structures, which melded patron-client relations and liberal democratic institutions. It shows the workings of racial power from the earliest years of the republic, despite universalist claims of Cuban social egalitarianism. Even as Spanish colonial structures were replaced by those of new national governance and republican representative democracy impinged on entrenched hierarchies, historic social tensions survived the end of colonialism. In some cases, they deepened after independence in response to both domestic and foreign encroachments on Cubans' socioeconomic rights. Chapter 2 reconstructs black activists' penetration of formal political structures and the machinations of black political elites, which most often occurred in neighborhoods and municipalities and even at the regional level. Despite numerous obstacles to black political participation, I argue here that black elites created politically expedient relationships for access to republican resources.

Chapter 3 begins discussion of cultural values among black civic activists by examining Africanist consciousness as but one among several articulations of black experience. By providing a history of alternative black civic communities and values, which existed outside the networks established by black political elites, the chapter reflects black political heterogeneity and coalition building. This focus on cultural values continues in chapter 4, where the discussion concerns the philosophical trajectory of black activism from the late nineteenth century to the republican period. Particular attention is paid to how activists simultaneously engaged blackness and bourgeois-liberal ideas about the "modern" Cuban nation. The chapter shows that a discourse of mass, black, racial consciousness was mitigated by diverse constructions of Africanist and Cuban identities.

The use of the black press to reinforce normative values as well as to build intimate ties with other activists and elected officials, at all levels of governance, is the subject of chapter 5. It argues explicitly for the centrality of cultural practices to black activism and republican politics (formal and informal). Starting with a historical overview of the turbulent 1920s and 1930s, the final chapter, chapter 6, delves further into black civic activists' ties to national leaders (such as President Fulgencio Batista) and simultaneously recovers the deepening ideological antagonisms directed at the island's black political elite by a new crop of black public voices, which forthrightly articulated gender, class, and even regional interests. In fact, understanding that the African-descended are dynamic historical actors, their life narratives must account for tensions, debates, and conflicts, that is, their heterogeneity and the multitiered political strategies that historically they have employed. Black experiences are frequently silenced by polarizing nationalist narratives and obfuscated by universalist interpretations that ignore micro-, local-level engagement. For the study of race in Cuba and in the Americas more broadly, local, national, and transnational developments are most revelatory when considered in tandem (though not necessarily on equal terms). Ultimately, this project destabilizes race as a static, analytical category by recovering the many ways black Cuban activism challenged misrepresentations of black life.

Sociability and the Scramble for Office

A meaningful starting point is acknowledging that black activists operated in cultural and political spheres simultaneously, as politicians who were also members of black civic organizations. A small but vital group of privileged blacks, who promoted themselves as civic leaders, were also entangled in mainstream parties in order to tap the opportunities offered by electoral politics. They promoted themselves at public events and in black periodicals and formed social and political organizations (also known as "societies of instruction and recreation" or, simply, "clubs") that were indispensable to entering formal politics. The clubs were political for a number of reasons, but primarily because club members actively endorsed politicians and in turn received rewards, such as subventions, land grants, and jobs. Club memberships (at times numbering several hundred) helped privileged blacks generate a robust public presence.

Arguably, black societies' exchange of political support for the resources controlled by political incumbents (that is, the clubs' integration of clientelistic electoral networks) helped more resources reach black hands than would have been the case had they not participated in this sort of patronage negotiation.[24] Certainly, the authority conferred by black club membership facilitated members' access to professional schools, lucrative jobs, reference letters, sinecures, contracts, and public works employment. More pointedly, the clubs' frequent endorsements of elected officials and the electoral system generally were important to elected officials of all colors. Part civic institution, part political cell, black clubs facilitated one's participation in the machinations of political sociability (a style of activism for which social relations and political activism overlapped). They reinforced black political ties and enabled black activists—politicians and clubmen alike—to integrate a cross-racial national community of political elites.

Yet the clubs' inspiration also rested on the politics of race. The clubs' genesis, in fact, was a response to public- and private-space segregation in the republic's hotels, parks, restaurants, housing, occupation, education, health care, and civic organizations. By organizing their own clubs, blacks advocated for improved Cuban race relations and challenged their exclusion from what were, unofficially, "white-only" civic institutions. And most clubs deliberately projected a public veneer of strict, civic activism in order to ameliorate historic fear of black mobilization of any sort. The idea was to generate social authority from the espousal of liberal, modernist cultural values and to argue on behalf of blacks' fitness for modern political leadership by espousing uplift, respectability, cultural refinement, and intellectual pursuits, and they were credited with (and themselves claimed to be) helping to advance the national project. Clubmen even supported racialist tenets attributed to the African-descended (and some whites) based on their cultural practices and social pedigree. For club members, "race" registered socially, at the level of behavior, and behaviors approximated either "European" or "African" norms. In fact, many black activists argued that a direct correlation existed between blacks' aspirations to ascend the socioeconomic ladder and their ability to distance themselves from the forms of cultural atavism embodied by Africanist practices. The clubs were often a mechanism to distance oneself from both Africanity (and Africanist blacks) and the widely accepted notion of deep cultural "blackness" (the "black" black). Black progressives did not dispute claims of racial difference. Rather, they insisted that race did not determine behavior, cultural proclivities, qualifications, or capacity. If racialists attributed most everything, from cultural affinity, social merit, worldview, and political authority, to biological "race," black liberalists insisted that modern cultural practices mitigated the determining force of biological "race." As cadre, the charge for black clubmen, politicians, and even intellectuals was to lead the island's black community out of its presumed degradation. They might be understood as "black modernists" who channeled civilization to masses of African-descended Cubans. Much of their authority was premised on embracing and spreading "modern" values (such as bourgeois liberalism, thrift, refinement, patriarchal norms, civility, and national patriotism) and exercising cultural influence over masses of lowly, unacculturated blacks.

Yet black leaders' authority also derived from masses of black Cuban voters. They cloaked themselves in the robes of leadership yet relied on the political potential of others. If they were to mobilize en masse, black adherents of one or another party threatened political incumbents and elite and foreign economic interests on the island.[25] Politicians of all colors hoped that black activists could sway black voters. To reinforce their authority, black activists almost always claimed to uphold black interests and to speak for Cuba's black masses. Thus, to integrate political networks and access power, they established both distance from *and* proximity to the majority of black Cubans. I label them "activists" to signify their practical struggle for resources rather than their investment in lofty, racial commitments or in swaying legislators to enact egalitarian and social justice legislation. As presumed spokesmen for one or another party as well as for the race, black leaders generally mediated between significant black frustration over lack of lucrative opportunities and antiblack media and/or restrictive government policies. Given the difficulty of reconciling such disparate agendas, black leaders' sonorous pronouncements of racial fidelity were, almost inherently, marked by profound contradictions. Although black clubs were subject to economic downturns and closures as well as government repression and antiblack media attacks, they discouraged overt racial militancy and sought ties to elected officials. They called for national egalitarianism among the nation's distinct racial groups while also, at times, remaining uninvolved in the face of racial violence. Finally, even though they consistently challenged racial barriers, they also hoped to engage a political arena that was, first and foremost, indifferent to socioeconomic disparity. This book is a history of black civic and political activists in the republic, who struggled tenaciously for resources despite complex mechanisms of racial subordination.

The Complexities of Racial Categories and Their Meanings

Scholars of the African-descended in Cuba wrestle with choosing or inventing the most accurate language to narrate faithfully the histories of racialized subjects. The disingenuousness of fixed terms applied to dynamic historical subjects only complicates scholars' best efforts. In fact, historical narratives should be fluid and consistently engage the dynamism of black life. I have adopted terms that I hope support these objectives. In general, I use the term "black" to refer to Cubans of African descent of various skin tones because the archival sources left by the African-descended do so, and because their actions suggest to me that they embraced an identity of historic "blackness." When paired with the term "mulatto," "black" refers to those people of African descent who in accordance with phenotypic assumptions of the republican period held a separate status from those presumed to have a mixed African and European parentage, although I have not always elaborated on how blacks and mulattos seemed to have experienced these differences. Further, historical records suggest that greater consciousness of marginalization emerged among black and mulatto intellectuals, who referred to all Cubans of African descent as "people of color," "the race of color," "the class of color," or simply as "black." For reasons of style and in part to emphasize broad relationships of expediency constructed among Cubans of African descent, I use the terms "of color" and "of African descent" throughout the book.

I use the terms "privileged blacks" and "elite blacks" or "black elites" to describe those of African descent with significant actionable social, economic, or political power. Thus, in referring to this segment of blacks, the terms "privilege" and "elite" refer only occasionally to elevated economic status and most often to their social and political authority. Privileged and elite blacks enjoyed greater economic wealth, sometimes to a far greater degree than did the majority of blacks, but this was not always the case. Most blacks were paid less than whites for equal work in the republican period, even when they worked as professionals, such as doctors, lawyers, dentists, teachers, pharmacists, and architects, and records do not show a significant presence of blacks with enough wealth to compete with or be classed comparatively to the sector of economically powerful, elite whites.

The term "white" refers to Cubans of European descent who claimed to be or would have been identified by others as the descendants of Europeans (primarily from Spain). This is true especially among those Cubans who seem to have enjoyed and defended racial privileges, as opposed to the privileges extended by the Crown to peninsular Spaniards to the detriment of island-born whites. During Spanish colonialism, peninsular Spaniards typically monopolized Cuban political administrative posts and those posts of significant remuneration, creating tension among the population of European descent throughout the colonial period.

I refrain from using the term "Afro-Cuban" to refer to the African-descended in Cuba. First, primary documents do not bear out this usage in any sustained way. Historical documents, in fact, show that, historically, in Cuba, the term "Afro-Cuban" was used overwhelmingly to describe *cultural practices* broadly construed as Africanist (that is, practices widely considered to have resulted from Africa's legacy in Cuba) rather than to refer to human beings. For most of the republican period (and, arguably, including the *Afrocubanidad* artistic movement), "Afro-Cuban" was a pejorative and dehumanizing term to describe blacks' presumed cultural degeneracy and to render them objects and national Others, an "improper" embodiment of nonnormative cultural modes detrimental to the new nation. Further, my sense is that scholars, more than historical actors ever did, conflate "Afro-Cuban" with terms common in the United States, such as "African-American," "Afro-American," or "Afro-U.S." Similar terms, such as "Afro-Venezuelan," "Afro-Peruvian," "Afro-Mexican," or "Afro-Latin," used to describe the African-descended of several national and transnational identities of the Americas, may be appropriate if they have resonance for black experiences in specific locales. Such terms may suggest certain relationships of the African-descended to their respective states and to indigenous people or the descendants of Asians, Arabs, Europeans, or others of the region's polities. One could also argue that these terms may reify nationalism and assign the African-descended an identity embedded in the construct of "nation." In turn, this could detract from a clear understanding of domestic and transnational historical processes or obscure the fact that the African-descended most often and according to historically specific formulae have engaged local, national, and transnational political processes *simultaneously*. An unreflective use of the "Afro" prefix collapses rather than explicates the dynamics of racial power, and historical trajectories are too complex and variegated, and racialized subjectivities still without sufficient scholarly elaboration, for such terms to be universally applied.

CHAPTER ONE

"Political Changüí"

Race, Culture, and Politics in the Early Republic

In January 1901, as constitutional delegates hammered out the new republic's architecture, even coming to ideological blows over such issues as North American occupation (1898–1902) and the restricted suffrage, the polemical Havana daily *La Lucha* ran an editorial derisively titled "Changüí Político."[1] The piece ridiculed ranking Republican Party activists in the capital busily campaigning for the island's first-ever general elections, to be held later that year in December.[2] Havana's Republican Party, representing white and some black Liberation Army leaders and their supporters, was one of several, disparate, Republican Party organizations dotting the island and competing against each other for political office. Rather than campaign nationally, as one, united Republican Party (as their common name would imply), these early party organizations were locked in contentious battle with one another, each founded under the aegis of a different, locally or regionally powerful *cacique* (political boss).[3] Such political fragmentation was common in republican Cuban politics; it contributed to the importance of local political developments and limited opportunities for mass mobilization through at least the 1930s.[4] Indeed, early twentieth-century parties might have been more truthfully described as foxholes scattered across the island. Like their colonial predecessors, political activists generally politicked most fervently at the local level to win endorsements and votes from organizations or neighborhoods.[5] When the Havana-based Republican activists came under *La Lucha*'s fire, they were in the midst of holding a public forum in the city's Pilar barrio, using a then-common, open-air style of neighborhood organizing.[6]

Though *La Lucha* blasted both white and black Republicans on the forum stage, accusing them of bald politicking to build party support, the forum's black speakers, including Juan Felipe Risquet (later Republican Party congressman from Matanzas province) and Juan Gualberto Gómez (career politician, founding editor of several newspapers, and later Liberal Party senator), were the objects of particular contempt.[7] The black politicians had apparently displayed a complete lack of cultural sophistication and political savvy during the forum, so much so that *La Lucha* was moved to a burlesqued recount. The editorialist accused one black speaker of being "so dark-skinned he was blond," another of "blathering delusions of grandeur," and a third black politician, Juan Gualberto Gómez, a former Liberation Army general and journalist at various life stages for French, Belgian, and Cuban newspapers, of circling his arms over the head of a fellow white party member in an African ethnic ritual cleansing ("Aquello parecía un simbolismo del Ecorio Efó").[8]

The relationship drawn by *La Lucha*, between impropriety and the black politicians, exists at many registers, especially given the headline, "Changüí Político" (Political Changüí), because *changüí* is a music form based on specific rhythmic patterns that are historically associated with both plantation slavery and the predominantly black, eastern city of Guantánamo. The editorial calls attention to the centrality of cultural practice in racialized discourses in Latin American and Caribbean histories, which use normative values to subordinate and alienate certain members of national communities.[9] It shows how cultural attributes (however invented) can both convey and reinforce racial identities (such as the racial connotations of *changüí* music or the racialization of political behavior), often without explicitly referencing biological race or phenotype.[10] *Changüí* music, which in Cuba references slavery as well as Arará (*rará*) African ethnic and Haitian cultural practices and which, historically, is performed primarily by black Cuban musicians (often of Haitian descent), is believed to have its roots on coffee plantations largely populated by the Arará, in Cuba's east.[11] Additional uses of the word *changüí* ("throng," "public squabble," "disagreement," "rabble") refer to behaviors that, presumably, stood in opposition to the rational debate of modern political culture (as both ideology and practice). In essence, *La Lucha* editorialists intimated that based on their phenotype, warped sense of entitlements, and Africanist cultural tendencies, black men brought to the forum qualities incompatible with its purpose, thus discrediting Havana's Republican Party (one of three parties that had edged out many others) and reinforcing (amid vigorous debate on how far to extend the franchise) a climate of negative judgments and propositions about black political participation. Black political authority was also harmed by the public disrespect and humiliation that was heaped on black leaders, such as when President Tomás Estrada Palma (1902–6) refused to meet with distinguished black Liberation Army general Quintín Bandera in 1905. Estrada Palma also excluded black political wives from presidential functions that year, when he failed to send invitations for an end-of-the-year reception to the wives of Antonio Póveda Ferrer, Generoso Campos Marquetti, and Las Villas senator Martín Morúa Delgado.[12] In essence, both North Americans and elite Cubans believed that even if blacks secured the vote, their ascendance to political leadership was an altogether different and unacceptable outcome of the new republican order.

North American occupation officials, for example, pushed for an elite franchise that excluded most Cubans, and they were even disdainful of the idea of a black voter. In 1900, they vacillated between scoffing at black political empowerment ("the Negro has never been a political factor in the land") and full-blown anxiety about the idea of blacks armed with votes (black enfranchisement would lead to a "second edition of Haiti and San Domingo").[13] A decade later, in 1912, on the eve of the Independent Party of Color uprising against the political status quo, the minister to Secretary of State Philander Knox, Arthur M. Beaupré, seemed unsettled when he surmised that "the negroes have always been the backbone of political uprisings in Cuba, but under white leadership . . . the negroes themselves lack the necessary leadership and talent for organization to bring about unaided a widespread revolt."[14]

Notwithstanding North American desires to control black political participation, especially black political leadership, Cuban elites were, if no less anxious, more pliant. Cubans' majority tendency across socioeconomic sectors was, for various reasons, to push for suffrage rights for all males—irrespective of class or color. Prominent personalities, ordinary citizens, town councils, and civic organizations all protested early attempts to limit the suffrage, such as the Territorial Council of the Veterans of Independence of Matanzas, which petitioned Governor General Leonard Wood in January 1900, or the white veteran general José B. Alemán, who insisted that for the Cuban people suffrage was an "acquired right."[15] White intellectual and statesman Enrique José Varona[16] supported universal male suffrage but argued for a "plural vote," which assigned additional votes to men of a certain status and wealth—generally white men who were educated, propertied, and legally married.[17] White veteran officer and ex-president of the Cuban Revolutionary Republic General Bartolomé Masó (who was widely supported by blacks in his 1901 bid for the presidency) argued in 1899 that universal suffrage would not serve to unduly empower or embolden the black population. He intimated to North American general James H. Wilson that blacks posed no political threat because in general they would avoid political assertiveness; they were, he assured Wilson, "humble and tranquil."[18]

In fact, black political aspirations seemed to cross the imagined borders of a modern Cuban political culture by blurring the ostensible boundaries between the habits of colonialism, on the one hand, and postindependence modernity, on the other. The "old" was often portrayed by intellectuals and lawmakers alike as Africanisms, corporate favoritism, patronage, and social hierarchy under the monarchy, whereas the "new" was imagined as Cuban representative democracy, rational engagement, flourishing civic institutions, strong local government, and the absence of social divisions (such as race). Yet this break between colonialism and independence was not so clean. Spanish ghosts were everywhere visible after 1898—militarily, in the old, imposing El Morro Castle (the one-time sentinel still presiding over the island, on the precipice between Havana's harbor and open sea); architecturally, in the island's plazas and baroque facades; in hagiographic street names, Cuban cuisine, and historic *décimas* music; and also in the exercise and exchange of power. The legacy of Spanish colonialism, especially late colonialism, left an indelible mark on the republic's social and political structures, including the exercise of racial power.

Historian Ada Ferrer argues insightfully that late in the year 1896, with the Cuban victory against Spain imminent and an inclusive and multiracial citizenry on the horizon, insurgent leaders began to contemplate the ramifications of a socially open, postindependence society.[19] She posits that on the eve of peace, high-ranking Cuban officers rethought the very profile of leadership (including authority, prestige, and enlightenment) that the thirty-year, racially inclusive independence movement had produced. They purposely ignored widely held ex-rebel expectations of meritocracy—that one's valor in war would become as obvious as cream afloat in milk and would be rewarded without regard for class or color. By extension, the nation's first civilian leaders would be plucked pro forma from among those who on old insurgent battlefields had proven themselves most noteworthy. Yet fearing the ramifications of this scenario, of political power sharing in what would soon be an independent, egalitarian republic charged with implementing the revolution's mandate, high-ranking rebel leaders (mostly white and of privileged backgrounds) reconfigured the bounds of republican political authority by deploying colonial hierarchies based on class, race, and gender norms.

In their deliberations, the officers chose not to speak openly or pointedly about their sense of vulnerability as men or the presumption of the failure of the black race. Rather, they ascribed to themselves the right to interpret behavior and assess the cultural requisites (such as refinement, education, comportment, civility, honor, austere self-sacrifice, and sexual restraint—if only in the public eye) of political authority.[20] Then in August 1897, for the crime of flouting the concepts and precepts of power, they stripped black general Quintín Bandera (a highly ranked and respected fellow officer) of his command. At the same time, they increasingly favored other, mostly white ("truly worthy, honorable, and civilized"), officers over black ones for seniority promotion.[21] Their actions helped to set in motion the social face of postindependence political administration, providing U.S. occupation officials and republican Cuban leaders alike with a refashioned demographic profile for leadership and a precedent for later administrative appointments that implicitly argued for who in the postwar republic should lead and who would indefinitely follow.[22]

Had republican elections for public office been a meritocratic affair, without racial considerations, many black political hopefuls would have fulfilled and exceeded the pedigree requirements of nascent public and political spheres. Juan Felipe Risquet and the erudite Juan Gualberto Gómez, for example, had traveled internationally. Gómez was Paris-educated and a key revolutionary ideologue and nationalist intellectual and had been exiled to Ceuta, Spain (at Spanish Morocco), by colonial forces for his radical oratory and revolutionary media during Cuba's "fecund truce" (1880–95). His prestige landed him an appointment to Havana's Board of Education and the Cuban Academy of History, as well as a delegate's seat at the constitutional convention of 1900 to 1901. And Gómez spearheaded a hearty but unsuccessful protest among fellow constitutional assemblymen to prevent the adoption of the U.S.-authored Platt Amendment in the new Cuban constitution. Moreover, he served in the House (1914–16) and Senate (1917–24).[23] By most measures, then, he was an intellectual, activist, and quintessential patriot with more than sufficient pedigree to enter the political arena.[24]

Juan Felipe Risquet also held political office after the war, and in 1900, in an almost prescient gesture, he wrote *Rectificaciones: La cuestión político-social en la isla de Cuba* (Rectifications: The Socio-Political Question in Cuba), in which he defended resolutely blacks' fitness for cultural and political leadership. The book examines the history of Cuban slavery, intellectual thought, and black activist-intellectuals and attests to blacks' ongoing efforts for cultural evolution and social justice after independence. *Rectificaciones* profiles writers, educators, doctors, politicians, and other black professionals in Cuba and the broader African diaspora, demonstrating, first, black Cubans' moral character, liberalism, and social and economic achievements, and, second, their significance for new directions in republican Cuba.[25] In theory, then, both Gómez and Risquet embodied the tenor of authority in progressivist politics. Further, in practice, civic leaders, aspiring professionals, and local politicians of all colors looked pragmatically to certain black men (such as black activists Gómez and Risquet) for their political connections, influence, favors, and counsel—even as antiblack voices challenged black leadership and alleged cultural impropriety in order to restrict black suffrage rights and limit black political participation.[26]

The suffrage controversy, which was at the heart of the debates about strong political leadership and representation and which raged among the republic's constitutional convention delegates as early as November 1900, had began decades earlier when the anticolonial insurgency was first under way. Alejandro de la Fuente and Matthew Casey note that the issue of universal suffrage was raised in 1869 by insurgent leaders who saw a broad franchise as foundational to both social and political emancipation. By the middle of the final War of Independence (1895–98), both Spanish officials and Cuban separatists had reached consensus on the issue, albeit for different reasons.[27] Colonial authorities even made a tactical decision to draft a new constitution (1897) granting Cuba and Puerto Rico autonomy and universal (male) voting rights, in an unsuccessful, last-ditch maneuver to gain popular support and save the colonial regime.[28]

With North American occupation (1899–1902), the franchise issue surfaced again. As occupation officials pushed to reverse suffrage rights gained under colonial rule and to limit the vote to propertied, literate, and wealthy Cubans, they suffered a sharp rebuke by local governments and communities across the island. Among Cubans, voices both likely and unexpected supported Liberation Army veterans' political rights and the installation of a universal rather than a limited suffrage. Among U.S. journalists and legislators, the justifications for a limited suffrage were varied, but these voices consistently disparaged Cubans' ability to self govern. As the *Nation* lamented in 1898, Cuba was a "territory . . . unused to self-government."[29] Officials especially feared the large percentage of blacks in the island's total population. In a February 1900 letter to Secretary of War Elihu Root, Cuba's military governor Leonard Wood stated his belief that black Cubans were an "illiterate mass of people . . . unable to become responsible citizens."[30] Writing to Root a few weeks later, he asserted that black Cuban enfranchisement would lead to a "second Haiti."[31]

Suffrage debates were fueled by idealisms such as egalitarianism, representative democracy, and especially (given the large population of Liberation Army veterans) revolutionary sacrifice. And in this context, universal male voting rights seemed to capture more of the general will than did a limited suffrage that enfranchised only an elite, pro-U.S. electorate. Moreover, in flaunting a powerful U.S. agenda for a limited suffrage, Cuban constitutionalists laid the groundwork for a potentially egalitarian body politic. Despite their hold on the vote, however, black men continued to be marginalized in the republic because they could not win much in the way of government jobs or elected offices.[32] In fact, as de la Fuente has argued, voting rights did not inevitably translate to access to public office—or even to the nation's resources.[33] As in the colonial period, public office conferred socioeconomic opportunity on the officeholder, giving politicians access to public funds, contracts, jobs, and other benefits and making political offices a jealously guarded asset. Thus, political fissures were an extension of competing interests: U.S. officials hoped to limit the participation of the lower classes and especially of blacks; domestic political rivals fought over elections and public office; and political parties struggled to have absolute control over blacks in the political arena, seeing them as essential to success at the electoral urns as well as a significant threat to the dominant parties' leadership and their hold on political office and its spoils.[34]

The "Changüí Político" article, then, placed in proper context, was an instrument of political rivalry in a competitive and fragmented political arena; it was also a commentary on cultural fitness used to brand blacks as incapable of true political engagement. Even as Cubans argued vociferously for broad access to the political arena via universal male suffrage, a parallel notion emerged that black political authority was inconceivable. The article's significance, then, runs deeper than racially offensive depictions of black politicians or racially motivated political rivalries. In fact, it was part of the larger context of Cuban elites, U.S. occupation officials, political party leaders, and black activists themselves, who all debated the profile, place, and ramifications of black political behavior in the early republic. Casting blacks as antimodern in the political arena helped to alleviate Cuban leaders' anxiety in the immediate postindependence period. As economic and political elites struggled to claim their status as moderns, they did so aware of an acute need to prove their capacity for self-rule. As much as the postindependence political arena was conceived as an important site of Cuban modernity, republican leaders shouldered a burden typical of societies under foreign control—that of proving their capacity for stability, political modernity, and self-government. In fact, Cubans were both newcomers to the global "family of nations" and former colonials in the throes of negotiating North American occupation of and withdrawal from Cuban soil.

To that end, the architects of early republican political culture embraced republicanism, electoral democracy, and a political structure modeled after the U.S. bicameral system. As suggested earlier, there was no absolute break between the colonial and republican political spheres; the structures erected after 1898 were more complex than can be explained by political idealism. Patronage systems bled into electoral democracy, and Cuba's national economy leeched into the electoral arena, making political office (and officeholders' ever-expanding public budgets) highly coveted and a motive for artifice. Winning and holding office became the main tool to siphon funds for personal gain and to grant favors to loyal followers and corporate groups in order to win their votes. The 1901 election season, for example, was rife with accusations of fraud regarding the checks and balances system in which political "majority" and "minority" representatives were appointed to electoral boards to ensure rational competition. Presidential candidate Bartolomé Masó and his popularly based political coalition accused adherents of the U.S.-backed presidential candidate, Tomás Estrada Palma, of stacking the newly formed electoral boards in order to guarantee success in the December general elections. In fact, Masó eventually withdrew his candidacy because he and his supporters believed they would be unable to win the presidency, given the blatant and widespread electoral fraud of the *estradistas*.[35]

The idea of political modernity (a structure of fair and democratic elections, public debate, civil institutions, and decentralized government) was an important aspect of *Cubanidad* (Cubanness) in the first years of the republic. This was especially true during the North American occupation (1898–1902), since at the very moment Cubans set about defining postrevolutionary society they did so within structures imposed by foreign powers. U.S. officials appointed the island's first postcolonial administrators, set new legislation, and designed new systems of education, sanitation, and social control. The definitions of *Cubanidad* that emerged from this context, then, were part nationalist propaganda, part cultural critique, yet heavily influenced by the presence of U.S. forces in "Cuba Libre."[36]

Cubans resented the doubt cast on their ability to self-govern and U.S. officials' self-designation as the arbiters of Cuban affairs. They even called the occupation a "civilizing invasion."[37] The first head of state, Tomás Estrada Palma (1835–1908), warned that Cuba's new, progressive governance depended on assuming heavy "responsibilities" and demonstrating Cuban preparedness for self-leadership by using "tact," "skill," and "prudence" in politics.[38] In part, U.S. occupation obliged elites to call for civic responsibility among the citizenry: public order, sanitation, urbanization, and eugenics were, they believed, the cornerstones of a modern Cuban society, which could elevate Cubans in relation to the West's other citizenries.

Nationalist intellectuals even theorized that Cuban political modernity could reverse the island's historical atavisms, such as inadequate political representation and overly centralized government. The "new science of local government," which focused on strong municipalities, was, for them, an important model for new national politics. These ideas were forcefully articulated by prominent lawyer and highly prolific intellectual Francisco Carrera y Jústiz, who insisted that urbanization and healthy political culture (buttressed by Spencerian notions of "social fitness" and survival, as well as by soundly structured city government) were common to all *culto* (cultured) countries of the modern world. Carrera y Jústiz placed Cuban society in this Western imaginary, suggesting that Cuba, like "all modern societies," grappled with global trends of urbanization, expansion, and political restructuring.[39] At the same time that Carrera y Jústiz lauded the West, he proclaimed Cuba to be a "Latin society," with European influences (particularly French and Spanish), and among the finest civilizations in the world. More than a tempest in a teapot, his contributions to theorizing and drafting local government policies were so highly esteemed by republican leaders that after the first Cuban Congress was elected in 1902, members of the House of Representatives postponed discussion of municipal laws until they had an opportunity to consult with him.[40]

Carrera y Jústiz focused on recovering the sociological dimensions of politics, arguing that as members of the "Latin Race," in a "sustained struggle between the [Anglo and Latin] races," Cubans should define their national identity and culture by adopting advanced political organization and strong local government. If they failed to build dynamic, microlevel systems of political organization, they risked annihilation by foreign powers. Importantly, for Carrera y Jústiz, racial identity shaped the political sphere and was integral to forming truly "advanced" societies. In 1904, he delivered the first of several conference papers to an audience at Havana's Association of Good Municipal Government, stating that "the struggle of the races is the basis of civilization" and a necessary act of "human progress."[41] Thus, in a global hierarchy, Cubans would be distinguished by their propensity for civilization. All modern polities adopted good government, he believed, which made them superior to inert, antimodern societies that rejected civilization. He theorized: "Races that do not struggle—such as, for example, the Indian and the Black—exist in Asia, Africa, and America as an immutable stagnation, fighting against civilization."[42]

These attacks did not go unanswered. Some blacks responded by challenging the continued use of any racial identity and by raising objections, as Nicolás Valverde did in 1900, to the government's use of historic, racial labels such as *negro* (black) or *pardo* (mixed-race), rather than the universal terms *Cubano* or *ciudadano* (citizen) in civil records.[43] Congressional representative Antonio Póveda de Ferrer broached this thorny subject again in

1903 by writing to President Estrada Palma and insisting that government dispense with all racial labels in its documentation. To use racial labels was, he argued, a reversal of more progressive, universalist policies instituted in the final years of liberalization during Spanish colonial rule.[44] Blacks also responded by building coalitions based on a variety of shared circumstances, including ethnic and/or cultural affinity, regional location, professional status, and familial ties. Though race-conscious mobilizations were at best infrequent if not rare in the republic, the most famous example of organized black protest was La guerrita del doce (the Little War of 1912, also called the Race War of 1912), in which hundreds of members of the Independent Party of Color, overwhelmingly of African descent, rose up between May and July 1912 to challenge the Morúa Amendment prohibiting race-based political organizing.[45]

Whatever the degree of racial consciousness, black activism must be analyzed in historic context, by considering Cuba's political economy, regional networks, and republican political culture. Most black activism was spearheaded by a small yet powerful group of black clubmen and politicians who generated significant opportunities for themselves and others by integrating the emerging structure of political patronage at both the local and the national levels. By doing so, they won a greater share of jobs, contracts, and appointments. Their activism, only partially motivated by racial consciousness, led many black politicians to work within mainstream parties, alongside whites, for greater socioeconomic opportunities. At the Republican Party forum of January 1901, for example, Juan Gualberto Gómez, Juan Felipe Risquet, and Martin Morúa Delgado campaigned not as racial activists appealing to an all-black constituency but in front of a multiracial audience and alongside their white coreligionists to recruit voters for their party and enhance their opportunities. Their activism, which granted some access to resources, despite continued racial exclusions in force since colonialism, was motivated as much by socioeconomic opportunity as by racial injustice, one issue trumping the other at different moments in republican history.

Political activists, including black political activists, most often engaged officials and political parties at the point of resource delivery, rather than lobbying local or national officials for legislative redress to racial injustice, such as punitive measures against racial repression or legislation supporting black employment, health care, education, and urban or rural planning and development. Ideologically speaking, political parties were nearly indistinguishable in the early republic, and ideology as an instrument of political consciousness took a back seat to the practical struggle for scarce resources. Historian Jorge Ibarra argues that social welfare benefits were almost nonexistent in the early republic; social services were distributed by ruling party administrators to their political supporters based on patronage agreements and client need.[46] This changed after the 1933 Revolution, when, for example, black activists and civic organizations pushed politicians to address black unemployment (in both rural and urban settings), public health (especially the high rates of tuberculosis among the African-descended), and education. In particular, black civic activists showed sustained interest in the passage of the so-called Complementary Laws to strengthen the antidiscrimination articles 20 and 74 of the 1940 constitution.[47]

Socioeconomic opportunities were almost nonexistent unless blacks engaged in formal politics—even organized black militancy for access to public office was untenable (as seen by the horrific response to the Independent Party of Color uprising in 1912). In fact, despite antiblack discourse, unofficial segregation of public space, discriminatory government hiring practices, police harassment, and repressive legislation (most prominently the racialist, anti-African laws of 1900, 1922, and 1925) presenting nearly insurmountable barriers to blacks' socioeconomic advancement, black activism never resulted in a mass, race-conscious mobilization or facilitated *strict* racial consciousness. Rather, black activist-intellectuals, professionals, and politicians in the republic focused on the goal of accessing socioeconomic resources.

As self-appointed black leaders, they articulated their belief in shared racial experiences among all blacks, irrespective of economic status. And they presumed to speak in the public sphere on behalf of mass black experience. On the one hand, their social justice discourse reiterated a common value expressed by many among the African-descended: They had done much (especially during the wars of independence) to create an independent Cuban nation and therefore deserved socioeconomic parity and full participation. On the other hand, their emphasis on racial self-help, cultural improvement, and bourgeois-liberal gender and family norms placed much of the blame for black marginalization on the backs of blacks themselves—particularly those who were less educated, professional, or economically solvent than the cadre class, which constituted just 1 to 3 percent of the total black population during the republican period and enjoyed a public presence disproportionate to their numbers. To disseminate their philosophical approach to racial injustice as well as to help their own advancement, many edited black newspapers, such as *Minerva: Revista Universal Ilustrada* (1910-15), a periodical devoted to blacks' engagement with politics and culture, including their social networks and organizations.[48] Black newspapers were integrationist and often blamed "the uncultured of

[our] race" for racial disparities. Further, the topics, contributors, and personalities featured in the black press articulated the experiences of blacks of relative privilege; they only presumed to represent a unified, cross-class African-descended population. Beyond articulating experiences of racial oppression, black activists participated in the island's political patronage networks. As we have seen, racial marginalization was a concern for black leaders even before the War of Independence ended. Despite the creation of socioeconomic "levelers" (such as national racelessness ideals and universal suffrage rights), administrative posts continued to be delivered into white hands. Black leaders, then, had to negotiate the mechanisms and machinations of formal politics, especially the pervasive patron-client relations.

The "Unjust Monopoly"

The 1901 Cuban constitution, drafted as a foundational writ of representation, extended the suffrage to all men, irrespective of race, literacy, property holdings, or other assets. Black men, representing from 20 to 50 percent of all voters (depending on the demography in a particular town or province), enjoyed formal political participation according to universal suffrage.[49] Because politicians of all colors depended on black voter support to win electoral office, electoral politics were integrated. The 1907 census conducted during the North American occupation states that the "element of color" constituted from 21 to 44 percent of provincial population totals for voting-age males.[50] For the island's six provinces, blacks' percentages of the total provincial populations in descending order were the following: Oriente, 43 percent; Matanzas, 38 percent; Santa Clara, 27.5 percent; and Havana, 23.4 percent, with Havana City at 25.5 percent.[51] In addition to higher concentrations of black voters, these provinces were significant in national elections because they were home to the greatest numbers of voting-age men, forcing politicians to appeal in one way or another to black constituencies.[52]

Simply put, without black votes politicians could not win at the polls. As de la Fuente has rightly suggested, black voters determined electoral outcomes.[53] No party dared to publicly reject black voters. Further, the island's dominant parties often recruited black leaders in a thinly veiled attempt to attract black voters and wooed black institutions, which were an important tool to reach black voters. In 1901, for example, during the short-lived presidential campaign of Bartolomé Masó, prominent black veterans, such as General Quintín Bandera, Generoso Campos Marquetti, Ramiro Cuesta, and Valdés Pita, stood inside the walls of the black club La Divina Caridad (Divine Charity) in Havana to call attention to Masó's presidential candidacy and attract black voter support.[54] Black politicians who served on Masó's campaign committee spoke publicly on his behalf and visited numerous black societies to drum up black support.[55] Bartolomé Masó himself made stops at key black institutions, such as the Centro de Cocineros (Cook's Club), in Havana.[56]

Yet however much politicians campaigned for black votes, they were far less interested in addressing the concerns of the black voting public. Mass black mobilization, demands for better employment, and full political participation were, in fact, discouraged by government officials, the media, and elite intellectuals, as dangerous and unpatriotic threats to national stability. Cross-racial patronage networks facilitated black participation, but actual black mobilization on behalf of "race issues" was unacceptable. Throughout the republican period, in fact, blacks were underrepresented among the ranks of elected officials and did not receive full access to a range of resources (quality education, health care, public works contracts, employment, and socioeconomic benefits) granted by patronage relations. Disparities such as these existed during colonialism and remained after independence, as numerous antiblack racial practices (such as limiting the number of black candidates on mainstream party rosters, failing to appoint blacks to government posts, and restricting those blacks lucky enough to land public sector jobs to the government's lowest echelons) served to keep blacks from accessing national resources. Despite their majority presence in the insurgency's ranks as foot soldiers, their strong representation in the Liberation Army leadership, their numeric significance in republican elections, and even the logic of racelessness ideology, black political authority was attacked following Cuban independence from Spain.

Take, for instance, the words of Ricardo Batrell, a black veteran of the War of Independence (1895–98), who recounted bitterly in his memoir that despite blacks' pivotal role in the insurgency's success, they were denied jobs and resources after the war ended. Black marginalization, he insisted, occurred in spite of the formal transformation of the colony into a sovereign and supposedly egalitarian republic: "The war ended and the empire or kingdom of Spain in Cuba was defeated, and with sadness I witnessed the rise of a cunning and unjust monopoly. In Matanzas province, where only men of color had waged war, following the Armistice those few white officers, who without fighting had skulked around [*majasiando*] in the background of the revolution, began to come out from their hiding places. The appointments that corresponded to us, we who had battled relentlessly, were given to those loafers."[57]

Batrell's memoir was published ten years after the birth of the republic and reveals the inequities in Cuban society, a continuation rather than an abatement (as promised by the revolutionary leaders) of social hierarchies based on race. Having fought in the war, witnessed the birth of the republic, and lived for many years in Cuba Libre, Batrell's personal account provides testimony of ongoing and uneven socioeconomic access despite widespread rhetoric on Cuban national unity, racelessness, egalitarianism, and self-determination. The narrative reveals the chasm between the discourse on national racelessness and the failure of the nation to achieve social equality. His work might be seen, in fact, as a way to measure social justice, much as environmentalists extract water samples at intervals along a river's bank to measure change, continuity, and patterns otherwise indiscernible in its course.

Many black public intellectuals assessed the results of revolutionary edicts of equality, some concurring with Batrell and others dissenting. Yet Batrell identifies the tenor of much black consciousness in the republic. Most blacks, across cultural orientations and economic status, expressed anger over black exclusions from the patronage system, but until the 1930s (and even then) they did so without insisting on legislative change. They articulated a continuing frustration about ongoing racial inequality in the dispersal of national resources, in light of blacks' disproportionate sacrifices in the war and their centrality to Cuban nationhood. Even after the war, black veterans raged about the failure of political patrons to distribute the favors owed them based on their political support.[58]

Black activism was rooted primarily in a desire to participate in vertical relations of political patronage. Patronage, a political system emphasizing individual and corporate access to resources rather than mass-based ideological movements, was deeply entrenched. Patronage relationships operated along vertical lines to promote hierarchical ties between patron and client and the demands of political loyalty rather than horizontal ties based on class and/or racial solidarity. In fact, black Cuban activists were generally more interested in resource acquisition as individuals and as corporate groups than they were in the distribution of government resources to all blacks. Certainly it is impossible to determine the motives of all black activists, but research shows that most were working to access patronage positions rather than to build a mass, antiracist black movement in the republic.

In the face of extreme social and economic competition during Cuba's transition from warring colony to republic at peace, patronage networks united political associates and linked politicians to their supporters, while also tying government bureaucracy to a variety of civic, political, and economic organizations. Patronage in Cuba facilitated the growth of a dense structure of legal and extralegal avenues for distributing local and national resources according to political loyalties or interpersonal relations, based on race, regional ties, occupation, or family.[59] Activists and political hopefuls of all ideological persuasions and pragmatic concerns entered Cuba's political sphere with the understanding that they, first, had to conquer its web of patronage and clientilist relations.

In the patronage system, certain clients (often family members, close friends, or political accomplices) were appointed to the government payroll without actually performing any real work. For their part, clients reciprocated by campaigning and voting for or attesting to the character of their patrons. These sinecures, called *botellas*, were an important component of a patron-client system that grew exponentially from 1899 to 1940, reflected in a sharp increase in public administration budgets and distributable government civil service jobs. In 1899, approximately 1 percent, or 1,300 islanders, worked for the government. By 1903, the public payroll had exploded to include 20,000 public employees.[60] In 1911, the figure jumped to 35,000, with one reporter alleging that both the national budget (25 million dollars) and the number of government employees were the highest ever that year and that at least 50 percent of the cost was unnecessary.[61] To illustrate, in fiscal year 1914-15, for a national budget of 38 million dollars, approximately 21 million dollars (55 percent) went toward the payment of salaries and wages.[62] Thus, elected officials were increasingly able to use favoritism to gain and maintain their power.

Yet, rather than define *botellas* and other aspects of patronage relations as "corruption" that threatened otherwise representative rule, these should be seen as integral parts of a particular political system that blended corporatist authoritarian elements with liberal democracy. In fact, given that patronage-clientilism was important to electoral and other political mobilizations, any significant voting or political bloc (or those who brokered in votes) received a percentage of the public treasury. The distribution of resources depended on reciprocal relations among patrons, brokers, and their clients. In fact, the element of reciprocity provided some limited inroads for otherwise marginalized sectors of the population.

Cubans of all colors were pushed into vying for limited government reserves. Municipal, provincial, and national officeholders gained access to a slew of resources, from jobs to contracts to funds that they could use to grant favors and ensure continued loyalty from their clients. This support, though cultivated through and highly dependent on social relations, was at times coerced. Political party members at the national and local levels, for example, expected various types of assistance from party coreligionists once elected, as did nonparty members who pledged their support to elected officials. Thus, party members and laymen both relied on patron-client reciprocal relations, when patrons brokered favors for votes and other support from clients. As key brokers and clients in patronage networks, blacks, too, expected political favors in exchange for their support of candidates of all colors at the local, regional, and even national levels, although racial hierarchies mitigated their authority in electoral politics.

Individuals often approached influential members of local society for aid in desperate situations. Reducing sentences, dropping charges, and attesting to moral character were all services that a well-placed prominent individual of respected moral character could provide. In 1903, the president of the African-influenced San Lázaro and Santa Rita Society wrote to black politician Juan Gualberto Gómez, possibly in response to raids on black clubs in the first decade of the republic, asking that he publicize the society's status as a duly regulated society with no political affiliations—explaining that its sole purpose was to gather regularly to fulfill religious obligations, as stipulated in the bylaws.[63] Thus, even as many blacks challenged the "unjust monopoly" identified by Ricardo Batrell, they tried to actively participate in that patronage monopoly for their own individual and corporate interests. For example, early republican activists called on elected officials to set aside civil posts for black Cubans. Indeed, as several historians have argued, the antiblack Race War massacre of 1912, when the U.S. military, the Cuban military, and white civilians joined forces to thwart a significant black political threat to their common interests, was sparked by blacks' demands for equal access to both civil employment and political organizing.[64]

Accounts such as Batrell's, of white "monopoly" of national resources and of the 1912 Race War launched against the Independent Party of Color insurgents and black civilians, have been given in previous historical narratives and with several intents.[65] Social scientists, for example, often cast early republican racial politics as a series of failed attempts to win racial equality. For the Race War of 1912, scholars have treated the racially conscious movement and the repression that brought it to a screeching halt as the two pillars of race relations in republican society. In this interpretation, black and white racial identities are stable throughout the republican period and disconnected from larger political processes. I argue that even racial identity was unstable, according to a variety of social, economic, and political factors. Thus, racial identities are historical, changing, and negotiated. Republican political culture was influenced by liberal democratic discourse, "racelessness," egalitarianism, patronage, local loyalty, personalistic ties, and nationalism—some of which first emerged during thirty years of independence insurgency while other elements surfaced after 1898. An equally important consideration in the history of black Cuban activism is the dense network of patronage relations that penetrated the republican political arena. As blacks participated in these networks—by wielding varying degrees of influence—they were, in turn, shaped by patronage relations. Thus, as blacks struggled for a greater share of resources, they engaged Cuban political culture (as both ideology and practice), which necessarily provided a structure for both black activism and racial consciousness.

Formal Politics in the New Cuba

Cuba's republican political system emerged from the old bones of colonialism as well as from wartime destruction, foreign investments and political control, labor militancy and social frustration, nationalism, and liberal democracy. While foreign control and militancy threatened to destabilize the island's fledgling government, these and other factors were part of the palimpsest that anchored government. The Platt Amendment, for example, drafted to protect rapidly expanding U.S. interests on the island, prompted Cuban economic legislation, such as the 1903 Reciprocity Treaty, which entangled the U.S. and Cuban economies and created development priorities based on sugar industry expansion.[66] And rather than reject out of hand North American coercion (which the Platt Amendment embodied), constitutionalists argued that autonomy and national development depended on the amendment's promulgation, if only to spur a U.S. withdrawal of occupation forces.[67] Thus, Cuban civil rights, national economic development, and domestic politics were all placed under the shadow of North American rule, with a debilitating loss for Cubans of political and economic control in domestic affairs.

Cubans saw an aging empire (Spain) go and an ascendant new one (the United States) come, and they looked on while North American, French, British, and Spanish investors rapidly acquired large portions of the Cuban economy. Even before the republic was founded in 1902, vast tracts of land and numerous estates—primarily in the east—slipped through Cuban fingers. In 1901, the United Fruit Company purchased nearly 200,000 acres of land in the eastern town of Banes; its subsidiary, the Nipe Bay Company, scooped up 40,000 sugar acres that same year, near Puerto Padre, also in the east.[68] The Cuba Company acquired nearly 50,000 acres of land between 1900 and 1901 to complete a Cuban Railway system in the east.[69] Foreigners controlled utilities, cigar manufacturing, mining (U.S. investors, in particular, were issued rights to iron mines in Oriente province by the U.S. occupation officials), and banking, an industry dominated by Spanish, English, French, and North American capitalists. In fact, by the time the republic's ten-year anniversary arrived, foreign economic investments had surpassed 300 million dollars.[70]

Aspiring but destitute Cuban capitalists suffered significant economic hardship. Widespread property losses occurred between 1895 and 1898 when as much as 88 percent of Cuban sugar mills were destroyed. Those mills that were not destroyed ceased operations, a fate also suffered by tobacco growers. Cuban mill owners and cane growers lacked capital to finance or jump-start their operations by 1899, which caused even mills intact at the war's end to remain inactive for lengthy periods and eventually become inoperable. This blow for domestic growth and recovery was further exacerbated when Spanish lenders retracted mill owners' credit lines. Further, many sugar haciendas (estates) were alienated through property sales and transfers. By 1899, most of the island's remaining hacendados (large landholders) were forced to sell their lands and mills to North American investors in an effort to recoup at least a portion of their losses. Thus, although wartime destruction had, following the peace, opened up land and industry to new development, these opportunities were primarily for non-Cubans. A small number of Cuban and Spanish hacendados who survived the war's destruction, weathered economic ruin, and avoided forced property sales to foreigners formed the Agrarian League to lobby for their interests with government officials.[71]

As foreign investments poured into the island, dominating the sugar, tobacco, mining, railroad, utility, and banking industries, and with few Cubans in control of the country's most viable and profitable enterprises, Cubans quickly turned to formal politics as the most lucrative, domestically controlled site of economic activity. Electoral politics was the central theater of competition and negotiation within the domestic economy, since winning public office or a government post translated at the very least into substantial pay and often into public treasury access—a fund from which to grant political favors. Public employment became the primary route to socioeconomic advancement in the republic. Government officials increasingly depended on public funds (in the form of public works contracts, civil service employee positions, subventions, the national lottery, and so on) for control of their lucrative public offices.[72] They drew on their budgets to attract and increase their political following. In so doing, the government bureaucracy expanded rapidly after 1902. In 1919, for example, the number of public employees was 26,000. By the decade's end, that figure had jumped to 51,000. So much did the government workplace resemble a marketplace that by

1921 social commentator Miguel Carrión called the arena of formal politics Cubans' "only industry."[73]

Since colonial rule, formal politics based on a patron-client system had operated according to expedient, transactional social relations.[74] "Practicing politics [*haciendo política*]," the act of pursuing politically expedient relations in order to bridge social divides and win votes, was important in order to navigate formal politics and attract and build a political following. Political relationships were often cultivated at the local level and included important social aspects (such as reciprocity and personal prestige) that, in turn, enhanced one's opportunities to win office.[75] Patronage politics coexisted alongside a new system of representative democracy as well as policies that served U.S. interests. The occupation government instituted significant structural changes, abolishing the old colonial *ayuntamiento* (town council) system in August 1898 and granting increased autonomy to municipal governments. During the late colonial period, local governments were appointed by regional authorities, a system supplanted by local, popular elections following independence. U.S. officials attempted to control political processes on the island by appointing Cubans friendly to their interests and capable of influencing popular opinion in key local and regional contests for councilman, mayor, and governor's offices.[76] U.S. officials struggled—with less success—over universal voting rights. In fact, in 1900, North Americans succeeded in imposing a limited suffrage law for the first municipal contests in June and for the September constitutional delegate elections for the 1901 convention.[77] Protest against the limited suffrage was so intense, however, that in late January 1901 constitutionalists voted to stop the installation of a limited franchise in favor of a universal one. By June 1901, the island's first popular elections for mayoralties were held.

Even as U.S. officials attended to their own interests by handpicking sympathetic appointees and passing out favors to supporters (Governor Leonard Wood in Oriente, for instance, distributed patronage resources to whomever would bend his way), the foundation of government in independent Cuba became a collaboration of political systems extant before, during, and after the 1898 revolution.[78] Some of the most socially and politically prominent men of the region had been active members of colonial political organizations, such as Club Moncada, constituted by men who had distanced themselves from insurgent fighting between 1895 and 1898 yet who had moved to the fore of local politics in Santiago during the post-1898 process of decolonization. Club Moncada members enjoyed enough prestige to propose to Governor Wood that collectively they act as a liaison between the general population and U.S. occupation officials. But even then they remained under the thumb of U.S. officials—Moncada members appointed men to local administrative office who were often rejected by U.S. military officials.[79]

Cuban leaders were highly ambivalent on the question of North American control. On November 25, 1898, after Governor Leonard Wood named prominent rum mogul Emilio Bacardí to be mayor of Santiago, Bacardí immediately called together a "Residents' Assembly," an advisory council for local projects and operations, including the creation of schools and hygiene and sanitation improvements and the paving of streets.[80] Among other issues, the Residents' Assembly serves as an important example of the blurred boundaries between civic activism and party politics, which were increasingly common in the republic. The assembly received public acclaim, such as support from Club Moncada, and reflected similar civilian roots and peacetime relations—it was made up of twenty prominent figures, many of whom had sympathized with, though not necessarily fought in, the Liberation Army. Led by Bacardí, the Residents' Assembly represented a significant early political bloc within the structure of provincial authority.[81] But nine months after its founding, in December 1898, the assembly disbanded when Bacardí renounced his position as mayor because of the contradictions he felt were apparent between the Cuban project of building a revolutionary society and the interests of U.S. occupation officials.

Other political groups emerged in the vacuum left by the Residents' Assembly, in a cycle of political factionalism and polarization that soon dominated the electoral arena. Two regional political parties based in Santiago— the Republican Democratic Federal Party of Santiago de Cuba and the National League of Oriente—were both founded in 1899. The National League's leader, black veteran general Quintín Bandera, was in ongoing dialogue with Enrique José Varona, the influential intellectual who had been named secretary of public instruction in 1898 and served as a board member of the Havana-based Cuban National Party. Bandera proposed to expand the Oriente-based National League to other provinces and suggested to Varona the possibility of a merger between the National League and the Cuban National Party.[82] These talks failed, yet by 1900 the island's first three political parties to emerge as national rather than strictly regional contenders had been founded (the National Party, the Union Democratic Party, and the Republican Federal Party), each of them sending delegates to that year's constitutional convention. The rise to national prominence of political parties represents a shift away from highly localized organizing, as regional *caciques* (political bosses) and their supporters extended their sphere of influence to other parts of the island. Yet notwithstanding the emergence of national-level political contenders, it is important to understand the machinations of republican politics and the context in which Cubans built political organizations and coalitions despite the presence of a U.S. interventionist government.

In the extreme flux of the postwar period, almost any attempt by Cubans to exercise political authority required gargantuan efforts. The war had been devastating, including loss of life, property damage, and increased debt. And it had helped to dismantle local political institutions, such as the *ayuntamiento* (town council), a central part of the Crown administration since the inception of colonialism. Also dissolved were the two Crown-sanctioned political parties that had provided Cubans with limited metropolitan political representation after 1878. Further, North American occupation officials supplanted Cuban leadership by placing themselves in key interim administrative posts at both the municipal and the national levels—such as Leonard Wood, who after the war served first as governor of Santiago province and, later, from 1899 to 1902, as governor general of the island. U.S. officials also frequently rejected local leaders who had been duly elected into office by Cuban municipal administrators, such as Alfredo Zayas in Havana in 1901. Alejandro Rodríguez was elected mayor of Havana in June 1900, serving only until April of the following year. After he left the mayor's office to assume a post as head of the Rural Guard, the town council voted to seat Zayas as his replacement. Zayas's appointment was vetoed by the occupation officials, however, because of his anti–Platt Amendment stance, and in a second-round deliberation, the town council replaced Zayas with Miguel Gener Rincón, who served out his term.[83]

Occupation officials also had the temerity to name Cubans to administrative posts and then restrict their authority and their assigned responsibilities, particularly at the local level. Such was the case in Santiago de Cuba, the capital of Oriente province and site of several decisive August battles against Spanish forces. Rafael Salcedo, for example, a former councilman for the city of Santiago under the Crown, who was appointed mayor of that city by the occupation government, suffered severe restrictions in the carrying out of his duties during his short term in office. Salcedo, whose duties were to oversee municipal payrolls and small public works expenditures, was summarily replaced by a North American after Salcedo appointed to local posts individuals unpopular with the occupation government.[84] In fact, U.S. officials made themselves custodians of early Cuban politics. In exchange for the favor of an appointment to public office by the occupation government, there was a clear expectation of political loyalty.

But North American officials had to contend with a population well steeled by the Revolution. Thirty years of conflict had produced widespread militancy and nationalist expectations among Cubans. Despite U.S. controls over postwar political structure, one factor that cut across racial and class lines and legitimated leaders and political hopefuls was one's participation in the wars of independence. (In some but not all cases, moral authority was also conferred on politicians based on their racial, class, and gender identities, for these factors also helped to define them as leaders.)[85] Veteran leaders were well represented among the early republican political elite. First, veterans moved easily into civilian jobs after the war commensurate with their former army ranks. In fact, U.S. military governor general John R. Brooke, head of the occupation army in Cuba, exchanged veterans' weapons for jobs and employed numerous other veterans in countless public works projects.[86] What is more, although General Brooke believed that the Liberation Army's vast veteran reserves were a threat to the island's political stability, he also reasoned that making veterans a part of republican leadership was an important way of establishing political authority.

Many early republican Cuban politicians and elected officials, such as José Miguel Gómez, Mario García Menocal, Quintín Bandera, Jesús Rabí, and Generoso Campos Marquetti, had been generals during thirty years of anticolonial struggle. As the logic went, their leadership in the insurgency had contributed to the birth of the Cuban nation and creation of a sovereign public. The legacy of political freedom, exacted through loss of life, starvation, and illness and the destruction of public and private property, was the chief rhetoric of the postwar period. Military sacrifice, but most especially leadership in the Liberation Army, was often touted as an irrefutable sign of political authority, something that U.S. occupation officials understood as well. Black Cubans, for example, having fought and died during the war in vastly disproportionate numbers, often based their own claims for social justice and political inclusion on this definition of valor, which conjured up patriotic self-sacrifice, strength, and courage in the Cuban collective memory of the independence wars. Given the large proportion of black soldiers in the ranks of the insurgency, blacks publicly voiced their frustration at failed reciprocity after Cubans won the peace. As black veteran Esteban Montejo remembered, "When the [1898] war ended, the talk started about whether the blacks had fought or not. I know that 95 percent of the blacks fought in the war."[87] What is more, historians argue that blacks were heavily represented as insurgent leaders.[88]

Liberation Army veterans General Clemente Dantín in Bolondrón, Matanzas, and General Pedro A. Pérez in Guantánamo were appointed as mayors in their towns, as was Clemente Gómez in Jovellanos, Matanzas.

Mayor General
Agustin Cebreco

Sr. Gregorio Galán
Ex-presidente de Aponte

General Silverio Sánchez Figueras

Sr. Miguel López
Presidente de El Casino Cubano

SR. EMILIO BACARDI
Senador por Oriente

Sr. Prudencio Dupin
Presidente de
La Luz de Oriente

General Pedro Yvonnet

Sr. Odioclato Carvajal
Teniente Coronel del E. L.
Ex jefe de Policía de Santia-
go de Cuba

Sr. José B. Callis
Vice presidente de Aponte

Black politicians, veteran officers of the Cuban Liberation Army, and clubmen. From Rafael Serra, *Para blancos y negros: Ensayos políticos, sociales y económicos, cuarta serie* (Havana: Imprenta "El Score," 1907). (Courtesy of Manuscripts, Archives and Rare Books Division, Schomburg Center for Research in Black Culture, New York Public Library, Astor, Lenox and Tilden Foundations)

Though military officials appointed numerous Cubans from elite families with conservative, even pro-U.S. leanings and openly supported the "better classes" in elections, they installed Liberation Army leaders in the early republican government to help safeguard North American policies. Officers of the Liberation Army were, in fact, a strategically important resource for occupation officials. An 1899 meeting, sponsored by the Neighborhood Committee of the Cuban National Party in Guanabacoa, a town just south of Havana, morphed into a mass rally after attendees decided to show public support for the mayoral candidacy of Liberation Army general Guillermo Acevedo.[89] The ongoing popular appeal of veterans, North American officials hoped, would ensure local and regional backing for their newly appointed civilian leaders and lend credence to the claim that support, not domination, was the central reason for U.S. intervention in Cuba.

Occupation officials felt it imperative to scrutinize the corps of ex–Liberation Army leaders in order to identify those individuals who seemed to support the central tasks of the occupation government: political stability, state consolidation, and U.S. economic expansion and to screen for those "obedient and faithful" applicants for jobs with the newly formed Rural Guard.[90] Civilians of considerable influence and followings were also named to posts, such as Matías Infanzón, named to the city council of Havana, and Emilio Bacardí, named mayor of Santiago de Cuba. Throughout 1899, the occupation government named veteran Cuban generals to all six of the island's provincial governorships.[91] As far as journalist Nestor González could tell, every former Liberation Army officer was holding a government position with some level of leadership responsibility.[92]

Indeed, from 1902 to the 1933 Revolution, with the exception of Tomás Estrada Palma (who ran unopposed and was heavily backed by Washington to become Cuba's first head of state) and Alfredo Zayas (whose running mate was a Liberation Army veteran officer), all subsequent elected presidents (José Miguel Gómez, Mario García Menocal, and Gerardo Machado y Morales) and vice presidents (Enrique José Varona, Emilio Núñez Rodríguez, and Francisco Carillo Morales) had served as high-ranking officers of the Liberation Army. Occupation officials believed it was more dangerous to exclude such men from leadership than for them to have some authority, assuming that after a U.S. withdrawal they would support the Platt Amendment and the ideals of the "protection of [North American] life, property, and individual liberty" in Cuba. U.S. involvement in domestic politics further complicated a national body rife with conflicting domestic interests. Competing political parties fought bitterly over control of government offices and counted U.S. occupation as a key tool in their arsenals, to remove from power incumbents reluctant to remove themselves—such as happened during the August Revolution of 1906.[93]

In fact, political parties in republican Cuba were difficult to sustain. Those that were successful in the electoral arena had to maintain followings of sufficient strength to survive political contests. Political coalitions were highly volatile and unstable and prone to factions, fragmentation, and dissolution whenever party leaders lost supporters and affiliates to other political coalitions. Although dozens of parties emerged throughout the course of the republican era (1902–59), at regular intervals they disbanded, reorganized, fused, and split under similar or different party names.[94] These political coalitions were often headed by *caudillos*[95] (political strongmen) of recognized authority and ability to garner and maintain followings. An example was the Union Democratic Party of the early republic, whose emblem was, in 1901, a coat of arms surrounded by a flag and the name "Masó," after their political hopeful, Bartolomé Masó.[96] In fact, more than coalitions that were grouped according to opposing ideological beliefs, Cuban political parties were pathways to social and economic resources.[97] Turmoil and flux were so common in republican formal politics that between 1902 and 1959 the party system was reorganized more than a dozen times.[98] Moreover, the formation of groups in support of politicians had less to do with individual party ideologies than with the socioeconomic interests of such groups and the ability of their leaders to distribute favors (jobs, political appointments, monies, letters of recommendation, and intervention in legal matters) once elected to office.

Patrons, Parties, and Friends

Political party organizing necessarily began at the local level, where a complex structure of patron-client relations linked local-level political behavior to national electoral outcomes. Even as parties assumed increasingly national operations, they remained connected to local *caciques* (local political bosses) with sufficient ongoing support to mobilize a local party branch of their national organization and deliver regional votes. Jorge Domínguez argues that this political localness relates to the early republican system of indirect election, in which each provincial board of electors cast their vote for the presidency. Thus, votes were aggregated provincially, not nationally, which in turn reinforced the authority of provincial politicians and their significance for national contenders.[99]

These are important considerations for understanding the history of political organizing in republican Cuba, particularly in the early decades.

Though certain sectors mobilized en masse according to horizontal relationships and common interests for structural change—primarily among trade laborers—most sectors of the population sought vertical social and political patronage ties to meet their socioeconomic needs. Activism among the African-descended, for example, largely followed this broad pattern of strategic appeals and reciprocity to well-placed local patrons in order to gain greater access to national resources. Black clients often approached black brokers (politicians, professionals, club administrators, civil servants, businessmen, and so on)—occasionally but not always invoking the bonds of racial fraternity—in order to exchange their votes for the goods and services that the brokers possessed. Black brokers also served the vital function of contributing to the twin myths of racial equality and black participation in republican democracy. José Guadalupe Castellanos, for example, a mulatto political boss in Santiago, built a respectable career in politics and in the local *santiaguero* civic life. He was in constant communication with the highly influential politician Juan Gualberto Gómez, was named councilman to the Santiago municipal assembly by the North American occupation government, and was later elected as the city's lieutenant mayor. Castellanos was also very active in the city's black civic clubs, serving on the board of directors of several organizations, including Santiago's Light of the East Political, Instruction, and Recreation Society; the Cuban Casino Instruction, Recreation, and Beneficence Society; the Martín Morúa Delgado Patriotic Cultural Center; the Provincial Federation of Black Societies of Oriente; and the National Federation of Black Cuban Societies.

Black veteran general Quintín Bandera enjoyed even greater political influence. Based in Oriente province, Bandera hoped to capitalize on his remarkable regional influence by working with highly regarded general Máximo Gómez. Together they planned to inaugurate the National League of Oriente, a national political organization based in Santiago that would seek constituents from across the island. In 1899, Bandera called a meeting at the headquarters of Club Maceo, a social and political organization in the city, which drew about 500 supporters. He outlined the organization's simple, forthright platform for the attendees: recognition by the U.S. government of Cubans' ability to self-govern, as well as a withdrawal date for U.S. occupation forces based on international law. Bandera also called for the creation of a Cuban militia for peacekeeping that would work alongside the existing U.S. militia.[100] Despite his regional prominence and organizing skills, the National League was unsuccessful, and, along with it, Bandera's bid for national leadership.

During election seasons, neighborhood, citywide, and regional political committees called on their party's faithful to support party candidates, to elect delegates to national meetings, and to clarify party platforms. In 1901, the National Party met at the presidential palace to articulate to the occupation government its support of U.S. economic policies.[101] Supporters of the presidential hopeful, Bartolomé Masó, who was endorsed simultaneously by the Republican Independent and Union Democratic parties, organized the Neighborhood Committee of Nuevo Pueblo to increase voter turnout for Masó that same year.[102] Before the general presidential election in December, neighborhood organizations across the island mobilized for the upcoming elections. In Havana, the San Lázaro Neighborhood Committee of the Republican Party met in October at the Cuban Lyceum to hear party leadership speak and rally broad local support; other neighborhood committees in city barrios (such as Jesús María, Santa Clara, Colón, Vivés, and Tacón) were equally active on behalf of their own parties.[103]

Patron-client relations, in fact, are based on individual or group political conduct in reciprocal exchange. Rather than attracting adherents with various competing ideologies, republican political organizations had the primary goal of enhancing adherents' access to resources.[104] Richard Graham argues that in the case of nineteenth-century Brazil, political party campaigns focused on maintaining (transactional) relations with loyal supporters rather than on fashioning and articulating political programs driven by ideology.[105] Party supporters expected that should their candidates be successful at election urns they would distribute the contracts, jobs or appointments, budgets, influence, recognition, and so on at their disposal to their clients (family members, friends, supporters, and the party faithful) in fulfillment of reciprocal obligations. In the months before assuming the office of the presidency, Tomás Estrada Palma summed up the basis for this style of clientilist party politics as "local affinities and personal affairs rather than principles."[106]

Favors that benefited a particular group or neighborhood formed the basis of republican clientilist exchange. Such was the case for a public works project to build workers' housing during the José Miguel Gómez administration. Where workers benefited from government housing they were expected to reciprocate by affiliating with the ruling government party.[107] In fact, many types of citizenship rights and government services in the republic were meted out by officeholders in the form of favors. Thus, rather than a set of government social welfare obligations to the citizenry, patronage services were rewards for loyal clients; and those who obtained benefits from elected officials demonstrated strong clientilist relations with their political patrons.

Political patronage drove many socioeconomic and political processes and impacted daily needs, as well as facilitated opportunity and mobility. Winning amnesty or favorable judgments for people who ran afoul of the law; exemption from fines or payments; a public service post in administration, education, public works, or a hospital; an educational fellowship or grant or admittance to private or postsecondary school; a coveted spot on the government payroll (*botella*), for which one received compensation whether or not work was actually performed; membership in exclusive social clubs, institutions, and organizations; public works budgets at the municipal and provincial levels; and gift monies from elected officials to certain institutions—all of these were typical forms of compensation under the clientelist system. Anyone failing to engage with this culture vastly reduced the likelihood of meeting many life necessities and aspirations. Further, patron-client political culture was as much based on social and personalistic ties (being "known by" each other) as on political relations (party affiliation), though both were important to formal republican politics, despite the ideological tenets expressed publicly by parties or candidates.[108]

In keeping with patronage leadership and a tradition of political sociability, political relationships often were forged at social venues and within social and cultural institutions. All sorts of organizations surfaced in the early republican years whose agendas were simultaneously cultural and political. This paradox is explained in part by the island's history of political activism within social and cultural organizations since the colonial era. Some of the earliest organizations espousing proto-nationalist ideals were the *sociedades filarmónicas*, liberalist societies dedicated to artistic production for the purpose of free thought and social and cultural development. These emerged in the early nineteenth century (1820–44), and their activities (such as pedagogy and teaching history) were monitored heavily by the Crown. In time, they became hotbeds of political activity bent on shifting and challenging colonial authority. Other societies, such as societies of instruction and recreation, were closely aligned with the anticolonial insurgency, and it was common for entire society memberships to close their doors and join the movement. Finally, the Abakuá secret society (an African-derived male fraternity) was believed by most to be a haven for collecting armaments and planning political revolt against Spain.

The lack of a party system during most of colonial rule also politicized social and cultural organizations. Not until Crown concessions articulated in the Pact of Zanjón (1878) was there a government stipulation allowing reformist political representation and the formation of political parties. Even then, party members enjoyed only a limited voice in decision making and had no direct control over metropolitan policies affecting the island's economy, politics, or officially sanctioned cultural practices. Colonial social and cultural organizations often did the real "work" of political activism, by making patronage appeals, for example, or by agitating against Crown rule. They also helped maintain political continuity during the late colonial period by organizing war efforts and forming political blocs in the early republic.

A case in point is the Santiago-based civic organization Club Moncada, whose members had coordinated their efforts during the war and, after independence, had reconstituted the institution. During the independence wars (1868–98), corporate organizations of all types, such as African-influenced religious organizations, recreation societies, and progressivist clubs, all devoted their energies to end colonial rule. Moncada members, for example, distributed medicines and munitions to anticolonial forces. For many corporate groups founded after Cuban independence, patriotic efforts such as these cut across class, culture, and racial lines and constituted an important ethos for institutional legitimacy after independence. Santiago's La Caridad de Oriente, a poor, black organization of Afro-Haitian origin, kept alive the *tumba francesa* culture among transplanted Haitian slaves who fled to eastern Cuba with their Euro-Haitian owners during and after the Haitian Revolution. La Caridad members boasted of their participation in Cuba's war to end colonialism in ways similar to the patriotic pride expressed by members of the black progressivist club Victory Society, of central Cuba, and the Club San Carlos, a white society of considerable wealth and standing in Santiago.[109]

In the republican period, social organizations had simultaneous political, social, and cultural aims and often blurred the boundaries of these ostensibly discrete sorts of activity. The San Lázaro Neighborhood Committee of the Cuban National Party in Havana, for example, held a three-hour, outdoor, patriotic celebration, complete with decorations, music played by the police band, fireworks, and speakers, in order to attract broad local support for the party. All were invited "without distinctions of any type" to enjoy the festivities and listen to speakers.[110] In this way, the San Lázaro Committee, like all organizational efforts of this sort, hoped to win sufficient support to gain a political office. The voting public, and committee members in particular, also hoped that their support would result in access to the resources controlled by the office won by their candidate and/or party members.

Political and social terrains were not, in fact, mutually exclusive in the context of early republican society. Political organizations mobilized their support in part by providing their members with recreational activities that in turn gave them a sense of cohesion; and members inserted themselves into formal politics by debating political ideas, providing electoral candidates with an audience, and issuing frequent public statements regarding contemporary issues of both local and national significance. As historian María de los Ángeles Fuentes Meriño argues about political parties in Santiago de Cuba—the island's eastern capital and the most prominent city after Havana—activists there slated candidates and ran campaigns by engaging a range of activities, many of which fell outside the purview of traditional concepts of electoral politics. These politically engaged associations had been in existence since colonial times, and their resurgence after independence constituted an important component of republican political structure.

Cubans of all colors inserted themselves into formal politics by establishing multipurpose corporate organizations to support their candidates, such as the flurry of political *círculos* founded after the War of Independence, which had a pronounced social character.[111] Such political institutions enhanced the local and national prominence of their members and leaderships by creating an increasingly wide net of social relations and a formidable public sphere presence. In turn, this renown helped officeholders/statesmen to identify individuals of prestige and influence who could mobilize public opinion and electoral support on their behalf.

Círculos: The Politics of Sociability

The political *círculos* (centers) that flourished in the first years of republican life were modeled after those of the nineteenth century. In one instance, a rash of them surfaced in colonial Oriente province, such as the Círculo Autonomista de Baracoa, founded in 1889. As the club's bylaws stated, its mission was to facilitate "relations between all autonomists of the immediate area, in order to invigorate and extend the propaganda of the Cuban Liberal Party, and to contribute to servicing the interests of all of those of Autonomist inclinations."[112] Among other objectives, members hoped to spread the doctrine of the Liberal Party (their institutional base) and to use any means at their disposal to serve the interests of all autonomist affiliates and sympathizers. They strove to provide leisure activities and scientific, literary, and artistic events.[113]

In large part, postindependence republican *círculos* served as institutions of voter recruitment by building social and cultural cohesion among the voting public and by generating a political following for candidates. The Círculo Nacionalista "Antonio Maceo" of Santiago de Cuba, for example, was the pulpit of a ranking member of the National Party in Santiago, Antonio Bravo Correoso, and others, helping them to disseminate their platform, including the need for an inclusive suffrage as well as the importance of both formal politics and the role of the National Party in republican government.[114] *Círculo* members debated politics and supported politicians, while also integrating cultural and social activities into their agendas. The bylaws of at least eighteen early twentieth-century *círculos* listed intellectual and moral development and licit entertainment and social activities as their goals. Many were concerned as well with national well-being and patriotic values. Several had established or planned to create libraries to foster scientific and literary talent among members and their families.

As political organizations, *círculos* were just as fervent. Members publicly identified with their political party and sought to strengthen their party at the local level, thereby increasing its chance of installing patrons with which they could establish reciprocal relations. To create reciprocal relations with political patrons, clubs took the names of electoral candidates or political parties, such as the Círculo Liberal "Valeriano Hierruezuelo" (first mayor for the town of San Luis, Oriente, under the occupation government) and the Club "Bartolomé Masó" (an early presidential hopeful for the 1901 elections).[115] As political organizations, these clubs followed a widespread pattern of fractious and unstable republican political organizations—that is, they were short-lived and often closed their doors permanently within months or even weeks after being founded. The long-standing Círculo Liberal "Martín Morúa Delgado" (revolutionary, congressman, Senate president, writer, intellectual, and black political activist) was an exception. It was active until 1952, according to government records. *Círculo* memberships allegedly swelled to several hundred (up to 700 or 800 in some towns).[116] And although their social compositions are undetermined (archival documents do not reveal the importance of racial politics in these organizations or whether segregationist beliefs informed member ideologies), given that their purpose was to strengthen political candidates and parties at the local and regional levels, *círculo* memberships likely had fluctuating percentages of black and white members, dependent on area demographics. Black *círculo* members would have likely worked for their party's success and, less publicly and less forcefully, advocated for racial equality.

Black political activists, however, also sought additional avenues for their activities, by forming social, cultural, and political organizations with all-black memberships (though these were not as overtly exclusionary as were many white civic organizations). It is also true that publicly very few of these had activist agendas and rarely were they overtly political. In fact, precisely because black mobilization provoked extreme anxiety in mainstream party leaderships and among elected officials, their bylaws almost always stated explicitly that they were apolitical. Notwithstanding such protestations, black clubs were important sites of political negotiation, filling a void in republican politics by creating a space for vibrant political activism. And they attracted politicians. Often labeled as societies or clubs of "instruction and recreation," they were nonetheless a vibrant site of political activity and concerned with more than responsible citizenship. In fact, they facilitated social *and* political networks. A principal goal of club leaders and members was to forge powerful local relationships and involve themselves and their friends, families, and organizations in local and national political processes. Thus, in everyday club activity, members and leaders purposefully developed relationships of trust and loyalty among friends, supporters, acquaintances, and family to strengthen their own standing and power. In particular, dynastic family relations predominated in clubs and contributed to the rise of local power brokers and strongmen.

All in the Family

The networks of political patronage were often dynastic, and their development and deployment was, almost exclusively, the purview of males. Black clubmen and their brothers, cousins, uncles, fathers, and grandfathers entered the political arena by running for office within the same political party, holding posts that had complementary authority in relation to each other (for example, a provincial governor and a local police chief within the same province), gaining a seat on the society boards, or receiving political appointments from elected officials. Often several members of the same family held board seats in a particular society. At times one person sat on several society boards. Black political activist Pablo Sánchez Gastón is an early example of this, holding leadership positions in three different societies in the 1900s—Club Aponte, Club Juan de Góngora, and the Sociedad "El Cocoyé"—while simultaneously working in local Santiago elections.[117]

More frequently, one family member was a board member and his brothers, cousins, uncles, son, father, and so on, were part of at-large membership—an arrangement that helped ensure ongoing support for his position on the board. Furthermore, some dedicated themselves to varying degrees of *haciendo política* (political brokering). They often belonged to clubs located outside their place of residence. Thus, in addition to creating dense local networks in black societies, family members might have ties to clubs in other towns or cities across the island, thereby increasing their sphere of influence.

Perhaps the most famous black family network in Oriente province was that of the politico Américo Portuondo Hardy. A native of Santiago de Cuba, Portuondo Hardy held numerous political posts during his lengthy career, including municipal council person (1920-22), delegate to the 1928 national constitutional convention, and congressional representative (1922-26, 1932). He was prominent enough to organize with the powerful black politician and clubman Miguel A. Capestany a 1928 tribute to President Gerardo Machado. From across the island, 187 societies attended the affair, for which intellectuals orated and renowned artists, such as Zoila Gálvez, sang opera and performed salon music.[118]

Américo's brother, Dr. José Guadalupe Portuondo Hardy, was involved heavily in black societies, serving in leadership positions for many years. In 1917, 1932, and 1933, a young José Guadalupe was elected vice secretary of Santiago's most prestigious black society, Club Aponte. He served as president of that club in 1934, and in 1945, 1947, and 1950-52 he was the club's vice president.[119] He was also vice president of the Provincial Federation of Black Societies of Oriente in 1950 and 1951 and served the next year as the vice secretary of recording for the National Federation of Black Societies.[120] Luis Mancebo Portuondo, cousin of Américo and José Guadalupe, was secretary of the nationally based Asociación de Veteranos (Veterans' Association) as well as an active leader in black societies. He served as a board deputy for Club Aponte in 1909, as secretary in 1918, and as president in 1928 and 1930. Another cousin, Arnaldo Portuondo, was an accountant for Club Aponte in 1955, the same year that yet another Portuondo, Fausto, was the club treasurer. Arnaldo also served as Aponte's vice secretary of correspondence in 1956, the same year that Efraín Romero Portuondo, cousin of Américo as well as his notary, served as Club Aponte's recording secretary.[121]

Oftentimes families that held multiple board positions did so in conjunction with other families, facilitating the possible creation of interfamily coalitions. For example, the Joubert brothers of Santiago were very prominent in Club Aponte as well. Germán Joubert served as secretary of Club Aponte during approximately the same years that members of the Portuondo family held key leadership positions, as did his brothers Rádames and Celso. In the city of Holguín, the Pupo family dominated the boards of the mulatto societies, the Unión Holgüinera and the Sociedad "Antonio Maceo de Gibara."

The Sociedad Unión Holgüinera was rife with familial dynasties. Besides the Serrano family, the family of Valentín Milord Zamora was prominent in society affairs. Milord Zamora and his brother, Benito, their nephew, Luis Milord Nápoles, and Valentín's three sons, Miguel, Victor, and Gabriel, dominated the Unión Holgüinera's board for four decades.[122] They served

PARADOS:—1.° Sr. Tomás Gastón, Vice Secretario. —2.° Sr. José Sánchez, Secretario. —3.° Sr. Marcelino Larrosa, Vice-Tesorero —4.° Sr. Ramón Gelis.— 5.° Sr. Serafín Budou, Vocal —SENTADOS:—1.° Sr. Manuel Figarola, Vocal.—2.° Sr. Mónico Echevarría, Presidente.—3.° Sr. Gregorio Galán, Tesorero.

Board of directors of Club Aponte, Santiago de Cuba, ca. 1907. From Rafael Serra, *Para blancos y negros: Ensayos políticos, sociales y económicos, cuarta serie* (Havana: Imprenta "El Score," 1907). (Courtesy of Manuscripts, Archives and Rare Books Division, Schomburg Center for Research in Black Culture, New York Public Library, Astor, Lenox and Tilden Foundations)

in a variety of capacities, from president to treasurer to deputy to secretary of correspondence. Often, members of the Milord clan occupied board slots simultaneously. Their presence was particularly intense during the years of the rise and fall of the *machadato* (the Machado administration).

Even those black societies that enjoyed less prominence and prestige in the public sphere created dynastic relations in their civic organizations. The Nápoles family of Santiago was particularly active among African-influenced societies, and many of the Nápoles were musicians. In 1919, José de los Santos Nápoles was president of the Cabildo Carabalí Isuama; his brother, Tomás, was vice president. José de los Santos was elected president again in 1924, the same year that other Nápoles brothers held board positions—Pedro was vice president, Alberto Nápoles was vice secretary, and Guillermo and Felix were first and fourth deputies. José de los Santos also served as president of the long-standing, African-influenced society, El Cocoyé (1868–78, 1888–1957) in 1925 and 1936, with brothers occupying board slots in those and other years as well.[123]

Some black politicians maintained ties to black societies as well as built family networks in public administration. In Santiago de Cuba, during the course of a decade, Pedro Salas Arzuaga served as board president, vice president, vice treasurer, and vice secretary of Luz de Oriente (Light of the East), the city's prestigious mulatto society. He was also deputy to the House of Representatives for the Liberal Party in 1942 and chief of police for the city of Santiago in the 1940s.[124] His brother, Justo, was active in Luz de Oriente as well, though he focused his energies on political office and went on to serve as alderman under the Liberal Party (1922), deputy representative to the House for the Liberal Party (1924, 1927, 1932, 1948), and mayor of Santiago under the Revolutionary Communist Union Party (1940–44).[125]

Although black civic organizations were, at several moments in republican history, supported by government officials such as Fulgencio Batista in the 1940s, before such ties were well established and during moments of political turmoil black clubs were the frequent targets of suspicion and state repression. And as some black activists took bolder political steps to challenge dominant parties, advocating that blacks withdraw from the mainstream arena altogether and unify as a race, they came under state-sponsored repression. At the same time, the republic's fledgling government adopted extreme tactics for political control, such as the ruling Moderate Party had done before, during, and after the 1905 elections. Even those activists not willing to take on the political apparatus were subject to harassment.

Police raids on black clubs in Santiago in 1906, for example, prompted José Vantour, a board member of the Luz de Oriente Society, to request help from Juan Gualberto Gómez. Vantour complained that after the confirmation of Colonel Federico Pérez Carbó, the newly elected Moderate governor of Oriente province, police raids on his and other black organizations had increased. "The raids spread us thin," he complained, "making our daily club operations increasingly difficult." It seems that the odious colonial Law of Association (1888) was still in force, permitting government access to clubs at will, in this case under the pretext of stopping illegal gaming practices. He then shifted to Gómez responsibility for the very life of the organization: "[The raids] make it difficult to raise funds to sustain our organization being this society one where the artisan finds entertainment and recreation. If these tactics that denigrate and humiliate us don't stop we will soon be forced to close our doors."[126] Vantour ended the letter with a plea that Gómez use his "considerable influence" to stop the raids.

That he wrote to Gómez in the first place suggests that, as members of a locally prominent black civic organization, they expected some assistance from the nationally prominent black politician. There is an implication, too, that in return for Gómez's much-needed assistance society members as a whole would reciprocate with political support.[127] What was not written in the letter but was likely understood by both was the two men's political connection—Vantour was a delegate for the Liberal Party nominating committee in Oriente province and had cast his vote in favor of the José Miguel Gómez–Zayas ticket. He was, therefore, an asset to Juan Gualberto Gómez—a party leader and staunch *zayista* supporter. Thus, Vantour functioned in Oriente province as a black broker: his direct line of communication with Juan Gualberto Gómez at the national level made him important to other Luz de Oriente members (to "get things done" for the club), while his local prominence made him useful to national politicians as a local point man for local backing (votes).[128] Given the force of antiblack repression and the government's fear of black political mobilization generally, the police raids (such as those about which Vantour complained) are not surprising. Indeed, at several moments in republican history, repression against black organizations of every ilk surged, such as police investigations of black clubs in Havana in 1910 in response to rumors of a black uprising.[129] This sort of repression was not unusual. In fact, many forms of violence were commonplace in the early republican political sphere, particularly when elected officials were struggling to retain their incumbency as elections drew near. Elections were so contentious because they could either maintain the status quo or open up the political sphere to new leadership. And, as suggested by José Vantour's letter, rifts among national organizations played out at the local level.

The political competition surrounding the 1904 partial elections, for example, was the source of violence and fraud. In the bitter rivalry between the Liberal Party and the newly formed Moderate Party (the party of the presidential incumbent, Tomás Estrada Palma), no tactic was too severe. Moderates used every possible resource at their disposal to control electoral outcomes. As the 1905 general elections neared, electoral boards were stacked in favor of Moderates, voter rolls (for elections in 1904 and 1905) were padded, and pro-Moderate police arrested Liberals on trumped-up charges or designed entrapment schemes to force their resignations and remove them from political competition. Local law enforcement, for example, harassed Liberal municipal officeholders with the threat of force and used other forms of coercion, including malicious gossip, to malign and publicly humiliate Liberal leaders and their family members, on occasion forcing them to resign their offices. Moderate judges were notorious for issuing warrants against Liberals and handing down unusually severe sentences to Liberal Party felons. Public employees were dismissed, teachers and school administrators were fired, and schools were abolished wholesale in areas with high concentrations of Liberal Party registrants.[130]

At times, the violence included property destruction and murder, as individual acts of terror were perpetrated against known Liberal Party members or their organizations. In the central city of Cienfuegos, Liberal Party leader Colonel Enrique Villuendas was murdered in September 1905 by local police, after they showed up at his hotel room under the pretext of searching for arms and dynamite.[131] *Círculos* in the region were especially vulnerable to Moderate attacks. As party predecessors had done in 1904 to the Rodas Círculo Liberal, Moderates in neighboring Cienfuegos attacked the local Círculo Liberal in fall 1905.[132] When the scale of violence caused Liberal candidates to withdraw in protest from the 1905 general elections, Moderates swept elections across the island. Tomás Estrada Palma and Domingo Méndez Capote were elected president and vice president, and their party took virtually every gubernatorial and congressional seat up for election that year.[133]

In the seven years between the Moderate-dominated general elections of 1905 and those of 1912, two related events affected blacks' trajectory in national politics. In August 1906, members of the Liberal Party rose up in arms against the ruling Moderate Party, and by 1908 an autonomous group of mostly black activists, the Partido Independiente de Color (the Independent Party of Color) (PIC), mobilized a national independent political organization. Following the Liberal Party uprising (the 1906 August Revolution), one of Governor Charles Magoon's first priorities after landing U.S. troops was to remove defeated and thoroughly discredited Moderates from office. By late September, the Moderate president, vice president, and congressmen had all resigned their posts, and in November the party was officially dissolved. Liberals assumed the position of front-runner for the 1908 general elections, but they were divided by internal factions, with one group, the *miguelistas*, supporting Liberation Army veteran general José Miguel Gómez as Cuba's next president, while the other faction, the *zayistas*, stood squarely behind the candidacy of lawyer-intellectual Alfredo Zayas.

For a number of black political hopefuls, the Liberal Party split became a golden opportunity. In the ongoing battle to dominate formal politics, parties could not afford to lose voters of any color, and practically speaking, black politicians helped mainstream parties to secure black votes. Despite the obvious need for black voters, most black activists were passed over for opportunities. Even though the Constitutional Army, an army containing a significant number of blacks, waged the 1906 August Revolution, for a second time since the republic's founding blacks were overlooked in the distribution of resources and were underrepresented in municipal and provincial elections.[134] Thus, the increase in black congressmen in 1908 notwithstanding, following the rebellion, blacks were largely ignored as new administrators divided up the spoils of public office.[135]

Historian Aline Helg has argued that if the dominant *miguelista* faction of the Liberal Party had lost black votes to the autonomous black political organization—the PIC—*miguelistas* would have lost control to either *zayista* Liberals or to the newly formed opposition Conservative Party that replaced the Moderate Party.[136] Liberal political dominance might also have been threatened by some black former Conservative Party activists who had formed part of the PIC leadership. The pressure for mainstream parties to secure the black vote was palpable following the 1906 August Revolution, a fact revealed by the number of blacks that stood for office. An unprecedented fourteen black candidates took congressional seats in 1908.[137] Presumably, putting forth black candidates on party rosters was done to increase public confidence in the party system's commitment to fairly divvying up resources, to undermine further black political mobilization, and to guard against a Conservative Party-PIC coalition.

Yet when Moderates vacated office in 1906 (they were forced to resign on September 12 by the U.S. occupation government), the ascendant Liberal Party was accused of continuing to deny blacks public sector employment opportunities.[138] Many black activists soon believed that no matter how decisive their level of participation in the independence wars or in the recent Liberal Party uprising, they would continue to be passed over for patronage jobs unless a checks and balances system for jobs and education was put in place and social recognition was given to blacks.[139] One organization with these objectives was the Camagüey Directorate of Citizens of Color, founded in August 1907 by thirty men, who penned a public manifesto decrying blacks' inability to access their rightful share of public resources. As the organization's manifesto suggests early on: "In the ill-fated hours of our homeland, in moments of danger to liberty, and under all critical circumstances, the race of color has been the shoulder to cry on, the bronze hand that breaks the chain of oppression, the one who has proportioned the largest contingent for the conquest of liberty yet who has had the least usufruct of the fruits of that conquest."[140]

Also during that August, outraged black Liberal Party leaders from the northeasterly seaport of Gibara wrote in frustration to Juan Gualberto Gómez, asking him to intervene in an unacceptable situation. White Liberals in Gibara were snagging local public sector jobs, for which black Liberals had petitioned, traveling as far as Havana to secure guarantees of local employment distributions to blacks from national party leadership. They had recommended a black man, Sr. Rafael Orozco, for the job of head of protection at the Gibara Customs Office, only to discover that a white man, Emilio Vega, was jockeying for the same position. The men charged: "Men of color in this locality are hurt. . . . Sr. Orozco was the only employee of color recommended for any [local public service] job and he is competent."[141]

Frustration ran high enough to cause some black activists to reject mainstream parties altogether. Members of the La Bella Unión Club in the central city of Santa Clara resolved to withdraw from mainstream political parties in order to join an all-black one.[142] In nearby Cienfuegos, rumors spread about blacks there forming an "independent party."[143] The 1906 August Revolution helped to shift the dynamic of racial politics as black leaders mobilized veterans and civic activists to win for a privileged community of blacks access to patronage opportunities. The Liberal Party's policy of handing administration appointments to white veterans of the Constitutional Army did not sit well with black former insurgents.

Frustrated blacks were, in turn, motivated to mobilize autonomously. That is, following several years of marginalization, particularly in terms of access to elected office and positions of political leadership, black frustration boiled over, and black activists began to agitate to improve their access to republican resources outside of mainstream political parties. As longtime black activist and recent general in the 1906 August Revolution Evaristo Estenoz suggested in 1908, "Barely established, the Republic has turned our concerns to anger, and done so to a greater extent and under worse conditions than in the most offensive moments of colonialism."[144] In August 1908, Estenoz, Gregorio Surín, and others founded the organization that would later be called the Partido Independiente de Color (the Independent Party of Color) (PIC). From its inception, the PIC struggled for political ground; party candidates performed disastrously in the 1908 elections, and in 1910 government opposition to the party resulted in the arrest of Estenoz. Legislation also passed that was damning for the party—the Morúa Amendment, authored by black senator Martín Morúa Delgado. Estenoz was imprisoned for about a month in 1910 before being released by President José Miguel Gómez—a prudent move after widespread protest broke out in response to Estenoz's arrest. Yet the Morúa Amendment to the national electoral law was passed by the Senate on February 14, 1910, and stood as a state-sponsored deterrent to black political mobilization. In essence, it outlawed political parties and independent groups made up "exclusively of people of one race or color."[145]

Two years later, Estenoz and other PIC adherents continued to voice their discontent over their exclusion from political appointments, lucrative jobs, and political office by crafting a three-point offensive to rescue their party. They decided in early May to move their actions to Oriente province, a region that had one of the highest concentrations of blacks and mulattos, constituting a large percentage of the province's voting public. Second, they reasoned that a fight to relegalize the PIC might energize black voters in the Oriente province and build party support. Finally, they met with President José Miguel Gómez, who was gearing up for the coming general elections and who purportedly promised to support the repeal of the Morúa Amendment.[146] The rebellion's driving force, however, was more heavily weighted toward securing access to resources than the lofty dream of defeating racial injustice. The PIC rose up in arms against the Morúa Amendment in May 1912, fighting for three months in what is now famously known as the Race War of 1912. As the historians Rebecca Scott and Aline Helg have similarly argued, it is highly likely that the *independentistas* hoped to use the conflict to secure North American intervention, thereby ensuring a reconfiguration of formal political power—either as shared power or, at the very least, to encourage redistribution of political control into hands other than those of the incumbency.[147] A similar strategy had played out quite well for the political underdogs several years earlier, when the Liberal Party's 1906 August Revolution precipitated a second U.S. intervention (1906–9) since Cuban independence in 1898 and brought down the Conservative Party monopoly on local and national political offices—from the president and both houses of Congress to local judges, mayors, and town councilmen. For the sake of gaining political leverage it is logical to think that the *independentistas* might have dredged up old, workable tactics as the 1912 elections approached. From May to August 1912, a few hundred disgruntled *independentistas* occupied foreign property and skirmished to protest obstacles to their full integration in republican politics. The Race War of 1912 began on May 20, the official date of the founding of the republic in 1902, and ended almost three months later, after PIC leadership members, along with thousands of black civilians, were killed by Cuban and U.S. armed forces as well as by white civilian brigades. Thatch-roof shacks were set ablaze, and blacks were hanged, decapitated, castrated, stabbed, and shot. In one horrific recount, a white government volunteer in Santiago de Cuba sported a bag of ears, lopped off of heads after blacks were shot to death.[148]

Where PIC leadership struggled to insert the organization into formal political structures by winning abrogation of the Morúa Law, the state and dominant press portrayed *independentista* grievances in the most vicious and racially polarizing light, arguing that black political empowerment meant the destruction of the nation as thus far defined.[149] In fact, in early June 1912, at the height of the war against the *independentistas*, President José Miguel Gómez felt that stability had been so compromised that he suspended constitutional guarantees for the entire province of Oriente.[150] Gómez launched a vitriolic assault on the *independentistas*, called the Oriente campaign, positing that their rebellion denigrated the nation and threatened its civilization and, in a thinly veiled reference to white patriarchal authority and the sexual propriety of white women, argued that the *independentistas*' actions were "outside the radius of human civilization." The insurgents were loath, even, to respect the "rights of the home [*los fueros del hogar*]."[151]

The president went one step further, suggesting that the rebels were subhuman. They personified nature and instinct, he insisted, embodying the rural, forested outpost where they had first launched their attack. In retribution, he called for their blood:

> For the honor and glory of [reclaiming the homeland] there are no great dangers; the enemy now moves in the thickening of the forest, attacking by surprise, avoiding [our] combatants; but, if there was danger [our] dignified and heroic people, who do not know how to tolerate threats to their honor now as always, now more than ever they will face with impetuous serenity those who, in Cuba's rural countryside between steaming piles of waste will with their own blood dye the strips and triangle of [our] homeland's flag.[152]

In many ways, Gómez also evoked myths that circulated in nineteenth- and twentieth-century Cuba as well as in other parts of the Caribbean, which placed the rural subject in opposition to the urban, modern one. Geographic and cultural proximity to urban bourgeois elite cultures, it was believed, encouraged compliance with government interests.[153] Rural blacks and whites, ostensibly tainted by country life, had dangerous tendencies of sensuality, boundless lust, sloth, and failure to adhere to the institution of marriage.[154] For example, racialist ideals in Puerto Rico intensified these characterizations; thus, historically, rural blacks were assumed to be murderers, sexual predators, nomads, and "monstrous mothers."[155]

The 1912 Race War massacre suggests the degree to which political elites (such as José Miguel Gómez) reached to squash political competitors and block blacks' efforts at full integration into the republic's political sphere. Yet black political elites were often just as keen as white politicians to close ranks against the PIC and the politics of racial consciousness. Rebecca Scott argues that this was based on black elites' desire to stay in the good graces of dominant political parties, rejecting the *independentista* tactics and exercising "a mix of principle and prudence."[156] In fact, many black activists, particularly representatives from black societies, wrote to local and national newspapers asking them to publish their indignation at the PIC uprising. They offered the sweat of their brows to help crush PIC insurgents. The black clubs Luz de Oriente and Club Aponte in Santiago de Cuba sent open statements to President Gómez testifying to their support of his repressive actions against the PIC and their willingness to help defeat them on behalf of "national unity" and "public order."[157] Blacks in Matanzas condemned the PIC uprising, as did members of Havana's Fraternal Union black society, who resolved in June to support the government response to the PIC.[158] During the short-lived massacre, black congressmen met with the president, complaining that the Cuban military had denied black citizens arms in order to defend themselves against the PIC and that the press should not use the appellation "black" to describe PIC members. To do so, they suggested, would increase the possibility of confusion between black civilians and PIC members, with dire consequences.[159] During the massacre, fear of being associated with racial nationalism undoubtedly drove these public condemnations of the PIC, yet black political insiders were also committed to maintaining their influence with and access to resources controlled by mainstream parties. The PIC's success would have threatened black political elites' power as well.

In fact, most black activists chose a different, more subtle, modus operandi than the PIC. Black civic organizations, also known as societies of instruction and recreation or simply as clubs, were sites not just of social but of *political* activity, even if not explicitly labeled as such. Clubs held balls, academic conferences, literary and beauty contests, patriotic commemorations, and fund-raisers. And although cultural activities evince a politics of bourgeois performance, the fact that politicians made frequent stops at clubs on their campaign trails, that clubs often endorsed publicly and privately certain political candidates over others, that they voiced publicly their analyses of race and elections, and that high-level government officials subsidized clubs also suggests that black civic organizations were fully integrated in republican formal politics.

Politicians courted black civic organizations, establishing the importance of black clubs to officeholders. In Santiago, for example, many prestigious club events were attended by socialites and public officials alike. Newly founded civic and labor organizations and newly elected boards of directors often issued press greetings to signal their entry into a broad community by saluting "Authorities, Press, Societies, Political Parties, and other persons that offer us their friendship." In fact, candidates and clubs devoted a significant amount of time to patriotic events and political and electoral campaigns. They were a frequent stopover on campaign routes by white and black politicians and were the site of political debate, politicking, and collaboration with elected officials at the municipal, provincial, and national levels.

For example, on June 15, 1899, black general Quintín Bandera issued a manifesto against U.S. military occupation of the island, calling for the "powerful invader to declare the exact date of the end of its interference in affairs that are the sole responsibility of Cubans."[160] Two weeks later, he spoke at the headquarters of the Club Político y Recreativo "Antonio Maceo," where he railed before an audience of 500 members against the occupation.[161] The first bylaws of Club "Antonio Maceo," written in 1900, stated that its organizational purpose was to provide a space for invited guests where political ideas might be debated and exchanged, by way of conferences, social gatherings, and other public celebrations "of a political nature." Further, the club was organized to contribute "personally, economically, and intellectually to all public acts that tend toward Cuba's wellbeing" and that develop the intellect of members and their families.[162]

In October 1901, during his brief candidacy for the nation's top executive office, aged Liberation Army veteran General Bartolomé Masó visited Havana's black society, the Centro de Cocineros (Cook's Social Center). The Centro was the site of his own campaign committee, perhaps because Masó counted black voters among the most significant supporters of his campaign.[163] Unlike Estrada Palma and later national politicians, Masó's speeches directly addressed black Cubans' place in republican society in order to win their support, demonstrating that he considered them central to his political success, a fact underscored by the number of prominent black war veterans and revolutionaries in his camp.

This dependency on black social and cultural organizations for political support continued after the first general elections. In 1903, after the rash of political and economic exclusions that had characterized his presidency since 1902, Tomás Estrada Palma visited Oriente province to stifle rumblings among disgruntled blacks in the east. During his stopover in Guantánamo, Estrada Palma dined at the home of black war general Jesus Rabí and visited Guantánamo's most prestigious black club, El Siglo XX. He also met with Pedro Ivonet, another ranking black veteran and president of the Veterans' Council for the city of La Maya.[164] Ivonet, a political activist from the earliest years of the republic, later become an important leader in the 1912 Race War uprising by the PIC. A year later, in 1904, Rafael Serra, a black journalist and veteran, launched a successful campaign for a seat in the House of Representatives with the National Radical Party, making sure to include many black, white, and Spanish social and recreational societies in Santiago on his campaign route.[165]

The clubs, in fact, organized a rally on Serra's behalf, together with several representatives of local labor organizations, including the Carpenters' Union, the Worker's Center, the Tobacco Workers' Union, the Dockworkers' Union, and the Farm workers' Union, which was covered by Serra's own press. Labeling him the "right hand" of the martyred revolutionary intellectual, José Martí, and an indefatigable warrior of "our" liberties, the predominantly black rally-goers who gathered called on Serra to continue his political mission in the House of Representatives and suggested that he was their candidate of choice because his patriotic loyalties to country were felt at least as deeply if not more deeply than those for his race. Serra, they insisted, fought for "Cuba" and "Cubans" and not for "races," making him a more viable politician. Reports relayed how the event closed with a round of support: "Serra lives in the People! Vote unanimously for him!!!"[166] Serra won their critical support and the election in February of that year.[167]

Where black voters were well represented in provinces and cities, local *caciques* actively courted black leaders for their influence with the local population. In one case, Liberation Army veteran Colonel Isidro Acea, a black broker from Guira de Melena in Havana province, was placed on the payroll of local Spaniards after he convinced them of his influence with black laborers. Despite the Spaniards' payments to Acea (presumably to win the workers' acquiescence to Spanish business interests), he secretly mobilized blacks for his own political aims and played local blacks against the Spanish, eventually incurring the Spanish merchants' anger and frustration.[168] Among other maneuvers Acea was alleged to have a supply of arms and to have incited a local, black protest.[169] Following the incident, Acea was arrested, no doubt in response to the threat of his authority among blacks in Guira de Melena, which local Spanish businessmen took seriously. In fact, Acea was seemingly able to mobilize local workers in support of or against local business interests based on political loyalty. His political authority was a powerful challenge to local political and economic structures and epitomizes the machinations of early republican political networks fueled by loyalty and favors rather than ideology. To the extent that black activists such as Serra and Acea could position themselves to participate in these networks, they received greater access to republican resources.

Conclusion

As the structures of early republican politics coalesced, the most viable forms of political activism stood in increasingly sharp relief. Blacks entered the political arena armed with the vote as commodity; and black civic and party activists—a relatively small percentage of the African-descended population—gained access to resources by negotiating in the electoral arena with those votes. Patronage relations were foundational to these machinations, as was a culture of political sociability. Both were the modus operandi of Cuban elections and were central to the pursuit of resources of one or another type. Institutionally speaking, *círculos* and clubs facilitated black political participation; they bridged social gaps between blacks and whites and encouraged political brokering between them. Even as officials, journalists, intellectuals, and political rivals, such as those represented by the *La Lucha* "Changüí Político" editorial, attacked black political participation in the nascent republic, a small number of black activists managed nonetheless to win access to resources.

Although some blacks managed to enter the republic's early political party system, this did not translate into across-the-board benefits or legislative change in favor of more equitable distribution of national resources. Rather, black participation in political parties increased the number of black brokers and held merely the promise of greater access to resources for their black constituencies. Clients offered votes during electoral contests and were important to obtaining political offices. In large part, then, black patrons and black clients both depended on and were fundamental to republican electoral politics and the rapidly expanding system of political patronage. In fact, black Cuban activism must be analyzed according to the political context of the early republic. Almost all black activists, except for those who formed the short-lived PIC, joined the ranks of mainstream parties. Contributing to this were important local (rather than mass-based or national) mobilizations, the culture of patron-client relations in Cuban politics, and rapidly growing public budgets where many Cubans at the local and national levels accessed resources. Other factors were the cleavages among rural, urban, native, and foreign-born workers and political party dependency on black figureheads in order to win black votes, all of which mitigated both mass- and race-based organizing. If the mandate of the Cuban independence movement had been national egalitarianism (and harmonious race relations), powerful forces worked to curtail these democratic impulses. Black Cubans, at once demographically significant, economically disadvantaged, and socially marginalized, might have been the inspiration of revolutionary egalitarianism in the republic rather than a frequent target of ridicule and attack, as was done by *La Lucha* editorialists and others.

The political landscape produced activists, including black activists, who by and large sought resources rather than rights. Black activists in Cuba engaged patronage relations and only partially addressed social justice issues. Their activism, which integrated republican political processes, must figure as a foundational aspect of twentieth-century black Cuban experience. The career of the highly influential black activist, Juan Gualberto Gómez, arguably the most powerful in republican history, provides some much-needed clarity on the question of black experience in early twentieth-century Cuba. His network of relations is important to understanding how privileged black activists infiltrated mainstream political networks and operated in the context of republican racial politics in an effort to dull the pincers of racism and win socioeconomic resources.

CHAPTER TWO

Black Patronage Networks

"The issue," said black political activist Juan Gualberto Gómez in 1902, "is to begin, and begin on the inside."[1] Gómez spoke with satisfaction after Cuba's new head of state, Tomás Estrada Palma, announced his intention to set aside one hundred public service jobs for "deserving" Cubans of color.[2] Government set-asides were far from novel in Cuban politics, particularly when used to cinch political loyalties. In fact, centralization of administrative resources (such as jobs and public works contracts) were long a convention of Cuban politics. Even before independence it was an important mechanism of corruption and control at all levels of Spain's colonial administration.[3] After the end of colonialism in 1898 and due in part to the policies of U.S. occupation officials (who appointed pro-U.S. supporters to key administrative posts and enacted U.S. Military Order 218 instituting a North American–style governance system on the island), similar artful uses of government resources emerged as common practice in "new Cuba."[4] What was without precedent after independence, however, was the new president's public promise of job distribution—across the races.

Estrada Palma had pledged to increase the number of blacks on government payrolls (as postal employees, clerks, messengers, inspectors, police officers, and rural guardsmen), a move that Juan Gualberto Gómez—arguably the island's most influential black voice in the early republic—suggested would bring more blacks into the "inside" of Cuba's new economic structures and would, in one sense, help to nullify segregationist policies established during U.S. occupation (1898–1902). Gómez and others believed that Estrada Palma's gesture was potentially important to igniting an egalitarian impetus following national independence in 1898. This promise of jobs, however, had come only after Generoso Campos Marquetti, the black veteran general of the Liberation Army, and several hundred other black veterans and civic activists demanded that the government end discriminatory hiring practices. Having fought side by side with whites in the independence wars (1868–98) in numbers disproportionate to the total island population and believing that the Revolution's triumph should confer on all not just citizenship status but real opportunity, the activists pushed to be included in the lucrative echelons of the emerging republican economy.

In fact, the Revolution's egalitarian rhetoric notwithstanding, in practice very few Cubans of color managed to win a public service job in the early republic.[5] Many fell short of infiltrating patronage networks at levels that yielded socioeconomic benefits, as was customary practice in the distribution of public resources. As argued here and earlier by historians such as Louis Pérez, Alejandro de la Fuente, and Jorge Ibarra, throughout the republican period ever-expanding bureaucracies and budgets funded patronage sinecures, nepotism, and favoritism at all levels of government.[6] Powerful foreign investments in Cuba limited domestic economic activity, relegating a significant amount of Cuban economic transactions to politics and public budgets. As state budgets mushroomed after 1899, administrators' power increased. Their capacity to appoint supporters to civil service jobs expanded, and they manipulated jobs and other resources in order to line their own pockets as well as secure political loyalty in the gamey exchange of favors for votes.[7] Although the number of state employees expanded in direct relationship to expanding state budgets, it was still difficult to obtain public sector opportunities. Fierce job competition (largely due to a sizable immigrant laboring population and thousands of out-of-work Liberation Army veterans) as well as race, gender, regional, and familial preferences further worked against equitable job distribution.[8] Thus, penetrating emerging republican structures and being on the "inside" of them, as Juan Gualberto Gómez described it in 1902, meant insinuating oneself into the dense web of patronage relationships that increasingly determined employment, protections, contracts, and favors in republican Cuba. Aline Helg argues, for example, that one's political affiliation was a likely source of employment, such as the jobs acquired by prominent blacks in the ruling Moderate Party between 1903 and 1904, including Rafael Serra's appointment to the post office, General Jesús Rabí's stint as forest inspector, and Manuel González's post in Havana's customhouse.[9] Socioeconomic success, even one's survival, then, forced Cubans of all colors to navigate the complex, arterial networks controlled by elected officials, whose power was safeguarded (at least for their term of office) by manipulating public resources.

Black activists in the early republic argued vigorously that despite a few, scattered appointments, the political system (and by extension Cuban representative democracy) had fallen short of guaranteeing equal opportunity or even respecting blacks' political significance. Even the black journalist and politician Rafael Serra, who had reaped some benefit from his ties to government officials, was so dismayed by postindependence resource disparities that in 1905 he called the situation a "soft war" against blacks.[10] Blacks agitated with mixed success for better opportunities (such as equal access to public space, quality education, formal professional training and careers, and civil service employment) and rightfully charged that the postindependence administration had acted unfairly, upholding inequality rather than revolutionary egalitarianism.

Thus, at a landmark assembly on May 25, 1902, just five days after Cuba's first president took office, black veterans and clubmen formed an "Action Committee" and raised the issue of blacks' lagging status in the new nation with government officials.[11] They chose to confront the new president about jobs, knowing that administrative turnover created a window of opportunity for political negotiations. Election seasons in general were strategic because of politicians' constant struggles to attract voters, and Estrada Palma, who had assumed the nation's highest office on May 20, 1902, needed black political loyalty. His administration was especially vulnerable to instability, given the recent protracted anticolonial war, North American occupation, and increasing barrage of foreign investment projects undermining Cubans' control of their own national economy. Further, a significant number of blacks had opposed Estrada Palma as president, backing instead his onetime political rival, Bartolomé Masó, who, before withdrawing from the 1901 presidential race, was generally perceived as the socially egalitarian candidate. Estrada Palma's political career, indeed his entire party, was brought down in August 1906, when the antigovernment Constitutional Army revolted. Many blacks participated on the side of the constitutionalists, whose revolution initiated the second North American occupation since Cuban independence in 1898 and precipitated Estrada Palma's resignation and the dissolution of his Moderate administration.[12] This sort of antigovernment militancy was unusual among black activists, however, with most seeking inclusion in government structures.

In fact, blacks often sought resources at the time of electoral contests, as several early actions attest: the Veterans and Societies of Color mobilization (1902), which challenged the newly elected administration on racially exclusive government hiring policies; the August Revolution of 1906, which challenged the Moderate Party bid to persist in office by any necessary means; the postrevolutionary initiative for a Race of Color Directorate in Camagüey (1907), which emerged from black frustration with the August Revolution leadership and its failure to follow through on political appointments;

the coordinated, island-wide protests that same year, for more black census takers to help conduct the U.S.-sponsored census; the Independent Party of Color (1908), founded following the disastrous August 1908 partial elections; the civic and political journal *Minerva: Revista Universal Ilustrada* (1910–15), which appeared in the months before the 1910 partial elections; and the Independent Party of Color preparations for the 1912 general elections (including a National Assembly meeting in March 1911 as well as the party's uprising in the summer of 1912). This congruence of black activism with key electoral events suggests that whether or not the activists were integrated in mainstream political party leadership, they believed that party activism was the most viable avenue to access political authority and, in turn, resources. It suggests, too, that they were actively engaged in the electoral system as voters, activists, candidates, and officeholders.[13]

Mobilizations such as these helped (if only briefly) to bend the arc of power toward black activists. The strategy worked, for example, after the August 1908 provincial and municipal elections boded ill for racial equality and black political success. Black mainstream party candidates running for office during the August contests failed to make inroads, which in turn provoked other black activists, such as Evaristo Estenoz, to form the Independent Party of Color (PIC).[14] In the wake of founding the PIC (first called the Agrupación de Color [Group of Color]), black participation in mainstream political organizations was boosted; the island's mainstream parties reacted swiftly to the threat of political competition from the PIC and put up a relatively large number of black candidates.[15] They fared comparatively well at the polls during the November 1908 general elections, revealing what was then a veritable rhythm of political call-and-response between electoral contests and the race for black votes.[16] That is, there is a history in republican politics of interplay between black activists seeking socioeconomic opportunities through patronage and the competition among mainstream politicians and parties for black support.[17] When blacks attempted to mobilize autonomously or to form competitive, racially inspired political organizations outside of the purview of the island's dominant parties, they often encountered violent opposition, such as against the PIC *independentistas* during the 1912 Race War or the ostracism to which the short-lived Friends of the People Party was subjected in 1915.

Black veterans' and society activists' primary concerns were racial exclusions in government hiring, and their principal mode of action was to make demands on officeholders. Black activists (such as the members of the Action Committee), emboldened by the galvanizing effects of the Veterans and Societies of Color mobilization, eventually sought out local and national officials to press their demands.[18] As previously discussed, the Action Committee, led by Campos Marquetti and veteran Liberation Army officers Julián Sierra and Evaristo Estenoz, met with the president in early June 1902, shortly after he was elected. Though initially hopeful, the presidential meeting degenerated quickly. After debating Estrada Palma in his office for more than two hours and pressing him for more widespread appointments in civil administration, the men left the talks disillusioned and dissatisfied.[19] The sparring became so heated during the encounter that among Campos Marquetti's final words to Estrada Palma were the following: "The truth is, Mr. President, this is not what we [blacks] expected from the Revolution and things cannot continue like this."[20] The men met that same month with the mayor and governor of Havana and presented the House of Representatives with a memorandum that called for the repeal of the antiblack U.S. military orders—including the "white-only" policy that limited police hires to whites.[21] Yet despite these meetings and the hundreds of black civic leaders, veterans, and private citizens who were behind these gestures, their efforts changed frustratingly little.

By late June, nationally prominent black veterans (Juan Gualberto Gómez, Campos Marquetti, Ramiro Cuesta, Silverio Sánchez Figueras, and Lino D'ou) again responded to rising black discontent over employment by organizing a second mass meeting and calling on the president to "maintain the unity forged [during the Revolution] by black and white."[22] The event's first speaker, political activist Ramiro Cuesta, felt compelled to dispel the rumors equating black demands for jobs with a "racial uprising." Lieutenant Colonel Lino D'ou approached the podium next, unabashedly calling black exclusions "a national embarrassment." War veteran Silverio Sánchez proclaimed that Cuba needed the efforts of both its white and its black sons and daughters, each one contributing in his or her own way. As the rally peaked, Campos Marquetti (whose political résumé included insurrection against Spain, exile to Spain's Ceuta penal colony, and following independence, a successful career in electoral politics) recounted bitterly to rallygoers that when he and others raised the issue of state employment for blacks with the president they were called "racists."[23]

The last person to speak, Juan Gualberto Gómez, charged that under Provisional Governor Ludlow, the U.S. occupation government had adopted a "white-only" policy in certain civil service sectors that sent a wrong-headed message to Cuban officials about the course of Cuba's postoccupation administration.[24] Gómez admonished white Cuban leaders, stating that they

Politician and civic activist Generoso Campos Marquetti. From Rafael Serra, *Para blancos y negros: Ensayos políticos, sociales y económicos, cuarta serie* (Havana: Imprenta "El Score," 1907). (Courtesy of Manuscripts, Archives and Rare Books Division, Schomburg Center for Research in Black Culture, New York Public Library, Astor, Lenox and Tilden Foundations)

held in their hands the possibility of realizing the principles of the Revolution. Thus, they should assume responsibility for unifying and integrating the constitutive, black and white "elements" of the Cuban people.[25]

When the dust finally settled, only a limited number of lower-level jobs in the police and postal services were granted to blacks. And notwithstanding the jobs awarded, both the president and the House of Representatives had ostensibly deliberated on this issue of black access to government resources, yet both had failed to design or institute the more far-reaching legislative reforms necessary to satisfy the demands of black and mulatto veterans and clubmen or fully ease tensions.[26] Further, officials' manipulation of civil service jobs, personally wielding state resources for political control, was in full force. Shortly after he set aside some one hundred municipal posts for black job seekers in and around the capital city of Havana, Estrada Palma inquired in personal correspondence to Francisco Sánchez Hechavarría, then governor of the island's far easterly Oriente province, about how best to control black malcontents there with token political appointments.[27] By 1902, then, officials had swept out to sea the wave of black activism that challenged unequal distribution of national resources. In the years leading up to the 1912 Race War, when a few hundred autonomous black activists rose up in arms over exclusions, blacks continued to demand a share of patronage appointments, though most gravitated to activism on "the inside" of the political structure rather than agitating at its margins.

The disparity between revolutionary democracy (the idea of "a nation for all" postulated by José Martí years earlier) on the one hand, and equal access to public resources on the other, did not dissuade black leaders such as Juan Gualberto Gómez from aligning with the national project. Gómez, in fact, continued to express hope that if afforded the opportunity the nation's leaders would answer black concerns, despite clear evidence of antiblack exclusions in the postrevolutionary government. He had, after all, supported Estrada Palma's paltry offer of set-asides in response to black frustration. And he was unquestioning about the president's public reference to the "deserving black"—the black veteran patriot who beyond the selfless act of fighting for national freedom also strove to improve his cultural orientation and professional "preparation."[28] Publicly, Gómez articulated faith in the Cuban nation and its captains. On numerous occasions, he suggested that in the wake of the Revolution, the most effective activist strategy for disaffected blacks was to make demands for inclusion, such as the Veterans and Societies of Color mobilization had done with President Estrada Palma and the new Cuban Congress.[29] In essence, in the face of race-based exclusions, the preferred strategy of many black leaders such as Gómez was to penetrate rather than challenge the republic's emerging socioeconomic structures.

Accused of being too radical because of its open challenge to government hiring practices, the Veterans and Societies of Color mobilization was quickly absorbed by a broader, parallel movement of veterans seeking the pay and benefits owed them by government officials. Yet how to participate effectively, in not just new Cuban democracy but also in older, more familiar and widespread systems of patronage, remained an excruciating question for black Cubans. They were generally squeezed out of opportunities, unable to effectively compete with whites for elected office, public service jobs, and even nongovernmental employment. And race-based black mobilization was increasingly delegitimized. Worse still, at times they were supplanted by foreign (generally Spanish) laborers, especially in trade occupations such as masonry and tobacco production.

Notwithstanding such difficulties, a small group of privileged black civic and political activists managed to penetrate government structures. The 1902 Veterans and Societies of Color mobilization represents an early, if largely unsuccessful, attempt by activists to win permanent access to the mechanisms of the republic's political economy. Though the vast majority of African-descended Cubans were not elected to office, politicians by necessity courted prominent black activists in order to attract black votes. As brokers of black political support, they wielded some measure of power in the political system. Election time was critical for these black activists, who took advantage of the opening afforded to them by administrative turnover and the frequent changing of the political guard after elections. As one black journalist described it, elections were the "hour of political wheedling."[30] Alejandro de la Fuente has rightly argued that electoral politics afforded blacks important opportunities because campaign seasons ignited the drive for votes and obligated political parties to place black candidates on their rosters.[31] Even after the 1902 Veterans and Societies of Color mobilization disbanded, black activists agitated within mainstream political organizations and black activist leaders saw their own stakes in the electoral success of the political parties within which they were working.

In the early republic, the majority of prominent black leaders (such as Silverio Sánchez Figueras, Genoroso Campos Marquetti, Rafael Serra, and Juan Gualberto Gómez) were, like their white counterparts, veterans of the anticolonial insurgency. During the first two decades of the republic, several young, postindependence black professionals began to grab at leadership as well, including attorneys Miguel Ángel Céspedes, Primitivo Ramírez Ros, and Américo Portuondo Hardy, physician José Guadalupe Castellanos, architect Aquilino Thorndike Lombard, and intellectual, journalist, and writer Juan Felipe Risquet. They represented an intimate corps of black civic activists who parlayed their notoriety and prominence into civil service posts, often eventually running for and winning public office. These politicians extended their reach into black civil society, maintaining a presence in the black press and among black clubs, associations, unions, and even multiracial public schools. They blurred the distinction between government and civil society. Despite scholarly debates that draw a clear line of distinction between state and civil society, constructing these as discrete and, at times, warring entities and insisting that civil society provides a system of checks and balances to state power, in republican Cuba state and civil society overlapped in critical ways. In fact, they often functioned as part of the same administrative apparatus.

In exchange for public prominence, black leaders largely eschewed overt racial consciousness and supported progressivist and bourgeois-liberal values, which were common in early republican society. Their actions suggest that scholars need to more closely examine the range of commitments of republican black civic leaders and political activists. Rather than espousing racial nationalism or black, cross-class unity in their public sphere speeches, events, and newspapers, this small sector of highly visible, self-selected black leaders professed a belief in progressivism, liberal democracy, uplift, and bourgeois respectability. Further, despite their elitist underpinnings or their incongruence with the experiences of most blacks of the early republic, privileged black leaders insisted that adherence to these social values would "advance the race." Simultaneously, they challenged a dominant presumption that as blacks they were culturally incompatible with the progressivism and bourgeois respectability necessary for national leadership. Their political strategy, then, was to assert their "fitness" both to occupy public office and to constitute a privileged black leadership cadre on behalf of black racial uplift.

At the same time, however, their power depended on the political strength of Cuba's black population. Numerically, black Cubans (estimated by census takers to be about one-third of the total island population throughout the republican period) constituted a significant segment of the population and represented a large cache of potential votes. In the highly competitive republican political arena, all votes were coveted and black support was important for politicians of any color to win office. Blacks' electoral influence notwithstanding, they contended with racial exclusions in formal politics. Although their votes were important to office seekers, dominant political parties put up few black candidates on their party rosters and even fewer held leadership positions within a party. More often than not, blacks failed to win political office in numbers proportionate to the black population.[32] This, in turn, limited their access to the public treasury.

Further, party leaders failed to engage in substantive discussion about blacks' difficult socioeconomic circumstances or to champion the antiracist cause. In fact, they generally avoided overt discussion of race and racial injustice. In fact, despite ongoing racial exclusions, the early republican political environment made overtly race-based activism a challenge. Because of this avoidance of talk of race, black leaders often spoke publicly in support of social "harmony" and racial fraternity instead of racial equality. With ongoing racial exclusions, the politics of representation (which was a significant but not overriding determinant of political loyalty) carried enough weight for black leaders to attract black voters by purporting to champion a racial cause. Black leaders, then, existed at the interstices of race and republican political structure. They worked for socioeconomic opportunities for themselves by harnessing the political strength of the island's black votes. And for a time they were able to navigate a climate of both black socioeconomic frustration and a dominant national philosophy that rejected race-conscious activism.

Returning to the Veterans and Societies of Color Action Committee and its 1902 skirmish with President Estrada Palma over employment, many of that mobilization's key public figures, such as Juan Gualberto Gómez and Generoso Campos Marquetti, were at the center of the action in large part because they were among the most visible black leaders of the early republican period. This is especially true for Gómez, who for almost three decades, until his death in 1933, served as one of the most influential politicians, spokesmen, journalists, and political brokers in republican history. In the words of Campos Marquetti, in the first years of the republic the paltry few blacks that had actually managed to land a state job in Havana had done so "owing to the influence of Juan Gualberto Gómez."[33] In fact, Gómez's candidacies, party endorsements, distribution of favors, voter recruitment, and contributions to nationalist ideology were nearly unsurpassed by Cuban leaders of any color for the period, and particularly for those of African descent. A close examination of the sort of power that he commanded and the tributaries he navigated in a network of political relations provides a nuanced understanding of black Cubans' political behavior and their engagement with formal republican politics.

Gómez was situated at the axis of two of the republic's most critical political questions. He vehemently endorsed a nationalist cause, even as foreign political and economic interests subordinated Cuban ones. In 1901,

Gómez led fellow constitutional delegates in a fierce repudiation of the U.S.-authored Platt Amendment to the Cuban constitution and editorialized in several political newspapers in defense of national sovereignty. A consummate nationalist, Gómez used political office, the press, and oratory throughout the early decades of the twentieth century to challenge foreign encroachments on Cuban sovereignty. Yet he also spoke for racial equality. As a mulatto Cuban, son of ex-slaves, and a respected activist in the ranks of black leadership, Gómez advocated social justice when this was attacked by politicians and the press. In the postcolonial peace, as Cubans set about building a new society, Gómez balked at a possible return to racial inequality and argued for a black political party.[34] He often used the press as a mechanism of protest both during and following colonial rule. In the early republic, pages from his newspaper, *La República Cubana*, for example, self-touted as the "organ of the colored people of Cuba," demanded greater patronage appointments for blacks. In 1915, following the 1912 Race War and on the eve of national elections, he campaigned for an island-wide network of black civic organizations. And during the witchcraft scare of 1919, when several black men were murdered in and around Havana, accused of the crimes of rape and anthropophagy of young white children, Gómez joined other black public figures in drafting a manifesto against the crimes and the rising anti-black press spree.[35]

Gómez the nationalist had organized politically among all classes and colors since the late colonial period, informed by both republicanism and racial consciousness. His years in France (1869–79) during the Paris Commune contributed to his republican leanings and caused him to proselytize— particularly among black and mulatto artisans—insisting that African-descended Cubans, especially former slaves, could win respectability and gain political inclusion through education and enlightened thinking and behavior.[36] Black participation was central, he believed, to the formation of a sovereign and democratic Cuban republic. Historians such as Carmen Montejo Arrechea and Oilda Hevia Lanier have documented his ability to mobilize black tradesmen during the late colonial period. Despite exile in Spain from 1880 to 1890, Gómez mobilized many artisan organizations to build a black civil rights organization, galvanizing hundreds of black and mulatto artisans and social-club members on the island and strengthening the Central Directorate of Societies of the Colored Race.[37] The nineteenth-century Central Directorate provided member organizations with high visibility and distinction, access to education and social networks, and a platform to demonstrate black cultural refinement, and it represented the colony's most powerful sector of African-descended Cubans. Much of his notoriety and prestige stemmed from the ten years he spent in exile after agitating against Spanish colonialism and participating in the Revolution that eventually ended colonial rule, but he also built a solid reputation as a newspaper editor, of such polemical presses as *La Fraternidad*, *La Igualdad*, *El Fraternal*, *Patria*, and *La República Cubana*, each of which debated nationalist ideologies and social justice issues during various moments of late colonial and early republican history.

Gómez again surfaced as a leader of black civic activism following the War of Independence. In June 1915, for example, he addressed an island-wide gathering of black societies. Then a Liberal Party congressman from Havana province, he urged hundreds of delegates gathered in Havana to strengthen black activism through civic involvement, cultural enlightenment, and "progress."[38] For Gómez, his revolutionary activism and career as a journalist and civic activist facilitated his emergence as *the* point person on national race issues in the early twentieth century and made him one of the most influential spokespersons for the African-descended in Cuban history.

Caciques, *Caudillos*, and the Black Broker

Gómez built an impressive public career in civics, journalism, and especially politics, serving as a constitutional delegate, congressional representative, and senator (1916–20). Highly visible in the public sphere and in municipal service, he was appointed to Civil Governor William Howard Taft's so-called Peace Committee following the 1906 August Revolution, to Havana's prestigious Academy of History (1908), and to the occupation government's Advisory Law Commission (1907–9), among many other honors.[39]

Gómez the radical leader was also a powerful national player, as demonstrated in a bloody clash that broke out in 1902 due to intense job competition. He mediated a truce between the Workers' League and government officials regarding protections for native workers, particularly in the tobacco industry, where foreign (Spanish) labor predominated at the expense of Cuban workers. A few years later, during the August Revolution of 1906, when Liberal Party members revolted against the Moderate government's monopoly of state offices, Gómez was the only black Liberal Party leader arrested. The Moderate president saw fit to corral other powerful, white rival Liberals accused of leading the revolt, such as José de Jesús Monteagudo, Demetrio Castillo Duany, and José Miguel Gómez (who would later become president).[40] Juan Gualberto Gómez's political stances on race, too, were published on numerous occasions, including during the 1912 Race War and the antiblack violence of 1919 in and around Havana. Between 1900 and

1930, in a politically volatile climate, on several different occasions Gómez mobilized political coalitions and often served in their leadership.

Paradoxically, despite his imposing public presence, Gómez's power stemmed from his critical role in the shadows, *away* from the public eye, where he agitated quite successfully as a politico and power broker. He made deals with clients and political party leaders and often was called on to distribute favors in exchange for political support. Much of his power, too, stemmed from his ties to black civic clubs, which publicly lauded his political activism and civic participation. The clubs also privately sought his support for their financial and social agendas. Gómez and other black leaders shepherded land grants, funds, jobs, and subventions to these institutions during the republican period in exchange for their organizational support. In fact, these organizations constituted a coterie of political agents that helped to enhance the reputation and prestige of black leaders. Archival records, for example, are replete with black club correspondence to Gómez, pledging public support, including informing him of his appointment as club "President," "President of Honor," "Honorary Member," or "Protecting Member," among other honorific titles. As early as 1900, for example, the secretary of the "Juan Gualberto Gómez" Recreational Club sent his organization's hearty congratulations to Gómez after he was slated with others to represent Santiago de Cuba at the upcoming constitutional convention.[41] Several black clubs on the island, in fact, venerated Gómez and confirmed his national prominence by taking his name. Gómez's political record represents a long-standing, active engagement with the complex machinations of building political authority in the early republic's political culture. His political influence was publicly acknowledged by the use of the title "Don" ("Don Juan"), a label of distinction used since the colonial period that was rarely associated with blacks.[42] Arguably, in the political parlance of the early twentieth century Juan Gualberto Gómez might have been called a *caudillo*.[43]

That Gómez had the power to influence a large black constituency was clear to U.S. occupation officials as well. Provisional Governor Leonard Wood intimated as much to President Roosevelt in 1901, when he noted that Gómez's so-called nationalist campaign against the odious Platt Amendment was, in truth, a thinly veiled attempt to hasten a U.S. withdrawal and to use the resulting political vacuum for his own benefit and to expand his influence among blacks. Wood likely suspected as much, because black Cubans had so resoundingly rejected the Platt Amendment as part of the Cuban constitution.[44]

The degree of racial affinity among the African-descended in Cuba has

Politician, journalist, and nationalist civic activist Juan Gualberto
Gómez. From "Anniversary Album," *Boletín Oficial del Club Atenas*
1, no. 9 (September 20, 1930): 4. (Author's private collection)

not been fully examined by scholars, leaving unanswered and interesting questions. How much confidence did prominent black figures inspire among the African-descended? To what extent did racialized experiences inform political behavior? One influential argument about political behavior among people of African descent in the United States has been asserted by political scientist Michael Dawson. Called "linked fate," his theory of race consciousness can be understood as the belief that one's socioeconomic interests are best served by allegiance to a group united in its common experience of racial oppression.[45] For blacks in Cuba, archival documents contain some expressions of racial affinity, but they do not support the assumption that blacks held an overwhelming sense of racial group allegiance. Some certainly desired to act on behalf of racial "linked fate," yet it is important to consider that this likely was not the only perspective informing black experience. Rather, a variety of motivations, identities, and circumstances mediated and even supplanted racial consciousness in Cuba. Rather than accept a facile understanding about the link between black activism on the one hand and black racial consciousness on the other, the nature and degree of racial group solidarity demonstrated by black Cubans demands further study.

Black Cuban leaders such as Juan Gualberto Gómez, Rafael Serra, and Agustín Cebreco were sought by political parties, ostensibly for their racial appeal. Their campaigning helped to secure electoral outcomes, and they served as important partisan spokespersons. Serra dedicated many of his final years to defending Tomás Estrada Palma. Several of his essays, which are gathered in his compilation of political commentary, *Para blancos y negros*, supported not only Estrada Palma but the reigning Moderate Party.[46] The National Liberal Party of Oriente managed to lasso Juan Gualberto Gómez in 1901 to work on behalf of the party's expansion. He served in the party's provincial directorate alongside several other prominent politicians, such as Alfredo Zayas, local black politician Alberto Castellanos, and distinguished white veterans Erasmo Regüeiferos and General Demetrio Castillo y Duany. A few years later, in 1904, he joined the newly organized Liberal Party (different from the 1901 National Liberal Party of Oriente) and almost immediately assumed party leadership.[47]

In fact, Gómez was behind the formation of several political parties that emerged in the early republic only to reorganize or fold quickly under new names and leaderships, including the Republican Party (1901), the Independent Republican Party (1901), the Liberal National Party (1903), the Liberal Party (1905) (which won the presidential election of 1908), and the Cuban Popular Party (1920) (which secured the Cuban presidency for Alfredo Zayas in 1920). Thus, not only did Gómez help build some of the most successful political organizations in republican history, but on several occasions he created the very parties within which he worked as a political activist.

Yet there were also limits to his success. His candidacy for the 1904 congressional elections, under the Oriental Independent Coalition banner in the largely black province of Oriente, was unsuccessful. Gómez was unable to beat Rafael Serra, who had joined the Radical National Party in Oriente under the leadership of National Party regional strongman and incumbent senator Antonio Bravo Correoso. Rampant fraudulent practices of political incumbents had rocked the 1904 partial elections, and Gómez was one of the many defrauded candidates who brought charges against government-backed electoral boards. As many as 7,888 votes were purportedly stolen from Gómez in his bid against Serra, which caused him to lose the congressional seat.[48] Current histories of the period are unclear about whether Gómez failed to win against Serra because of the strength of the reigning political party in Oriente and its ability to lobby among blacks in the region, or if what blocked his election was electoral fraud. Either way, by 1905 a history of dirty elections had galvanized a significant, popularly based movement to overthrow conservative rule. Known as the August Revolution of 1906, the Liberal-led civil war drew together political opposition of all colors against electoral fraud and the impenetrability of public office for political contenders.

Thus, as the 1905 elections approached, in response to a series of flagrant electoral-board illegalities favoring the newly formed Moderate Party (August 1904–August 1906), traditional National Liberal Party supporters mobilized, forming a new Liberal Party in April 1905 led by Juan Gualberto Gómez and two future presidents of the republic: José Miguel Gómez (1909–12) and Alfredo Zayas (1921–25). Moderates, however, refused to relinquish their hold on government office, using their control over the courts and electoral boards and even thugs to intimidate and oust their Liberal political competition. Battered Liberals rose up in arms in and around Havana in November 1905, asserting their right to occupy public offices and to challenge electoral malfeasance. The revolt soon spread to other regions of the island. The Liberal Party's uprising lasted almost a year, peaking in August 1906. During its course, Liberal leaders were jailed; a heroic, if controversial, black general, Quintín Bandera, was brutally slain; the president and his cabinet resigned their offices; the United States occupied Cuba (1906–9) for the second time since Cuban independence in 1898; and the Moderate Party was dissolved.[49]

Historian Thomas Orum has argued that many of those who participated in the revolt on the side of the Liberal Party were black, especially those insurgents in the capital city and in the western and central portions of the island. He suggests that Liberal Party frustration grew from the problem of access to public offices and Moderates' relative failure to distribute civil jobs to all Liberals, but especially to blacks. After the Liberals successfully ousted the Moderates and ended their monopoly on state offices, for example, black Liberals Juan Gualberto Gómez and Martín Morúa Delgado—both appointed after the August Revolution to the new Committee on Claims and Jobs by provisional governor Charles Magoon—pressed the governor for a remedy to the recurrent issue of civic employment for blacks.

One question unanswered by historians is why Moderates—notorious for their reluctance to include more than a smattering of blacks on their election rosters—had counted on a significant black support base in the east, presumably spearheaded by a solid show of support from black veteran army leaders and soldiers.[50] One possible explanation is that Moderates were successful in recruiting black veteran independence leaders from Oriente province. Given the importance of regionalism to Cuban political mobilization, as demonstrated in the history of deeply rooted regionalism among political parties, if Moderates had attracted black regional strongmen this in turn would have brought to the party a locally identified base of supporters.

Loyalty and "the Local"

The republic's first political parties were organized according to regional (municipal and/or provincial) political dynamics. They operated under the auspices of local political strongmen, who counted on localized voter support. Many of these leaders were veterans of the Liberation Army, and black Cubans were fully represented among veteran leaders. Historians such as Pérez and Ibarra have argued that blacks in the Liberation Army accounted for as much as 40 percent of commissioned officers and 60 percent of soldiers.[51] Like all military leaders, black officers (such as Quintín Bandera, Lino D'ou, Guillermo Moncada, Agustín Cebreco, Silverio Sánchez Figueras, Generoso Campos Marquetti, and Juan Gualberto Gómez) commanded loyalty even after the war ended, and this loyalty often translated into notoriety and popular votes when former military leaders stood for civilian political office. Some fallen black war heroes, Antonio Maceo and Guillermo Moncada, for example, were commemorated by black social organizations. Veteran officers enjoyed lasting loyalty, such as General Quintín

Bandera, who mobilized his local base of support on behalf of the National League of Oriente, a proposed national party to be based in his native province of Oriente.[52]

A group of notable black women provides another example of how important localized identities were in Cuban political behavior. In Santiago de Cuba, these women founded the Admiradoras de Moncada (Admirers of Moncada) organization, which drew many black women civic activists over the years.[53] The club began as a mobilization of working-class black women, and as the century progressed, black women of privilege joined the organization's ranks. In 1946, for example, the club roster included Nelsa and Nacarina Portuondo, the daughters of the preeminent black statesmen Américo Portuondo Hardy; Sara Mancebo, the sister of Luis Mancebo, a powerful, longtime secretary of Santiago de Cuba's veterans' association; as well as teachers and pharmacists and a doctor of pedagogy.[54] That these women considered themselves distinguished local patriots is particularly clear when in the early 1940s they changed the club's name to Asociación Patriótica de Damas Admiradoras de Moncada (Patriotic Ladies' Association of Admirers of Moncada). In 1923 the Admiradoras engaged in a public performance to express patriotism and commemorate black general Guillermo Moncada, himself a revered native of Santiago de Cuba. The women collaborated with the black, Santiago-based Aponte Social Club to honor the memory of insurgent general Guillermo Moncada on the twenty-eighth anniversary of his death.[55] Although the Aponte Social Club sponsored the event, the primary actors were members of Admiradoras, including its board of directors and affiliates from several neighborhood branches. On April 5, at four o'clock in the afternoon, the women departed from Club Aponte's social center en route to Santiago's Santa Efigénia Cemetery. Even the aged and infirm daughter of the "Ebony Titan," as Moncada was known, was present, and she required assistance throughout the days' events.

Imagine the scene—a parade of local female dignitaries walking solemnly through the narrow brick streets of Santiago, each one cradling a metal crown and wreath of fresh flowers. They passed blacks' and whites' homes along the way, drawing residents to their windows to stare. The women took center stage as state officials, such as provincial governor José Ramón Barceló, Lieutenant Colonel Luis del Rosal, Captain Enrique Corona, provincial councilmen Justo Salas Arzuaga and Antonlín Callejas, and newspaper editor Daniel Fajardo Ortiz, as well as representatives of the local veterans' association, civic institutions, and a large crowd of *santiaguero* onlookers trailed behind.[56]

At the Moncada Mausoleum, the district military band played ceremoniously while Admiradoras members deposited their flowers at Moncada's tomb. A series of speeches then ensued, delivered by Club Aponte members and local politicians. Later that evening, a gala was held in honor of Moncada, the "Ebony Giant" (as he was also known), at which the municipal band played the national anthem among other patriotic scores. It was proposed that the Moncada home be bought as a "pearl" of local collective memory and an important pedagogical tool for future generations.[57]

Such a regional show of patriotism often served the dual purpose of reinforcing political relationships among local organizations and politicians and of elevating the status of a sector of local society. A show of regionalism is clear in the pomp and circumstance surrounding the remains of Mariana Grajales as well, one of the few female martyrs of the anticolonial insurgency. Grajales (1808–83) was the mother of several anticolonial combatants. She is remembered as a national heroine because two of her many children figured among the most powerful national military leaders of the anticolonial insurgency: generals José and Antonio Maceo. In 1922, her bones were shipped from Jamaica to her native city, Santiago de Cuba, and once received, were duly commemorated by local officials and organizations.

Members of the mulatto Sociedad Luz de Oriente, for example, involved themselves intimately in the very public and solemn process of authenticating and repatriating Grajales's sacred corpse. They used the event to express their own patriotic commitments to one of the only black heroines from Oriente province to be recognized in the nation's pantheon of independence heroes. A full team of doctors and public officials, including several councilmen, José C. Palomino (the vice president of the city council), and members of Luz de Oriente and other local societies of color spearheaded the official transfer of the martyr's bones home. Group photos of these key political players, portrayed as guardians of the national patrimony, appeared in several newspapers.

More than articulating fidelity to an imagined localized political community (even when that community's sons and daughters—such as Guillermo Moncada and Mariana Grajales—reached national prominence), identification with the "local" also emanated from the localness of blood ties and dynastic family relationships. Building familial networks within local civic organizations and government served at least three purposes for local leaders and politicians. Family members constituted an important and particularly loyal pool of political supporters; they helped to shore up a family's social standing; and they worked to expand the families' economic status and cache of resources.

As I have argued previously, black politicians created networks in both civic institutions and government offices, effectively bringing local civic and state operations into the same sphere of influence. Familial relationships facilitated the process. In Santiago, from the 1920s to the 1930s, Pedro Salas Arzuaga was a board member of the Luz de Oriente Society in various capacities. In the 1940s he served as Santiago's chief of police and as a Liberal Party deputy congressional representative. His brother, Justo, was active in Luz de Oriente as well, yet more of his energy went to political administration. Justo served as a Liberal alderman (1922) and, on four separate occasions between the 1920s and the 1940s, as deputy congressional representative. He was also mayor of Santiago from 1940 to 1944 for the Revolutionary Communist Union Party.[58]

National political parties used local-level organizing to their advantage, such as the National Party, which recruited many black veteran officers to its ranks, including Nicolás Guillén, Agustín Cebreco, and Quintín Bandera. After 1902, when national, rather than local political parties began to gain prominence, they continued to rely on localized mobilization to garner support. The Liberal Party stronghold, for example, was in the western, not the eastern, part of the country, and Moderates in Oriente province enjoyed significant support in the early years. Liberals there wanted to expand their influence, a fact born out by numerous letters penned by local politicians such as Juan Estrada Portuondo, Dr. José Guadalupe Castellanos, and José Vantour. They asked Juan Gualberto Gómez to use his political influence to build the local Liberal cluster in Oriente.[59] Writing to Gómez just before the 1904 elections, Vantour suggested that Gómez could be of great use to Oriente's Liberal Party because his balanced leadership style and distinguished reputation would likely invigorate the party and attract followers.[60]

Power's Reach

Even late in his life, calls for the Havana-based Gómez to intervene in local matters came from all corners of the island. In this sense, he might be compared to other *caudillos* in Cuban history. In 1923, for example, Luz de Oriente wrote to Gómez asking that he block an unwanted transfer of Head Comptroller José Bueno to the distant city of Camagüey, because Bueno was "a man important to the interests of 'our social class.'"[61] Luz de Oriente wrote to Gómez on another occasion, requesting that as in the past, he use his influence on behalf of Dr. Francisco Bermúdez Rodríguez, ex-president of Luz de Oriente, to win Bermúdez an appointment as head of sanitation for the town of San Luis in Oriente province.[62]

Requests for help were not always cordial and at times were even threatening, suggesting that within the patronage system, those who appealed for favors expected results based on the principles of reciprocity. In 1924, a black club from the town of Baracoa in Oriente province wrote to Don Juan (Gómez), in essence stating that it had supported his candidacy as senator yet he had failed to deliver on his promise of an automobile for the club to raffle. The club needed the car, the writers charged, to acquire funds sufficient for their club headquarters. Members had had to seek support from another person of influence, and they implied that their ongoing political support of Gómez was withdrawn.[63] Black appeals to Gómez began soon after Cuban independence. In the months immediately after the war in 1898, members of the black Sociedad La Unión of Matanzas drafted a letter to him expressing their deep concerns. Identifying themselves as "free Cubans, unstained" (presumably a reference to their distance, as free people of color, from slave labor), they requested Gómez's assistance, "knowing the unbearable need that our compatriots and brothers of the race, who liberated the homeland, have come to suffer."[64] They proposed a committee, under Gómez's tutelage, for black advancement in the "new order of things that the country is about to undergo." Their letter, however, was particularly provocative for two reasons. First, they suggested that the committee's purpose would be to "prepare the *sane element* [emphasis mine] of our race" so that it would "know how to rise as one in aid of the firm aspirations of our lives." Further, the society members suggested that black Cubans had lost in war "our most beautiful hopes, José and Antonio Maceo. That has made us suffer!" Thus, the group pinned its hopes on its moral force (as elevated people of color) and on the power wielded by Juan Gualberto Gómez, perhaps the state's most highly placed person of color at the dawn of the republic. The members asked Gómez whether as blacks they should be strict racial activists, separate from whites, or whether they should offer their support unconditionally to a broad effort to build the republic. Pledging their support to him, they intimated that whatever political action Gómez planned to take he could count on their numbers—"the sane part of the black population of Matanzas"—and that they would not take any steps as activists without his instructions.[65] At the same time that they pledged their fidelity to the prominent black leader, they also identified themselves as a political bloc, capable of supporting or abandoning political hopefuls. For this relatively privileged group of people of color, political empowerment was at once a matter of developing networks among the island's many black and mulatto clubs, such as the La Sociedad Unión, and of obtaining formal education, demonstrating the accoutrements of refinement, cultivating ties to the state, and articulating publicly a sense of racial consciousness.

Two years later, on September 15, 1900, Juan Estrada Portuondo, a school council member in Oriente province, wrote to Gómez in Havana for his help. He wanted Gómez to use his influence in a local, provincial political struggle over civil jobs, a request that stemmed from the general problem of the island's rapidly growing state bureaucracy (including the number of civil service workers), which challenged local politicians' control over an expanding army of state employees and threatened their political power and influence. As mentioned earlier, in 1899 only 1 percent of the population worked for the state, a number that increased exponentially in the course of six decades of republican politics. By the 1959 Revolution, the state bureaucracy had grown ninefold.[66]

Juan Estrada Portuondo first apprised Gómez of the political ambitions of Eduardo Yero Buduén, a rising politician from Oriente who had been recently named provincial superintendent of public instruction by Governor General Leonard Wood and who had been elected as an alternate to the constitutional convention just two weeks earlier.[67] According to Estrada Portuondo, Yero Buduén meant to remove him and other men from the local school council because they were not of his same "school of thought." Presumably, the men posed a threat to Yero Buduén's monopoly over state posts. Estrada Portuondo believed that Yero Buduén planned to sabotage the U.S. occupation government's new educational reforms, which had been initiated under the direction of the North American superintendent of schools, Alexis E. Frye, who was working with local, Cuban officials to overhaul Cuban public education. Apparently, Frye meant to reduce the total number of teachers across the island in a move to improve the efficiency of the education system.[68] As a by-product of downsizing, Frye would decrease the total number of teachers in Oriente province (Estrada Portuondo estimated that Oriente province had 3,000 to 4,000 teachers on the state's payroll), thereby decreasing the state jobs that Yero Buduén controlled as superintendent.[69] Estrada Portuondo urged Gómez to "neutralize" Yero Buduén, by pulling the coattails of the island's secretary of education, José Enrique Varona, as well as school superintendents in Havana, who could, in turn, rein in Yero Buduén.[70]

José Guadalupe Castellanos, a politically influential mulatto and leader in the eastern club movement in Oriente province, wrote to Gómez as well, in 1902, urging him to intervene in the upcoming provincial council elections.[71] Castellanos, who in 1898 had been appointed lieutenant mayor of Santiago by U.S. occupation officials, suggested that in Oriente province a political vacuum existed due to a rift within the National Party between rank-and-file supporters and party leadership. Castellanos believed Gómez might use this split to win political support and increase his power. Despite his residence in Havana, Gómez could even be put up as a National Party candidate in Oriente if he secured significant local support among Oriente's popular voters—many of whom were of African descent.

Factions had developed around two local white politicians, Ambrosio Grillo Portuondo and another "Yero," Manuel Yero Sagol, both of whom were in line to represent the National Party in their respective political districts. Both men also were vying for leadership of the Provincial Council of Oriente. The popular vote, suggested Castellanos, backed Grillo, and National Party leaders were behind Yero Sagol. Though National leaders had at one time supported Grillo publicly, he had failed to win Provincial Council elections. Instead, it seems, National Party leaders had acted according to the wishes of the powerful senator Antonio Bravo Correoso, leader of the National Party in Oriente, and had elected Yero Sagol as head of Oriente's Provincial Council, a move that alienated and angered many voters from the province.[72]

Castellanos suggested that Gómez could commandeer National Party support, based on widespread dissatisfaction and ruptures at the local level. He suggested to Gómez that frustrated voters were powerful enough to quash Yero Sagol's campaign. According to Castellanos, if Yero Sagol lost the popular vote he would lose the top spot on the Provincial Council, a position he coveted for good reason since doctors had revealed that the health of Oriente's first appointed Cuban governor, Francisco Sánchez Hechavarría, leader of the anticolonial insurgency in Oriente province, was so poor that he would not last for a full term. When Sánchez Hechavarría died shortly after assuming office in 1902, Yero Sagol (who years later was elected as a Conservative Party senator from Oriente province) assumed Sánchez's post, donning the governor's mantle on December 24, 1902.[73]

In 1904, two years later, when Moderate intimidation tactics against Liberals spread across the island, Gómez was called on to help Liberal activists at the local level. In Oriente province, for example, where Moderates predominated, Liberals were on the defensive and mobilizing whenever possible to preserve their political influence.[74] On July 20, 1904, a black Liberal Party organizer from Oriente province, José Vantour, sought the help of the party's ranking black leader, Juan Gualberto Gómez, in a matter of "vital interest" to local party members.[75] Vantour had moved swiftly to contact the Havana-based Gómez after his own local Liberal Party chairman had died that same day in July, leaving Liberals—in a region dominated by Moderates—without a leader to organize on behalf of the party or to spread publicly "the propaganda so necessary" to political success.[76] And in the months before the December 1905 general elections, Liberals in Santiago de Cuba agitated within black civic organizations such as Club Aponte and Luz de Oriente for political support.[77]

Yet Gómez's power extended beyond the manipulation of regional party factions or formal political structures. Importantly, he provided opportunity for voters of all colors and especially black voters to enter into reciprocal relations with him to receive political favors. People turned to Gómez for his assistance in securing funds for civic organizations and getting individual jobs, for his support in applications to elite and professional education programs, and even for improved political representation. In return, they supported his bid for various political offices throughout the first decades of the republic. High-ranking officials requested his help, too, such as in 1910 when the white presidential secretary, Dr. José Lorenzo Castellanos, asked Gómez, in his capacity as the director of *La Lucha* press, to assist one Señora Rosina Esponda, the daughter of a good friend, most likely in her quest for job placement.[78]

Gómez's vast political influence undoubtedly led to rivalry. For instance, he is said to have had an intensely antagonistic relationship with another highly influential black politician, black senator and one-time Senate president Martín Morúa Delgado. Yet despite rumors of animus, the two joined forces after the 1906 August Revolution. Both Gómez and Morúa Delgado had participated in the revolt against the reigning Moderate Party that lasted from November 1905 to fall 1906. Perhaps this history had provided them with enough common ground to work together and offer each other patronage favors. On May 15, 1906, for example, Morúa Delgado wrote an urgent letter to Gómez, asking him to support his recent Senate proposal for electoral reforms and advising him, "If you agree with my proposal, then hand to the wheel and let's get cracking on our colleagues!"[79] In another letter, dated November 6, 1906, Morúa Delgado asked Gómez to support a recent civil service nomination by Alfredo Zayas, which would appoint Evaristo Estenoz (who a short time later spearheaded the Independent Party of Color movement) as head of sanitation and transportation for the Department of Public Works in Havana. Morúa Delgado said he had a "vested interest" in the appointment and its approval by U.S. occupation governor Charles E. Magoon. As a fellow member of Magoon's important Jobs and Claims Commission, he wanted Gómez's support for the Estenoz nomination.[80]

Historical documents link Gómez to several other black leaders who were *caciques* in their own right. On March 7, 1899, Rafael Serra sent Gómez a letter of recommendation for J. A. Lucerna, vouching for his revolutionary principles and work ethic and asking Gómez to help him in any way possible.[81] The long-standing relationship between Juan Felipe Risquet and Gómez serves as another example of black participation in patronage networks. In December 1899, Risquet, a black intellectual and politician from Matanzas province, used his relationship with Gómez to help a white colleague, Mr. Antonio Genova de Zayas, also from Matanzas province, to find a teacher's post in the Havana school system.[82] Though archival documents are sparse regarding Genova de Zayas, he seems to have been building his own political career by seeking work at the board of education, as teaching could be a highly respected and well-connected post. Within a decade, in fact, Genova de Zayas was elected to public office, serving as a House representative for the Liberal Party from 1908 to 1912.[83]

Risquet the politician used his relationship with Gómez to place Genova de Zayas. He counted on Gómez's high-profile appointment to the Havana school board and, after pledging his support of Gómez, asked for his help to place friends. A year later, in 1900, Risquet again requested Gómez's assistance in obtaining a position for Mrs. Elvira Barboza Onido as a school caretaker. Risquet confessed to Gómez that he had promised Mrs. Onido a recommendation, trusting that Gómez would oblige the favor. And in February 1901, Risquet again used his relationship with Gómez to secure the appointment of Mr. Nicolás Muñíz as the secretary of the Committee on Shipyards.[84]

Risquet was a prominent member of the Matanzas-based Republican Party from 1901 to 1904. No doubt, in order to cultivate the strong *relaciones* instrumental to his own success, he needed to move agilely up and down a vertical continuum of patronage relationships.[85] He would have interacted with those people who owed him favors and with those, such as Gómez, to whom he was indebted. Indeed, for the chain of patrons-brokers-clients of the patronage system (where brokers cultivated loyalty from clients and sought resources from their patrons), a broker such as Risquet used his ability to grant favors to win success at the same time that he deferred to someone like Gómez. His *relaciones* with a powerhouse such as Gómez would have been critical to his own political base of support. Indeed, his tenure in Congress from 1901 to 1904 and from 1908 to 1912 serves as a testament to his success in the patronage system.

Shortly before joining Gómez in the Cuban Republican Party, Risquet paid proper respect to the patron, requesting that Gómez approve his plans to launch a republican political newspaper ("before anything else, I want to ask for your utmost approval") to support the Cuban Republican Party. According to Risquet, the proposed newspaper would follow "the principles of liberty, equality, and fraternity, upheld by the Cuban Republican Party."[86] Both Risquet and Gómez would be central to Havana's Republican Party by 1901, and Risquet had set about identifying a group of like-minded activists to attract other potential Republican Party affiliates through printed propaganda. Risquet suggested that his group of adherents expected Gómez to "design" the press—to set its tenor and agenda. After clarifying that he, Risquet, also enjoyed significant *relaciones* and "acquaintances," he assured Gómez that even as he energetically mobilized activists to support the new press he was able to discern who was of the same political bent and who embraced the same school of thought as he and Gómez, and thus he would choose adherents well.[87]

Gómez also launched the career of Miguel Ángel Céspedes, a lawyer, congressman, and elected officer of the most prestigious black club in republican history, Club Atenas. The sapling Céspedes, in the nascent stages of a highly successful career in national politics, had enrolled at the University of Havana Law School in 1903. Céspedes must have represented the promise of resources for a network of black workers back home, in his native province of Camagüey, because the secretary of the Camagueyan Workers' Center, Liborio Vega, wrote to Gómez in December 1903 promising the center's support of Gómez so long as he provided, in turn, his support to the young law student. Intimating that Céspedes was looking to become politically well connected, Vega insisted that Céspedes needed the help of "generous men." Vega also let it be known that days earlier, at a Workers' Center meeting, members voted to support Gómez. That is, they pledged him their political support in the upcoming February 1904 elections under the assumption that Gómez would give their rising star a much-needed hand—both during and after law school. Important to note, too, is that Vega wrote to the *cacique* precisely when Gómez needed that *camagueyano* support. Having recently launched a congressional bid under the multiparty Independent Coalition of Oriente, the Camagüey Workers' Center members represented a critical bloc of voters for the upcoming election in an important provincial territory.[88]

Gómez and Céspedes both eventually became important leaders in the black club movement, working together on many projects in the 1910s and 1920s. In 1912, several years after the Workers' Center had appealed to Gómez on Céspedes's behalf, the up-and-coming law student was elected to Congress under the Patriotic Conjunction Party banner—a faction of the Liberal Party. He was also a key organizer of the movement to unify black societies across the island in 1915 and in the largest black society in Havana, the Fraternal Union (Unión Fraternal). He was also influential among the island's black elite. By 1925, he was elected president of the well-known and prestigious Club Atenas.[89] Even as colleagues, however, a sense of reciprocity dictated their interaction. In March 1922, Céspedes, seeking a public office nomination, pressed Gómez to intervene on his behalf with Cuba's president, Alfredo Zayas, even questioning Gómez's swiftness—or lack thereof—in pleading his case with the head of state.[90]

Gómez's influence reached black societies, including the smaller, often less economically solvent ones in the island's interior. As the 1908 campaign season approached, Evaristo Landa, provisional secretary of the black society Unión Lajera, located at Havana's outskirts, in San José de las Lajas, wrote to Gómez decrying the club's lack of political representation.[91] The members complained that in general in San José de las Lajas, blacks held very few positions of real power; only two had been elected to the city council and another headed a local factory. San José de las Lajas was then a midsized town in Havana province with a population of 11,988, about 10 percent of which (1,248) was of color.[92] Unión Lajera members sent out a call for the "race of color" to unite for socioeconomic advancement, intimating in their letter to Gómez a willingness to support him politically with their votes so long as he reciprocated. As a clear sign of their effusive yet conditional loyalty and their desire to cultivate a reciprocal relationship with Gómez, they noted, "After extending our thanks in advance we would like you to please accept our embrace, your defenders, who truly love you."[93] Unión Lajera's letter to Gómez clarified what was also obvious to politicians: black civic organizations were willing to throw their institutional support behind responsive candidates, and as the cases of Gómez, Evaristo Landa, and Miguel Ángel Céspedes suggest, many black politicians and civic organizations together created patronage relations of mutual benefit.

Conclusion

Despite a recent surge in studies of race in republican Cuba, scholars have not fully examined the relationship between black clubs and politicians. Further, they have paid scant attention to the theoretical potential of a serious examination of race, black consciousness, political organization, and patronage in republican Cuba, the focus of this study.[94] In fact, as the most visible site where blacks created political community in the republican period, black civic institutions were deeply involved in the republic's patronage system.

Black clubs were included on the campaign routes of politicians at all levels and colors throughout the republican period. Politicians such as Tomás Estrada Palma, Rafael Serra, Juan Gualberto Gómez, Quintín Bandera, Miguel Ángel Céspedes, Mario Menocal, and Gerardo Machado lobbied among black civic organizations during their campaigns. Black politicians seem to have visited black societies more often than white ones, but evidence shows that both black and white politicians courted black clubs. It is unclear whether the "attraction" between black clubs and black politicians was based on a shared sense of racial experience (a political community based on "linked fate") or on the expectations of black voters generally that black politicians should court them and represent their interests in republican society. Also murky is whether or not black political success in electoral politics resulted in general economic gains for black Cubans. What can be more easily discerned in republican history is that during moments of political crisis and competition, black activists and government officials sought to strengthen political ties with one another and build greater intimacy.

Conversely, if powerful figures such as Juan Gualberto Gómez, Rafael Serra, and Miguel Ángel Céspedes were distinguished in their political careers, their success was due in large part to their ability to mobilize a clientilist base of black civic activists. Unión Lajera, for example, one of hundreds of black civic organizations that existed during the republican period, was one locale of many on a speakers' circuit for candidates and political parties. Black club conferences, meetings, and rallies gave prominence and prestige to politicians of all colors, providing them critical access to a black public sphere as well as a platform for attracting political support. Political success on the "club circuit," however, was not solely due to one's prominence as an elected official. It also resulted from the ability to accommodate and publicly represent a particular set of cultural values, which shaped the structure, social composition, and agendas of these clubs. Black leaders such as Serra and Gómez insisted on their significance for a black club constituency based on their ability to promote progressive, black, civic values. And they often defined themselves as black public figures who epitomized progressivist, even "modern" values, and who, therefore, were able to help advance the modern national project. Their role as "race men" representatives of the island's entire black population was rendered largely symbolic by the elitism of the black progressivism that the men practiced, and their ties to a broad black Cuban public were generally more implied than concrete.

In fact, there were other forms of black civic institutions in the early republic that drew from progressivist ideals in conjunction with a highly politicized African diaspora consciousness and an allegiance to African ethnic identity. The definition of political community for these organizations diverged from that of mainstream black activists. Further, there is only limited research on the history of patronage relations between African-influenced societies and white elites and elected officials. Lists of Africanist society administrators show that certain club officers installed themselves on the boards of both African-influenced societies and less prominent, progressivist black clubs. Some scholars, such as Judith Bettelheim, argue that elite white Cubans cultivated loyalties among working-class black club members by underwriting certain of their cultural activities.[95] One Africanist society, the Sociedad Carabalí Isuama, always participated in carnival activities throughout the republican period. Because of high participation costs for elaborate costumes, floats, musicians, food, and drink, local businessmen sponsored clubs' participation, presumably in exchange for their political support.

Members sustained a vision of political community, however, that was at the same time nationalist, progressivist, and Africanist. By doing so, as the next chapter shows, they centered their own experiences as people of African descent, a fact that can, in turn, expand scholars' understanding of the range of black political response to early republican society.

CHAPTER THREE

Inventing Africa and Creating Community

In the months following the republic's inauguration, Domingo Julia and Leon Escobar, both self-proclaimed Africans, used newly granted constitutional rights to petition the governor of Santa Clara province. At the heart of their request was a plan to repatriate to the African continent with government assistance. The two claimed to represent about one hundred Africans—ex-slaves—living in and around the central coastal towns of Remedios and Caibarién in Santa Clara province, a historic stronghold of sugar production since the mid-nineteenth century. African laborers, brought throughout much of the nineteenth century to work the region's cane fields, had increased the population of African descent. The 1899 census, for example, reports that about a third of *remedianos* were the descendants of Africans, while significantly fewer were African-born. The men's petition, submitted to local officials on the heels of Cuba's shift from colony to nation, suggests that for these diasporans one's political identity was newly subject to negotiation. As ex-colonials in a postrevolutionary context, they opted, it seems, to take the new nation's leaders at their word and advance a new, black, republican subjectivity.[1]

Domingo Julia and Leon Escobar were among many Africans brought to Cuba to work as slaves. Most obtained their freedom by 1880; those remaining in bondage were emancipated during Cuba's gradual process of abolition (1880–86), which coincided with intensive political upheaval on the island, including fervent anticolonial insurgency and the liberalization of the Spanish colonial state. This coincidence of emancipation and war suggests that the political status of these laborers figured centrally in colonial politics and was part and parcel of Crown maneuvers in a war with insurgents. The Moret Law (1870), for example, passed a decade before abolition in 1880, during Cuba's Ten Years' War (1868–78) against Spanish colonial rule, includes a Crown concession to Africans who sought repatriation to their homeland communities. Colonial authorities offered to return to the continent all free Africans who wished to do so.[2] At its core, the African repatriation clause—motivataed by the island's significant African presence, fear of African political mobilization, and desire to win African loyalists at a time of heightened anticolonial insurgency—was meant to promote partisanship. That is, given the real possibility of recruitment by the insurgency, colonial authorities sought to bind diasporan loyalists to a colonial political community. Arguably, the policy also dismantled the moral integrity of slavery and expanded the range of possibilities of African political response by supporting, at least in theory, the emigration and extraterritorial movement of the African-born. Though the Crown sought their loyalty, circumstances leading to the 1870 Moret Law made Africans' emigration—and their absence from colonial politics—preferable to their remaining on the island in opposition. Thus, while hoping to win the loyalty of the African-born and their children, authorities were also politically willing to unfasten the knot between African partisans and the colony.[3]

During new political opportunities of the early twentieth century, again created by domestic turmoil, officials this time called for a national community of a "modern" political culture (liberal democracy, republicanism, and progressivism) that, as we shall see, would reject the notion of African participation in the national political community, even as these officials asserted that it was a representative democracy. For Leon Escobar and Domingo Julia, their relationship to this nascent community and its modernist political appeals was laced by nostalgia for an extranational (and ostensibly antimodern) "home," making their identity in the new nation particularly sophisticated and complex. That is, their desire to return to the African continent related as much to republican democracy and "freedom" as it did to memories of home, to a history of transgression against their humanity, and to vesting their futures. As the men's petition read: "In their condition as Africans, having suffered the rigors of slavery, they desire to return to the country that witnessed their birth. To that effect they ask that the Cuban government undertake the necessary studies and procedures to consider apportioning a set [annual] amount in the national budget for ship's passage to repatriate all black Africans who wish it, knowing that in this district there are one hundred petitioners, among them the undersigned."[4]

The spirit behind Domingo Julia and Leon Escobar's petition, in which they claimed kith and kin in Africa ("the country that witnessed their birth") *and* individual rights as Cubans, placed them at the crossroads of two seemingly distinct yet deeply enmeshed identities in the early twentieth century.[5] At the same time as they appealed for citizenship rights guaranteed by the new Cuban constitution, they also sought to be able, as Africans, to preserve an allegiance to an extranational patrimony. Paradoxically, when at the dawn of the republic Julia and Escobar requested state aid to return to Africa, they identified and mobilized allegiances on the island and practiced the machinations of forming a particular, Africanist, political community.[6] They drew boundaries, asserted commitments, and identified compatriots who in the early republic seemed increasingly at odds with the construction of a modern, homogeneous, and ostensibly raceless nation.

Like these petitioners from Remedios, many African-descended Cubans of the early republic drew on this sense of commitments and compatriots to build formal networks. These networks (unlike those previously discussed, which linked prominent black activists to mainstream politicians) were intensely corporatist and less focused on achieving intimacy with elected officials. Yet they were the foundation of black sociopolitical communities alternative to the mainstream. Early twentieth-century archival documents attest to the formation of Cuban Africanist civic communities, many of which were the continuation of African ethnic societies (*cabildos de nación*) of the colonial period. Beginning in 1900 and for several decades, hundreds of African-identified diasporans gathered across the island in various corporate organizations to write bylaws and set agendas on behalf of religious beliefs, cultural practices, and financial projects. These organizations, also known as "clubs" or "societies," put forth ideals and values that were at once patriotic and African-ethnic. In the style of older, colonial generations of African ethnics, these ethnically defined communities professed allegiances to, even a diaspora consciousness of, among others, Yoruba, Calabar, Congo, and Bibí cultural sensibilities, while simultaneously embracing territorial nationalism.[7]

The postindependence rekindling of these societies and the Julia-Escobar case, then, suggest the need for scholars to make diaspora beliefs and activism historical by unraveling the context in which social and political commitments emerge, beyond static assumptions about racial identity or political loyalties. Both the existence of Africanist societies in the early republic and the petition that these self-proclaimed Africans in Remedios filed with local authorities raise questions about multiple imaginings of Africa and their role in the formation of republican political identity. In fact, such activism underscores that political communities are formed out of what Michael Hanchard has termed the "premises and machinations of coalition."[8]

Indeed, these Africanist mobilizations highlight a growing tension between Afro-diasporan experiences and the methods used during the sovereign republic's protracted process of decolonization to define virtuous citizens. This juncture of diasporan belonging and displacement was initiated in 1898 by a massive political shift from colonial territory to sovereign nation, a shift inexorable for all people residing on the island and complicated by a mounting push among statesmen and intellectuals to create domestic stability and a modern national identity. Yet this crossroads is also where African-descended Cubans sought to reconcile the disconnect between Cuban modernist imaginings (civilization, cultural refinement, nationalism, representative democracy, economic progress) and their experiences, first as ex-slaves and later as citizens. Their experiences contribute to the location of diasporan sensibilities well beyond the confines of dominant nationalist paradigms. That is, in their transition from colonial subject to republican citizen they set about formulating a new relationship to state and society, one that contended with the evolution of white supremacy in Cuban nationalism and the neocolonial presence of the United States in Cuban affairs, and one that acknowledged African ethnics' loyalties to multiple patrimonies. For all Cubans, this moment of defining postindependence identities involved imagining a collective *and* divergent sense of pasts as well as futures. For diasporans such as Julia and Escobar, the early republic provided a political opportunity to assert their connection to an African body politic, however vague were their ties to continental Africa. At the same time, the two men and the one hundred *remedianos* they purported to represent began to reject the confines of a delimited, national community in favor of a more expansive political vision.

Inventions and Coalitions

In many ways, the two men drew on an invented Africa to constitute their community. Moreover, they put this invention to various political uses by elevating their experiences as diasporans alongside negotiations with government and by identifying an Africanist body politic. Many white Cuban elites did the same, to different ends and for completely different purposes, by drawing on assumptions about the African continent and its descendants. Whereas Julia and Escobar saw the compatibility of "Africa" with conceptualizations of the national body, white Cuban elites believed it antithetical to the new nation. Thus, they also put "Africa" to good political use, primarily as a tool to bring the republic's modern political community—itself a racialized construct—into sharp relief. As V. Y. Mudimbe has argued, community practices stem from a "zero degree discourse." That is, according to Mudimbe, each society has a popular interpretation of its "foundational events" and historical becoming.[9] Certainly the wars of independence (waged between 1868 and 1898) in their aggregate were universally understood as bedrock events of modern Cuba's "becoming." And though the participation of Afro-diasporans during thirty years of anticolonial insurgency was undeniable, their philosophical contributions to national culture was, a priori, subject to impassioned debate. Elites argued that Africa was beyond the pale of Cuban history and that diasporans were the antithesis of the modern Cuban subject. Diasporans, in fact, were increasingly racialized by national discourse, generally placed in a monolithic racial category, *negro*, even as they made sharp distinctions among themselves in various social, economic, and cultural communities. Indeed, at this historical moment of racial homogenization, when, for many, Cuban racial divides hardened, some among the African-descended perpetuated ethnic distinctions and African memory rather than embracing an identity based principally on race.

Africans such as Julia and Escobar, having lived in Cuba for decades, most likely had little information about their ties to the continent, and their connection to Africa was arguably more symbolic than tangible and an important facet of diaspora imagination. Indeed, in 1902, the African homeland to which they might have returned was a vast continent at war, a series of killing fields where invading foreign and autochthonous armies clashed over human and material resources such as diamonds, rubber, ivory, palm oil, coffee, cocoa, and the labor necessary to extract and process these resources.[10] Europeans had negotiated territorial entitlements in Africa during the infamous Berlin Conference (1884–85) and then sent imperial militias to stake colonies and enforce increasingly global, imperialist projects. Backed by their militias, European rulers gradually took control of approximately 90 percent of the continent.[11] As Germany's Kaiser Wilhelm II declared in 1901 regarding overseas expansion, "We have conquered for ourselves a place in the sun."[12] Thus, had Julia and Escobar left Cuba following the protracted and bloody thirty-year anticolonial insurgency and arrived in the "land that witnessed their birth," they would have entered yet another theater of war and exploitation. Their 1902 petition, in fact, coincided with Britain's attack and repression of Nigeria's northern Muslim populations and Leopold II of Belgium's brutal use of the armed Force Publique to bring terror and crush anticolonial resistance among Belgian Congolese rubber workers. African responses to European imperialism abounded in the early twentieth century, such as the wars that erupted over colonial taxation laws in present-day Angola, Sierre Leone, and Southwest Africa. Other populations, such as the Ashanti, Herero, and Zulu peoples along Africa's western and southern coasts, likewise suffered a series of military defeats.

Notwithstanding such events, archival documents allow more for supposition than for conclusion about Julia's and Escobar's intentions. Consistent with extant data on repatriation among Cuba's African diaspora communities, the men may have filed their petition with an urgent sense of exodus, and perhaps not solely for themselves but for family members. In the late nineteenth century, for example, black *criollos* (those born in Cuba) had repatriated with their African-born families, such as the two African men, two African women, and four African descendants who in 1895 applied for passports to repatriate to Portuguese Luanda.[13] Further, following independence, many on the island claimed African birth in order to enhance future survival and opportunities. In 1900, a group of self-proclaimed Africans in Cuba petitioned British authorities for status as British subjects. Born in African territories that had fallen to British colonial rule, they desired colonial status in order to gain certain protections and "privileges." Although the petitioners could not furnish documentation to prove their African births, British authorities surmised that they were, indeed, African because of certain cultural traits, particular "dialects and customs" that ostensibly marked them as "African."[14]

Moreover, mounting prejudice toward cultural practices deemed "African" and, by extension, toward many of the island's African-descended may have prompted Escobar's and Julia's desire to leave Cuban territory. Within months of their request for repatriation assistance, Remedios law enforcement raided a home at the outskirts of town, on the grounds of the Adela sugar mill. Police surprised a presumed society of black *brujos* (witch doctors), likely sugar workers, gathered in religious worship. After conducting a sweep, they accused those apprehended of using skulls, jawbones, spurs, human teeth, and a wooden doll to perform their rites therein. The men were arrested and brought to town for processing, where a Remedios judge sentenced them to six months in prison.[15] This sort of raid on black congregations intensified after 1900, and Julia and Escobar may have rightly believed that their professed allegiance to Africa, on behalf of a group of one hundred others, made them vulnerable to state repression.

Alternatively, many blacks of the early republic articulated outrage toward the government and the antiblack characterizations of the national body, due to Cuba's unique process of development and independence. As Julia and Escobar expressed in their petition, blacks were aware of the wealth that their labor had generated and, by extension, their singular importance to the colonial economy. Yet more to the point, given the postwar climate, many African descendants argued that Cuba was indebted to them for the decisive role they had played in Cuba's anticolonial insurgency. According to Jorge Ibarra, blacks had constituted at least 60 percent of the Liberation

Army's fighting forces.[16] Further, anticolonial nationalists during the wars had often linked the fight to end Spanish colonialism and claim Cuban political rights to the struggle for individual rights, irrespective of color and including slaves. Thus, Julia and Escobar likely believed their requests were justified, particularly if they had seen combat or had lost loved ones in the island's theaters of war or in its slave labor system.

The men's claim was also supported by new citizenship rights in accordance with the 1901 constitution, article 27, title 4, section 1, on individual rights, which stated: "All persons can direct a petition to authorities that will be resolved and the results communicated to the petitioner."[17] And they, like many diasporans of the period, understood the implications of claiming rights according to concomitant and overlapping communities. As the African Lucumí "Santa Bárbara" Mutual Aid and Recreation Society stated in 1913:

> We declare that we are native Cubans, advanced in age, who from infancy have practiced the Lucumí religion, without neglecting the Catholic religion; that we have never nor will ever deny that our ancestors were African; that we respect freedom of religion and the laws of the republic. . . . There is a need that the rights that the Constitution has granted to all inhabitants of the Republic be guaranteed by the forces of law and wherever it appears; that Cubans with unjust intentions try to interfere with the sincere democratic sentiment of the Cuban people who support liberty[,] not a corrupt bureaucracy pushing [Cuba] toward a new slavery; let us beware of the microbes infecting this social body. Let us think about and study the progress of nations without hatreds and resentments.[18]

In their pro forma claims, however, the "Santa Bárbara" society members, like the two Remedios men, adopted a unique and by some measures unthinkable sense of entitlement, which placed the modern nation on a par with the African continent, a comparison that did not work for many in an age of stepped-up forays into Africa on behalf of imperial expansion. In fact, in the broader context of republican Cuban society, their allegiance to Africa and their exercise of individual rights constituted an ideological divergence rather than a crossroads. That is, at the beginning of Cuba's process of decolonization, Cuban journalists, lawmakers, and scientists cast the African legacy (the island's diaspora population, its ethnic-influenced cultural practices, its slave-labor economic system, and its ideological allegiances) as antithetical to nation building and modernity. It was illogical that the African continent and its descendants—who had surrendered to aggressive slave trading and European colonization efforts to exploit human resources and raw materials and as the most backward part of the world—should be recognized as the equal of a modern nation-state. That the government would underwrite the men's desire to return and support such an allegiance among Africans in Cuba was rejected by authorities, and the men's petition was summarily denied.[19]

Cuba joined the global "family of nations" upon winning independence and becoming a sovereign territory. For many Cubans, the global dimensions of Cuban nationalism—the location of their nation in the world—rested on modernization. That is, they believed that Cuban modernity could be accomplished according to the ability of Cuban society to distance itself from savage and atavistic cultural practices as well as "disorder." Government officials were charged with protecting the national project, and any challenges to their authority were labeled anti-Cuban, especially political mobilization rooted in black consciousness. During the Race War of 1912, for example, when black political activists (the Independent Party of Color) rose up to challenge their party's proscription, President José Miguel Gómez called the black insurgents "savages." He suggested that for their gall in deigning to mobilize for black political rights, placing these above the will of the nation-state, they deserved annihilation and that their blood should be used to dye the strips of the Cuban flag.[20] Gómez's call to contain the black activists also reveals his need to thwart U.S. occupation, since the terms of Cuban modernity and national sanctity were profoundly influenced by international politics. Indeed, a critical task for the nation's new leaders was to unite a Cuban body politic that was sharply divided by race, class, gender, region, and occupation while also struggling to achieve domestic stability and maintain sovereign rule. It was widely understood that any incidence of unrest could easily bring the return of North American occupation forces, given the U.S. interest in Cuban affairs.

This eagle's shadow over Cuban domestic affairs was also used effectively in domestic political struggles. An opposing political faction, for example, might attempt to harness or align itself with U.S. forces—or even to use the specter of occupation in order to threaten or beat its opponents. In 1904, for example, rum mogul and Santiago mayor Emilio Bacardí led a short-lived campaign to raise government funds for municipal sanitation. Bacardí invoked the Platt Amendment, arguing that proper sanitation, especially for the island's port cities, was critical to protecting both public health and the future of U.S.-Cuba trade relations. To prevent possible U.S. military (rc) intervention brought on by epidemics and contamination, which could reduce or stop trade, the national government should underwrite the cost of municipal sanitation improvements. The request was denied by Secretary of

State Diego Tamayo on the grounds that it was prejudicial to the republican government's prestige, public order, and international relations.[21]

North Americans poured nearly 205 million dollars of investments into Cuba by the end of the republic's first decade, in sugar mills, agriculture, railways, mines, shipping, banking, mortgages, and public utilities.[22] Besides massive investments, occupation officials implemented restructuring programs meant to build stability and modernize the new republic and instill certain "North American" social and cultural values in Cuban society. As discussed in chapter 1, occupation officials made political appointments, passed legislation, appended the constitution, and developed and oversaw systems in local government, public education, social engineering, sanitation, and prostitution regulation. Louis Pérez has recounted in detail how the U.S. presence greatly impacted Cuban culture, self-perceptions, and autonomy throughout the twentieth century and even before the end of colonialism.[23] Thus, after peace, in 1898, U.S. officials influenced the development of nascent political communities by installing U.S. systems in the foundations of the new republic's structures.

Bodies Politic

The cornerstone of Cuba's nation-state project was the 1901 constitution, a document that interpreted specific political events and their actors according to Cuba's contemporary political order. Legislators and national leaders framed the constitution as the end product of thirty years of anticolonial insurgency, billing it as a revolutionary document that safeguarded individual rights and equality. According to their imaginary, the constitution provided a template for Cuban democracy, modeled heavily on the U.S. bicameral system and demonstrating a clear ideological transition from colony to liberal republic.[24] But Cuba's 1901 constitution was also overshadowed by foreign (particularly U.S.) domination and the threat of occupation if and when domestic tensions or policies strayed from North American interests on the island. This policy, perhaps the most odious symbol of Cuban domination by a foreign power, was introduced to the U.S. Congress in 1901 by Connecticut senator Orville Platt (1827–1905). The Platt Amendment to the new Cuban constitution infringed on the sovereign authority asserted in article 1 of Cuba's 1901 constitution ("The people of Cuba constitute a sovereign and independent state") and rendered the constitution's force as a writ of republic and nation building at least as figurative as it was concrete. North American encroachment on Cuban sovereignty was harshly criticized by constitutionalists and the general population. When the writers of the constitution effectively were forced to add the amendment, one faction campaigned vigorously against its passing and mass protests were ignited across the island.

In the broadest sense, the writers of the constitution began the process of defining free Cuba by including a declaration of the parameters of Cuban national territory and a delineation of individual rights, responsibilities, and protections under the law—including individual property rights and universal male suffrage. The constitution also included a concise explanation of the new, democratic political system; a declaration of national independence and sovereignty; and extensive clarifications regarding the civil status of those residing on the island. Of these new constitutional guarantees, those that had to do with nationality were clearly stipulated: those born to Cuban parents on or outside of republican territory were Cuban. Those born on Cuban soil to foreign parents were also Cuban, as were those born abroad who claimed Cuban parents, even in cases where parents had lost their Cuban nationality.[25] The constitution also outlined freedom of association, religion, public education, and speech, when these did not offend Christian morality, personal honor, keeping the peace, or social order. In fact, the writers of the constitution defined the terms of citizenship and national inclusion in part because of the large number of extranationals on the island after 1898—immigrant laborers (Chinese, Spanish, and Antillean), Spanish veterans and merchants, and North American speculators, merchants, retailers, technicians, and occupation forces—a significant portion of the Cuban social milieu.

Government officials had to contend with these challenges and face the task of developing the legal criteria for the body politic. The terms of naturalization were also clear: those not born in Cuba but who had demonstrated certain attributes of loyalty or had contributed to the national project earned the right to naturalize under the terms of the 1901 constitution. Foreigners who had participated in the nationalist insurgency against the Spanish Crown could be naturalized. Specifically, any foreigner who had fought for the Liberation Army or had resided continuously in Cuba since at least 1899 was qualified to apply for Cuban citizenship for a period of up to six months following the constitution's promulgation. Spaniards who showed signs of loyalty to Cuba, not Spain, were also granted naturalization rights if they did not register their Spanish national status. Finally, as indicated by authorities ruling on the Julia-Escobar petition, Africans who had been emancipated and those who had been granted their freedom according to an 1835 treaty between Spain and England were also eligible for naturalization.[26]

These constitutional guarantees are critical to a greater understanding of republican cultural identity in general and racial politics in particular.

Consider, for example, that Cuban census records since at least 1899 do not list Africans by ethnicity. Those considered "white" were also classed as either "foreign" or "native-born," and often according to national denominations, but this was not true for nonwhites, who were listed as *negros* or *mulatos* or *de color*, whether foreign-born or not. Further, census enumerators began to measure and record the Asian population according to a new category—"yellow"—in 1899 and to lump "yellow" Cubans with the African-descended in the category "element of color." This suggests that diversity notwithstanding, from the point of view of census officials, the act of grouping Antilleans, Africans, Cuban-born blacks and mulattos, and to a lesser degree, immigrant and Cuban-born Chinese in the same "colored" category was an adequate, socially meaningful way to mark them.

Further, for those on the island claiming African birth, nationality was even more complicated. The first, second, and fifth clauses of article 6 of the constitution regarding naturalization suggest anti-African exclusions. The fifth clause, for example, implies that those who claimed African birth occupied a space neither foreign nor Cuban in the national political community. Since Africans were not included in naturalization provisions granted to other foreigners, such as recognition of loyalty to the anticolonial insurgency against Spain or continuous residency on the island since at least 1899, they were neither foreign nor Cuban. As soldiers during the wars of independence, some of the African-born fought for Spanish loyalists. Most, however, fought on behalf of the anticolonial insurgency, where the ranks were heavily populated by Africans and their descendants.[27] Thus, Africans should have been protected by the first clause of article 6 granting citizenship to those who had fought with the Liberation Army. Those Africans not covered by the terms of the first clause should have been naturalized according to the terms of the second clause pertaining to residency before 1899.

In fact, most African-born Cubans had arrived in Cuba at least three decades before the Spanish-Cuban-American War ended due to a resurgence in slave trading in the 1860s (approximately 12,000 African laborers were imported each year between 1860 and 1866). This was one of several spikes in slave importation during the first half of the century, due to the contraction and expansion of agricultural production. The numbers of African laborers imported fluctuated from 2,000 or 3,000 to 35,000 per year.[28] In 1866, a royal antislavery decree stating that any illegal trafficking would result in slave seizures and owners' arrests dealt a serious blow to slave traffickers and effectively ended the slave trade.[29] Without continuous reinforcements, the African population on the island declined significantly. By the end of Spanish colonialism, Africans made up only 3.5 percent (7,948) of the island's total foreign-born (228,477) and less than .05 percent of the total island population (1,572,797).[30] The island's total native-born population of color (505,443), about 32.1 percent of the total island population, can be compared to the African-born using an approximate ratio of 64-to-1.[31] That is, in 1899 for every sixty-four native-born Cubans of color, there was one African in Cuba.

This suggests that the idea of an "African" presence was politicized—an idea used more for constructions of national identity than to explain Africans' impact on early republican society. There were more foreign-born Chinese than Africans on the island in 1899, having arrived as early as the 1840s to work as contract laborers. By the end of the nineteenth century, they represented 4.9 percent of all foreigners; the Chinese and their descendants were fully integrated in the economy as merchants, day laborers, salespersons, and laundry workers. In general, foreigners constituted 11.2 percent of the total population, the largest segment by far being Spaniards— about 81 percent of the total—who worked in all sectors of the economy, especially in publishing and retail and as merchants and salespersons. According to the 1899 census, there were only slightly more Africans on the island than people from the United States.[32] Yet the writers of the constitution came up with an ambiguous civil status for Africans, although many had lived on the island for decades.

Authorities' fear of an exodus of African-descended Cubans is one explanation for Africans' complex position in relation to the national community. In the wake of thirty years of warfare, authorities and local and foreign investors alike hoped to recoup, rebuild, and expand. The final War of Independence (1895–98) had destroyed much of the island's infrastructure: agriculture, roads, schools, hospitals, towns, railways, bridges, and buildings. The issue of cheap labor for the many reconstruction projects was urgent, and African-descended Cubans constituted part of a valuable labor force. Historians have surmised that employment conditions and living standards for black Cubans were worse in the first years of republican life than during the colonial period. As veteran black activist and future rebel leader Evaristo Estenóz declared in 1908, "Barely established, the Republic has turned our concerns to anger, and done so to a greater extent and under worse conditions than in the most offensive moments of colonialism."[33]

It would be logical to think that Cuba's African-descended population had earned the right to full citizenship in the nation after its significant contribution to the anticolonial insurgency. Yet the African-descended were also central to Cuban modernist discourse on egalitarianism, an important feature of Cuban nationalism. A comparative case, arguably, is postrevolutionary Mexico, where the country's newly appointed minister of educa-tion, José Vasconcelos (1921–24), devised the now-infamous racialist theory known as the *raza cósmica* (the "cosmic race"). Rooted in historic racial, ethnic, and class differences between Mexico's ostensibly pure "Indian" and pure "Spanish" races, the "cosmic race" theory put forth that Mexico's *mestizo* or hybrid racial identity allowed for the social transcendence of the Mexican nation. *Mestizaje* (race mixture) seemingly resolved the social and political tensions based on race, region, class, and ethnicity that had played out so viciously during Mexico's bloody and protracted revolution (1910–20) and throughout Mexican nationalist history. This theory of *mestizaje* was fueled by the postrevolutionary Mexican elite and served as an ongoing, im-portant component of Mexican national discourse.

Yet cross-racial alliance, not race mixture, served as a linchpin of Cuban postrevolutionary national discourse. In the Cuban case, rather than empha-sizing racial hybridity, many national leaders and elites stressed the impor-tance of sustaining the cross-racial ties formed during the wars of indepen-dence. Others among them drew clear boundaries between white and black Cubans, reinforcing racial differences and arguing that national resources were rightfully earmarked for whites. In September 1915, in response to rumors then circulating that blacks were meeting quietly to launch a second racial uprising following the 1912 Race War, the secretary of the interior on government, Colonel Aurelio Hevia, scoffed that there was "no conspiracy." What is more, he clarified, "this Republic is [and will always be] for the whites and not for the blacks."[34] For those endorsing a more fluid vision of community than this one, racial harmony and even Cuban racelessness were avenues to Cuban egalitarianism. National unity, so the logic went, precluded race-conscious activism. For the African-descended, their tenu-ous positions as citizens were partially a result of the denial of racial discord and even the significance of race to Cuban national identity, which served to silence the outcry against Cuba's socioeconomic disparities among the races.

Declaring the National Body

The task of constructing an enduring national community was shouldered by several early republican intellectuals, who in many cases placed racial relations at the center of national stability. Historian and veteran Rafael Martínez Ortiz recalled in 1921 that when the republic was founded,

> no significant problem divided public opinion; all were in prior agree-ment. Slavery had been abolished for several years and though the gen-

eration that had experienced slavery for years still lived, the two races that populated this country—one of them dominant over the other—co-existed in peace on the bases of mutual tolerance and even confraternity. Together the races made independence, thereby erasing the natural antinomies that surged from the very character of the institution under whose regimen they had developed. Those deep racial antagonisms, which in Cuba have been largely unknown, even made illicit the marriages between whites and blacks, as happens in some states of the North American Union. The time will come to erase boundaries and establish Cuban equality and fraternity on an unshakeable foundation.[35]

Martínez's particular national ideal stressed redemption. That is, he argued that allegiance to national harmony resolved historic tensions among Cuban racial groups and ensured Cuban national advancement. In the most straightforward interpretation, these beliefs were held widely across racial and class sectors. Rafael Serra, for example, a black intellectual, revolutionary activist, and journalist, also sounded the call for a unified nation just two years after the republic's inception. In 1904, he published an eloquent editorial in support of Cuba's national project, the ruling Moderate Party administration and its cooperation with the United States, and the precept of a unified and homogeneous Cuban nation:

> Thus to create a progressive and robust nation of sure existence and broad liberties; to create a contented nation, where our own and foreigners live freely enjoying the benefit of rights; to create a nation, finally, where we may all have a fortunate and tranquil home; for that and not for any other thing we have carried our part of the collaboration; for that and with the luxury of fortune, thanks to indescribable efforts that are at times strengthened by the valiant protection of a friendly nation, thanks to all of this we have been able to constitute the Republic on the bases of respect, and we have not had to fall according to cowardice, frailties or submission of spirit, fueled by the sin of temptation to convert the *patria* into mere prophetic statues.[36]

Serra echoed Martínez's vision for national unity and his belief that Cuban progress depended on the stability that a unified populace could provide. Yet, whereas Martínez focused on fraternity among Cuba's disparate racial groups and on harmony (rather than equality), Serra's ideal national unity emphasized individual rights and universal access to resources. Harmony and political stability were of great concern to government, as demonstrated by communication between Cuba's soon-to-be president, Tomás Estrada

Palma, and Havana's civil governor, Juan Ríus Rivera, on the eve of the republic's inauguration in 1902. Estrada Palma cautioned that "there should not be the least doubt how much prudence, tact, and skill will need to be displayed before and after the republican government is constituted."[37] He urged the governor to be mindful that "on assuming the responsibilities of an independent people, they should have a clear idea of how important it is to our country's future to consider ourselves as members of the same family, not only Cubans without any exceptions, but also the Spanish residents on the Island, citizens or not, and the foreigners who have interests here."[38] Like appeals for national harmony, Estrada Palma's entreaty for Cubans to be "of the same family" reveals the government's burden of proof to resolve domestic tensions in the face of ongoing occupation by North American forces. Almost six months passed before the United States withdrew its troops from Cuban soil and Estrada Palma took office, making Cuban authorities aware of the importance of domestic peace to avoiding foreign occupation.

Certain elite notions of the national community drew from a pantheon of prominent elites, public intellectuals, educators, and revolutionary leaders of the nineteenth century who had "stupendous intelligence, vivifying warmth, and great hearts," such as priest and educator Padre Félix Varela; liberal editor, writer, and activist José Antonio Saco; rich sugar hacendado and freer of slaves Carlos Manuel de Céspedes; and educator José de la Luz y Caballero.[39] After 1898, poet and intellectual José Martí was awarded the status of national hero, as was the famous mulatto military leader of the insurgent army, Antonio Maceo, among the very few men of color admitted to this roster. This sense of national community also relied on liberal and post-Enlightenment ideas about restraint, industry, order, economic progress, and the "family of nations." In late April 1902, as Tomás Estrada Palma sailed from the United States to Cuba aboard the *Reina de Los Ángeles* to assume the presidency, he argued that national advancement rested on key principles, such as "work which ennobles, peace which enriches, order which secures . . . and the discreet exercise of liberty."[40]

Yet few of the African-descended were admitted to the elite national pantheon of heroes. Those few added, such as Antonio Maceo, could not fully represent the breadth and numeric contribution that blacks had made during the war. As historian Marial Iglesias suggests,

In [early republican] *habanera* society the excessive emphasis on symbolic transformations, evidenced in the placement of tags, labels, and ceremonies, hid, perhaps, the survival behind the revolution of independence of oppressive structures and practices of exploitation and discrimination. In this sense, those of the same race as Maceo, many of whom had their share of glory in the war, soon understood that in the new state of things, far from being recognized or publicly promoted, they were to be excluded and hidden, as if an uncomfortable presence, threatened with being "civilized" as a price of their integration in society.[41]

Further, in addition to the omnipresent celebration of white Cuban patriotic figures in the nation's capital, in the form of busts, plaques, statues, and dedications, liberalist names for streets and stores were also adopted, such as Progreso (Progress) and Porvenir (the Future), as part of a larger Cuban, modernizing project.[42] Historian Louis Pérez has even argued that throughout the republic, at particular moments, Cubans judged standards of character and modernity according to prevailing norms in the United States. Cubans "saw themselves," he suggests, "through the eyes of North Americans."[43]

Notwithstanding currents of white supremacy in early republican nationalist discourses, some leaders of the early republic supported black political empowerment rather than absolute racial subordination, so long as it was in coalition with whites. White veteran general Bartolomé Masó, for example, enjoyed massive black support in his early bid for the presidency in 1901, including from black revolutionary leaders and war veterans, such as Lieutenant Colonel Lino D'ou, General Quintín Bandera, and Juan Gualberto Gómez. Masó ran on the National Party ticket against Tomás Estrada Palma, and before retiring from the race in December 1901, he saw fit to characterize blacks as "humble" rather than dangerous political subjects. Unlike those of Estrada Palma and later national politicians, Masó's speeches show his belief that blacks were central to his political success. This is a fact underscored by the number of prominent black war veterans and revolutionaries in his camp. As he suggested in the weeks before the December 1901 elections, "The race of color has been an essential factor in our social existence and has proven itself an ordered element, despite great suffering, and they represent a respectable force in peace and to work, just as they have always been ready to take part in our struggles; they have in their family heroes of all classes and martyrs of all types. We cannot abandon these heroes now, denying them participation in our political body and taking from them the right to take part in our public life."[44] By calling for black participation, Masó demonstrated a radical break from the segregationist politics of the occupation government and from many elitist Cuban officials. Yet his concept of the nation nonetheless relied on a normative vision of a modern, white, body politic: "The race of color has been . . . an ordered element . . . ready to take part in our struggles; . . . we cannot abandon them . . . denying them participation in our political body . . . in our public life." Further, his overt compartmentalizing of the body politic ("our," "we," and "them") qualified black political participation; black activism had to be sanctioned and legitimated by whites.

Black participation in formal politics was perceived as a clear threat to elite power, and many insisted it be controlled or even eliminated. The threat of reoccupation, for example, motivated Cuban elites to respond to U.S. concerns over broad political participation by the popular classes (where blacks figured prominently), since for both U.S. and Cuban leaders the need for stability stemmed from their mutual interests to maintain domestic control and protect U.S. property and investments. During the constitutional convention (held from November 1900 to September 1901), the issue of universal-versus-restricted suffrage moved white writer, philosopher, and statesman Enrique José Varona to propose a series of voting requirements that included class and social criteria such as "education, property, and legally established families."[45] These requirements were defeated, but had they been passed they would have restricted or eliminated black participation in the electoral process.

Elites often accepted the dual burden of proving their fitness for leadership and shepherding the progress of the nation. In some instances, they legislated social behavior and public order in an effort to extirpate social elements that threatened national advancement and civilization, led by a cadre of the "better classes." A case in point is municipal legislation, passed in Havana in 1900, that declared that "prohibited from passing through the streets of this city are groups or *comparsas*, known as Tangos, Cabildos, and Claves or whatever other things convey symbols, allegories, and objects that conflict with the seriousness and culture of the inhabitants of this country."[46] In fact, certain cultural practices and their practitioners, seen as the antithesis of modernity, were necessary to defining the national community. If, for example, Africanity was increasingly cast as dangerous, it was also central to the nation. The legacy of Africa was an imagined threat to the Cuban nation, and Africanist cultural practices (religious celebration, dance, and music) and leaders (often referred to as *brujos* or sorcerers) contaminated the island with atavistic, Africanist practices. These practices had the potential to infect the national body, and their eradication was necessary to protecting the nation. As *El Diario Cubano*, a daily newspaper in Cienfuegos, on the island's southern coast, editorialized in 1905, "*Brujería* (witchcraft) has spread in our Southern Pearl at a notable pace. There are neighborhoods of the city where only *brujos* live. . . . There *brujos* and *brujas* work as quacks and pose a grave risk to [locals] who believe in their remedies."[47]

In 1915, the Havana daily *El Día* lamented that despite the recent death of "Papá Silvestre" (a local *brujo* and Lucumí Santa Rita de Casia y San Lázaro Society founding member), the urbane, capital city of Havana was still vulnerable to Africanist culture. Many innocent habaneros, *El Día* reported, representing a wide socioeconomic spectrum of Havana society, had succumbed to Silvestre's manipulation. While Silvestre lived and delivered ritual services of one or another sort, their desperate trips to seek his counsel and "uncivilized" treatments had resulted in their suffering from "decomposing organs" and "atrophy of the brain." The article also suggested that Africanist activities were tantamount to political mobilization, since *brujos* like Silvestre and organizations such as Santa Rita de Casia y San Lázaro had attracted a significant following of impressionable and unfortunate habaneros seeking solutions to personal problems. Accordingly, promised *El Día*, the Tribunal of Justice was well aware of the danger presented by these activities; they knew of Silvestre's successor, another *brujo* popularly referred to as "Papá Colás," and planned to prosecute his and all *brujería* crimes to the full extent of the law.[48] Such anti-Africanist beliefs, which informed government policies, also buttressed attempts to discredit black political mobilization. The vicious depictions of blacks—as savages, rapists, and murderers—that circulated during the state-sponsored Race War of 1912 are examples.

Many racialist scientists and journalists believed that Cubans of African descent maintained a direct connection to Africa. Blacks facilitated a vigorous and ongoing African presence because of their Africanist cultural expressions and retrograde worldview. Inherently, they both embodied and perpetuated Africanisms on Cuban soil. As Cuban anthropologist Fernando Ortiz argued in 1906, "Witchcraft is a deficiency of evolution. Those who believe in it, if Africans, follow the same beliefs of their country or, if Creoles, they are the children of Africans and have suckled on these same beliefs; likewise are the white fetishists who are so close to the Africans psychologically even if they do not identity with them. If African and Cuban witch doctors are not the same person, there isn't more than one step between them, one generation."[49] Arresting the spread of such practices, excising them through research, legislation, vigilance, and violence, was a way to police the body politic and safeguard national development. Thus, despite calls for unity, national "racelessness," and harmony, non-normative cultural modes and their practitioners were repressed in the new republic. Brackette Williams has previously argued this point, suggesting, "This Other comes to represent an improper embodiment not merely of nationality but of universal humanity that has vanished into a racio-national configuration."[50] Thus, for Africans and their descendants, even as they served as fodder for criminal justice agents bent on "civilizing" the body politic (and, in a way of thinking, as a barometer of Cuban modernization efforts), their claims to Cuban citizenship correlated to their relationship to "Africanist" practices. That is, it related to how distant they were from Africanity and disconnected from the continent and/or the valorization of Africanist practices. People such as Julia and Escobar and other Africanists on Cuban soil who recognized Africa and embraced simultaneous Cuban national and African identities threatened the modern, civilized Cuban nation.

Some blacks sought to dismantle racial identity in the rising climate of nation building by protesting the continued use of racial categories, such as Nicolás Valverde, a black man from the city of Cienfuegos. In April 1900, as Havana officials outlawed certain Africanist cultural practices, Valverde petitioned the governor of Santa Clara province to change existing policy regarding racial categories in the civil registers, arguing that consistent with the principles of equality under the law, the term "citizen" was the only one that should be used in public records.[51] Similarly, Antonio Póveda Ferrer wrote to President Tomás Estrada Palma two years later to protest the continued use of racial labels in government records; the existing practice for public employees was to record one's civil status using racial nomenclature, such as *blanco* (white), *pardo* (mixed-race), and *moreno* (black). Póveda commented that the practice "deeply disgusts and humiliates the social classes who deserve and have a perfect right to demand that they be treated with all due respect."[52]

In fact, the ongoing use of racial nomenclature in government records suggests the importance of race in early republican national identities, including emerging beliefs about national *belonging*. Normative notions of racial identity emerged that placed some within and others outside the body politic. If the Cuban nation was increasingly defined according to attributes such as civilized, harmonious, and "modern," Africa's legacy in Cuba and African-descended Cubans were deeply implicated in the construction of these signifiers. In fact, little political space existed for Cubans of African descent to articulate allegiances to their African past. There was, perhaps, no other group as committed to defining the social needs of the modern Cuban nation as the island's social-scientific community. And no other scholar was as renowned (and prolific) as anthropologist and criminologist Fernando Ortiz (1880–1969), who in his early career championed Cuban eugenics and social engineering projects.[53]

Ortiz received his doctoral degree in Juridical Law from the University of Madrid in 1901 and later studied criminology with noted Italian criminologist César Lambroso. He devoted his early career to research on black Cuban socio-psycho pathology, publishing in 1906 the first book of a two-part series that launched his career: *Hampa-afrocubana: Los negros brujos* (Afro-Cuban Underworld: Black Witchdoctors). Ortiz argued that understanding the Cuban "underworld"—its inferior classes—helped to explain "Cuban psychology." That is, Cuba's African legacy was central to Cuban exceptionalism and to how the island differed culturally from other countries. Throughout his prolific career, he wrote thousands of entries, articles, and books on Africa's legacy in Cuban culture, folklore, politics, and national identity.

In many ways, the work of Ortiz and other social scientists informed government policies regarding the regulation of cultural practices and affecting the African-descended population generally. In fact, practices associated with Africa were at the core of a mounting battle between government agents and ethnically identified diasporans concerning their right to claim an Africanist ethnic identity and the government's control of civic life. The island's Africanist social clubs protested their marginalization repeatedly in the early republic by publicly announcing that their member activities conformed to the nation's highest order of civil laws and moral sentiments. Silvestre Enice, for example, in his capacity as president of the Africanist Sociedad San Lázaro, requested that a prominent black leader vouch publicly in Havana newspapers for his organization's legal constitution and moral conduct. He entreated leadership to make known the club's intent to "honor" the republic and to understand the orderliness of its members, as well as their abhorrence of political activism and refusal "to mix in any sort of politics whatsoever."[54]

For Cuban elites of all colors, however, Africanist practices seemed to be an obstacle to national progress. Many national leaders, intellectuals, scientists, and journalists chafed at the implications of Africanist practices for their own status as moderns, what anthropologist Stephen Palmié calls "a national embarrassment with respect to Cuba's accreditation as a civilized state."[55] The notion that Africanisms (African-influenced cultural practices) deviated from the standards of a civilized nation and endangered Cuba's future progress were ideas held by many elected officials, informing their views of the African-descended generally and African-influenced cultural practices more specifically.

In creating a harmonious and united national community, Africa's legacy presented Cubans with a conundrum. On the one hand, lawmakers and intellectuals recognized the vital importance of incorporating blacks into the republic's society and economy, even if according to hierarchies and with disparities. On the other hand, those who claimed an allegiance to Africa in Cuba compromised their individual credibility as loyal and progressive citizens. As Pérez has discussed, the dominant pattern for articulating Cubanness in postcolonial popular culture was both racialized *and* white.[56] Republican legislation reflected the belief that the descendants of Africa were to be increasingly relegated to the republic's lower socioeconomic rungs as well as cast in sharp relief to the white, Cuban, modern nation.

If the nation as defined by elites was both exclusionary and dependent on an invented notion of Africa and Europe, how might a notion of Africa have figured in alternative political communities constructed by the African-descended? Given the push to eradicate cultural practices deemed "African" from the modern Cuban nation, what was the response of the African-descended to these tactics? In what ways did their notion of political community challenge, reinforce, or complicate cultural norms and ideas of national community? If those who identified with Africa rejected Cuban national identity, as had Africans in Remedios, what sort of political communities did African descendants embrace? The black club movement, the most visible mobilization of blacks and mulattos in the twentieth century, was a system of civic activism, a set of sociocultural organizations that had emerged during colonialism, usually called "societies" or "clubs," which were created according to specific interests and social and economic factors. How Africans and their descendants organized themselves to confront cultural repression and racial polarization can be discerned, in part, by examining Africanist organizations within the club movement, which emerged in the colonial period and morphed after 1898 according to a shift in the broader republican context.

Politics and Africanist Communities

In the colonial period, Africanist organizations emerged in at least two forms, as religious *cofradías* and as *cabildos de nación*. These organizations helped to mediate relations between ethnic Africans and their descendants and colonial authorities, while also perpetuating African ethnic cultural practices.

Cofradías, Catholic brotherhoods organized by ecclesiastical authorities for the purpose of proselytizing, performed civic and religious charitable acts as well as promoting African ethnic culture. They existed throughout Spanish colonial rule, as did *cabildos de nación*, which were civic organizations that also encouraged ethnic religious practices.[57] Many Africans arriving on the island joined these organizations according to their ethnic identities. The first documented ethnic African organization was a *cofradía* founded in 1598 in Havana, called Nuestra Señora de los Remedios.[58] Both *cofradías* and *cabildos* were created by colonial authorities to maintain control over masses of African laborers because they encouraged ethnic division among African laborers.[59] In time, however, *cabildos* became important to Africans and their descendants as a place where they engaged in ethnic cultural practices and politics and pooled financial resources for economic self-help.

Cabildos de nación (based on African ethnic "nations") date to fourteenth-century Spain and were juridical and economic institutions that facilitated the state's political control of Seville's African labor force.[60] These early organizations addressed the needs of their African ethnic members, many of them slaves, by providing them with assistance in case of illness, funds for funeral arrangements, and gift monies for the families of deceased members. Often, they accumulated sufficient capital to purchase members' freedom. Members used them as spiritual refuge and for celebrations, including dances and vigils for the deceased.[61] *Cabildantes* (members) worshipped collectively in closed ceremonies, and *cabildo* leaders were generally the only members privy to religious and healing techniques. The colonial state recognized *cabildos*, and together *cabildo reyes* (kings) and *capataces* (cabildo captains, second in command after kings) acted as liaisons between *cabildantes* and local authorities. *Reyes* and *capataces* oversaw *cabildo* activities and resources. They resolved grievances and wielded tremendous power by participating officially in state structures. Although *cabildos* encouraged ethnic divisions among the island's African-descended population, they were also important sites of cultural engagement (including spiritual practices) in the lives of the African-descended.

After the end of colonialism in 1898, these organizations resurfaced with religious and/or civic names, often calling themselves the "continuation" of specific African ethnic *cabildos* from the colonial period. Generally called *sociedades* (societies), they created political communities premised on Africanist cultural practices, which drew on imaginings alternative to the nationalisms envisioned by José Martí, Juan Gualberto Gómez, and others. They adopted elements of dominant nationalist discourse while also addressing national politics in highly complex ways.

Africanist societies had both cultural and political implications. Although the scope of their activity appears to have been limited to events for members, these organizations were part of a broad, heterogeneous black club movement. Like the population of African-descended more generally, blacks founded organizations that mirrored their divergent social, economic, and political identities in the republic as well as their varied cultural practices. The privileged sector of black societies, for example, held fancy balls and prided themselves on ostentatious displays of cultural refinement and relative material wealth. They commemorated nationalist heroes associated with Cuba's recent thirty-year anticolonial insurgency, including José Martí, Antonio Maceo, and Guillermo Moncada, and were secular in both their organizational agendas and their club goals. Further, they participated in an important black press network, and many enjoyed significant support from the republican government. Privileged black societies of instruction and leisure were made up of intellectual, skilled, and professional blacks; and the widespread use of the words "instruction and recreation" in their names belied an organizational ethos of modern and liberal commitments, understood as paramount for participation in the mainstream political arena as well as for broad recognition among Cubans of all colors. Their ideological commitment to bourgeois liberalism, too, placed these elite blacks squarely within the confines of a national body politic, which though discursively imagined as a series of horizontal and egalitarian relations, unfettered by race, gender, or class differentiation, was nonetheless highly polarized along racial, gender, economic, and cultural lines. These clubs promoted economic prosperity, marriage, cultural advancement, morality, highly proscribed gender roles, mutual aid, and engagement with formal politics. Further, even as they spoke of black advancements and lauded certain blacks' intellectual and cultural achievements, they also believed that as African-descended Cubans, their suitability for participation in the national project depended on their vehement rejection of a continuing relationship to Africa. In particular, elite blacks' adherence to modern political culture and patronage was necessary for participation in formal politics.

Ethnic African societies embraced many of the same liberal, progressive values espoused by privileged black club leaders and broader republican society, including education, moral improvement, and economic prosperity. Yet their principal task, to protect and perpetuate their ethnic community, ran counter to liberal individualism and middle-class constructions of modern social values. Government officials attempted to control African-influenced clubs even before the beginning of the republican period. In 1881, for example, Cuba's governor, General Ramón Blanco, proclaimed that colonial authorities would permit black societies to function so long as they pursued scientific, literary, and benevolent activities. He was clear to distinguish these acceptable practices from those that were supposedly antithetical to the modernist colonial state, positing that "if [societies] evoke the memory of Africa, they will not have my consent, because they do not benefit the culture, civilization and general interests of this country." In 1888, colonial authorities also attempted to inculcate new cultural values among *cabildo* members by mandating the explicit use of Catholic denominations in *cabildo* titles and discouraging the use of African ethnic appellations such as Cabildo de Lucumí or Cabildo de Carabalí.[62] The law remained in force after the end of colonial rule, and though similar naming practices prevailed in the republican period, the available evidence does not fully reveal their precise meaning among Africanist organizations.[63] Even though former *cabildo* members complied with these regulations after 1902 by adopting Catholic names, in most cases *cabildos* also retained African ethnic appellations, constructing bulky titles in the process. For example, the Cabildo Carabalí Olugo adopted the name Society of Our Lady of Carmen, Formerly Cabildo de Carabalí Olugo. The Cabildo Lucumí became the Society of Instruction, Recreation, and Mutual Aid, "San Emilio," Continuation of the Cabildo Lucumí of Santiago. Africanist clubs, then, complied with the law while also asserting an ongoing, public commitment to African ethnic identity and resisting nationalist homogeny and vilification of the African continent. In their process of building community, the clubs rejected characterizations of Africa as the antithesis of modern Cuban society as well as monolithic constructions of the Cuban nation. Instead they declared commitments to both Cuba and Africa.

The Nation's Alchemists

Take, for example, the members of the "San Benito de Palermo" Religious, Instruction, Recreation, and Aid Society of Africans and Their Children (later to be called the Society of Jesus the Nazarene), who were self-proclaimed Africans and poor residents of Santiago de Cuba. They named their organization for a lay brother of the Franciscan Order, born of African descent in Sicily in the sixteenth century, who had moved multitudes with his miraculous cures and pious acts. As a symbol, Saint Benito spoke to them as Africans and African descendants and to their economic condition, given that organizations such as these were founded to accumulate collective, corporate resources and furnish members with the social services that the republican government would not. As day laborers, bricklayers, washerwomen, housewives, street peddlers, dockworkers, tobacco workers, small farmers, and cooks, San Benito de Palermo members were mainly the unskilled, the underemployed, and the underpaid.[64]

The San Benito de Palermo Society bylaws reveal members' needs as they defined them, including benefits for ill, unemployed, and deceased members and their families. To fortify their community, members also helped wrongly incarcerated coreligionists, visited their sick, and allotted small budgets, when possible, for artistic and scientific conferences. Regular religious meetings were also written into their bylaws, as was an annual celebration on December 4 in honor of Santa Bárbara or, depending on one's perspective, Chángo, in the Yóruba-derived, Regla de Ocha pantheon.

San Benito de Palermo members mixed many elemental faiths, using the descriptors "Africans and Their Children," "Religious," "Instruction and Recreation," and "Mutual Aid" in their group label, suggesting that in their minds the breadth of these seemingly disparate elements was necessary to capture the scope of their beliefs and organizational purpose. In fact, the members of Africanist organizations such as San Benito de Palermo might be seen as the alchemists of a race, because they went to considerable lengths to define themselves in contrast to early republican racial identities. They mixed various discourses of early twentieth-century Cuba and spun these in ways that were contradictory and transformative. Take their inaugural bylaws, which declared: "There is constituted in this city [of Santiago] a religious association of Africans and Their Children, for the purpose of education and leisure. By the morality of its character this association offers bylaws consonant with the aspirations of all modern societies."[65] In fact, the notion raised by such organizations, in advancing their claims to political coherency while gathering under the same social rubric "Africans and Their Children" and "Modern Aspirations," originates not from the members themselves but from the early republic's context of anti-African repression and visions of national community that subordinated, vilified, and occasionally rejected Africa's legacy in Cuba.

By joining modern nationalist and Africanist commitments, understanding these as duality rather than as dichotomy, the members of San Benito de Palermo asserted a worldview that was particularly challenging to white republican elites. Not only did they stand in opposition to the statesmen and scientists who tried to create a continuum that located Africa at one barbarous end and Europe at its civilized other end. The members rejected these efforts at their criminalization. In essence, they repudiated implicitly much of Cuban scientific research that was then devoted to quantifying blacks' (especially poor blacks') social practices and physical characteristics, a way, ostensibly, of measuring their criminal tendencies and civic deficiencies. Instead, they pledged allegiance to an Africa irreducible to a binary. Their expansive sense of identity placed them both within and at the margins of the national political community.

Despite widespread discourse about Cuban "racelessness," the early republic was a racially divided society. Many of its most prominent and widely respected intellectuals, such as Fernando Ortiz and Israel Castellanos, were hard-line adherents of scientific racism. Well into the republican period Ortiz and Castellanos conducted meticulous, and now discredited, anthropological work measuring skulls, noses, lips, hair texture, speech, and cultural production, such as dance, music, and song. Blacks' religious rites and ritual objects were also measured as putative proof of the danger African-influenced culture posed to both government and the national body. Described by mainstream reporters and legislators variously as "cancerous," "diseased," "leeching," "vicious," and "infantile," those engaged in African-influenced practices became the targets of government repression. Government agents and scientists focused in particular on those black Cubans who they believed embraced primitive ontologies and posed the threat of spreading depravity to the polity. By 1906, social scientist Ortiz had recommended in his now-infamous text *Hampa Afrocubana: Los negros brujos* that black "witch doctors" be incarcerated, cautioning authorities to pay particular attention to their isolation and work routines in order to limit their contact, scope of influence, and "parasitic behavior" with fellow inmates.[66]

In fact, in 1900, before the constitution was drafted or the republic inaugurated, the mayor of Havana outlawed dances and traveling street festivities, called Tangos, Cabildos, and Claves, as well as the use of African-derived instruments, such as drums, whether these were used in public or in private spaces. Two years later, a scandal erupted, on May 20, 1902, when, in the waning hours of the republic's inaugural festivities, Havana police raided a group of men gathered in ritual celebration in a working-class neighborhood at the city's outskirts. Both police and reporters labeled the men *ñáñigos* (a pejorative term for those of Abakuá, African-derived, religious faith). The police confiscated ritual objects, arrested the group's leaders, and charged them with illicit association. At times, police also raided privileged black societies, whose cultural practices were ostensibly less threatening yet whose racial status alone seemed to suggest illicit activity. This was the case in 1904, when José Vantour, board member of Luz de Oriente, the elite mulatto society in Santiago de Cuba, complained to mulatto statesmen Juan Gualberto Gómez about the matter. Vantour charged that the governor of Oriente province targeted black and mulatto society members, using local police to conduct frequent raids against these organizations under the pretext of clamping down on illegal gaming. As a political favor, Vantour asked Gómez to use his substantial influence to stop local repression against decent clubs such as his.[67]

As we have already seen, self-identified Africans and their descendants founded clubs as a powerful strategy of community formation. Despite the repressive racial context and reprisals against Africanism, these club members continued to maintain certain ties to an African past (however mythic) and to cultivate political allegiances to other Cubans who embraced African ethnic practices. From 1900 through the 1940s, the bylaws of at least nineteen African-influenced societies, many based in Santiago de Cuba, declared that they would provide "protection" to club members, which, arguably, was an important tool to sustain cultural norms and group viability. Some organizations, such as the Society of Mutual Aid, Formerly the Council of Carabalí Agro, indicated that their only objective was to provide mutual aid in case of illness or death. Yet most clubs defined their missions more broadly. They emphasized mutual aid, community formation, celebration of African ethnicity, and "protection," in conjunction with collective spiritual worship, education, and the inculcation of modernist and patriotic values.

For the members of the "San Emilio" Society of Instruction, Recreation, and Mutual Aid, Formerly the "Cabildo Lucumí"—which was the target of police harassment in 1924 and in 1934 was forced to close by the provincial governor—protection meant offering sickness and burial benefits as well as pensions to the families of deceased members. Their community life also encompassed instruction, leisure activities, and religious celebrations in honor of San Emilio.[68] The bylaws of Cabildo "El Cocoyé" stated that the club would "protect" its members as well as celebrate the Virgin of Charity, patroness of the society and patron saint of Cuba, and would provide educational opportunities and organized leisure activities.[69] Similarly, "El Tiberé" Society of Instruction, Recreation, and Mutual Aid sought to offer its members protection, education, and leisure activities and, according to the bylaws, aimed to "celebrate simultaneously religious festivals in honor of the Virgin of Charity."[70]

Members of these societies believed in an ongoing connection to Africa, which represented for them a unified body politic as well as a connection with past generations. Often, bylaws stipulated that they honor their deceased ancestors and provide mutual aid for descendants of their particular ethnic African group. Many also sought bonds with other societies that were likewise invested in African connections.

Though most African-identified societies did not clarify whether their members were African-born (records, for example, show only one organization listing African-born members and these constituted about 25 percent of the total roster), they still imagined an African homeland.[71] This sensibility served to unify members and challenge dominant norms of bourgeois individualism, without rejecting patriotic nationalism. Africa was at the center of a nationalism that represented belonging, despite and because of the context of extreme Afro-phobic aggression in the early republic.

A *rezo* (collective song or prayer) of the African-influenced Carabalí Isuama Society of Santiago de Cuba articulates these African-identified Cubans' nostalgia for homeland as well as their harsh everyday experiences. In particular, this *rezo*, composed sometime in the early republican period, relies on a circular narrative of lived experience. Here, the trope of blood— both the letting of it in violence and its power to redeem and win justice— invokes birth and freedom. Drumbeats-are-heartbeats-are-blood in this lyric prayer, which is suffused with longing:

Si por siempre he podido olividar
Siendo libre la sangre [de] mi abuelo
Los trabajo que pasé por ella
Eso nunca lo puedo olividar
África, África, África,
La tambora me hace recordar.
[If I have forever forgotten being free,
it is the blood of my grandfather, my blood
the work endured,
that I will never be able to forget
Africa, Africa, Africa,
The drum makes me remember.][72]

In this *rezo*, club members describe their political loyalties to an imagined African homeland and to a broader global diaspora community. They affirm that their experiences, though harsh, were valuable. Connection to Africa (through bloodlines and cultural practices) was central to their own selfhood and to black subjectivity more generally.

Yet Africanist societies also divided themselves along ethnic lines. Ethnic identity was a significant criterion for group participation, and members often conceived of their ethnic lineage as "nations." The archival records of African-identified societies show that they claimed loyalties to the continent as well as to their specific ethnic community. Members of the Society of Our Lady of Carmen admitted only those who were of Carabalí lineage and who had frequented the club since childhood in the company of their Carabalí parents. The Cabildo Carabalí Agro Society stated in its bylaws that only Carabalíes of the Agro "nation" could join the association.[73] For the Congo Club Juan de Góngora, both cultural identity and corporate insularity were prerequisites for membership. Its 1902 bylaws stated that potential members had to win three-fourths approval to join and had to be descendants of Congos.[74] Most clubs did not require publicly acknowledged lineage in order to join, though leadership positions required proper ethnic pedigree. For instance, the Society Carabalí Isuama stated that though others could join the organization, only descendants of Calabar Africans could hold leadership posts. For members of the Society of Our Lady of Carmen, leadership eligibility was open only to those Carabalíes who were the descendants of the founders and builders of the original *cabildo* headquarters during colonial rule.[75] The San Salvador de Horta Society, Formerly Cabildo de Viví, stated in 1909 that it was a "continuation of the Cabildo Viví and its purpose is to meet in the cabildo house that belongs to all the children of the [Viví] nation to protect each other mutually, in all necessities of life."[76] Members even stipulated a lifetime pension of two pesos monthly for the "Viví, Señora Justiana Ferrer," whom they identified as the last survivor of the Viví "nation" in Cuba. The Admirers of San Miguel Archangel Society stated in 1929 that its primary goal was for African descendants and those who identified as such—but especially those from the "Lucumí territory"—to meet in the society's social house for spiritual and secular activities.[77]

Although the discourse of sovereignty and independence permeated the early republic, African-influenced clubs' insisted on a political strategy rooted in cultural practice and real or fictive kin ties (rather than in ideological commitments to the rights of the individual, mass action, liberalism, or specific political parties), thereby exposing the shortcomings, at least for club members, of the liberal-democratic model in addressing their concerns and interests. Their support of certain tenets of Cuban modernity (such as literacy and education, morality, and nationalist patriotism), however, also reveals their engagement with and tacit endorsement of racialist ideologies. It reveals a desire to challenge those ideas based on their own experiences of racial, ethnic, and economic oppression and as underpaid laborers of African descent. Finally, it reflects their wish to engage on their own terms in their roles as citizens and in their access to the socioeconomic resources of the early republic, where conformity to liberal-bourgeois norms was a prerequisite for politically expedient relationships and often for access to the benefits of patronage.

Despite club members' commitment to both ethnic lineage and a broad diaspora community, there were significant internal divisions in these societies. Power struggles erupted over organizational assets and elections. Among club leaders and at-large members, factions emerged. At times, these factions were rooted in ethnic difference. In the majority of cases, members appealed to government agents to intervene and correct alleged wrongdoing, such as in 1910, when the outgoing president of the Club San Juan de Góngora in Santiago, Felipe Boudet, was at the center of a legal battle over misappropriation of funds. Charged by a club member, Gonzalo Planas, with graft of the monthly rents from Góngora-owned properties and other club real estate investments, Boudet had refused to relinquish monies or explain how they had been allocated. Charges against him were dropped, however, due to lack of evidence and testimonies by the tenants of club properties.[78] A similar case surfaced in 1913, when the president of the Santa Bárbara Society, Jerónimo Díaz, stood accused by the society's at-large membership of embezzling society assets. In 1902, members of Club San Salvador de Horta complained to the provincial governor that their board of directors refused to make the club's balance sheets public, as the bylaws required, suggesting misappropriation of funds, revealing a lack of confidence in the integrity of the board leadership to safeguard club interests. In 1920, this board again stood accused by members. This time members wrote to the governor regarding election fraud, insisting that he send a "delegate" to force new elections.[79]

In many ways, ongoing ethnic identification challenged group cohesion and harmed the development of a broad, grassroots club movement to improve the socioeconomic position of all poor black Cubans, the sector that most often populated African-influenced clubs. A particularly bitter electoral battle in Club Juan de Góngora in 1915 is illustrative. Three self-identified Congos, Gil Esteve, Felipe Boudet, and Serafín Hernández, all members of the club's board of directors, protested to Oriente's provincial governor in December—the month that regular administrative elections were held. The men accused their president of naming non-Congo *criollos* (the island-born) as treasurer and secretary to his electoral slate (as well as reappointing himself for a second term) in the upcoming elections. Esteve, Boudet, and Hernández charged that the president had failed to respect the Congo authority specified in club bylaws.

The Congo men were not just concerned about the flouting of the bylaws that ensured that a Congo presided over operations. They were as much angered by the fact that *criollos* might attain an administrative post, since they did not trust their leadership. As the men wrote, "We don't want criollos because they lost us our best property." Furthermore, they stated, "no criollo son or grandson of a Congo can be in this club if they have failed to pay dues and been marginal, even absent to daily club life. The president neglects Congos that have years with the club in favor of criollos. . . . We therefore annul these elections, asking you, governor to approve of this annulment so that it be legal."[80]

Just as ethnic identity was an influential factor in club agendas, regional and national values at times determined club goals. The members of both San Benito de Palermo and the Our Lady of Mercy Association stated that their desire for fraternal ties with other organizations extended throughout Cuba's eastern Oriente province and even the entire republic, with the goal of creating a network among all organizations with similar agendas. The Regional, "San Lázaro" Society, founded in 1934, characterized itself as an African religious society whose objective was to offer fraternity to both the children and the grandchildren of Africans and to similar organizations residing in Oriente province. Even though the bylaws stated clearly that members were engaged in religious activities, not in political ones, the members chose to identify with both Cuba and Africa, slating weekly "traditional African" as well as "Cuban" dances.

African-influenced club members were interested in political participation, which they knew to be predicated on a political culture rooted in modernity. In fact, in their organizational charters—reviewed and approved by provincial authorities—they often declared preparedness for citizenship based on their adherence to "modern" social practices as a goal. Their bylaws demonstrate an allegiance to the republican and liberal values—such as a concern for moral character—that many early republican political figures expressed.[81] For example, members of the Our Lady of Carmen Mutual Aid Society suggested in their 1913 bylaws that the organization was to be made up of Congo descendants, recognizing the importance of and lamenting the deaths of their forebears. Yet they also rejected and resolved to bury with the deceased their old, ostensibly uncivilized, customs. "Our ancestors, having died," they wrote, "and wishing to cast off their old customs because of the degree of civilization that we find ourselves in today, this Society will henceforth be named, Our-Lady-of-Carmen-Formerly-Cabildo Carabalí-Olugo, because [the society] is the Cabildo's continuation." Other societies supported the development of culture and education, such as did the San Benito de Palermo and the Admirers of San Miguel Archangel Society, which stated that their organizations would provide books, newspapers, and social events, according to the traditional and contemporary custom, with the strictest morality, decorum, and civilization and according to the law of order.

The Our Lady of Regla African Society, founded in Santiago in 1939, intended to help members study, learn, and disseminate spiritual doctrine as well as to provide night school in order that members would be educated and therefore useful to the Cuban republic. The members of the Our Lady of Mercy Association pledged themselves to the moral improvement of its members, by cultivating intelligence and morality in both public and private lives. Except for San Benito de Palermo, the Congo Club Juan de Góngora made perhaps the strongest statement among African-identified societies in support of republican political culture as well as ethnic identity. In 1902, these self-identified Congos pledged an allegiance to both the Cuban and the Congo "nations." They offered their club headquarters for social and political gatherings, to be used "to celebrate parties, conferences, and other public gatherings of a political nature that contribute economically and intellectually to all public and private acts that aid the progress and absolute independence of Cuba."[82]

Conclusion

These societies demonstrate that identities among Cubans of African descent are historically contingent rather than monolithic and that the social and political communities that they created contributed to expanding republican narratives of the meaning of Africa. On the one hand, the mainstream media and government officials insisted that the island's population of African descent, particularly poorer blacks, thwarted republican social and political advancement and were antithetical to the formation of a national body fully qualified to join the "Family of Nations." On the other hand, even though the agendas of African-influenced clubs differed significantly from those of the privileged black clubs and mainstream political activists, many Africanist societies such as San Benito de Palermo insisted that they were fully part of Cuba's nationalist ethos and development, although on their own terms. As such, they moved beyond racial binaries to enrich the articulation of blackness in the diaspora. They sharpen, in fact, our understanding of republican Cuban political discourses.

At a moment in the history of the early republic, when the government, public intellectuals, scientists, and most media homogenized and even criminalized black Cubans, Africanist society members struck back at the core of this logic, that is, at the validity of excising imaginings of Africa from the developing political lexicon of the Cuban republic. In this sense, they pushed against a highly delimited vision of Cuba's modern political world, practicing what political scientist Michael Hanchard has termed "Afro-Modernity," that is, the "negation of the idea of African and African-derived peoples as the antithesis of modernity."[83] In early twentieth-century Cuba, the myth of national racelessness helped to perpetuate the teleology of the forward-looking European and the backward-facing African. In the process, the interdependency of these historical inventions and their development was obscured. When Africanist societies did accept, in part, the disparaging notion of lineal atavism, they still remained committed to the belief that phenotype did not obviate cultural evolution, again dismantling the logic that black subjectivities were necessarily static and ahistorical. In rescuing their vision of Africa as a redeemed, moral homeland, compatible with modernity, nationalism, and liberalism, they challenged the portrayal of Africa's legacy as a menace to Cuban society.

CHAPTER FOUR

Africa in the Privileged Black Imaginary

If Africanist club members struggled to assert complex and dynamic definitions of selfhood and to merge Afro-diasporan sensibilities with Cuban patriotic nationalism, privileged black Cuban leaders, such as Juan Gualberto Gómez, journalist Miguel Gualba, and journalist and politician Rafael Serra, were nearly unanimous in their public disdain of "Africa." Africa's legacy in Cuba, they asserted, was an obstacle not only to national progress but to black Cubans' socioeconomic status in the nation as well. Long a source of conflict and controversy among sectors of the African-descended population, for republican black activists the island's African legacy seemed to work against rather than help in their struggle for public resources. They believed that embracing "savage" Africanist practices was counter to their interests. In fact, they were generally in tacit if not open agreement with many racialist architects of Cuban nationalism on the need for a modernist intervention among the popular classes. A leadership cadre, they often asserted, would promote among blacks "civilized" behavior and normative values such as self-denial, refinement, civility, and respectability, as well as order, industry, and thrift. As black war veteran, journalist, and progressive Rafael Serra counseled in 1904, by pursuing formal education, professional training, and legal marriage, postindependence blacks could repudiate outmoded "savage practices."[1]

The antithesis of their modernity was in part *lo Africano* (things African), a social force that was, primarily, cultural in its articulation, perpetrated by atavistic blacks, and influential in creating gradations of blackness. That is, "race" registered at the level of behavior. One's behavior could approximate cultural norms that were either European or African. In this sense, and according to the logic of progressivism, Africanity, and even blackness itself, were choices. Black club members argued that a direct correlation existed between blacks' aspirations to improve their social and economic status and their ability to distance themselves from the cultural backwardness embodied by Africanist practices. If, according to the island's social-racial continuum, Africanity was an articulation of deep blackness (the "black" black), then to the degree that black Cubans embraced Africanity they condemned themselves to social and political marginalization. Many privileged Cubans of African descent felt that "cultural improvement" was the best remedy for racial subordination. Arguably, self-actualized "cultural improvement" was impossible to achieve due to the concept's amorphousness and imprecision. Rarely was "cultural improvement" tangible. In fact, when black public intellectuals, politicians, and others called for improvement, they were talking about the mainstays of social ordering, engineering, and control—emphasis on marriage and patriarchal unions, participation in industrialized wage labor, compliance with state ordinances and regulations, circumspect social, cultural, sexual, and economic behavior, and formal education. Africanist cultural practices—generally viewed as those that respectable citizens of any color avoided—were vigorously attacked and legislated against at several moments in republican history.

Rafael Serra's strategy for black socioeconomic advancement, like that of many other black public sphere activists and intellectuals, was to adhere to certain cultural norms in order to improve his access to opportunities. In fact, he sparked one of the earliest twentieth-century public sphere debates about black Cubans' African heritage and its significance for blacks' socioeconomic advancement. Though he railed against Cuban leaders who failed to support black civil rights and equal access to socioeconomic resources, Serra also condemned Africanist cultural practices, which like most Cubans, he saw as anachronistic and antithetical to national civilization, civic life, and, ultimately, progress. In broad terms, his brand of race and culture mirrors that of other black leaders struggling under the constraints of circumscribed, often racialist, norms in their push to access republican resources. Arguably, his perspective on race, politics, and culture derived from his unusual personal history of travel and journalism, as well as from his political ambition, patriotic nationalism, and high-stakes political ties.

Born in Havana to free black parents in March 1858, Serra spent his early years training as a tobacco apprentice. His work as a *tabaquero* elevated him to the ranks of the black artisan class, a population segment that in the nineteenth century enjoyed relatively lucrative employment as carpenters, barbers, drivers, bricklayers, musicians, wheelwrights, and blacksmiths, among other trades. A tireless advocate of formal education as the principal strategy to win socioeconomic advancement for Cubans of African descent, Serra founded and directed a free school for black children in

Matanzas province during the years of the Little War (1879–1880). He then went into exile, moving to Key West, Florida, by 1880, where he contributed extensively to the civic life of Cuban Floridians, even founding the patriotic society Centro San Carlos, before later relocating to New York City. During his years in New York, Serra joined an anticolonial, exile community of Cuban intellectuals and activists. When anticolonial activists needed to step up their efforts, Serra and other Cuban exiles traveled abroad to raise funds for Cuban independence.[2]

Returning to New York City in 1887 at the age of twenty-nine, Serra once more became a vital figure among exiled Cubans there. By 1890, in addition to his continued support of Cuban anticolonialism, he cofounded the civic organization La Liga (The League) with fellow exile José Martí and twenty-eight others. La Liga mobilized black Cubans in New York City behind the separatist cause and provided them with formal education and civic involvement. Serra returned home to Cuba after colonialism ended in 1898, though not before meeting future president of the republic Tomás Estrada Palma (1835–1908). After his own exile in the 1870s, Estrada Palma had made his way to Central Valley, New York, in 1879, where he founded a school for Latin American children and served as its director. In April 1902, he, too, returned home to Cuba to become the new republic's first head of state.

Until his death in 1910, Serra built a successful journalistic and political career in Cuba. He was a staunch supporter of Estrada Palma's administration (for which he was awarded a job in the postal service), which provided him access to formal politics. In 1904, shortly after winning a congressional seat under the conservative-leaning National Radical Party banner, he founded *El Nuevo Criollo*, a newspaper that from 1904 to 1906 urged black voters to support the national administration.[3] By 1905, Serra's efforts on behalf of Moderates were crucial, given that party leaders were otherwise known for supporting U.S. involvement in Cuba and for their disdain of black political leadership. Serra provided public support for officeholders while simultaneously articulating a particular vision of the nation that united the island's various social and economic sectors ideologically and morally. He often appealed to Cubans across the races to commit to the national project. Cubans, he insisted, had to close ranks and support state consolidation: "We who are dedicated to serving our country are convinced . . . to take seriously the changing times and the change that comes always with new needs and desires to be satisfied. We should be loyal and insistent on contributing to a modest labor . . . because the harmonious efforts of Cuban compatriots can bring rational and healthy change to aged [Cuban] institu-

Politician, journalist, and author Rafael Serra. From Rafael Serra, *Para blancos y negros: Ensayos políticos, sociales y económicos, cuarta serie* (Havana: Imprenta "El Score," 1907). (Courtesy of Manuscripts, Archives and Rare Books Division, Schomburg Center for Research in Black Culture, New York Public Library, Astor, Lenox and Tilden Foundations)

tions, bound to latency and, [which stand] against the innovative spirit of our days these erroneous practices that run contrary to the development of a people."[4]

At the core of Serra's activist vision was a preoccupation with the self and an individual commitment to progressivism, self-denial, and industry. His philosophy, which ultimately depoliticized black activism, was embraced by most privileged black leaders in the early republic. That is, rather than call for socioeconomic restructuring, these leaders argued that black Cubans should focus their energy on *self*-improvement. Thus, Serra urged "enlightened" blacks to declare war on cultural backwardness. As he stated in *El Nuevo Criollo* in 1904, "We would be some renegades and apostates if we were not to . . . launch a tough battle against everything that clashes with culture, civic awareness, and love of good and beauty."[5] For Serra and other like-minded black activists, progressivism, enlightenment, and civic-mindedness defined modern national culture, a culture that at least in the abstract all Cubans could adopt. They also drew sharp distinctions among blacks, so that even as they fought for blacks' access to jobs, they criticized those blacks who engaged in non-normative practices, holding them at least partially responsible for their low socioeconomic status. Blacks' social acceptability, then, was judged according to cultural practices, and Cuba's Africanist legacy was vigorously debated, given its implications for defining blackness, articulating black identity, and constructing the modern, black subject. Rafael Serra published one such polemic in 1904 in *El Nuevo Criollo*, which featured two dissenting, ostensibly black, voices grappling with their sense of black political inspiration. Their central point of contention was the value of legacy for blacks, including Africanist beliefs and practices, in assuming their place within the island's "modern democracy."[6] Should they venerate earlier generations of blacks (for their lofty as well as atavistic cultural achievements), or should they denounce those pasts in order to face squarely forward and focus on creating a new generation more fully compatible with the modern republic? But this debate served largely to define and reiterate black political authority.

Africa and the Legacies of Blackness

Two black intellectuals carried out this debate under the noms de plume "El Negro Falucho" and "El Negro Oriental."[7] At the heart of the debate was the politicizing of blackness and black consciousness and the view that Africanity and Western modernity, two invented, symbiotic tropes of Cuban national identity, were not compatible. Even the noms de plume suggest a view of Cuban national identity separated between the ideas of tradition and modernity. El Negro Falucho, from the capital city of Havana, evoked militarism and progress; El Negro Oriental (who self-identified with the blackest and most rural region of the island—the east was home to a significant concentration of African-descended people) aligned himself at least partially with black Cuban tradition. The pair argued with intensity about black Cubans' connection to Africa, including whether blacks should embrace their ancestral lineage and African-influenced culture or whether they should claim a progressive identity and support the tenets of self-help.

One of the primary concerns of both El Negro Oriental and El Negro Falucho was the obstacle Africanisms posed to black Cubans' progress. El Negro Falucho disdained the African legacy that informed black cultural practices; El Negro Oriental believed these constituted foundational elements of black Cuban identity:

> "To be or not to be" is the question raised by my brother, El Negro Falucho. My brother, El Negro Falucho, believes that yes, it should be that we *break* with the old mold and the old uses and customs of our parents and that, having resolved [these anachronisms], we should place our spirits at the height of the progress, culture, and civic duty provided by those among us, descendants of Africans, who serve as exemplary, luminous beacons in the diverse order of human knowledge. . . . Yet we, born in these parts, the most beautiful and enlightened in America, [are to believe that] we owe absolutely nothing to Africa, birthplace of our parents?[8]

In fact, though he concurred with El Negro Falucho's disparaging assessment of the Africanist cultural practices and their place in Cuba's national future, El Negro Oriental also suggested that black Cubans' attachment to their African past was an important aspect of their place in the modern Cuban nation. Paradoxically, he highlighted what could be gained by a modernist vision that took note of, rather than ignored, Africa's legacy in Cuba. El Negro Oriental pointed to black diaspora excellence in economics, the arts, and public life. This was a tribute, he suggested, to the cultural and intellectual leaders who came out of a glorious past from which black Cubans could draw their nationalist inspiration, much as many white intellectuals drew on their own foundational national myths. As he suggested in a rebuttal to his fellow polemicist:

> As much as we would like we cannot extricate ourselves from all connection to Africa. Even if [Africa] was unable to give us culture, it has at

least given us the trunk of our family tree, just as the Caucasian has given that to our white kinsmen, which causes them much pride and joy, and for whom there are so many distinguished Varonas, Luz and Caballeros, Zayases and Sanguilys; our [black] tree also has a distinguished branch, such as the many Plácidos, Whites, Brindises, Booker T. Washingtons, Gómezes, Morúas, and even Alexandre Dumases.[9]

Thus, for El Negro Oriental, a rich legacy of black cultural achievements was the foundation of black Cuban patriotic nationalism. He echoed many of the same themes that early black nationalists of the Americas did and placed black Cuban patriarchs on a plane equal to white ones. Unlike many privileged black Cubans of the era, El Negro Oriental drew on a model of political community rooted in (black) national homogeneity, purity, and distinction. Rather than imitate or accept the dominant nationalist pantheon of the period (with its invention of a white national cadre of intellectuals, politicians, nationalists, and educators), El Negro Oriental was inspired by an alternate nationalist pantheon, a political community based on the impressive intellectual lineage and glorious past of Cubans of African descent who had succeeded publicly as intellectuals, activists, politicians, artists, and businessmen. This, for him, was the legacy that the African-descended offered black Cubans in the early twentieth century and from which they should draw for their cultural and political inspiration.

El Negro Falucho, however, rejected Cuba's African legacy and racial nationalism more generally. He believed unequivocally in the trope of the African savage and that African-descended Cubans should resist African influences. He suggested, too, that El Negro Oriental's excessive interest in blacks' Africanist heritage made him blind to the danger posed by Africanist religious leaders:

> El Negro Oriental has lived in a moral atmosphere very different from that which, by necessity, this poor "Negro Falucho" has [lived and] breathed. Oh! I would take him by the hand and, acting as a blind man's guide so that he would not stumble or fall, I would make him pass through these dens of inequity, where vice presents itself in all of its impudence so that he sees how, under the conspiracy of the ignorant fetishist, a disgusting gang of co-conspirators wallows and dedicates itself to the most savage African practices, people of all ages, of all sexes, of all colors, and even of all races.[10]

El Negro Falucho insisted that Africanist blacks were marginal to the national community, while blacks who adhered to dominant cultural norms were in a position to secure their full citizenship rights. El Negro Falucho's rebuttal to El Negro Oriental asked:

> What is modern democracy? Is it not progress, light, much light, ennoblement of human individuality, elevation of one's intelligence to the highest grade? Or is it obscurantism, ignorance, brutish intelligence, feeding these with extreme and absurd beliefs that cause one to drag himself miserably to the feet of a shameless drone, a disgusting and repugnant satyr, insatiable in his clumsy desires, demanding from those of his fanatics, possessed by that devil's influence, the very sacrifice of their honor, just as have the despotic, barbarous, and insignificant kings from the most impenetrable regions of equatorial Africa?[11]

Proper cultural practices, then, determined one's proximity to a modern and racially inclusive Cuba and made one fit to be represented by the new, post-independence democratic political system.

El Negro Falucho's views correlated closely to those of many privileged blacks in the early republic—that black advancement was best served by turning away from the cultural backwardness perpetuated by colonial slavery, toward modern intellectual pursuits, decorum, civic duty, and loyalty to the state and the nationalist patriotism implied by all of these. However close to the slave condition and inherently antimodern were the African-descended, many black public intellectuals insisted they could overcome social stasis. Each new generation, they argued, promised relief from the human degradation caused by slavery. As successive generations widened the chronological divide between slavery and freedom, black Cubans were increasingly likely to integrate into modern Cuban society. Longtime black journalist and civic activist Miguel Gualba argued:

> Given our necessity, those of us who are parents, to not lose our efforts and sacrifices, so that these may be offered to the flesh of our flesh along with a future that differs absolutely, not only from our past but from our present, we must hearten and fortify the difficult struggle. . . . We need to continue to support and emulate by example so that our youth carry on with ardor and without shameless cowardice and weakness, in that path that if narrow and abrupt in its beginnings will widen as it is traversed and will undoubtedly bring us [blacks] to possess the highest and most noble social respect.[12]

Further removed from the slave "condition" than their forebears, black youth had a better socioeconomic outlook; the founding of the independent republic in 1902 was the beginning of Cuban democracy and at least in theory marked the dawn of a new chapter of black opportunity. Many hoped that the end of slavery (1886), bound so closely to the end of colonialism (1898), would open new avenues of participation for Cubans of all colors—in particular for the African-descended. They predicted that although the degradation of the slave experience hindered cultural development, it did not make black subordination inevitable. In fact, concern for black advancement was not so much heightened by the watershed of the republic's legal birth in 1902 as by slave emancipation, accomplished more than a decade and a half earlier. Thus, the legacy of Africa and the importance of shedding the stigma of slavery weighed on the minds of black civic activists and laymen alike in the late nineteenth century, motivating them to construct self-help ideologies that later informed early republican advancement strategies.

Transcending Servitude

Though few black voices joined the political debates during the protracted anticolonial insurgency, those that did argued publicly over how, after the abolition of slavery in 1886, African-descended Cubans could enhance their political, social, and economic participation.[13] These voices often blamed colonialism (characterized as Cuban political slavery), deeply rooted racial injustices, and a dire need for black cultural improvement as the principal causes for the lowly status of the island's former slaves. Martín Morúa Delgado (1856–1910) and Juan Gualberto Gómez (1854–1933), the most renowned black intellectuals of the late nineteenth and early twentieth centuries, wrote extensively in the period before Cuba's final and triumphant War of Independence (1895–98) about freedom and the relationship between racial emancipation and Cuban political sovereignty. As black public intellectuals, they argued that at the heart of black Cubans' political strivings were both the continued political subjugation of the island itself and the injustice of human bondage.[14] As Morúa Delgado posited in 1879: "The Africans that were brought to Santo Domingo in 1506 could no longer bear the weight of despotic servitude by 1522, and they rose up in earnest. . . . Although the Spanish saw this only as a despicable act of insubordination, our vision reaches beyond this and we see the intuitive dignity of Man, striving always to break the yoke of despotism and arrogant domination."[15] Morúa Delgado, like Serra and many other black activists of the late colonial and postindependence periods, enjoyed a long career as an intellectual and politician. In three decades of public life, Morúa Delgado published fiction, served briefly in the presidential cabinet as the secretary of agriculture, commerce, and employment, was elected to the Senate, and became

Senate president (the only nonwhite to hold that post in republican history) in 1909. What had been an impressive professional career for any Cuban, however, came to an abrupt end when he died on April 28, 1910. He was for many a highly controversial figure, particularly during his days of distinguished public service at the national level. He was often in vehement disagreement with Juan Gualberto Gómez, another powerful politician and race activist. Morúa Delgado believed that blacks should acquire liberal-bourgeois values of citizenship and enter mainstream politics in order to end political isolation, a gradualist approach that he also took regarding the political freedom of Cuba itself: "Can a people adjourned at night under the oppression of a despotic government awaken to the tight embrace of liberty, of independence without so abrupt a change causing harm?"[16] According to Morúa Delgado, this preparedness came from the pursuit of knowledge and the assimilation of modernist values in order to lead a new, independent society. He argued that formal education and "modern" values, such as rationalism, social restraint, civility, political liberalism, civic activism, and economic advancement, constituted freedoms in their own right, and that these were the best avenues for black Cubans to advance. As he suggested after the end of the Ten Years' War (1868–78): "An educated man cannot be subjugated; an enlightened man is a free man. This is all that we want." Further, he stated: "Nothing can be gained if the most terrible of servitudes is not destroyed, the servitude of ignorance."[17]

Juan Gualberto Gómez, in his own lengthy career as an anticolonial activist, politician, and journalist, was a leading exponent of Cuban nationalism and antidiscrimination. Gómez worked among black civic organizations, leading an island-wide federation of black clubs in the 1880s and early 1890s. The clubs were important tools of black enlightenment, he believed, which could help the island's ex-slave population cultivate rational values, cultural refinement, and civic participation; he felt the clubs represented the best hope for black empowerment.[18] Several Havana-based organizations of the time were in agreement. In 1886, just one month after slavery ended in Cuba, they founded the Directorate of Societies of the Colored Race to celebrate abolition. The collective held a sense of hope similar to Gómez's and a desire to join colonial Cuban society on the strength of their civic values. As the Havana-based La Divina Caridad stated in a letter to Juan Gualberto Gómez, written to him on behalf of all societies in the collective, "[The Directorate was] a consequence of abolition . . . to organize a great, civic procession . . . of all [clubs] that belong to the [black] race."[19]

Notwithstanding this call for black civic unity, the directorate represented only a small segment of the island's black civic organizations. And even

Martín Morúa Delgado and daughters Arabella and Vestalina. From Rafael Serra,
Para blancos y negros: Ensayos políticos, sociales y económicos, cuarta serie (Havana:
Imprenta "El Score," 1907). (Courtesy of Manuscripts, Archives and Rare Books
Division, Schomburg Center for Research in Black Culture, New York Public Library,
Astor, Lenox and Tilden Foundations)

though members in 1886 had called on all societies of "the race" to join the directorate procession, only thirty of the island's estimated seventy-five African-descended civic organizations of the time participated in the celebration. Further, by July 1887, almost a year after the inaugural parade, a much smaller collective gathered (some thirteen societies) at the Centro de Cocheros (Drivers' Club) in Havana to formalize the directorate.[20] The smaller group gave new shape to the organization, elbowing out societies of Africanist cultural orientation, even as the collective officially claimed to represent the needs of the race of color. The following year, in 1888, the directorate's organ, *La Fraternidad*, edited by Juan Gualberto Gómez, insisted that Africanist practices were untenable in a progressive society and condemned Africanist organizations as unacceptable. *La Fraternidad* ridiculed those of African descent who celebrated in Africanist ways, such as the *ñáñigos* (Abakúa secret society members), who gathered on Three-Kings' Day (January 6, 1888) on Havana docks to "contort ridiculously in raw savagery."[21] *La Fraternidad* even chastised Havana police for not intervening and arresting those gathered at the waterfront, suggesting that Gómez drew clear distinctions among the African-descended.[22] He called for the gradual eradication of Africanist organizations and their customs by permitting only Africans, and not their descendents, to join African *cabildos*. In time, he implied, the organizations would expire slowly as the deaths of those who first brought them to Cuban shores occurred: "Note that we, for reasons easily understood, are not in agreement that here [in Cuba] the dances and habits of Africa are perpetuated. It pains us that those born in Cuba, even though their parents are African, direct their gaze to the beaches to which they will not return. This is why we believe African *cabildos* should be solely for Africans."[23]

On occasion, Gómez departed from anti-Africanist opinion, such as his 1892 stance in *La Igualdad* (a periodical that supplanted *La Fraternidad* as the directorate's organ), which criticized Havana police for their repression of Africanist *cabildos de nación* as they routed Africanist *ñáñigos*.[24] Then Gómez defended the right of Africanist *cabildos* to meet and practice according to their customs, since they had "nothing to do with groups of *ñáñigos*."[25] He believed that *cabildo* associations should be protected and that their rights to meet and to participate in Cuban associational life should be preserved, based on recent reformist legislation of the liberalizing Spanish colonial state:[26] "But since these [*cabildo* members] cannot be prohibited from their predilection for the songs, dances, and distractions of the place where they witnessed first light, besides this in our minds the Africans have rights because they combat a [police] infraction of legal rights and we will always combat arbitrariness. Although the authorities believe they pursue a likely outcome, if we feel that in pursuing this end they violate the law, then we believe in the right to censure this violation."[27] More than seeing any inherent value in Africanist practices, Gómez upheld liberalist principles and the Law of Association granted by the colonial state in 1886, and in broad terms he challenged anti-African repression. He insisted that associational activism, an important tool of modern Cuban political culture, was critical for the African-descended in enlightening and preparing themselves for participation in Cuban politics and society.

Nonetheless, the extent to which Gómez indicted Africanisms as barbarity is clear in an editorial debate between two newspapers in 1893. The fray, concerning the terms of Cuba's political relationship with Spain, erupted after slave emancipation (1886) and preceding the final War of Independence (1895–98) between *La Igualdad*, Gómez's anticolonial, separatist newspaper for black Cubans, and *La Vanguardia*, a procolonial periodical whose readership was, presumably, privileged and of European descent. A third press, *El Diario de la Marina*, Havana's conservative daily, characterized the journalistic factions as "two *caudillos* [strongmen] of different races that are mortal enemies and want to do away with each other."[28] The heart of the matter was the uncertainty regarding the postcolonial social order. The threat of black political participation, even political mobilization, in independent Cuba took on importance because the strictures of colonialism might soon be lifted. *La Vanguardia*'s attack, based on a racialist logic, was a ploy to discredit the separatist movement on racial grounds. Gómez fired a swift riposte in a now-famous polemic titled "Cuba Is Not Haiti." Part palliative, part political anthropology, the essay argued that black violence, although possible in other parts of the Caribbean region, especially in Haiti (which had a history of large-scale, armed black resistance), was impossible in Cuba due to Cuban social and cultural developments. Gómez, in fact, repeated similar arguments made by Cuban planters in 1812, anxious in the wake of the 1804 triumph of the Haitian Revolution. Planters then argued that unlike Haiti's bondmen, Cuban slaves were "treated as men," and that whites' numbers, civil laws, and benevolence toward Cuban slaves made slaves too "happy" to revolt.[29] Eighty years later, Gómez drew on similar logic to insist that at the time of the Revolution, blacks on Saint Domingue (Haiti) outnumbered whites twenty-four to one. Demographics had made it possible for blacks in Haiti to overpower whites, a feat impossible in Cuba. He also posited that Haitian slaves came from particularly "savage regions" of Africa, such as Senegal and Dahomey (aggressive regions in his estimation), an important factor in slave violence against Haiti's planter class. Africans in Cuba came in large part from the more "passive" Congo and Guinea regions. Gómez suggested that the Senegalese, the Dahomey, and other "aggressive Africans" were still "tenaciously resistant" to the civilizing effects of Europe. He also emphasized that Cuba had the largest free black population in the Antilles, making for a hefty population of color that, *over time*, had become quite "civilized."[30] Gómez indicted Africanist practices but, like Morúa Delgado, also argued that nationalist consciousness had furthered blacks' cultural progress.

Both Gómez and Morúa Delgado stressed that one's cultural "condition" and political aptitudes were environmental, not biological, a position supported by the anticolonial insurgency's most vibrant philosopher, José Martí, who in 1895, on the eve of war, wrote: "To he who has all my vices and virtues I say, you are my brother. To he who comes from below me and rises because of his intelligence and honor and abnegation as great as mine, I say, you are my brother. . . . Cuba does not need to elevate the black; his share merits truth that the white needs elevation as much as the black might need it. In Cuba, for humanity and foresight, we must be just."[31] Gómez and Morúa Delgado attacked the widespread notion that recently emancipated blacks were unable to transition from slaves to freemen. They insisted that, should they choose to, emancipated blacks were capable of shedding their previous "condition" as part of a concerted effort to progress toward modern socialization. They did not question that blacks could become *culto* (cultured).[32] Stated more succinctly, the descendants of Africans held the possibility, though not the guarantee, of cultural evolution.

Even the laws promulgated during the so-called fecund truce (1880 to 1895), promoting civic freedoms and abolishing slavery (1886), placed in greater relief the problem of how to incorporate this sector into the colony's civic and political arenas, a concern echoed by Morúa Delgado and Gómez. In 1890, a highly concerned Gómez wrote: "The black man came [to Cuba] in ignorance from the African jungles to the slave [plantation] where he was isolated. It is logical that this produced intellectual atrophy; 'culture' and 'slave' are terms antagonistic to each other."[33] And in 1893, two years before Cubans' final bid for independence began, he stated bleakly, "Novices of public battles, little accustomed to political projects, it comes as no surprise that on entering public life [blacks] appear on the social scene without any cohesion or unity."[34] Morúa Delgado and Gómez defined their activism as the struggle to combine Cuba's anticolonial movement with one whose implications for them were equally sweeping: black, postemancipation civil rights in colonial society. This was especially true for blacks who belonged to directorate member societies, who sought to distinguish themselves from the masses of former slaves in order to retain their privileged status. Historian Rebecca Scott suggests that following emancipation castelike divisions among the African-descended "blurred."[35] As all blacks were granted equal legal status, the socioeconomic lines formerly separating urban, rural, free, and enslaved black populations dissolved. For blacks of traditionally privileged socioeconomic status, retaining that privilege vis-à-vis the island's at-large black population was a difficult (and often contradictory) endeavor.[36]

One way in which Morúa Delgado and Gómez claimed distinguished status was to reason that although all blacks deserved absolute freedom, most were not ready to take part in universal freedoms and liberal democracy. Both men suggested that uncultured blacks had a big task: to educate themselves in order to acquire the civilization necessary for full civic participation.[37] He aptly reiterated this politics at an 1887 conference in Key West, Florida, when he declared that blacks were "revolutionaries" in the midst of a "social revolution" whose guiding forces were "reason" and "moral persuasion."[38] Most privileged blacks believed that Cubans of African descent had to shed their pasts before they could participate in the coming "modern" order, and that those pasts would be best buried through formal instruction.

In keeping with liberalist and nationalist ideals, women were society's consummate educators, a tenet of patriarchal norms that black leaders readily embraced. Black women were often assigned the task of black cultural regeneration and formal instruction, and their sexual behavior, morality, and social relationships were scrutinized and proscribed to a greater extent than were those of men. The success or failure of the race was often laid at black women's feet; among the African-descended women were often cast as moral beacons who were poised to impart wisdom, sensitivity, restraint, and chastity. In fact, throughout the nineteenth century, educating the island's non-elite population was the purview of women of color, and public teaching posts allowed many of them a modicum of social and economic mobility, although they were poorly remunerated and often looked down on by elite Cubans. In the 1820s, the Public Instruction section of the Sociedad Económica de Amigos del País (Friends of the Country Economic Society) (SEAP) even characterized the education of Cuban children as the task of women of color and of "unfortunate [white] widows, barely literate themselves, [who were] asked to be the country's *minervas* of the fair sex."[39] Not surprisingly, the magazine *Minerva: Revista Quincenal Dedicada á la Mujer de Color*, which first went to press in 1888 and which was written expressly for women of color, was organized by activists of the Central Directorate of Societies of the Colored Race. Juan Gualberto Gómez wrote that the magazine would serve as the organ "of studious youth" and would "awaken love for things beautiful and true." Its founders strove "to offer to all those that aspire to a vocation in letters and arts a magazine in which they can come to know their productions."[40] Gómez applauded the editors of *Minerva*, who, he said, rejected "vulgar things, those of doubtful morality, bad taste, or crudeness [which] are the only things that will always find closed the doors of *Minerva*."[41] *Minerva*'s editors believed that black women were uniquely able to promote cultural achievement and liberal family values among newly emancipated slaves: "One of the things that today we most need," wrote a contributor in January 1889, "is the education of women, because they are called to contribute in great part to the moral improvement of our families. What is the man whose wife is not educated? What can she teach to her children?"[42] Dedicated to the cultivation of domesticity, morality, virtue, and motherhood among women of color, *Minerva*'s editors insisted that black and mulatto women of standing were natural activists for the "improvement" of black men and children.

The relationship between social advancement, sexuality, and gender propriety was also a theme addressed by *Minerva*, and regular contributors to the magazine, such as Cecilia Onatina, suggested that black women were as able as white women to fulfill bourgeois-liberal norms of chastity and morality. In fact, many of the magazine's pieces concluded that black women could cast off the stigma and shame of slavery (and perhaps of forced sexual relationships with slave owners) through outward displays of virtue. Their practice of chastity and moral behavior disproved presumptions about their inferiority as true women:

Á Onatina
Woman is most beautiful demonstrating her elegance
Without spreading about her fragrance
But conserving, in particular, one thing: virtue.
It is a lovely gift, the most cherished treasure
That she has to guard with decorum, if she has sane reason.
What is it that should be done to unearth vice?
Be always willing to educate, woman.
To triumph today, it is important to combat ignorance
To kill arrogance where it roots
Our daughters, what pain!
Abandoned, lost, many corrupted by their infamous seducer,
Degrading but shamefully true results,
The effects of the damage of that famous institution.
Why did so many wrongs result from slavery?

Because heinous mortals did not teach virtue.
For the [slave] institution to triumph
You [were denied] the sacred right of education
The venturous day of redemption has arrived
As has the long-dreamed hour of our happiness.
The woman to whom the air habitually pledges itself is glass.
Clean she must remain because that is, for her honor's sake, a duty.[43]

For the editors of *Minerva*, socioeconomic advancement was not only the result of professional success and racial equality. They also believed that intrinsically blacks' social value depended on adherence to cultural norms such as domesticity, sexual propriety, and patriarchy. Further, black political empowerment hinged on proper education, circumspect behavior, restraint, *and* civility, the onus of which, for bourgeois liberalists like the editors of *Minerva*, was borne by black women.

The emphasis on education relates in part to blacks' minimal access to formal instruction until the late colonial period. In fact, blacks were not granted the right to education beyond primary school until 1878, when the Superior Council of Public Education granted blacks legal access to secondary, professional, and university instruction. But they were de facto barred from higher education by school segregation, since few institutions existed to educate black children and adults.[44] Nonetheless, following emancipation, most blacks placed their faith in the power of a formal education to create job opportunity and provide the tools necessary to claim legal rights and fulfill civic duties. In this sense, they believed that education compensated for the cultural deficiencies of the African-descended. Blacks of privilege also understood it to be a critical factor in distinguishing themselves from a lower class of blacks.

Black societies of instruction and leisure often identified education as an urgent need; during the so-called fecund truce period (1880–95) several of them opened schools. Arguably, no other theme rang so intensely in the late colonial and early republican periods. An 1892 letter written by a black club near Havana to Juan Gualberto Gómez, then president of the Central Directorate of Societies of the Colored Race, suggested as much. Victor Vázquez, writing on behalf of what he called an "unaffiliated corporation" from Colón town, a predominantly black town at Havana's outskirts, aired his organization's extreme frustration on this point. Although the law mandated black primary schools in towns larger than 10,000 "souls," officials had not ordered any black primary schools to be built so that "black children might receive the principles of enlightenment."[45] Members of the black Sociedad

La Bella Unión near Havana met in July 1892 and were in general agreement that "the need that exists in our town specific to the class of color is instruction, and given our circumstances we lack the elements necessary to achieve that." For these members, education was critical to black advancement and to breaking socioeconomic barriers. Their common aspirations, as they expressed them, were to be "free and respected as citizens and according to pacifist means to break the lines of division that contribute to dissidence ... because there is no difference between one [race] and the other ... and achieving this we will arrive at the point where our aspirations lie."[46] In clarifying their goals, they also intimated that the pursuit of education was less motivated by their own perceived backwardness than by a belief in its utility to win justice and economic opportunity.

For the class of aspiring blacks and mulattos in the postemancipation period, the concept of "uplift" only partially encapsulates the paradox of the moment's racial politics. As they struggled to remove racial barriers to their own education and employment and against the state's attempt to group African-descended Cubans into a singular, homogeneous community, they perpetuated class and gender hierarchies among Cubans of African descent. In fact, throughout Cuba's history of slavery, privileged blacks and mulattos practiced social exclusions among themselves and with other, less-privileged Cubans of African descent to help their own social and economic advancement. In the postemancipation period, education was one of the most important avenues for social and professional advancement, and blacks seeking privileged status sought the opportunity for education at the same time that they called for the removal of racial barriers to opportunity. This complexity of Cuban racial politics would be borne out in the republican period, for Cubans of African descent were faced with a number of factors in the formation of their political strategies. The aspiring class of blacks, for example, called for black unity while distinguishing themselves from the masses of black Cubans, in one sense, as previously suggested, using these distinctions to fulfill their own aspirations.

Black republican activists supported the idea that, given blacks' African lineage, time spent in the slave "condition," and ongoing economic disadvantages, many were still socially and culturally unfit to participate in formal politics and civic life. Generoso Campos Marquetti and the black veterans' Action Committee suggested as much in 1902 when they met with President Tomás Estrada Palma to demand more government appointments, specifically for those blacks of "real merit." This, in turn, correlated with a poor prognosis for their social and economic advancement unless, so the theory went, they changed their cultural behavior. "We should break with the old mold, the old customs and practices of our parents," suggested one black intellectual in late 1904, "and resolved we should put our spirits toward the elevation of progress, culture, and civic activism as demonstrated by those among us of African descent who are luminous beacons in diverse orders of human wisdom."[47] Not surprisingly, they insisted that they themselves constituted a black cadre ready to lead the masses of blacks toward self-improvement.

This call to break the "old mold" was penned less than a year after black American intellectual W. E. B. Du Bois wrote "The Talented Tenth." A writer of uncommon eloquence, insight, and clarity, Du Bois was particularly articulate on the topic of black experience, and his writing reflects a post-Enlightenment preoccupation with developing the self. Given the context in which he wrote, of imperial expansion and the concomitant ordering and ranking of the world's populations, Du Bois also challenged the myth of the immutability of the human condition. In September 1903 he pronounced: "The Negro race, like all races, is going to be saved by its exceptional men. The problem of education, then, among Negroes must first of all deal with the Talented Tenth; it is the problem of developing the Best of this race that they may guide the Mass away from the contamination and death of the Worst, in their own and other races."[48] Black Cuban leaders such as Serra would have received these words as logical and righteous, having defended a similar philosophy decades earlier, in the late colonial period. Black Cuban activists also argued that cultural advantages were not limited to "exceptional men" but could be obtained by education and normative behavior. Privileged black Cubans identified themselves as vanguards for the black masses, mentors of self-improvement. According to their progressivist narrative, to the extent that the African-descended could adjust to dominant values, blacks would improve their social and economic status. They argued vigorously throughout the republican period that cultural backwardness could be changed. Even as scientists of the era generated numerous studies to "prove" that blacks were inherently degenerate and inclined toward backward practices, black leaders reiterated that all Cubans, irrespective of their race or cultural tendencies, were able to transcend atavistic culture. Obtaining formal education and gradually accumulating wealth, for example, would improve one's socioeconomic status, and in this sense cultural practices were less determined by biological "race" than by individual choice; a shift in blacks' choices could place them on socioeconomic par with whites. As Serra wrote, "The inferior races should elevate themselves to their [racial] superiors by way of education and instruction. Intelligence is the great leveler of the human species."[49] *La Estrella Refulgente*

(The Shooting Star), a black literary, cultural, and political magazine, argued similarly in a March 1906 editorial: "There are two capital problems . . . that we [blacks] are obligated to resolve gradually and completely, if it is true that we desire (and of this there is no doubt) our social improvement and due consideration from all of our [white] compatriots. . . . These two problems are education and economy."[50] Arguably, black activists were faced with a third problem. Beyond inspiring "due consideration" in their compatriots, as equal citizens they had to prove their fitness for social and political leadership. For so public a role—whether as head of a civic organization or in government service—black activists had to publicly demonstrate redemption and the capacity to lead. Even those who could recall the horrific conditions suffered by slaves and unskilled agricultural laborers in colonial history, describing in detail the "whistle of machines," the "twenty-hour work days of the sugar mills and other work farms," and the "crack of the overseer's whip," insisted that with refinement and education former slaves could advance national progress: "One day, beloved homeland, you will be the crucible that with the fire of reason and consciousness purges the false tinsel that degraded the purity of your birth. . . . From today on, Cuba, you will be blessed for all eternity because freed, those of your sons that howled in the most cruel servitude, in the curve of your loving breast [they] will be, in short years of constant study, men of benefit to family, society, and the homeland."[51] In fact, as Sidney Mintz has argued and black Cuban writer África Céspedes here suggests, it was precisely because of whistling machines, grueling work schedules, and the overseer's order that slaves developed "modern" sensibilities. Céspedes argues that these sensibilities could be capitalized on by freedmen, whose best chance at modernity was acquiring civic values through education and healthy family life.

For many privileged blacks in postemancipation society, from newspaper editors to civic activists, formal education was conflated with social respectability, political engagement, and economic opportunity. Such liberal-bourgeois ideologies did not fade with the island's switch to independent rule. Rather, they influenced early republican black activism and definitions of leadership. In April 1906, for example, in the midst of a revolution that eventually toppled President Tomás Estrada Palma and his Moderate-run administration, the Havana-based Booker T. Washington Institute of Popular Education held a conference on racial politics, titled "The Cuban Social Question." The institute's director, Emilio Céspedes Casado, was the keynote speaker. As an educated black man, Céspedes Casado proposed several strategies for black advancement, though he first clarified that his speech was not meant to advocate for "any class or race in society." He hoped to contribute to the education of the popular working classes, most especially "the black race; making use of the opportunity to elevate the public perception of [black] women and children."[52] Framing much of his argument according to prevailing gender norms, the director insisted that blacks had earned certain rights of citizenship based on their inspired call to serve the mother country, "offering their hand and declaring, 'Oh, Mother! Here we are.'"[53] Yet however much black men had shown valor in defending the nation (in the independence wars and in the anti-Moderate Revolution then under way— the August Revolution of 1906), Céspedes Casado insisted that blacks' full political participation depended as much on intellectual development as on military prowess. They needed to raise their current level of culture and instruction in order to advance, pointing to education as the most important strategy for improving blacks' status in the republic. Formal education was the hope provided by institutions such as the Booker T. Washington Institute, yet cultural inspiration for present and future generations was, he asserted, found at home. In this realm, argued Céspedes Casado, black women were the principal players; they were the conduits of black cultural improvement.

Céspedes Casado articulated a common belief about race progress and the role of black women, one that, as we have seen, prevailed in the late colonial period among black civic activists. Of those black civic organizations financially able to publish their own periodicals, many featured women's photos and their domestic achievements as evidence that the organization promoted refinement and respectability. Women, in general, did not join black societies but were important to reflecting black privilege and respectability. They were central, in fact, to proving black authority and to the *performance* of black civic respectability and refinement in broader society. In 1930, for example, in a commemorative issue of the Club Atenas bulletin, photographs of club members' wives and children were as prominent as photographs of male club leaders featured for their professional achievements or as candidates for one or another political office.[54]

The logic that black Cubans needed education and cultural improvements in order to progress was undergirded by a widespread, racialist belief that Cubans of African descent (particularly those with few economic resources) were socially and politically unprepared for civic participation. Describing them as unenlightened, uneducated, and culturally backward, Céspedes Casado echoed a common sensibility regarding the dire necessity of forming an enlightened black cadre, a select few, those "cultured blacks, educated, decent, rich, and respectable," who could serve as leaders of the republic's African-descended population, preparing blacks to actively participate in the national political community. In fact, he suggested that the masses of black Cubans clamored to be led by black elites, based on their longing for cultural fitness, fraternal desire for national progress, divine inspiration, and the welcome subordination of Cuba's unenlightened black majority to the few privileged blacks:

> But for that multitude that anxiously waits for a supportive word, council, and guidance; for that multitude that due to causes unnecessary to enumerate here have found themselves isolated in a desert without examples and without teachers; for those masses that hold in their hearts a gleam of love and in their spirits the need to improve their condition, it is to them that we direct ourselves, in the manner of teachers with the quality of soul-mates, to whom we open our arms and stretch them out as brothers, and for whom I desire rapid and healthy regeneration, that they do not die without having touched—as we have—the sweetness of spiritual life. We will help all with this great work and we shall receive the blessings of God.[55]

Conclusion

Integral, then, to theories of black improvement was a call for a black cadre with the political authority and cultural attributes to successfully lead. Although akin to Du Bois's notion of a Talented Tenth, this call for black Cuban improvement had its roots in advocacy for black civil rights in the late nineteenth century, during the "fecund truce" between 1880 and 1895 and in republican political culture. For blacks active in formal electoral politics, this was especially true. Black political hopefuls endured intense pressure to prove their capacity for political authority and allegiance to the developing nation-state; they also understood that suspicion and harsh judgments abounded regarding their particular motives for political participation. As Emilio Céspedes Casado lamented, "I know well that many will criticize our [black activists'] work, hiding under a censurable lack of concern over the shame that they should have regarding the disconcerting spectacle that is offered by social disparities in this country."[56] A critical aspect of black civic and political leadership, then, was public image and the projection of power.

Black civic and political activists used a range of tactics (attire; press announcements; forums, contests, sporting events, and dances; and public conference and lectures) to perform normatively, disprove racialist theories about their lack of social "fitness," and anoint themselves as leaders. Like privileged blacks of the nineteenth century, those of the republic insisted

that their cultural practices distinguished them from the masses of culturally "backward" black Cubans. Cultural practices seemed to offer proof of
one's fitness for public office in the early decades of the republic, since to
be politically active and/or to occupy public office depended heavily on the
perception that one possessed respectability, accomplishments, and refinement. In fact, the relationship between normative performance and political
aspirations and endorsements shaped black activism in powerful ways in the
early republic and helped to establish the tenor of black political leadership.
Black political authority also rested on public sphere debates, where black
politics, identity, and strategies were discussed. Most black newspapers and
civic organizations enabled black leaders to propagandize on behalf of their
political interests and to assert power, yet at times these venues also gave
voice to their detractors and, beyond revealing deep tensions and disparate
motivations among black leaders, challenged the myth that all black Cubans
in the early republic were grouped together in uncomplicated social, political, and cultural ways.

CHAPTER FIVE

Power and Great Culture

In the first three decades of the twentieth century, black leaders and civic activists advanced the idea that refinement, patriarchy, and bourgeois respectability should be the basis of Cuban leadership, irrespective of a leader's race. Black civic organizations promoted this ideology and enabled black leaders' public performance of the cultural practices (respectability, refinement, and adherence to normative values) that reinforced their political authority. Dr. Miguel Ángel Céspedes, a politician and board member of Unión Fraternal, one of the largest black civic organizations in Cuba (and brother of Emilio Céspedes Casado), advocated for the use of education to modernize and uplift aspiring blacks. In November 1914, he proposed to use the club's salons to create a "Popular University," "in the French tradition [of learned institutions] that today are founded in all nations of great culture."[1] Political scientist Luis Roniger has described how under clientelism, which is characterized by intense competition for political office, public performance and power are related. He argues that in the struggle to secure elected office, political actors strategically project specific modes of "appearance, reputation, credibility," and so on, to more successfully compete for power within formal political institutions.[2] The connections among civic activism, modern cultural values, political leadership, and elections are clearly visible for the early republican period, and black civic activists and their organizations and presses carved out a critical niche in the public sphere, particularly in black print media, where journalists reported on the politics and culture, political behavior, and social graces that were on display at numerous black social gatherings. A critical yet largely unexamined case is *Minerva: Revista Universal Ilustrada* (Minerva: The Universal Illustrated Magazine), the black periodical that ceased publication after a brief run (1888–89) in the shadow of the abolition of slavery, only to begin a second, five-year run from 1910 to 1915.

Though *Minerva*'s nineteenth-century run had focused on civil rights activism, targeting black women as the population segment most critical for civilizing, educating, and integrating the formerly enslaved in colonial society, *Minerva*'s tenor in the early twentieth century reveals a significant shift in focus toward the electoral arena. For the African-descended, participation in formal elections was severely limited by suffrage restrictions, in force for Cubans of all colors until 1897. After independence, with citizenship rights and universal male suffrage granted in January 1901 to all Cuban men irrespective of race, new political concerns took hold among the African-descended, namely how to participate fully in formal politics beyond the mere exercise of casting a vote. The new *Minerva* seems to have been multipurposed: to feature the careers of prominent blacks in the public sphere, to highlight black cultural refinement, to expand and solidify a network of black society activists, and, perhaps most important, to promote activism to support specific local and national politicians. Though self-identified as a journal of "Science, Art, Literature, and Sport," *Minerva* often published political propaganda in support of incumbents as well as opposition candidates, an unsurprising practice given that several of the journal's editors were active in electoral politics or were career politicians. In fact, *Minerva*'s resurrection in 1910 coincided with intense national debates on race and politics during the drafting and promulgation of the Morúa Law (May 1910), as well as mass arrests of black activists and vigorous black electoral activism, primarily from the Independent Party of Color (PIC).[3] As a propagandist press, *Minerva* helped to shape readers' interpretations of rising black electoral participation by the end of the first decade, along with a rise in antiblack activity. As a literary journal, it advocated normative culture and social authority for the public figures that its editors endorsed. In fact, the reemergence of *Minerva* and its role in formal politics as well as in civic life was not unusual, given the historic relationship in Latin American contexts in general between political leadership and formal culture.

Ángel Rama argues eloquently in *The Lettered City* that the *letrados* (the learned class) in colonial Latin America associated closely with the state apparatus and enjoyed special access to power. He posits that this stems historically from the importance of administrative (legal and religious) writing to the largely illiterate societies of early modern Europe, where literacy, a necessary facet of governance, was used by powerful elite classes to safeguard their power and maintain social hierarchies. In the Latin American colonies, a close association of literacy with royal authority persisted. Rama argues that after Latin American colonies won independence, literacy and intellectual pursuits continued to convey authority. He argues, further, that the prestige attached to intellectuals and to public displays of erudition increased in postcolonial Latin American societies, because as the influence of the Catholic Church declined, "the secondary religion of letters was poised to take its place."[4] Following independence, literacy and intellectualism were at least as important as nationalist movements, as many socioeconomic sectors gained access to political leadership and authority: "Letters seemed to offer a ladder for the upwardly mobile, conferring respectability and access to the centers of power, as well as a greater relative autonomy regarding those centers of power, thanks to the new diversity of sources of wealth and the broadening economic base of the period's developing bourgeois societies."[5] Thus, in various newly democratic Latin American political systems, advanced formal instruction was prized for its intimate relationship to political authority.

Rama's adroit analysis has an application for the postindependence sector of privileged black Cubans and their use of print media to fulfill political and cultural goals simultaneously. Though the black press was not monolithic, funded as it was by a variety of sources for diverse purposes, some elements common to early republican black periodicals such as *La Estrella Refulgente*, *Minerva*, and *Labor Nueva* (New Labor) were shows of refinement and intellectual prowess, promoted bourgeois-liberal and patriarchal values, and demonstrated participation in the island's "modern" political culture. The black press, then, sought to confer on black leaders an authority that many white elected officials, mainstream newspapers and journalists, and intellectuals did not. For black leaders, the press served the Janus-faced purpose of attracting followers by propagandizing about their capacity to lead, even as it helped black activists convey their political authority to dominant party leaders, suggesting to them that in the battle for electoral votes it behooved them to draft black politicians. On occasion, the black press also bridged racial divides. Mainstream parties and high-ranking white officials, such as President Mario Menocal (1912–20) and president of the House of Representatives Orestes Ferrara, expressed their opinions and agendas in the black press in order to reach a black readership.

The black press audience cannot be easily identified, since black newspapers generally kept few operational records. Judging by the editorials, images, and feature articles, however, the editors, reporters, and readerships were a small, self-selected group, concerned mostly with endorsing bourgeois liberalism and domesticity and displaying their refinement and civic activism. Further, their editorial boards often envisioned a black "imagined community," bound together by their relative privilege when compared to other Cubans—and in particular to other blacks. Newspapers often described in detail the lush and erudite events held locally and nationally by black clubs and civic organizations. Black press pages were filled with marriage announcements, travel plans, and fashionable modes of dress; also described were banquets, conferences, public readings, nationalist commemorations, and dances—including attendees' elaborate dress and libations. Prominent were descriptions of literary and sport competitions and the names and photos of distinguished individuals and families. This all contributed to the general perception that there existed a clearly distinguishable group of ascendant privileged blacks.

Thus, part of defining a delimited, corporatist community was to emphasize black leadership capability: the photos portrayed black refinement, intellectual capacity, and patriarchal norms as necessary for bourgeois-liberal respectability. Black clubmen and civic activists often posed elegantly for photos, seated in chairs, with legs crossed and noses angled slightly upward. Black women and children were photographed in demure dress and poses, suggestive of bourgeois-feminine domesticity. Children often held musical instruments and were well-groomed, with hair and clothes typically adorned by bows and ribbons, suggesting that they came from respectable families. They generally gazed serenely off-camera, signaling to readers that they pursued leisure activities and pastimes relegated to privilege.

The black press also brought public attention to black politicians, constituting a political platform that they used to speak to black voters. Black periodicals were, in fact, heavily enmeshed in formal politics—influenced or controlled by political aspirants and government officials. *Minerva* featured prominent clubmen on its board and maintained affiliations with well-placed black politicians, veterans, and club leaders, such as Juan Gualberto Gómez, Juan Felipe Risquet, Miguel Ángel Céspedes, Lino D'ou, and Juan Canales Carazo. This mix of clubmen and politicians, individuals who as activists publicly called on the state to uphold socioeconomic equality but as elected officials worked as state agents, was typical of the early republican black press. I found no conclusive evidence to identify the presses' financial backers, but it is highly likely that editorial boards (made up of both regular and "special" or honorary members) were responsible for attracting investment capital or otherwise funding their operations. Given the intimacy of the relationship between politicians and black editorial boards, it is also likely that political parties, individual politicians, and mobilized political groups founded black newspapers for propaganda purposes. In this sense, the black press and the black public sphere did not operate independently of public officials. In fact, elected officials' political agendas appeared regularly in the press thinly veiled as editorials. Further, whole runs of black periodicals and electoral campaign seasons were congruent, such as *Previsión* (1908), *Minerva* (1910–15), and *Labor Nueva* (1916), which suggests their usefulness for persuading voters or influencing political behavior in times of increased electoral activity.[6]

Perhaps it was because of this intimacy between the black press and formal politics that only infrequently would black public-sphere voices challenge the era's standard bearers of black leadership as well as the myth that black political activists acted on behalf of "the race." One journalistic forum, which was inaugurated in 1915 in the months leading up to the 1916 general elections, discussed formal politics and "the [black] race." The series editor, mulatto journalist Ramón Vasconcelos, had managed to convince a Havana-based political rag, *La Prensa*, to run a weekly column on race issues. The editorial series was aptly titled "Palpitaciones de la Raza de Color" (Palpitations of the Colored Race), and during its two-year run a variety of black-life topics were discussed.[7] Each week, contributors opined on the plight of the masses of black Cubans—about their socioeconomic status, their place in the modern Cuban nation, and their best political response to ongoing racial inequities, often perpetuated, they insisted, by a political machine that benefited black political elites. Vasconcelos also spent considerable energy denouncing what he and others believed were the recurrent machinations of a black, political, old guard.

He was particularly keen on challenging black leaders who were cogs in a corrupt political system. For several weeks in the fall of 1915, for example, Vasconcelos attacked an incipient campaign to strengthen the public presence of prominent black politicians and club leaders, such as Juan Gualberto Gómez and Miguel Ángel Céspedes. Gómez, Céspedes, and others sought to "unify" black societies in and around Havana, even across the island, by consolidating resources and building a mass institutional structure. Vasconcelos railed against black society leaders (and black politicians) whom he felt were lobbying for black societies' unification in order to be able to lead a large black civic network as "supreme pontiffs" or point men of influence among the masses of black voters. Their ultimate goal, he surmised, was to broker black votes for dominant political parties during the coming electoral season. According to Vasconcelos, the unification effort was one way they hoped to create political visibility. In the end, the campaign fizzled out, in early 1916, shortly after it had emerged. Its death as a political project was celebrated by Vasconcelos, but many proponents of black civic activism, such as Domingo Mesa and Primitivo Ramírez Ros, were not phased by the movement's demise and remained active in electoral politics for many years.

The Politics of the Black Public Sphere

In the months before the 1916 election, Domingo Mesa and Primitivo Ramírez Ros, prominent black clubmen and politicians, initiated a new black weekly, *Labor Nueva: Revista Semanal Ilustrada* (New Labor: Weekly Illustrated Magazine), dedicating the first issue to presidential incumbent Mario Menocal. *Labor Nueva* was one of only a few black periodicals that existed in 1916, perhaps the only one of national prominence. Editors Mesa and Ramírez stated that their three-fold purpose in launching the paper was to inspire the colored race to improve its morality, intellect, and economy; to work hard to improve relations among all sectors, black and white, of Cuban society; and to use the journal to showcase the accomplishments of certain members of the colored race, in order that they serve as an example for colored and noncolored alike.[8] Mesa and Ramírez insisted, too, that *Labor Nueva* would not be a publication cordoned off by racial loyalties. Instead, they sought a racial alliance where the best white Cuban thinkers enlightened the black race with their advice and spurred blacks on with their cooperation and incentives. Further, they assured interested white elites, their words would not fall on deaf ears and their "generous efforts will bear fruit luxuriously, as ripe seeds in fertile lands."[9]

Although the newspaper targeted civic-minded blacks, the editorials promoted nationalist racelessness and argued that both racial consciousness and challenges to state power were unacceptable. This position was underscored by the political prominence of its white Cuban contributors, such as Dr. Enrique José Varona (then Cuban vice president in the Menocal administration), Orestes Ferrara Marino (former member of the House of Representatives, director of the national newspaper *El Heraldo de Cuba*, and long-standing member of the professional staff of the University of Havana), and President Menocal himself, who held forth in *Labor Nueva* on the need for peace and unity in order to safeguard the nation-state. Menocal even published a letter in *Labor Nueva* that condemned the PIC's 1912 Race War as a despicable and irrational act—but despite the newspaper's black target audience, he neglected to mention the state's brutality against PIC members and black civilians. Orestes Ferrara sermonized that the colored race should be the "most patriotic," more patriotic than whites, even, given that that was one of the few qualities they offered their country.[10] And with clear reference to the 1912 uprising, Varona suggested that "the most patriotic act that the illustrious among the race of color can do is to help advance their race and to persuade [them] that violence will do harm to whites yet is [a strategy] without hope of helping their own."[11]

LABOR NUEVA

⮞ REVISTA LITERARIA ILUSTRADA ⮜

Año I.

Núm. 1.

| REDACCION:
Zulueta 71, por Dragones | Habana 20 de Febrero de 1916 | ADMINISTRACCION:
Empedrado 43 |

EL GENERAL MENOCAL Y
"LABOR NUEVA"

El General Mario G. Menocal, Honorable Presidente de la República, designado candidato por el Partido Conservador para un segundo período presidencial, nos ha honrado con la carta que aparece en fa. símil en esta plana de honor, en la cual carta, expresa los generosos sentimientos que le animan respecto al progreso de nuestra raza y a la compenetración que debe existir entre todos los componentes del pueblo cubano. En sucesivos números iremos publicando el sentir de nuestras figuras presidenciables, en relación con el propio asunto, pues siempre resultará de interés conocer el criterio de los llamados a dirigir los destinos de la Nación.

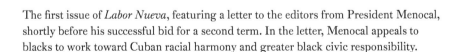

The first issue of *Labor Nueva*, featuring a letter to the editors from President Menocal, shortly before his successful bid for a second term. In the letter, Menocal appeals to blacks to work toward Cuban racial harmony and greater black civic responsibility.

Labor Nueva editors dismissed structural solutions to the problem of Cuban racial inequality. In March 1910, for example, one month after the first issue had been published, they argued that the problem of racial inequality could not be solved but only managed, since, at its base, inequality was pathological:

> The problem [of inequality] cannot be resolved by the force of laws and will always constitute an ill in what are called hybrid democracies, such as is ours. . . . Although the race of color is not satisfied with the qualitative and quantitative distribution of public offices among blacks and whites, since they have not received the better part or even a part proportional to their patriotic ballast. This is not the most bitter or bothersome of their troubles. They are much more hurt and indignant about their treatment among families, in daily life, and in their love life.[12]

That racial inequality (or even inequitable job distribution) could not be resolved by government was a central tenet of *Labor Nueva*. Similar to a significant current in black leadership ideals of the time, the newspaper sought to elevate blacks' moral condition, educational levels, and economic status, even as it condemned them to a marginal socioeconomic position and articulated clear doubts about their capacity for improvement.

Labor Nueva was so sympathetic to elected officials, in fact, that despite being a black-run newspaper focused on the experiences of the African-descended, among the most prominent voices on its pages were those of white Cuban elites. At least one of the editors, Primitivo Ramírez Ros, was tied to the Conservative Party and seems to have reaped benefits from his relationship with the party. When Miguel Arango Mantilla won a congressional seat for Matanzas province under the Conservative Party banner in the November 1916 general elections, he abruptly resigned his post and was quickly replaced by Ramírez.[13] It is likely that both Domingo Mesa and Ramírez hoped to join the ranks of the ruling Conservative Party by encouraging a black readership to support Menocal and national government.

Black political activists (who were often also civic leaders) initiated several public endorsements of mainstream politicians in the republican period, such as Rafael Serra's frequent defense of President Tomás Estrada Palma in *El Nuevo Criollo*, or the tribute that black civic societies paid to President Machado in 1928, eighteen months after he amended the constitution to "extend" (*prórrogar*) his presidential powers.[14] These tacit gestures promoted mainstream politicians and parties among black voters and reinforced black political activists' utility to high-ranking politicians, including the president. More important, however, they were reciprocated: Tomás Estrada Palma appointed Rafael Serra to a post office public sector job in 1902, and in January 1904 Serra was nominated by the National Party to run for Congress, a seat he won a month later during the 1904 partial elections.[15] Several decades later, President Gerardo Machado appointed a relatively significant number of blacks to his administration. He placed General Manuel Delgado in the top spot as secretary of the interior, Manuel Capestany as undersecretary of justice, and Benjamín Muñoz Ginarte as chief of section in the Secretariat of Agriculture.[16] Further, several blacks served in Congress during the *machadato*, after political parties increased black candidacies, including representatives Felix Ayón (Havana), Aquilino Lombard (Matanzas), Prisciliano Piedra (Matanzas), Manuel Capestany (Las Villas), Marcelino Garriga (Pinar del Río), and Pío Arturo Frías (Havana). It is important to note that all of these men were board members and/or at-large members of the island's highly prestigious, black Club Atenas, and their sepia-toned pictures with elegant font captions in the Club Atenas bulletin served as symbols of black achievement.[17]

Traditional black political elites were supported by black newspapers such as *Labor Nueva*. Its editors' brand of activism was to exhort black readers to vote for black candidates on the basis of racial solidarity while making little effort on behalf of blacks' socioeconomic status. Less than a month before the general elections of November 1916, the editors insisted that for black voters, "it is our turn to defend these dignified [black] candidates who actively participate in the development of our parties. There are so few of us as candidates, it is a good thing that we are not on ballots as mere [token] decorative figures."[18] Further, at every turn, the magazine editors cautioned against black political mobilization in the style of the PIC uprising of 1912. "We are not those [PIC] racists," the editors suggested. "Peace, peace is what we need, for the enhancement of our present and future generations!"[19] The editors insisted that blacks should have faith in black politicians working within the dominant political parties. Many black presses supported prominent black politicians because of their belief that the interests of black political activists aligned with those of the black masses. They also insisted that black civic activism and a vital black club movement were the common terrain where all black interests merged. Located ideologically between espousing absolute black consciousness and utter silence on the question of Cuban racial inequalities, black civic organizations were vocal about racial disparities, although they offered few solutions for changing the structural inequalities, except for black self-improvement. In fact, black clubs had claimed a window of opportunity for building their movement following the 1912 Race War and before the 1916 general elections were held. Black politicians and club leaders in Havana, recalling late nineteenth-century black civic activism, campaigned to create a black club directorate.

Clubmen Unite!

In June 1915, Havana-based clubmen began organizational efforts for a black club directorate modeled after the late nineteenth-century Directorate of Societies of the Colored Race.[20] Although the new organizing committee (the Comité Gestor) had envisioned a club network that spread beyond the capital city to other parts of the island, most societies at the meeting were based in and around Havana.[21] Veteran club activist Juan Gualberto Gómez gave the keynote address in which he insisted that black societies had to unite for strength, cultural enlightenment, and educational opportunities. Unification of existing black societies would build on earlier black advancements. Yet he also spoke skeptically, maintaining that black clubs were fragmented and unorganized. "Black Cuban unity," he admonished, "was threatened by factions and self-interest: [the clubs are] organized in small, segmented groups," "preferring that to the unity of our energies in order to raise a great cathedral where we might cover our foreheads and kneel before the god of progress and culture."[22]

Gómez echoed what all black public intellectuals seemed to agree upon in the early twentieth century, that progress and culture were critical to the advancement of blacks. And many, like Gómez, argued that the best way to fight for black progress was to form black civic organizations. The 1915 rally was not the first effort to mobilize blacks in the twentieth century nor would it be the last. In August 1907, almost ten years after Cubans won their bid for independence from Spain and one year after the island's two dominant political parties had come to blows over access to political offices and state funds, thirty men created the Directorate of Citizens of Color. The manifesto that the directorate penned was but one tactic among many to address in the public sphere blacks' fears that the racial politics of the newly constituted republic were the same as those of the old colony.[23] Based on the widespread belief that blacks had fought the lion's share of battles in the wars of independence, one of the decree's main principles was that blacks deserved full consideration as citizens and leaders. As the directorate's manifesto suggested: "The race of color has been . . . the one who has proportioned the largest contingent for the conquest of liberty yet who has had the least usufruct of the fruits of that conquest."[24]

The manifesto called for increased educational opportunities for blacks, including state-sponsored international scholarships to promising black students, and for blacks to build on the economic resources that some already possessed by demanding that state legislation help the African-descended population to make sound financial investments, file claims for land and other assets belonging to them since colonialism, acquire property, and receive instruction in economic management.[25] The 1907 directorate also argued for an extra-partisan coalition that would work with political parties to hold them accountable on black issues.

The 1907 directorate made clear that the intention was not to interfere with blacks' participation in patronage networks. On the contrary, members felt that practically speaking, blacks should develop the sorts of benefits provided by clientilist politics, using whatever pressures possible to demand lucrative jobs in public service. In true elitist fashion, the manifesto called on its members and others to champion black issues by assuming "supreme leadership" in the fight for race progress. They were uniquely poised, they insisted, to "lift up the race of color" from its "current condition" and impart the values of liberty and democracy. The 1907 directorate faded almost as quickly as it appeared. Yet in the half decade that followed its brief appearance, a more famous example of black political mobilization took center stage. The PIC, established in 1908, represents a five-year effort by black Cubans to gain greater power in the republic's structure of formal politics. After being outlawed in 1910, the party's 1912 uprising, the Race War of 1912, in which black activist Evaristo Estenoz led hundreds of party members to seize foreign property, signaled deeply felt discontent over black exclusion from political appointments, lucrative jobs, and political office. As Estenoz suggested in 1908, "Barely established, the Republic has turned our concerns to anger and done so to a greater extent and under worse conditions than in the most offensive moments of colonialism."[26] The Race War of 1912 began when disgruntled *independentistas* occupied foreign property in protest. It ended in mass bloodshed, primarily at the hands of Cuban and U.S. armed forces and white civilian brigades. The war invoked mass hysteria among many sectors of the Cuban populace and led to massive violent repression. Many lives were lost, even though the party itself had only a few hundred members. Almost 5,000 blacks, party members and otherwise, lost their lives.

Both during and following the uprising, the Cuban press embarked on a rampage of antiblack and racist coverage of events, casting the PIC and all blacks as inherently dangerous to society. The worst media depictions suggested that blacks were lawless savages; the best deemed them antiwhite and anti-Cuban. A common practice in republican news reporting was to cast race-conscious activists as backward and libertine. They were a plague of witch doctors and Africanist religious practitioners threatening national safety, a social poison from within. In September 1915, *La Prensa* reported that black political activists in Santiago who were seeking to form a political organization were meeting clandestinely for the purpose of witchcraft and African cult beliefs.[27] A brief examination of early republican press accounts of black mobilizations shows that they were almost always paired with journalists' rumors of heinous acts by black "witch doctors" and their followers, as well as of blacks' "racist" political gatherings.

Newspaper accounts of alleged *brujería* activity were common in 1915, the year former members of the defunct PIC were rumored to be organizing a short-lived political group known as Amigos del Pueblo (Friends of the People). This same year the Unification of Black Societies mobilization was under way in Havana. Both efforts coincided with mass preparations for the general electoral contests of 1916, though only the Amigos del Pueblo organization was overtly political. As early as January 1915, the newspaper *La Prensa* reported that ex-*independentista* Abelardo Pacheco had called on blacks to join him. Pacheco, the paralytic Eugenio Lacoste, and other veterans of the PIC uprising were, ostensibly, spearheading efforts to build an Amigos del Pueblo party in Oriente province.[28] Pacheco's rumored call led authorities to arrest thirty-nine blacks on charges of illicit association.[29] By September, reporters declared Amigos del Pueblo unsuccessful in gaining any substantial black support. Lacoste's health may have been a factor, since he died in October of that year. In a derisive response to black political leadership, several newsmen smirked that his funeral was poorly attended, with little pomp, few mourners, and no sympathetic outpouring.[30]

No doubt the extreme repression of the 1912 Race War had succeeded in its principal goal of intimidation, and many blacks considered the Amigos mobilization too risky. *El Día* even surmised that the rumors of a black uprising were part of a Liberal Party plot to wrest black support from the Conservative Party, given that Conservatives had a stronghold among blacks from Oriente province. A September report claimed that Liberals were spreading rumors of a new, racially conscious uprising—led by Amigos del Pueblo—in order to raise the specter of antiblack violence, just as the 1912 uprising had led to mass government-sponsored killings of blacks during the José Miguel Gómez administration. And just as Gómez's Liberal Party government paid a heavy political price in 1912 for that violence and for alienating blacks (Liberals lost the 1912 presidential race), *El Día* reasoned that blacks would abandon Mario Menocal's Conservative government (1912–20) following its repression of black Cubans. Editors argued that

Liberals hoped to use blacks' considerable fear of the repeat of government-sponsored antiblack violence to alienate blacks from Oriente province and elsewhere and weaken their historical support for Conservatives and the party's predecessors.[31]

Yet the 1912 Race War and the repression that followed it also represented an effort to establish boundaries on the use of both antiblack *and* antiracialist discourse in political mobilization. If the PIC members had discovered the outer limits of state tolerance for black consciousness politics and political mobilization, they had paid in blood for their discovery. And if state agents had hoped to stem blacks' demands on state resources, they learned that eventually some black Cubans were willing to take up arms and rally on behalf of equality in the distribution of resources. If, during the 1906 August Revolution, Moderates and Liberals were merely testing the waters regarding control of state posts, by 1912 the use of race and racial ideas in republican politics—to galvanize people for or against social equality—was also tested. In 1915, neither the state nor black activists were as willing to step up to oppose one another as they had been in 1912. The state had to accommodate some level of black access to its resources, and black activists understood that cross-class, race-based mobilization for resources was largely unacceptable. They learned from the 1912 racial massacre that black activism had dire consequences if it did not take place within the confines of republican bureaucracy. Black activists seeking socioeconomic justice not only threatened foreign investors' supply of cheap agricultural labor and raised the possibility of losing black electoral support. They also opened up the possibility of more black claims-making on elected officials, a prospect that was largely unacceptable to administrators. Instead, state agents and black activists bartered for resources, using the language of national egalitarianism, black advancement, and Cuban racial transcendence in their negotiations. To appeal to and attract the black voting public, black activists used charges of racial inequality. To bridge the divide that stood between them and a largely white republican administration, they spoke of racial improvement. Many white politicians recruited black politicians to secure support from black constituents. In fact, since the 1908 elections, state agents had consistently recruited among the black leadership to boost individual and party political success, and the state and black civic organizations were often closely aligned.

The short-lived mobilization of the Amigos del Pueblo (whose very name, "Amigo," suggests a benign, depoliticized stance) serves as an important example of the ongoing negotiations that characterized republican racial politics. The group emerged in 1915 under President Mario Menocal's Conservative Party administration—Menocal was honorary president of Amigos del Pueblo and he enjoyed the group's public support of his administration. Abelardo Pacheco, an Amigos leader, was candidate for congressman in Las Villas province and hoped to attract political supporters to the Amigos del Pueblo Party.[32] *La Prensa* alleged that the Amigos organization was a group of black political bosses who played on the sympathies of "the uncultured" of their race to win votes, bartering with political parties for money for votes.[33] Several sources charged that one of the organization's founders, Eugenio Lacoste, was on the government payroll as an "electoral agent," due to his alleged influence with black voters in Guantánamo. These dubious ties led mulatto journalist Ramón Vasconcelos to call Amigos del Pueblo a "political hook" meant to attract blacks to the party of President Menocal.[34]

Even as the Amigos del Pueblo movement sparked salacious press accounts of *brujería* in the east, the effort to unify respectable black societies in the nation's capital, led by highly lauded black leaders, also spurred press rumors. For leaders such as Juan Gualberto Gómez, the Unification of Black Societies project and the Amigos del Pueblo organization were worlds apart. During the PIC uprising in 1912, he and other black leaders had condemned the sort of racial activism endorsed by the Amigos del Pueblo. Yet the mainstream press saw the Unification of Black Societies effort as equally dangerous. *La Lucha* editors suggested that the unification was perpetrated by a nest of destructive, antinational, and racist black Liberal and Conservative congressmen and called on Cubans to "destroy the [club unification] shrub before it grows."[35] Two decades into independence, blacks were still marginalized and locked out of full political participation, making it increasingly clear for many that black leadership was largely ineffectual.

Unification and Its Discontents

There were other reasons besides the specter of libertinage that Havana's Unification of Black Societies mobilization provoked outcry among black Cubans. In fact, many black Cubans insisted that behind the rhetoric of racial progress were politically ambitious black leaders who, to secure their own political positions, relied on racialist campaigns and manipulation to supply political parties with black votes. The call to unify black clubs, which lasted from late summer to October 1915, was indeed led by black politicians and clubmen. Even after the Unification of Black Societies effort failed, many of its organizers joined the leadership of black civic institutions.

The most outspoken opponent of the Unification of Black Societies movement was young mulatto journalist Ramón Vasconcelos (also known as "Tristán"), who used his highly polemical column, "Palpitaciones de la

Raza de Color" (Palpitations of the Colored Race), to raise issues relating to black leadership and political strategy. His agitation may have derived from a desire to join the coalition created by prominent Unification of Black Societies organizers. Indeed, in the 1936 general elections, the first such elections since the 1933 Revolution, he emerged as a leader of the Liberal Party and won a senatorial contest for Havana province.[36] Thus, had he been a political outsider during the Unification of Black Societies effort he did not remain so. After his election to Congress in 1936 he went on to serve as Fulgencio Batista's minister of communication during the 1952 coup. According to Tristán, in 1915, however, far from being an example of black racial solidarity and advancement, the Unification of Black Societies was a bid for power among the black political elite. His public challenge of the elite in *La Prensa* in 1915 and 1916 called into grave doubt the commitment of black leaders to the socioeconomic inequities inflicted on the African-descended population. Further, he created a public forum where readers submitted their critiques about black experience and politics in relationship to Cuban society as well as questioned the accountability of black leaders to the masses of blacks in republican politics.

Tristán published reader comments about politics, culture, and society in addition to his own, which were often scathing. In a public sphere culture known for flowery (and sometimes disingenuous) language, as well as circumspect political commentary, his biting prose was a challenge to many powerful black leaders. In summer and fall 1915, in the midst of an outpouring of support among black civic organizations for the Unification of Black Societies project, Tristán editorialized that black leaders' campaign for a black societies unification served the sole purpose of creating funds (such as monthly dues) for their personal use. Labeling the organizing committee of the unification (the Comité Gestor) the "Negro-Electoral Trust," Tristán charged that committee members hoped for the passage of new legislation granting state aid to civic organizations. In almost prescient fashion, he predicted that unification leaders would move quickly if the legislation passed to request state aid and be placed on the government payroll. Indeed, two decades later, during Fulgencio Batista's first presidency (1940–44), many black societies were officially on the state's payroll. By implication, he meant that the unification leadership would pocket resources rather than channel them toward social improvement projects.[37] Further, he posited that the Unification of Black Societies was a platform for its leaders to broker black votes. They would use the united black civic organizations to court black supporters and influence how they cast votes, in exchange for monies and their own political candidacies.

Alejandro Sorís was among several outspoken blacks who challenged the Unification of Black Societies movement in Tristán's "Palpitaciones." In a September 1915 editorial, Sorís expressed a deep skepticism about the Comité Gestor's motives, insinuating that these were purely political. "When," he harangued, "have they worked selflessly on behalf of our race?" Calling the Comité Gestor a "social gangrene," Sorís posited that honest black activists needed to extirpate these leaders from their ranks.[38] Other readers penned similar eloquent statements rejecting the Comité Gestor and *caciques* generally, as organizations that assumed an "absolute authority" to represent all black Cubans vis-à-vis the state.

According to Sorís, those behind the Unification of Black Societies were largely the same men who had attempted to organize a Black Societies Directorate in 1907. In fact, Sorís charged that since the organizers of the 1907 and 1915 movements were essentially the same men, there were no significant political differences in the two campaigns. The 1907 effort for black political mobilization had faded quickly, after organizers rethought the need for social equality and greater black access to jobs. They had stated publicly that the anticolonial Revolution had won rights for blacks and whites and attacked inequity in the distribution of state resources, only to abandon the call for justice rather quickly. Why, then, did the organizers want to initiate a black societies unification project again, in 1915?

Given that both the 1907 and the 1915 efforts came just before major national elections (general elections were held in 1908 and 1916) and that both unification efforts followed on the heels of black independent political mobilization, several differences in republican history help to explain why the effort to unify black organizations was abandoned in 1907, only to be revived in 1915. First, for the election of 1908, more blacks were put up for and won national offices on both the Liberal and Conservative tickets than had happened earlier in the republic's short history. This suggests that as the 1908 general election approached, national parties likely hinted at their intent to include black politicians in state structures, thus encouraging more patronage resources to flow to black clients and possibly helping to neutralize the 1907 directorate and other independent black mobilizations. The nascent PIC movement, in turn, would have placed additional pressure on mainstream political parties, causing them to recruit more blacks to their ranks in order to discourage independent black political organizing.[39]

Black brokers were also likely part of a patronage apparatus that flourished in conjunction with an increase in state revenues and state bureaucracy. European beet crops in Germany, Austria, Belgium, and France were affected by World War I, and the rapid increase in Cuba's sugar production helped to generate greater revenues as global demands were met. Both the price per pound and production levels of Cuban sugar increased—creating a steep rise in growth that culminated in 1919 with the "Dance of the Millions." That trend began in 1914 and ended six years later. By 1914, American- and Cuban-owned *centrales* (sugar mills) were producing 2.6 million tons of raw sugar annually, an amount that by 1915 increased by 400,000 tons sold, for a total of 3 million tons that year.[40] Further, the maturation of the National Lottery system, initiated in 1909, provided additional state funds.[41] President Mario Menocal and members of Congress used hefty state budgets to increase their own salaries and, importantly, to neutralize political opposition. Menocal, in fact, alienated some of his own administration by presiding over an era of political and economic capriciousness that included delaying contracts and siphoning off funding for public works' projects, as well as increasing the salaries of high-ranking officials and *botella* sinecures.

Indeed, the intimacy of Unification of Black Societies organizers and dominant political parties is clear upon close inspection of the unification leadership, which included members of the Liberal Party and the Conjunción Party (an offshoot of the Liberal Party that supported Ernesto Asbert). Juan Gualberto Gómez, Miguel Ángel Céspedes, Generoso Campos Marquetti, and Saturnino Escoto Carrión, all members of the unification's Comité Gestor, won congressional offices in the general election of 1916 as well as in the previous general and partial elections (1912 and 1914, respectively). Moreover, at the unification's inaugural meeting in 1915, organizers had held forth on black unity and accomplishments and on the need to create federated black corporate organizations. Although Gómez suggested that blacks had made enormous "progress" in the republic and had demonstrated their love of "homeland and, by extension, institutions," it is likely that organizers saw political benefits in a federation of black societies.[42] That is, they hoped to capitalize on the threat of black autonomous mobilization (as had happened during the 1912 Race War) to suggest their usefulness to political parties by arguing that a club federation would position them to harness widespread black political discontent in order to influence black political behavior.

As a tactic of black civic mobilization and political opportunity, the unification effort failed to produce much for black politicians. In fact, black politicians had fared better earlier on in new republican politics. The Liberal Party, for example, used the tide of popular support, including black support, forged by the 1906 August Revolution to win at the polls in 1908. Liberals ensured electoral victory by helping a record-breaking number of blacks win political offices. In 1912, however, a smaller number of blacks won office, and by 1914 and 1916, under the Conservative Party administration of Mario García Menocal, very few blacks other than Juan Gualberto Gómez were elected. This helped to fuel a third civil war in the republic's short history—the Lollipop War of 1917, which began in February of that year after angry Liberals rose up against the Conservative government's ill-gotten monopoly on political office, achieved through the stuffing of ballot boxes and political violence and intimidation during the 1916 general elections.

According to Tristán, the unification effort failed because Havana's less-powerful black societies feared domination and perhaps control of their assets by the most powerful black unification society, the Unión Fraternal. Further, he suggested that the leaders of the network of societies, influential men such as Juan Gualberto Gómez and Miguel Ángel Céspedes, planned to use the network for their personal benefit. They would exchange the political loyalty of unification member clubs for money from Havana's municipal government, thereby enhancing their positions within the dominant political parties.[43] Whether or not Tristán was correct in his assumption, black civic activists continued to participate in state processes, in a relationship of mutuality based on the desires of black politicians to win political offices as well as the need of political parties to secure black votes.

Black brokers such as Juan Gualberto Gómez hoped to preside over the negotiations between elected officials and black voters. In the case of Gómez, he granted favors and worked within political parties behind the scenes, while continuing to represent publicly the push for cultural self-improvement and, less often, black civil rights. Gómez also continued to use black societies as an important site of mobilization, attempting in 1915 to unify prominent black clubs in Havana under one umbrella. When other prominent blacks continued to mobilize after 1915, undaunted by the failure of the Unification of Black Societies effort and the near absence of black officials in regional or national office from 1914 to 1920, Gómez did so as well. In particular, he supported Club Atenas, a black elite society founded in May 1917. For several years, Gómez would use his power as an elected official to help funnel land, money, and other assets to Club Atenas members (many of whom were black political activists belonging to one or another party and power brokers in their own right) and maintain his place at the pinnacle of black civic leadership and political power.

Most of Club Atenas's founding members had participated in the Unification of Black Societies movement, and many of them were career politicians and professionals. The roster of founding members, for example, included *Labor Nueva* editors Domingo Mesa and Primitivo Ramírez Ros (also congressmen from Matanzas province), José Gálvez (friend of President Menocal and political appointee to the Department of Public Works), Pío Arturo Frías (politician), Ramiro N. Cuesta (congressman from Matanzas), Dr. Oscar G. Edreira (editor of *Minerva* and public servant), Miguel Ángel Céspedes (politician and attorney), Lino D'ou (journalist and politician from Oriente province), Aquilino Lombard Thorndike (politician from Matanzas province), Alberto Castellanos (politician from Oriente province), Policarpo Madrigal (politician from Matanzas province), Hermengildo Ponvert (politician from Las Villas province), Manuel Delgado (politician from Las Villas province), and many others.[44] Club Atenas was, in essence, a collective of black movers and shakers bound across party lines into one civic organization. Members publicly showed refinement, financial savvy, social status, and political authority.

Further, Club Atenas emerged as the Lollipop War ended, suggesting that the political crises had provided an opening to strengthen ties to government officials by supporting their policies and working to calm discontent (such as when black clubmen repudiated the 1912 Race War or when Rafael Serra supported the increasingly unpopular presidency of Tomás Estrada Palma in the months leading up to the 1906 August Revolution). Black politicians used such opportunities to capture prominent positions in local and national leadership, despite vehement antiblack sentiments. As the rules that linked power to public performance dictated, as Club Atenas members emphasized their refined culture, bourgeois-liberal respectability, and commitment to intellectual pursuits, they also intimated their role in the success of dominant political parties. Ironically, they did so by disclaiming radical political activism and reinforcing their role as cadre, a force of cultural models for the masses of black Cubans. Regarding black political mobilization, the first issue of the club's official bulletin demurred: "Politics is the riotous information that attracts many . . . but there are still a few who value softer things that touch the soul. . . . We propose to contribute, although a small effort, to please those from this group and to convince others, each day a bit more, increasing the number of 'amateurs' that reach glory in the sciences, arts, and whatever other branch of knowledge."[45] The black Liberals and Conservatives who founded Club Atenas created a black civic organization of political privilege and, as expected of them, meticulous standards for public behavior. As electoral activists and less frequently as political party leaders, they adopted the most important tactic of formal politics in the republic. Their cultural commitments seemingly demonstrated fitness to lead *and* distinction from the masses of Africanist blacks. They were committed primarily to resource acquisition for personal gain and less so to an ideology of cross-

Prominent former board presidents of Club Atenas. From "Anniversary Album," *Boletín Oficial del Club Atenas* 1, no. 9 (September 20, 1930): 8. (Author's private collection)

class racial solidarity, described by Michael Dawson as "linked fate." At the same time, however, a discourse of racial uplift was crucial to merging goals of resource acquisition with those mired in black, antidiscriminationism. The 1902 Veterans and Societies of Color militancy, the 1907 Camagüey Directorate of the Race of Color manifesto, the 1915 Unification of Black Societies campaign, and the hundreds of black clubs founded throughout the republican period are all instances in which the twin goals of removing racial barriers to political participation and participating in patronage networks coincided.

Conclusion

The intimacy between black civic activists and government administrators increased in the 1920s and 1930s, due to increased multiparty organizing, black political candidacies, and political use of the black press. Though Cubans of all colors enjoyed patronage appointments and access to public office, to varying degrees, formal subventions for black clubs increased under the Menocal administration, when expanded public budgets made it feasible to control racially conscious political mobilization. Such control was increasingly part of the status quo of national administration. In May 1917, the same month that Liberals of all colors (including many blacks) had risen up during the Lollipop War, the House of Representatives voted to award the Unión Fraternal, one of the most influential black clubs in Havana, a large land grant to build a so-called Popular University and library on its grounds. The club president, Pedro Calderón, wrote to newly elected senator Juan Gualberto Gómez on May 9, reminding him that the proposal had yet to pass the Senate and that they would continue to be grateful to him for his ongoing support of their organization.[46]

Black civic organizations such as Club Atenas were of critical importance to subsequent presidencies, including the authoritarian administrations of Gerardo Machado (1925-33) and Fulgencio Batista (1940-44, 1952-59). Black club members, in fact, continued to agitate among elected officials for access to republican resources. Following the Revolution of 1933, black clubs again moved to join together. This time, however, rather than the conservatism of the Menocal administration, club leaders were pressured by a new political climate, of popular front ideologies and postrevolutionary militancy, to address, if only rhetorically, the dire straits of the masses of black Cubans. During the 1930s, efforts to unify black societies necessarily responded to this political climate. After the 1933 Revolution, the ability of both the club movement and traditional black political elites to achieve socioeconomic parity came under fire. The public sphere was muddied by new political voices that advocated more radical strategies for black advancement. Indeed, the radical, postrevolutionary political context in Cuba placed black leadership in sharp relief, exposing its motivations and ties to high-level officeholders, the subject of the next chapter.

CHAPTER SIX

We Come to Discredit These Leaders

Political Change and Challenges to the Black Political Elite

In May 1936, on the eve of Cuba's first constitutional elections since Gerardo Machado took office in 1925, the editors of *Atómo* (The Atom), a new youth-run black newspaper, threw down the gauntlet. They called out the political machine that had dominated Cuban politics since the republic's inception and that had betrayed blacks: "There are those corrupted by experience . . . and their thirst for sinecures . . . who seek to . . . exploit the collective anguish of a Race."[1] Speaking to politicians of all colors generally and to black politicians in particular, *Atómo*'s editors blasted Cuban leaders who placed their own individual interests above those of the racial collective. In leveling their accusation against black leaders, they also asserted their right to a more actualized relationship to kith and country: "We come to discredit these leaders in the name of youth who know that our parents, having paid in blood currency their contribution to winning the republic, give us the right (inalienable as are all things dignified) to demand from the Patria, or its administrators that we [blacks] be permitted, without psychological coercion, to fully develop all of our faculties."[2] *Atómo*'s demands fit in with a wave of radical nationalism sweeping the island by the 1920s. A coalition of activist groups expressed deep resentment and frustration with the national government and called for structural change, such as agrarian reform, national economic development, public health programs, and jobs. Within a decade, their wrath had swelled to revolution.[3]

Arguably, no issue better bound them in common struggle than the government corruption and political mismanagement that had taken hold at the republic's birth in 1902. As social commentator and economist Alberto Arredondo lamented in 1938, "Our politics has been a trick. . . . Parties without programs, without principles, without intimate links to the pressing needs of our country; vehicles of utter laziness and apathy have traveled the field of Cuban politics."[4] Arredondo might have been speaking ten years earlier about the political frustration and antigovernment sentiments already brewing among Cuban capitalists. Their appearance as a political constituency coincided with the sugar industry's postindependence resurgence during the years of World War I, which facilitated growth among domestic investors (entrepreneurs, manufacturers, professionals, and industrialists).[5] To safeguard their interests against damaging government policies, several sectors of domestic commerce, industry, and business joined forces under the banner of the National Federation of Economic Corporations, which represented Cuban producers, property owners, and two organizations: the Chamber of Commerce, Industry, and Navigation of the Island of Cuba and the Friends of the Country Economic Society.[6] As early as 1922, for example, investors founded the National Association of Cuban Industrialists and quickly urged protectionist policies to protect domestic Cuban industry from foreign interests. That same year, a group of young businessmen established the Committee of One Hundred, which almost immediately demanded an end to political misconduct.[7] These local Cuban business executives expected government trade policies to reflect national economic interests rather than the interests of those who were plundering Cuban resources from abroad. For example, the 1903 Reciprocity Treaty had reduced tariffs on Cuba-U.S. trade, ultimately undermining national economic development.[8] From the vantage point of these young businessmen, lively economic activity would strengthen the national economy. And they expected to have an increasing role in national political affairs. Cuban political elites, however, who scarcely tolerated political challenge from among their own ranks, were unwilling to respond to domestic capitalists on the issue of national economic protections.[9] When, in late spring 1920, sugar prices plummeted, sending the economy into a downward spiral, Cuban capitalists were among the many infuriated antigovernment camps. Cuba's economic crisis continued a boom-bust cycle through the early 1930s, when it crashed, leaving many unemployed, underemployed, and even those fully employed without pay.

For sectors clamoring for greater political participation, the year 1923 was especially portentous. In March, Julio Antonio Mella, Carlos Baliño, and others formalized Cuba's first Communist organization. In April, the first National Congress of Women met in the National Theater in Old Havana.[10] In August, the Veterans' Association gathered en masse in Havana to fight rumored pension cuts.[11] Attacking "Yankee imperialism" and promoting "new vernacular art" were the agendas of prominent elite white youth groups, such as the Grupo Minorista (1923–28).[12] A few years later, in 1927, University of Havana students founded the Student Directorate (Directorio Estudiantil).[13]

Many organizations called for administrative *regeneración* (regeneration) or, more precisely, a return to idealism, political honesty, and domestic economic development. In April 1923, the Junta Cubana de Renovación Nacional-Cívico (Cuban Committee for National and Civic Renovation), led by Fernando Ortiz, a former congressman who renounced his seat to protest congressional corruption, issued a lengthy manifesto signed by hundreds of nonpolitical civic leaders, which called for congressional "renovation." The manifesto condemned all branches of government for legislating congressional immunity, inheritable pensions, and amnesty to the "worst sort of" criminals and for "unbridled legislative activity in the grant of fabulous credits."[14] Earlier that year, the government's dubious purchase of a Havana convent provoked a vociferous response from young activist artists and intellectuals. Thirteen members of the Grupo Minorista staged a protest of government corruption during a public meeting of the Club Femenino, held at Havana's Academy of Sciences. The solemn event, a presidential commemoration of Uruguayan writer Paulina Luisi, who was scheduled to receive an award for her work, was presided over by President Zayas's minister of justice, Erasmo Regüeiferos Boudet. When Regüeiferos stood to speak, the Grupo Minorista leader, Ruben Martínez Villena, suddenly yelled out a denunciation of the Zayas administration and then ceremoniously walked out of the building, accompanied by twelve other members. Their act, called the Protest of the Thirteen, represents one of the first public challenges by intellectual and artistic youth to republican government corruption.[15] Intellectuals were, in fact, increasingly politicized, and their organizations, such as Ruben Martínez Villena's Falange de Acción Cubana, Fernando Ortiz's Junta de Renovación Cubana, and García Vélez's Movimiento de Veteranos y Patriotas, operated outside of traditional parties and labor mobilizations to fight corruption while also embracing patriotic nationalism.[16]

In decrying the failings and excesses of government and demanding greater political participation, activists from most sectors challenged the assertion that elected officials had represented the body politic in good faith. In fact, by the 1920s, formal politics had been all but discredited by widespread and growing frustration with electoral fraud and the misuse of political control. Since 1900, both had been integral to deciding political control and had provoked civil war (the 1906 August Revolution, the 1912 Race War, and the 1917 Lollipop War). Thus, elections less and less often resulted in a political mandate or moral victory for elected officials and their administrations.[17] Indeed, by launching such vigorous challenges to the legitimacy of the national administration, activists cast public doubt on the integrity of elected officials and undermined the traditional political elite's control over the national political arena. Robert Whitney argues that "by the early 1930s social protest from the *clases populares* [popular classes] became so widespread that the established mechanisms of social and political control no longer functioned."[18]

Black intellectual-activists, including young black civic activists (such as those later responsible for *Atómo*), stepped into these swirling waters. In fact, by 1933, Cuban political culture was more broadly defined and it accommodated many national sectors, including the *clases populares*, within which Whitney has argued were new "traditions of struggle" and "forms of political practice."[19] This resonates with new and vociferous challenges to black political elites by their black political rivals, who shifted the philosophical base upon which claims for black rights rested. These black rivals leveled pointed and quite public charges against black political elites. In their estimation, the black elites had failed to represent those they had claimed to represent since the republic's birth: marginalized blacks. Since the republic's founding, most black leaders had professed their responsibility and moral commitment to advancing the socioeconomic status of the "class of color." Yet even as they made such claims, black elites forged intimate ties to the structures of patronage politics. Further, since the birth of the republic, they had monopolized the leadership of black clubs. The tenor of their activism, in fact, raised concerns about whether their commitments were, in essence, to their black brethren or to themselves. Although traditional black leaders claimed a sense of responsibility to the "race of color," black political outsiders increasingly questioned their motivations and ties to corrupt administrations. As brokers, black politicians' task was, historically, to influence black political behavior. From the 1900s to the 1930s, using various avenues (such as the black press and public black patriotic commemorations), they worked to influence the black voting public and its commitment to the national project and its captains. The island's black citizens were, however, continuously caught in socioeconomic strife. Thus, the racial justice goals that they claimed (largely by dint of black community membership) were increasingly impugned. By the third decade of republican life, politics-as-usual rang falsely in the ears of Cubans of all colors, including black voters. As the youth-run newspaper *Renacimiento* stated in the weeks following the 1933 Revolution, "Our ethnic youth has to orient its steps to new paths; their moral and intellectual capacity lack collective integrity. . . . We need new directors for the old [black] societies or new societies for the present youth."[20] The best new hope for black socioeconomic improvement, the editors insisted, was to "break from the past."[21]

But many black activist newcomers were themselves faithful to the decades-old tactics and philosophies of patronage politics (such as political sociability) and racial uplift ideology (bourgeois-liberal values and demonstrations of cultural refinement) that Cuba's political old guard had so consistently engaged in since independence. In some cases, even as this tradition was called into question, new activists were reluctant to advocate for a revolutionary transformation of long-standing socioeconomic hierarchies. As activist Pedro Portuondo Calás editorialized in the youth-oriented black periodical *Renovación*, "The domestic calamities . . . that confront our [black] ethnic entity deserve solution. Logically, this [solution] should be . . . sponsored by those whose condition is most socially, politically, and economically advantageous."[22] Thus, the radicalism of maverick black voices of the period is difficult to gauge. With few exceptions and despite the heavily polarized political climate, they were neither avowedly revolutionary nor entirely accommodationist. Further, by the third decade of republican life, black activism had bifurcated, proliferated, and morphed. Without fully divorcing themselves from uplift ideology, new black political voices "broke from the past" by sharpening their critique of antiblack racism, defining political participation in more inclusive terms, and voicing dissatisfaction at the extent of black leadership ties to the machinations of political patronage.

Black elites had relied on cultural practices to judge black advancement as well as assert their own political authority, and now black political outsiders challenged them on the lack of progress in removing obstacles to economic opportunity. For decades, prominent blacks had actively distanced themselves from Africanist culture and embraced racial uplift; now their detractors began to rethink such Eurocentrism. Both groups frequently reiterated the myth of national racelessness (as articulated by José Martí, Juan Gualberto Gómez, Martín Morúa Delgado, and others), but one group advocated patience and decorum in the face of black marginalization, and the other demanded quick resolution to ongoing socioeconomic inequality.

The self-blaming premise of racial uplift ideology depicted blacks as whites' social inferiors. Its tenets created a social stalemate, an impossibly amorphous self-improvement goal of approximating Eurocentric and elite norms. Yet new philosophies of black political identity redefined cultural propriety and merit to include, for instance, women's political participation and their active role in civic life. Journalist and editor Gustavo E. Urrutia suggested that black Cubans and their Africanist roots should be celebrated. Other emerging black activists, such as Lázaro Peña and Jesús Menéndez, joined leftist movements and advocated for workers' social and economic rights through labor mobilization.

After the 1933 Revolution, along with a renewed struggle over the legitimacy of national leadership based increasingly on expectations of honesty and economic prosperity for all, new black activists and civic organizations chose to rethink the venerable old discourses.[23] For the most part, they moved beyond the traditional themes of black redemption, morality, and racial self-improvement—and the familiar retelling of blacks' sacrifices in winning independence—beyond even the idea that blacks had not yet received what a group of black National Party affiliates in 1904 called "their rightful share."[24] Rather, they insisted that as blacks and as members of the body politic, they expected their leaders to pay attention to their needs.

Outside of the inner circle of black political elites, then, black activists for years expressed their hope that socioeconomic parity might be possible. For this reason, the early Veterans and Societies of Color rancor (1902), the Citizens' of Color Directorate manifesto (1907), and the Independent Party of Color (PIC) activism (1907–12) all were struggles for black access to resources. These activists assumed that black politicians were at least as committed to black access to resources as they were invested in the machinations of formal politics. But by the end of the second decade of republican life, these hopes had been all but dashed. Black optimism had dissipated over the course of twenty years of political disappointments. Barely three decades old, republican Cuba witnessed three civil wars in which black participation was critical. Yet blacks gained little from these struggles. And black politicians and civic activists had, despite promises, failed to improve the social status of the overwhelming majority of blacks. Finally, republican administrators had responded almost exclusively to the needs of the privileged over those of the masses of Cubans of any color, and even less often to those of blacks.

Thus, by the mid-1920s, as the national administration battled on several fronts against a common perception of illegitimacy, a parallel phenomenon was true for black leaders. The promise of racial harmony, egalitarianism, and racelessness embraced by blacks at the beginning of republican life had lost its luster. The presidency of Gerardo Machado (1925–33) provided a fleeting hope. Machado's political success during the 1924 presidential election was largely driven by his Platform of Regeneration to end political corruption and give life to his populist declarations. These were demonstrated in public works projects such as constructing the Central Highway; in making high-level black political appointments; and in designating the anniversary of the death of black general Antonio Maceo as a national holiday.[25] Once in office, however, Machado fell short of this populist vision

when he unilaterally extended his presidency six additional years and relied on increasingly autocratic and repressive measures to suppress opposition. In 1928, for example, he initiated a political strategy that forced the
three main political parties to support his candidacy as president. Known
infamously as *cooperativismo*, the policy was meant to guarantee his continuing role as Cuba's head of state.[26]

The *machadato* (Machado's administration) was threatened by an unstable national economy. Depressed sugar prices on the global market
undermined Cuba's already volatile sugar industry, which collapsed in 1930,
devastating every population segment and economic sector. Both rural agricultural laborers and urban public employees suffered reduced or lost wages
and unemployment. Businesses closed. Government health care, education,
and postal services in many parts of the island were shut down. Rising repression took the form of stepped-up arrests and torture. Newspapers were
closed and editors were arrested. At the same time, laborers organized into
unions, increasing the size and political presence of organized labor. Between 1925 and 1932, labor organizations, such as the National Confederation of Cuban Workers (CNOC), the National Union for the Sugar Workers'
Industry (SNOIA), the Union of Workers and Staff of Electrical Plants,
and the National Federation of Cigar Workers, strengthened in both numbers and political presence. The number of strikes also mushroomed, and in
1930 the CNOC organized some 200,000 workers across industries, bringing everyday operations to a standstill. In the end, in late July 1933, strik-
ing workers sparked the Revolution.[27] After Havana bus drivers brought
transportation services to a halt and clashed with police, a rash of sympathy
strikes broke out across the island, paralyzing general operations from coast
to coast. In early August, the Liberal, Conservative, and Popular parties
turned against Machado, as did the army, leaving Machado little choice but
to flee to the Bahamas.

After the *machadato* fell, in September 1933, postrevolutionary reform-
ists gained even greater access to the political main stage, calling for a new
constitution as well as nationalist labor laws to create jobs for native workers
and to provide greater political accountability. Further, political developments that began after the Lollipop War (1917) and ended with Machado's
cooperativismo (1928) signaled the end of a traditional model of political
competition. That is, instead of two dominant parties vying to win and maintain their hold on public offices (at times seeking U.S. intervention as an
effective, divide-and-conquer strategy), new political tactics emerged. Party
allegiance became even more tenuous, and cross-party coalitions became
more viable. Party lines were not drawn according to specific ideologies,

and they hardly represented competing socioeconomic coalitions. Rather, the emergence of new political actors and tactics rendered the old political elite all but obsolete.[28]

Because political allies valued mutual benefit and access to resources more than ideological loyalties, electoral candidates of different parties strategically crossed party lines. They often created extraparty political coalitions for the purpose of ensuring each other's success at the polls. Initiated during the general elections of 1920, this interparty system of alliance, which predated the *machadato*'s *cooperativismo*, is represented by the infamous *piñas dulces* (sweet pineapples, i.e., powerful groupings).[29] The *piña* was a form of electioneering in which strongmen candidates controlled electoral results by banding together, irrespective of their party affiliation. For example, gubernatorial, mayoral, and senatorial candidates from different party tickets might agree to support each other's campaigns, across party lines. With the help of the *sargentos de barrio* to gain voter support and funds to purchase votes, these strongmen obtained votes according to their perceived power as individuals and as members of a highly influential coalition, rather than according to voters' ideological commitments or party loyalties.[30] Their collusion also depended on cooperation with a member of Cuba's Electoral College. In fact, in an electoral contest, the competition within a party was often greater than that between political parties, and *piñas* were frequently created within the same party against fellow candidates.[31] As long as individual candidates retained an Electoral College member on their payrolls and could reasonably claim a winning number of votes, they were assured of winning an election.[32] Writ large, the *piña* system mirrors the challenges and disparate political sensibilities raised against the old guard, which emerged even outside of traditional political parties, before and after the 1933 Revolution.

The political arena, in fact, opened up to new actors, among them black activists, who challenged traditional political elites' hold on the republic's political economy. Their ideologies were readily articulated according to a generational divide between old guard factions and new political organizations, and they complicated ideas about black leadership and political consciousness by calling for "modern" attitudes, expressing class consciousness, criticizing the self-blaming aspects of black uplift, and (especially after women received the vote in 1934) calling for the inclusion of women as political actors. The editors of *Atómo*, then, as much joined as complicated the storm of antigovernment outrage.

Postrevolution Black Politics

Black leadership had, historically, distinguished itself from the black masses on the basis of cultural practice and economic status. Privileged blacks always maintained that their suitability for leadership rested squarely on their bourgeois-liberal commitments, which, they argued, distinguished them from black Africanist practices. By the 1930s, however, black activist-intellectuals, such as black journalist and social commentator Gustavo E. Urrutia, increasingly embraced Africanisms as an important element of black Cuban experience; it was cultural production that was best cele-brated. This may have resulted from the vogue for all things black, known as *Afrocubanidad* (Afro-Cuban culture), which was celebrated by Cuban scholars and artists of all colors, such as Fernando Ortiz, Nicolás Guillén, Ramón Guirao, Lino D'ou, and Rómulo Lachatañeré, as a central compo-nent of Cuban national identity. Thus, many privileged blacks continued to argue for rejecting Africanisms and pursuing education and cultural re-finements as necessary to black advancement, but black political outsiders argued that Africanisms were an important part of the black Cuban experi-ence. Gustavo Urrutia, for instance, maintained that black elites, especially those who publicly espoused cultural distance from Africanisms and dem-onstrated bourgeois-liberal cultural refinements, had an "inferiority com-plex." They looked to whites, he argued, for social validation, even though European culture had proven to be bankrupt and had become, in Urrutia's words, "savage." Europeans, he insisted, looked to black cultural traditions for rejuvenation.[33]

This last critique was searing, given that the most recent, significant, anti-racist, public protest by black leaders had occurred during the "*brujo* [witch doctor] scare" in 1919, when authorities stepped up antiblack repression and dominant newspapers reported salaciously on the presumed threat of Africanity (African-influenced culture), whose practitioners demonstrated an "insatiable thirst for blood and [white] children's flesh," inciting racialist responses from whites. In the midst of the antiblack climate, several black men were killed just outside of Havana, causing black civic leaders to meet at the prestigious Club Atenas to publicly repudiate the lynchings in Regla and the shooting in Matanzas.[34] Black congressmen and the presidents of several Havana-based black societies—men such as Juan Gualberto Gómez, Juan Felipe Risquet, and Lino D'ou—blamed the violence on the inflamma-tory press and the *brujo* myth-making. They resolved to meet with Presi-dent Alfredo Zayas about their intent to publicly respond to the killings.[35] The "Manifiesto Al País" that they produced accomplished the difficult and contradictory task of attacking antiblack violence while also condemning the alleged Africanist cultural practices that had supposedly caused the vigilantism in Matanzas and Regla.[36]

The men argued that both blacks and whites had contributed to the nation's well-being and were, therefore, social equals. Thus, the actions against the black men had to be interpreted as crimes against the Cuban body politic and punished accordingly. As they argued, "Bloody reprisals and the [Africanist] crimes that inspire them both belong to the dominion of barbarity."[37] Endorsing an unspoken yet powerful racialist ideology, they argued throughout the document that despite blacks' African slave heritage, blacks had contributed to the nation's birth to a greater extent and with results more worthy than was commonly acknowledged.[38] In essence, although they rejected antiblack, racialist ideals and the violence that they ignited, the black activists failed to defend black humanity or to challenge government officials for their lack of response toward the men's murders. Their reluctance to challenge this official indifference reflects their own tenuous position in the arena of formal politics, especially as they themselves were vulnerable to racialist media attacks.

Black political elites backed down from publicly addressing the myth of national racelessness and blacks' socioeconomic status, particularly where public, antiblack violence was concerned; they were hesitant to call for a more socially equitable government distribution of resources. Rarely, for example, did they support black mobilization against racialist policies or ongoing racial marginalization. Their reluctance to speak more forthrightly on the issues confronting the vast majority of blacks, such as rising unemployment, repression and violence, and the lack of educational, professional, and social opportunities, cast them as disconnected and unconcerned. Both the broad historic context of radical demands and the continuing irresoluteness of black leadership helped prepare the stage for new black political voices.

Several black civic organizations developed sharp class critiques, such as Asociación Adelante (1936) and Renacimiento (Renaissance) (1933). For both groups, the radicalized political scene of the mid-1920s was highly influential. In 1925, the Cuban Communist Party and the CNOC were founded. Both argued for the protection of all workers, irrespective of race and nationality—immigrant black Cuban, Chinese, West Indian, and Spanish workers alike.[39] The Communists' platform articulated a position on race for the first time in 1928, after the Sixth World Congress of the Comintern. Cuban Communists followed the Comintern's position on "black self-determination," which argued that blacks had a right to organize autonomously where they existed in large numbers—such as in Oriente province in eastern Cuba. Blacks slowly entered the ranks of the party's leadership and were instrumental in mobilizing labor.[40] Then, too, from the early 1920s through at least the 1930s, continuing economic crises resulted in massive unemployment and underemployment across the board, including for state office workers, for police and military, for tradesmen, and for agricultural workers. The labor sectors that had the least cushion—among them sugar, tobacco, masonry, and carpentry—were among the most devastated. Black civic organizations claimed to represent the "class of color" and had to be involved, since the nation's economic crisis affected blacks disproportionately.

Globally, black consciousness, which was often tied to international labor movements, was on the rise. Italy's invasion of Ethiopia, for example, ignited, as few political dramas had, intense global black support for Ethiopia—seen as the last bastion of political independence and black freedom in the face of Western imperialism. The invasion was followed by the founding of pro-Ethiopia organizations throughout the world, including an eighteen-member Havana chapter of the World Pro-Ethiopia Federation (1939).[41] About the same time, the International Society for Black Defense was founded in Santiago de Cuba.[42] Activists were also galvanized by racial consciousness at the local level. The Buena Vista Social Club, for which a Cuban musical album (1997) and documentary (1999) were named, was founded in 1932 to provide "instruction" to members and contribute to "elevating" their "moral and intellectual level," while also "combating false concepts of racial superiority" and "working to end in the nation all racially discriminatory practices."[43] And by 1938, the National Permanent Committee against Racial Discrimination was organized.[44]

Differences in class ideologies among blacks grew sharper in the turbulent 1920s and 1930s. The new Asociación Adelante worked to protect black immigrants, but privileged black and mulatto Cubans were generally unsympathetic to the plight of economically vulnerable, foreign Afro-Antilleans. In fact, the 1931 congressional proposal for limiting immigrant hires through the use of quotas generated the following response by the editorial board of Havana's exclusive Club Atenas: "Our constant concern is to always care for the collective interests of our brothers, each day more threatened by competition, ruinous for natives in the arts, trades, and professional positions, by foreigners and those that are naturalized, so that what *we* gain, we all gain, and when we reach a goal, it will be enjoyed by all Cubans, white and black. . . . Partisans, now more than ever, we believe in a 'closed door' economic policy."[45] In fact, during the brief reign of President Ramón Grau San Martín of "100 days" between October 1933 and January 1934, when

Cuban nationalism, political unrest, and economic crisis resulted in popular demands to give preference to native Cubans over immigrant workers, many black Cubans called for Antillean workers to leave and encouraged Cubans to close ranks against foreign blacks. At the same time, however, they objected to the many racialist characterizations that justified immigration quotas and the eventual deportation of Jamaicans, Haitians, and other West Indian immigrants. In the public sphere, however, the Nationalization of Labor decree (the so-called 50 Percent Law), passed by President Grau, which stipulated that half of all jobs in industry, commerce, and agriculture would be reserved for native Cubans, provoked violent attacks against both foreign Antillean workers and Cubans of African descent. The 50 Percent Law was of great interest to black Cuban workers, who in November 1933 gathered in large numbers in Havana to hear Grau speak on the subject.[46]

The law also inspired concern among other groups. The conservative Havana paper the *Diario de la Marina* suggested that the law would encourage the growth of the black population and create a racial imbalance in the population as a whole, which could threaten to overwhelm the white Cuban population. This contention hinged in part on the proposed quotas for foreign workers, in which Spaniards were not given as many slots as Antillean laborers. Cubans of color fired back. The editors of the progressive black publication *Adelante* challenged the piece: "There is no such thing as black danger." In response to the *Diario de la Marina*'s contention that "white women control their childbearing while black women bear more babies," *Adelante*'s editors charged that this was absolutely false.[47] They posited that certain intellectuals were trying to "exploit racial prejudices" rather than use their "pens . . . at the service of a pure and fecund Cuban fraternity."[48]

Black intellectuals' and civic activists' willingness to see politics through a racial lens was consistent with a new concern for all things black among many black intellectuals and leaders, such as Gustavo Urrutia and Nicolás Guillén. Guillén, for example, a renowned poet and writer in the *Afrocubanismo* movement, celebrated *lo Africano* (all things African) in Cuban national culture. Though far more white artists and intellectuals produced *afrocubanista* literature, the mulatto Guillén lent considerable talent to the movement, creating poems with an "African" aesthetic. His now-famous collection, *Sóngoro cosongo* (1931), contains many pieces in his onomatopoetic, *afrocubanista* style, such as "Pregón" (Street Cry") and "Canto Negro" ("Black Song"):

¡Yambambó, yambambé!
Repica el congo solongo,

repica el negro bien negro;
congo solongo del Songo
baila yambó sobre un pie.
Mamatomba,
serembe cuserembá.
El negro canta y se ajuma,
el negro se ajuma y canta,
el negro canta y se va.
Acuememe serembó,
aé
yambó,
aé.
Tamba, tamba, tamba, tamba,
tamba del negro que tumba;
tumba del negro, caramba,
caramba, que el negro tumba:
¡yamba, yambó, yambambé![49]

The literary meanings of the poem portray black experiences as ethnography: *baila* (dance), *repica el negro* (the black man drums), and *repica el congo* (the drum beats). But Guillén's emphasis was on racial tropes—on rich syncopation and rhythmic patterns that articulated his sense of Africanist Cuban experiences.

In contrast, other artists and intellectuals eschewed such celebrations of black cultural expression in favor of strict class consciousness. Regino Pedroso, one of the period's most eclectic Cuban poets, who boasted about his Chinese and African heritage, argued for political activism based on economic status and class unity as well as on the struggle for workers' rights. In his estimation, this precluded a strictly racial consciousness. Indeed, his poems generally subordinated race to class consciousness.[50] In one poem, he urged his black compatriots to shun Africanist cultural identity and embrace class consciousness. For Pedroso, in fact, Africanist practices were the root of black exploitation. As his famous "Hermano Negro" (Black Brother) cautioned:

For their enjoyment
The rich man makes a toy of you.

. . . .

Black man, black brother,
silence your maracas.
And learn here, and look there,

and listen there to Scottsboro, in Scottsboro,
in the clamor of slave anguish,
in man's anxiety, man's anger,
in the human pain and longing of the raceless man.

. . . .

Black man, black brother,
cloak a bit your bongó.[51]

Recognizing the dire straits of black Cubans generally, both Pedroso and Guillén used the arts and letters to create a new political ideology for black Cubans, one they hoped would be responsive to black experience. Both believed that Africanist cultural practices (one poet celebrated these while the other cautioned against them) were at the center of that marginalization. Black youth organizations did not celebrate *lo Africano* or *Afrocubanismo*, and in this sense they mimicked the old guard ideologies of black civic leadership. The most widespread ideology among these groups, in fact, was bourgeois-liberal uplift ideology, self-improvement, and cultural refinement—all for black progress. As *Renacimiento* suggested in 1933, "We avoid these wrongs [done to us] with perseverance to extirpate ignorance from our [black] social sphere."[52] This ideological divide—between old and young, between "tradition" and "progress," and between "ignorance" and "enlightenment"—took root in the greater club movement, among young professional blacks, who worked within their own organizations or formed separate, youth-oriented clubs beginning in the early republic.

Black Youth Civic Organizations

One of the earliest privileged black youth clubs was Jóvenes de L'Printemps (Youth of Springtime), founded in 1908. According to its own propaganda, the "best" of their sector gathered there. In 1915, the Booker T. Washington Society was founded on the principle of promoting education on behalf of morality and on avoiding the corrupt ways of earlier generations that trafficked black votes.[53] Other organizations, such as Juventud Minerva (Youth of Minerva) and the Sociedad Instrucción y Recreo Les Printemps, were founded in Santiago de Cuba in the 1930s. The Hermandad de Jóvenes Cubanos was an international organization founded in the mid-1930s for the purpose of "fighting against illiteracy and the lack of culture of the popular masses . . . and [to] further sports . . . such as creating sports camps, [and] organizing sports equipment. . . . This organization [is to be] far removed from any party, that is, political or religious affiliation."[54] Other black youth organizations, such as Juventud Minerva (1921), Club "Los XXI" de Santiago (1927), Sociedad de Instrucción y Recreo "Les Printemps" (1921) (not to be confused with earlier clubs using a similar name), and Sociedad de Asaltos Instrucción y Beneficiencia "Ilustración Juvenil" (1923), were all founded during the national wave of youth civic and cultural activism in the 1920s.[55] Most of these organizations openly attacked "traditional" politicking and the "old sort" of social organization from previous generations, calling them a detriment to blacks' general interests. The Camagüey province's black youth newspaper, *Renacimiento*, for example, declared on the eve of revolution in 1933 that elite black clubs with their highly cultured professionals were not using their skills for the black race. Rather than on ostentatious displays of wealth, *Renacimiento* editors insisted, blacks' survival depended on a new tactic: regaining the positive values of their recent forebears. These parents and grandparents had, at the dawn of the republic, realized the importance of habits such as thrift and savings to black socioeconomic advancement.[56] The young black editors insisted on the need for black cultural development (thereby upholding a long-standing theory of the cause of black degeneracy) and simultaneously denounced blacks' public sphere treatment. Mainstream news journalists, who "turned a deaf ear to kindness, protection, and human affability," were not interested in black concerns, they charged.[57] *Renacimiento*, they insisted, represented a worthy response to pressing black concerns, and it offered the promotion of positive values, cultural development, and refinement *and* a challenge to the political monopoly of black, old guard politicians.

Although club politics often mirrored national political struggles, black clubs had their own internal tensions, typically expressed in generational terms; clubs were unsettled when junior club members challenged the entrenched power of older members. Typically, club elders had founded the organizations, held majority seats on their boards, and perpetuated patronage culture in club administration. Historian Jorge Ibarra argues that generational conflicts between 1898 and 1958 most likely resulted from divergent experiences between older and younger men in the workforce, pointing out that young Cuban men had disproportionately high unemployment and underemployment rates when compared to more marketable older men. Drawing on census figures, Ibarra calls attention to a trend of deepening unemployment among Cuban youth, from 1907 to 1953.[58] Their economic frustration translated into political action, and Cuban youth, historically active in republican politics, were particularly powerful players by the 1920s. Their impassioned support of Ramón Grau San Martín, the first president to hold office following the 1933 Revolution, led some to call his regime a "youthocracy."[59] Even though younger black club members were often folded into the very bosoms of their organizations—particularly via clubs' sports competitions—their tension with established leaders often created factions that addressed specific youth interests. Youth committees within clubs were the most vociferous protesters against the old guard. In 1936, for example, Juventud Apontista, the youth committee of Santiago de Cuba's Club Aponte, criticized authoritarian club leaders, calling them false apostles and *caciques*.[60]

In keeping with progressivist values, youth societies attacked the "old" ways of *caciquismo* (the rule of strongmen) by emphasizing new things in all spheres—representative voting, cultural evolution, sports activities, and competitions with other clubs. Youth clubs typically suggested that black leaders should reject past political practices. They expressed new concerns for the masses of blacks—focusing significantly less on cultural differences among blacks than had previous black civic activists—though they rarely, if ever, espoused revolutionary change in Cuba's social and economic structure or in the distribution of resources. In the struggle for black advancement, young civic activists argued for "new" (progressivist) leaders to energize long-standing black clubs. Black youth organizations also articulated a challenge to the traditional black political elite through a gendered lens, arguing that new political strategies required a reconfiguration of black women's place in the black club movement.

"New" and "modern" politics also emerged from an increase in black women's presence in the public sphere and an increase in Cuban women's public sphere presence generally. Women won suffrage rights following the 1933 Revolution, at about the same time that black women began to formulate a black feminist ideology that intermingled domesticity, challenges to the public/private split, frustration with attacks against black femininity and womanhood, and the desire to professionalize. And although new black radicals of both sexes called for modern, inclusive politics, black women expressed their rights as newly arrived political actors. Gendered politics were complicated for black civic activists, since historically women were counted as appendages to male activists and seen as participants at black club dances, conferences, and other social activities. Yet they were invisible in leadership. By supporting the activism of males and fulfilling gendered responsibilities, they were central to the definition of black civic activists as "male." At the same time, black female voices challenged the constraining social norms enforced by black civic organizations. Thus, at the same time that they continued to extol the virtues of caretaking and domesticity, they also insisted on black women's public sphere presence.

Gender and the Old Guard

Cuban women entered the formal political arena on February 3, 1934, when article 38 of the provisional constitution granted them the right to vote.[61] Women went to the polls for the first time in the island's history in March 1936. The most visible sector of women—elite, white, bourgeois liberals—had agitated in the 1920s and 1930s for voting rights, along with their calls for morality, children's rights, and the end to hunger and homelessness.[62] Their movement had cast suffrage rights as an important way to heal Cubans' colonial past and to bring the nation into the modern era.[63] Many feminists argued for women's political participation. Among black women, that activism often translated into a forceful challenge to old guard politics. Black women increasingly rejected their peripheral roles in black clubs and called for inclusion in black civic organizations rather than the exclusion that upheld class, gender, and cultural hierarchies.[64] Black societies were elitist, they insisted, even though their leaders claimed to represent Cuba's "class of color." Given widespread manipulation in the political arena and civic organizations, black women could be denied true empowerment if they were not discerning. Following the January 1936 general elections (the first elections since the 1933 Revolution), black journalist Calixta Hernández de Cervantes called on black women to make responsible political choices. During the recent elections, she lamented, black women had gladly hopped into fancy cars ("greys") chauffeured by local political captains, who shuttled them to the polls to mark their "x" for unsavory, unaccountable politicians.[65] Hernández urged women to not sell their vote to politicians and to vote "independently" and "wisely" for the sake of all black women.

In truth, the vote was the most readily wielded political weapon they had. Given Cuban women's historic absence from the formal political arena and black civic organizations' strict gender norms, black women had few activist alternatives, despite having won their suffrage rights. The norms of black civic activism supported patriarchal social relations and provided little or no space for female political authority. Gendered repression, in fact, was difficult to circumvent, even for black men. For example, admission to prominent progressivist clubs required prospective members to fulfill several prerequisites. First, members had to be "known," that is, a current member had to vouch for the candidate's familial lineage and his appropriate conduct had to be widely acknowledged. Bylaws prevented new members from engaging in "inappropriate" behavior, such as arguing, yelling, or swearing, or behavior board members construed as inappropriate, leaving members open to behavioral policing according to historically contingent notions of decency, morality, and civility. For instance, members had to distance themselves publicly from African-derived religious and cultural practices. They had to be financially solvent so as to be able to cover membership costs. And a widespread rule among black clubs—that clubmen had to be married to hold administrative office—reinforced the clubs' patriarchal structure.

The rigid standard of conduct in traditional club life limited men's behavior, as well as women's participation—casting the latter as valuable only in relationship to men. Generally unable to join clubs as individuals, women were nonetheless critical to the form and function of club life, the common ideology being that without the modern woman there could be no modern man. In fact, the legitimacy of prominent clubs was predicated on class, gender, and racial notions of conduct and morality, as men's patriarchal domain. A particularly poignant poem, "To My Race," which appeared in 1933 in the black newspaper *Renovación*, is telling:

> The time has come my dear race,
> now that servility has ended;
> we have proven our civic-mindedness
> and must claim our true lives.
>
> And it is time to understand
> —what is a proven fact—
> that rights are impossible to achieve,
> if duties are unfulfilled.
>
> And, what duty shows us
> in this solemn moment,
> is that we must redouble our efforts
> to improve the race.
>
> It is not the black race, no,
> even if spoken in such terms
> that should be held responsible
> for the "time that passed."
>
> But neither can you avoid
> the responsibility
> that today is yours
> for the future.

We can avoid past wrongs
with perseverance
which will eradicate ignorance
from our social sphere.

More to the point,
if we are to achieve
such noble aspirations
we must all follow them.

Men must study;
vice must be abandoned
and the abyss lessened
where they might plunge.

Understanding this logic,
they will come together
so that united they
acquire the greatest possible enlightenment.

And, we women
to fulfill our mission,
are obligated
to understand our duties.

If we all, equally,
—without there being obstacles to that—
search for, in progress
our moral perfection,

Perhaps we will achieve glory
and the world will be astonished,
to record our name
with honor and distinction in History.

And if our success
is as great as the noble efforts we will undertake,
we will erase the stigma
that society has thrown upon us.[66]

This highly gendered and racialized understanding of black feminist activism, which distinguished between black masculinist ideals (such as modern political participation, industriousness, intellectual development, civic activism, racial improvement, and patriarchy) and those of the *feminine* black woman (circumscribed behavior, responsibility to home and society, domesticity, morality, and virtue, all to neutralize the effect of slavery), reinforced as well as challenged the public-private divide between black men and black women. Black female civic activists, then, grappled with racial and gendered tensions and tried to assert their public presence, while also formulating a model of black femininity that was culturally acceptable. Powerful racial and gendered ideas informed the shape of their model and defined the social mores and behavior of black women and men.

Gender and Black Modernity

Although women were not part of club leadership, they were critical to black respectability and the clubs' social standing. Most club activities (such as dances, beauty contests, patriotic events, and children's programming) depended on black women's participation. Moreover, club leaders were often expected to be married. The clubs' reliance on gendered social norms meant that in general club members were pressured to engage in such practices as nuclear family life and public order and decorum. Even racial acceptance rested on the fulfillment of highly proscribed gender roles (especially as black women took on these roles), which were necessary to refuting common racialist perceptions about black clubmen's inherent lack of civilization. Black leaders even argued, as black editors of *Minerva* had done in the 1880s, that black women had to raise the moral standards of all blacks. Black journalist Ramón Neyra insisted that whenever black women fell, they dragged with them the honor of all women and the respect that black men deserved.[67] Another disparaged black women as "the greatest obstacle [to] black regeneration."[68] Further, black male and female purity relied on the trope of the nuclear family and a commitment to legal marriage and legitimate births in order to distance black civic leaders from a racial culture that pitted imagined "Africanisms" against progressivism, modernity, and civilization. As the logic went, blacks were degenerate, judged so due to their birthing and conjugal union practices. According to the 1907 and 1931 censuses, whites formed twice as many legal unions as blacks and blacks bore far more illegitimate children than whites—about two-thirds of all illegitimate Cuban children were of African descent.[69]

That gendered and racial discourses converged to shape black "respectability" is captured well by Ramón Vasconcelos (under the pen name Tristán), the mulatto journalist whose polemical weekly column on black issues (titled "Palpitations of the Colored Race") appeared in *La Prensa* newspaper from 1915 to 1916. Tristán argued that black female behavior was a measure

of black respectability because during slavery women had been horribly degraded by the sexual violation of their masters. Centuries of dehumaniza-
tion had instilled in them self-defeating behavior, he hypothesized, including poor choices in love and an ease with white men that was unbecoming
and irreverent. When black women learned to become serious and develop
their intellects they would, in turn, propel the race forward. Further, Tristán insisted that black redemption depended on embracing patriarchy. One
of the most important acts for black women to undertake, he moralized, was
to demand legal unions.[70] Calling black women the "deciding factor" for
the race of color, Tristán argued for cultural improvement in explicitly gendered terms and placed the responsibility for improving black morality on
women's shoulders. Conversely, if black women were unable to demonstrate
respectability by demanding marriage from men, the race could still improve
by embracing male leadership. So long as black men embraced education,
refinement, and self-abnegation—practices that made them true men—they
would be capable leaders.

Black club organs (such as those published by the Sociedad Renacimiento
and Club Atenas in the early 1930s) often insisted that to win social acceptability clubmen and their families had to exhibit masculinist values and
fulfill obligations related to citizenship (political engagement and education), morality (circumspect behavior and marriage), and female domesticity (care of children, home, and spouse). This in turn would mitigate
racist depictions of blacks, which undermined black political authority. In
essence, black women bore responsibility for black redemption. But gender
relations in which men controlled women's daily lives were also reinforced.
Some black periodicals even presented black women as the social property of
black civic leaders. Visible in the shadows of many black clubs, women were
often cast as a counterbalance to self-actualizing men, the embodiment of
subordination, and the bedrock of black bourgeois-liberal family life. Scattered throughout the 1930–31 edition of the official bulletin of Club Atenas,
for example, are photos of women and children, under titles such as "Damas
de Atenas" (The Ladies of Atenas) and "Nuestros Hijos" (Our Children).[71]

Class and racial discourse as well as gender norms were heaped on black
Cuban women in the republican era, casting them as the self-sacrificing
partners of black men and the bearers of morality and sexual chastity—
even sexual submission—of aspiring black men. In the words of Dr. Miguel
Ángel Céspedes, president of Club Atenas, spoken in 1920 on the occasion
of the club's second-anniversary celebration, "Our women . . . must be self-
sacrificing and long-suffering. As girls, they must be the angels of our happi-

Sra. Concepción Argudín de Matienzo y sus dos graciosas hijas Srtas. Juanita y Mercedes Matienzo y Argudín.

Srtas. Josefina y Delia Bachiller y Ordóñez, con su amable mamá Sra. Avelina Ordóñez de Bachiller.

"The Ladies of Atenas," featuring the wives and daughters of Club Atenas board members. From "Anniversary Album," *Boletín Oficial del Club Atenas* 1, no. 9 (September 20, 1930): 18. (Author's private collection)

ness, as young ladies, the source of our sweetest dreams, as mothers, loving and protective of our collective health and education, as wives, finally, faithful to sacrifice, and, similar to the vestal virgins of pagan Rome, always careful to keep burning in our chests, with their praise and caresses, the lamp of their love's holy flame."[72] Thus, clubs saddled black and mulatto women with the responsibility of upholding blacks' public standing, using women as the vectors of black civilization, morality, and distance from backward cultural practices. Women were to demonstrate these attributes through their sexual conduct. The paradox of invoking "vestal virgins" and "burning chests" and "holy flame" simultaneously to describe female duties is a telling component of black clubmen's dilemma. At the same time that masculine purity was a marker of leadership fitness, male virility imbued black clubmen with the potency demanded of leaders. The need to control black female sexuality, for the sake of presenting to the public an empowered and respectable community of black leaders, unified in a project of black uplift, was critical. They also may have been struggling to reassert their traditional control over women; Miguel Ángel Céspedes's public assertion of black male control of black females came just two years after the Cuban Congress passed no-fault divorce legislation, which weakened the absolute authority of male patriarchs in nuclear families by providing for asset distribution among guiltless parties and divorced mothers' rights over their children.[73]

Even as they upheld patriarchal norms and a cult of domesticity, in the aftermath of the 1933 Revolution some privileged black women asserted their right to political participation and argued for a public role in the fight for black advancement. In this sense, they, too, sought to challenge the strict divide between private domesticity and public political engagement. María Luisa Vélez, a contributor to the black newspaper *Renacimiento*, argued that for black women, public sphere activism *complemented* domestic duties and women's role as a moral, maternal force within the patriarchal family unit: "It is undeniable that in public life, the [black] woman was an effective defender of all progressive ideas that helped to maintain institutional solidarity. . . . If we refer to the home, she was the loving and caring mother of her children. . . . We see then that women cannot limit themselves in any way in their activities, and if her talents allow her to stand out in social and public life with more experience and better preparation and culture, she will bring a greater percentage of knowledge to her home."[74] Thus, as articulated by *Renacimiento*, progressive black women worked both inside and outside of the home, challenging the traditional public/private divide of patriarchal politics that barred women from public political participation. Yet at other moments the press also continued the idea that black women were to maintain that divide and in doing so created a paradox for black women activists.

The most elite black clubs insisted on strict control of women's behavior. In order to ensure that females "behaved appropriately," some prominent clubs built into their structures a "department of moral interests," sometimes called the "family department." The members in charge of this department—generally lesser members of the board of directors—kept their eyes and ears open for evidence of social misconduct among male and female at-large members. Under pretexts, they visited the homes of prospective members and invited guests (particularly women invited to social events) in order to observe their conduct, cultural environment, and economic possibilities.[75] They used this reconnaissance to blackball prospective members and to wield power against others of their social circle, especially young aspiring single women whose financial success depended less on entry into the job market as women of color and more on marrying successfully. For these women, participation in club social events was fundamental to marrying upwardly mobile black men and to securing economic stability.

A short story on this matter appeared in the April 1933 edition of *Renacimiento*, a youth-oriented black newspaper published in the central region of Camagüey. Fabio Luaces's "La Borracha" (The Female Drunk) is a supposedly fictional account of sex and gender politics and of the power black clubmen held over black women. The story was centered on a young single woman of color (whether black or mulatto is unclear) living with her single mother. The unfortunate young woman spurned the attentions of a board member of her local civic organization. In turn, the jilted man devised a cunning scheme to destroy her reputation, making it appear as though she received drunken men nightly at her home. She soon became the object of public gossip and disdain. Consistent with the practices of many black societies in the republican era that regulated women's sexual conduct, the board member claimed that he served the club's interests by exposing the young woman's unsuitability for club life and thereby protected its reputation. Arguing that her transgression violated codes of conduct and appropriate club behavior, he convinced the board to judge her unfit for club membership or participation in club events. Such public humiliation ruined her chances of being courted by other black clubmen of standing. Indeed, her tainted reputation barred her from relations with any socially acceptable male of standing or economic position. Given her impoverished life chances, the young outcast degenerated rapidly. Public humiliation and lost socioeconomic opportunities drove her into a downward spiral of alcoholic despair and dishonor. Her powerful admirer successfully ruined her life.[76]

Although very few clubs even admitted women, in "La Borracha," Luaces quotes the bylaws pertaining to female behavior and preconditions of club membership. Given that female members were, generally, single (since married women did not join but rather participated in club activities as an extension of their husband's membership), the behavior of female members was particularly important to clubmen and subject to strict control. The provision makes clear that mere speculation was sufficient for board members to unilaterally withhold or withdraw membership, without opportunity of appeal: "When it comes to the attention of the board that a female member is not found to be of [moral] condition appropriate to continue in the bosom of the society, her club registration will be erased [from club records] and she shall receive no explanation regarding the ruling; but, if she persists in asking for one, this article will be invoked which makes the decision irrevocable for the parties involved."[77] This provision underscores the degree to which class and sexual politics both undermined single women's power and placed them outside their community's protection against innuendo and scandal, which formal attachment to males, whether or not they were club members, could provide. Luaces continued his appeal, calling on young Cubans of color to pledge their allegiance to progressive and "modern" values: "To the coming youth, less prejudiced, more enterprising and reformist than are we, or were those that came before us, I dedicate the following narrative, so that in designing the programs of new societies, they do not copy those that exist today or have already gone."[78] Even more than a challenge to masculine abuses of power, however, the short story was an attack on the traditional hierarchies in societies of color. Ageism, clientilism, and *caudillismo* had, traditionally, provided impunity for club leaders, especially those who used their influence outside of clubs to secure resources (such as letters of recommendation—critical for admission to schools or clubs—political appointments, and jobs). Further, in the era of renewed populist nationalism of the late 1920s and early 1930s, "La Borracha" was a rallying cry against traditional forms of power (antidemocratic clientilism and corruption) within black clubs, which stifled communities and ruined lives. The tale also suggests the ways that class, sexuality, gender, and racial politics unfolded in daily club operations and permeated the sensibilities of privileged blacks. *Renacimiento*, however, offered its readers a reformist message regarding structures of power in Cuban society that called out corruption without espousing a structural redistribution of power in Cuba.

Although some black clubs' progressive tendencies, such as those of *Renacimiento*, attacked the sort of old boys' power wielded by club board members, many black progressivists contended that black women contributed to black male inertia, while characterizing black men as the forward-moving, potent, and regenerative force among the African-descended. According to this ideology, women of color were particularly vulnerable to public accusations of being backward and traitors to the race in preventing worthy black males from advancing socially and economically. Mulatto journalist and politician Ramón Vasconcelos made this point in 1916, when he argued that the moral and intellectual deficiency of black women was an obstacle to the regeneration of all blacks.[79]

Black women's mobility and social freedoms were almost always regulated by black clubs, either through bylaws or through the private aspersions cast on women's characters—and, depending on men's social and economic standing, even on the political standing of their partners. Black clubwomen often referred to these disparagements in club newspapers and in the black press by calling on their sisters to exhibit irreproachable morality, instructing black women about education and mothering and urging them to become a public presence through professionalization and cultural activism. For black women, early feminism was indeed complicated. Isolated from the almost exclusively white Cuban women's movement and cloaked by the patriarchal conceits that underpinned most blacks' versions of patriotic nationalism, black clubwomen nevertheless pressed for recognition of their roles in black political strategies, in ways both complicit with and challenging to masculine power.[80]

In 1930, María Teresa Ramírez illustrated the contradictions of black feminism within the black club movement. In Club Atenas's *Boletín Oficial del Club Atenas*, Ramírez challenged the idea of the modern black woman as backward and morally bankrupt, arguing that women's move toward professional independence had not eroded their moral and psychological fortitude or their traditional place in society. Rather, suggested Ramírez, women of color were able to contribute to society by professionalizing at the same time as they functioned as the devoted partners of modern men by remaining their "sweet friend[s] of heart and mind."[81] Thus, Ramírez decoupled womanhood from domesticity, defending women's right to enter work spheres while simultaneously appealing to women to subordinate their social power to men.

Many prominent clubs' publications had women's columns in which one black woman addressed another, advising on the necessity of being well groomed and having political aspirations, professional goals, domestic tasks, and impeccable moral standards. In progressivist clubs, then, black women helped to define the cultural orientation of black men; their participation was effected through men, by attending dances and other social functions, forming ladies' committees, and acting as caretakers of patriarchal family units. Not until the 1940s were black women able to join prominent clubs as independent members, and even then very few joined and even fewer actually participated in the leadership of such clubs. They did, however, form female-only civic organizations, such as the Asociación Patriótica de Damas Admiradoras de Moncada (Ladies Patriotic Association for Admirers of Guillermo Moncada) and the Legión Maceista in Santiago de Cuba.

Black clubwomen were at the center of clubmen's self-definitions yet marginal to political authority among black progressivist societies. Their public sphere debates about the role of black women in postrevolutionary society challenged this public-private division of gender roles, even as it reinforced bourgeois-liberal feminine norms. Yet gendered struggles notwithstanding, most challenges to the old guard were based on what many blacks believed to be its historic failure to respond to blacks' socioeconomic issues. The most visible clubs and politicians, in fact, seemed to be the least reliable as advocates for the large, beleaguered black population. Even after the Revolution, the tenor of national politics offered black clubs greater opportunities to expand their networks, and certain black activists called on traditional leaders to support the highly vulnerable black population. One organization in particular, the Sociedad Renacimiento, launched a biting attack on black political elites. Founded immediately after the 1933 Revolution, Renacimiento melded black consciousness, populism, and progressivism into a new, postrevolutionary philosophy.

Club Radicals and Postrevolutionary Patronage

In 1934, one year after the fall of Gerardo Machado, the members of Renacimiento penned a manifesto in which they claimed to be the "true voice" of blacks. They called themselves the Revolutionary Social Directorate—Only Front of the Republic's Societies of Color, and their manifesto outlined a multipoint plan to end divisions among blacks and between blacks and whites. They also pledged to fight for black education and for advancement, gender equality, and the unification of black societies.[82] Renacimiento insisted that to achieve black rights, the island's black societies needed a unified structure. They argued that in the new, politically open, postrevolutionary era, a national convention of black societies was the first step toward justice. Defining themselves as authentic race activists, they insisted that in order to succeed, the black club movement should oust its traitors, that is, those clubmen who failed to make good on their professed commitments to the interests of the black masses.[83]

Renacimiento's attack on "race traitors" focused on Club Atenas, the island's most prestigious black society, going so far as to charge that Club Atenas members had maintained intimate ties with the former Machado dictatorship, pointing to the many black politicians and Machado supporters on Atenas's leadership roster. Renacimiento discounted Atenas's claim that its members spoke for the race of color, arguing that they had shirked their responsibilities to the masses of black Cubans. Worse, charging patronage abuse, Renacimiento accused Atenas members of first using Africanist dance and music fetes to build a constituency among the masses and then, as political brokers, of selling their supporters' votes for their own gain.[84]

Renacimiento's self-declaration as a group of genuine black militants was not unique in the revolutionary era, and neither were ongoing accusations of patronage. Nationalist and populist activists attacked patronage as a holdover from Cuba's corrupt colonial past. But patronage continued to be an important factor in republican politics, including in black activism, through successive presidencies, in part because black votes were still necessary for political success. Politicians continued their efforts to entice black voters by canvassing and electioneering among them, as well as by cultivating reciprocal relationships. Novelist Gerardo del Valle captures the power of reciprocity to work for both patron and client in a tale about a *ñáñigo* (a pejorative term for a member of an African-influenced male secret society) named Candela, the head of a local *ñáñigo* association. A white political boss in Havana won the nomination for political representative, thanks to campaign support and voter mobilization generated by Candela, and in return, as custom demanded, the boss nominated Candela for town councilor.[85]

In fact, public knowledge of black activist intimacy with government officials grew after Gerardo Machado was elected in 1925. That year, Club Atenas received a donation of 50,000 pesos plus a parcel of land for their new headquarters.[86] Atenas inaugurated the building constructed with those funds in May 1929, although construction costs had exceeded the original allotment by nearly 25,000 pesos, causing the club to request additional monies toward cost overruns from the city of Havana. In public defense of both the state's initial gift and the club's extra debt, club president Cornelio Elizalde asserted that he had not benefited personally from the construction project. Rather, he insisted, the additional expenses had been necessary in order to maintain Club Atenas at the level of luxury that corresponded to its reputation and distinction accorded by the national government.[87] In fact, Machado's own political philosophy encouraged the division of Cuban society into corporatist organizations, much as it had been organized politically during colonial rule, which in turn facilitated group appeals and negotiations with elected officials. Machado cultivated patronage relations with black societies, and black societies responded in kind.[88] He was so confident in his relations with black civic and political leaders, including with the black masses generally, that he boasted as late as 1931 that there could be no real threat of revolution because many key segments were "with" him. Despite simmering unrest and imminent mass protest, Machado's relations with the clubs caused him to surmise that in the event of a large-scale political uprising "the Negro, whom I have done so much to dignify, would side with me."[89]

His confidence, however misguided, stemmed at least partially from relations cultivated several years earlier. In 1928, for instance, as Machado's struggle for political control intensified, black clubmen paid public tribute to the president, a move that yielded significant benefits. When Club Atenas sponsored a black clubmen's gala to honor Machado, involving nearly two hundred clubs from across the island as well as local and national elected officials and artists (such as Zoila Gálvez, who sang an opera solo in Machado's honor), several Atenas members were duly rewarded.[90] Machado named club members Manuel J. Delgado as secretary of the interior and communications, Manuel Capestany as undersecretary of justice, and Benjamín Muñoz Ginarte as chief of agronomic engineers within the Secretariat of Agriculture.[91] Black clubmen's ties to high-ranking administrators were ongoing; a decade later, in 1938, on the eve of the election for the 1939–40 constitutional delegates, Antonio Bravo Correoso, a white delegate from Orient province to the constitutional conventions of 1900–1901 and 1939–40 and a Conservative Party senator (1920–24), sponsored, with black clubman Mario Lacret Paisán, a conference to debate political issues. Lacret was then president of the provincial federation of black societies in Oriente province, also called the Plenum Social.[92] Entrenched in the realm of formal politics, black clubmen deliberately cultivated intimate ties to elected officials for their own interests.

Patronage relations also took the form of clubmen's appeals to politicians for aid in resolving internal organizational disputes, a strategy not unlike the long-standing practice in republican formal politics of requesting North American intervention in disputes between political parties to help sway political outcomes.[93] After the fall of Machado in August 1933, several members of the black Nueva Era Society of Guantánamo formed the Joint Commission of Revolutionary Administration. Almost immediately they wrote to the new interim provincial governor, lavishing him with praise for the progressive role he would soon play in office. They also informed him that they

"General Machado and his retinue on arrival to the National Theater to attend a recent homage hosted by Societies of Color." From *Bohemia* 20, no. 38 (September 16, 1928): 29.

had recently initiated a *golpe de estado* (coup d'état) against existing club leaders because that administration had enjoyed "intimate relations with the despotic regime of the *machadato*." By 1934, the backlash against the Joint Commission of Revolutionary Administration's *golpe de estado* resulted in their removal from Nueva Era leadership by the mayor of Guantánamo. Two years later, however, they again wrote to the governor, this time asking him to reinstate them as board members. In fact, one reason that black clubs' old guard structure remained so tenaciously intact throughout the republican era was the expeditious ties between black clubs and politicians. These ties were, in the early republican years, more unspoken than overt, a fact that slowly changed, especially after Mario Menocal's administration sponsored black press initiatives. By the 1940s, however, Cubans' assumption that clubs and government officials at all levels were closely linked was so widespread that relations were publicly and openly celebrated. By dropping the pretense of detachment from government officials and as an increasing number of black elected officials came from the ranks of the club movement, clubs were less able to claim righteous objectivity. It was harder, in fact, for them to claim a role as watchdog against racial injustice or a commitment to the plight of the masses of black Cubans.

Oscar Ortiz Domínguez, a consummate club leader and political organizer in the city of Holguín, left records that attest to ongoing patronage relationships between elected officials and black clubs. Like many club leaders, too numerous to mention here, Ortiz's political aspirations and sphere of influence reached beyond club life, evident by the positions he held in public office and on the boards of several prominent black societies.[94] Ortiz served as president of the city's most prestigious mulatto society, the Unión Holgüinera, from 1945 to 1948, and during this same period acted as delegate of culture for the Provincial Federation of Societies of Color of Oriente (1947–48) and as a deputy to the National Federation of Black Societies (1950).[95] During the 1940s, he was a representative to the House under the Unión Revolucionaria Cubana Party (1942), and in 1944, 1946, and 1948 he landed a spot as an alternate to the House of Representatives under the People's Socialist Party banner.[96]

In 1948, as part of his duties as outgoing president, Ortiz wrote his *memorias* (institutional memoir) for the Unión Holgüinera membership, which included a detailed record of his three-year stint as society president. Extolling his own leadership, social significance, and prestige among black and mulatto Cubans, Ortiz asserted repeatedly that his and other members' efforts toward club operations were done on behalf of "our families" and "our youth." But rather than being a history of collective club battles and triumphs, he used the memoir to tout his own local authority and boast about high-level political maneuvering. The document offers insight into the machinations of black club leaders in the formal political structure.

First, Ortiz himself served as alternate to the House of Representatives in 1942 during his time as club president. When fellow People's Socialist Party incumbent César Vilar gave up his post, Ortiz assumed that congressional seat.[97] He was also an alternate in later years at the same time as other prominent men of color of his party, such as the famous labor leader Jesús Menéndez, who organized the SNOIA, and the leftist labor leader Juan Taquechel. Further, Ortiz disclosed that on two occasions his political ties had led to personal meetings with head of state Fulgencio Batista and that those meetings had resulted in three separate state donations for Unión Holgüinera of 5,000, 10,000, and 30,000 pesos.[98] The last and largest grant, he revealed, had been brokered by Jesús Menéndez—member of the House of Representatives for the People's Socialist Party in Las Villas province—during Ortiz's final year in office.[99] At the end of his report, Ortiz exhorted society members to seek help from prestigious locals (from among Holgüín's "cultured elements") who were in a position to offer financial support. Ortiz urged members to do as he had done for the club: seek out well-connected, well-resourced people for favors and to generally create beneficial reciprocal relations. In fact, he argued, relationships such as these were fundamental to the club's socioeconomic advancement. Ortiz believed that members should both expect and work to cultivate expedient relations with local black and mulatto power brokers who could exercise influence on the club's behalf.[100] His *memorias* underscore that clubmen actively engaged formal politics by cultivating patronage relations in order to win resources.

Although historians such as Helg and Gott have argued that the infamous PIC uprising and subsequent massacre by the Cuban state and white civilian "volunteers" (the Race War of 1912) signaled an end to black political activism, as we have seen for the 1910s and 1920s the clubmen continued to work to federate and strengthen their influence through such efforts as the 1915 Havana-based campaign to unify black societies. More than a decade passed before black societies again convened to build their networks. In May 1928, several Havana-based organizations met with local white politicians, including Havana's mayor as well as the governor of Havana province.[101] Five years later, in 1933, black societies' efforts to federate took on national significance when members of the black club Unión Social of Santo Domingo, a city in the island's central region, held an informal national black societies meeting. Though their efforts were short-lived, they succeeded in consolidating many black societies' provincial operations. Finally, in 1936, after attempting to do so for decades, a national federated structure for black Cuban societies was formed in Havana. The first planning meeting of the National Federation of Black Societies was held in September.[102]

Race Men and "Black Jesuses"

Despite consolidating in 1936, external pressure was almost immediately exerted on the National Federation of Black Societies. In fact, its founding after the 1933 Revolution was both logical and inopportune. It was logical because serious flaws in the republican political system had been met with a response by organized labor and other political groups so forceful that it bolstered the grievances and authority of traditionally marginalized segments of the population, including blacks. After 1933, activist workers and the *clases populares* emerged as significant political players.[103] The federation's emergence was also logical because the political claims of all black Cubans (who were assumed to be constitutive of the *clases populares* by virtue of their race and irrespective of their social, economic, or political status) were given new resonance by postrevolutionary politics. Ironically, radical and populist voices buoyed black clubmen and political elites in their move to create a national black federation. Their focus on anti-imperialism, popular participation, and the rights of workers of all colors, in fact, provided a new social and political opening for blacks in Cuba and gave the black societies' federation movement new viability.[104] A federation would, they hoped, expand their social and political presence.

One significant issue that black clubmen confronted in the federative process was how to best sustain their penetration of formal political networks. The vertical nature of their patronage relationships as well as their corporatist ethos discouraged the expansion of their membership base to include blacks from across the socioeconomic spectrum—which might have been the basis of a class-conscious racial movement in the postrevolutionary period. Further, their ties to government and ideological emphasis on self-help preempted any long-term demands for socioeconomic change. When more radical concerns or reforms were articulated by clubmen, internal divisions among them prevailed and silenced that radicalism.

The federation also swam in troubled waters, because the postrevolutionary political climate emphasized populist reforms, and the very foundation of black clubmen's and political elites' traditional authority (as self-proclaimed cadre *and* advocates for marginalized blacks) was called into question. For emerging black activists and intellectuals who worked outside the club movement or elected office, Cuba's new, radicalized political context weakened traditional black leaders' hierarchical approach to political representation and rendered their traditional leadership style increasingly superfluous. Old school black leaders continued to insist on black strivings for rehabilitation despite their revolutionary context: self-denial, social purity, formal education, wealth accumulation, patriarchal authority, and refinement. Given the reformist, even radical political tenor based on anti-imperialism, political renewal, agrarian reform, workers' rights, women's rights, state-sponsored health care, and national economic protections, such politics-as-usual was intolerable. Blacks were among the central protagonists of popular struggle, which caused the architects of the black societies' federation movement to reflect the national mood and refashion the old self-blaming arguments according to new political circumstances. As black leadership ideals accommodated the country's political fervor, traditional leaders were compelled, albeit temporarily, to inject greater resonance into the federation's activist discourse.

On the other hand, given that the 1933 Revolution had successfully challenged the traditional political structure and imperialist interests on the island, the move to federate nationally was inopportune. Black federationists generated fear and speculation about black activism at a moment of real official concern about any political change.[105] Even though the Revolution changed who was politically significant (and made feminist, labor, anti-imperialist, and black civic activists important, if only in rhetoric), long-standing fears about the potential outcome of black political participation provoked a racial backlash to the 1936 organizing convention of black societies. As the ground shifted, the political use of antiblack racism remained a powerful check on black (and, by extension, popular) activism. In fact, irrespective of many black clubmen's status as political elites and the emergence of new black political voices, they nonetheless contended with tactics to curb their political authority.

Public officials and national media justified antiblack repression, using the allegation that black demands for a fair share of national resources endangered national stability. For example, when PIC members rose up in 1912 to win greater patronage participation, they were demonized by the media and by government at its highest levels as dangerous black *brujos*, lascivious rapists, and unpatriotic men. Shortly after the government violently repressed the *independentista* uprising, President José Miguel Gómez called the insurgents unpatriotic cowards. They "roamed the countryside," he raged, "in hiding," among "steaming piles of waste."[106] In the years after the 1912 Race War, a handful of black survivors created the Partido Amigos del Pueblo (People's Friends Party) to build an independent political movement, beyond the control of mainstream political parties, which ignited media allegations that organizers were libertines who "insulted white women" and admitted Haitian and Jamaican immigrants to the organization.[107]

By the early 1930s, as the Cuban revolutionary crisis came to a head, black political activism was attacked continuously. In its first manifesto (October 1933), the newly formed Ku Klux Klan Kubano, for example, attacked blacks' ideological compatibility with the island's new revolutionary order. KKKK affiliates charged that blacks had supported the *machadato* dictatorship as one of its "strongest pillars."[108] The KKKK's portrayal of black political engagement was consistent with the way that black activism had historically been portrayed—as ideologically out of line with the national project as well as provocative and dangerous for the body politic. Yellow press reports indicated that black violence against whites was on the rise; and newspapers accused blacks of plotting to take control of the island.[109] Based on long-standing antiblack fears, rumors that blacks in Santiago de Cuba were planning to attack whites there were fomented by a story of how, during the Machadato, Oriente province's then chief of police, Dr. Emilio Soto Barranco, had once sent twenty-four-hour evacuation orders to white *santiagueros*, requesting that they leave the city for their own safety.[110]

This issue of black compatibility with the national body politic—a common accusation leveled since the 1900s—was reiterated during the 1933

Revolution. A story about black *curanderos* (religious quacks) who were alleged to have killed eight white children was even recounted in the international press in lurid detail. In an article titled "Smiling Changó," *Time* magazine reported that Cuban children had died at black hands—that Africanist religious practitioners had dismembered their bodies, collected their blood, and in ritual appeasement, sprinkled it over a *Changó* idol."[111] Among the few voices that defended blacks by testifying to their national patriotism was a group called the Revolucionarios Auténticos (Authentic Revolutionaries). The group charged the mainstream press with spreading antiblack propaganda and accused yellow journalists of making false reports about the rise in antiwhite violence. The group cited one such case involving black women *porristas* (hired thugs) who had supposedly assaulted white officers' wives gathered at Havana's exclusive Hotel Nacional, after the officers and their families had sought refuge there following the September 4, 1933, so-called Sergeants' Revolt.[112]

In light of chaos and economic crisis in the 1920s and 1930s, few blacks interpreted such portrayals as anything other than attempts to control their political participation. In January 1931, a group of local black clubmen wrote to Havana's prestigious Club Atenas to express concern regarding an ostensible plot to cast blacks as supporters and henchmen of Machado, making them vulnerable to reprisals. In particular, the clubmen decried a scheme to recruit incarcerated black women from a jail in Guanabacoa (near Havana) for the purpose of attacking anti-*machadista* white women. Using the ongoing political crisis to foment racial divisions, they insisted, was dangerous to blacks' safety as well as national unity, and they hoped that Club Atenas could stop such "odious" political manipulation of black women.[113]

Thus, it is not surprising that in 1936, as black clubmen made plans to hold the federation movement organizing meeting, antiblack propaganda challenged organizers' political intents. In the months before the scheduled national black societies' organizing meeting, antiblack police activity increased and newspapers reported on police raids of "dangerous," African-influenced, religious *brujo* activity.[114] Justifications for black marginalization varied, from disdain for ostensibly non-normative cultural practices to contempt for supposedly false political philosophies. By the time the first official National Federation of Black Societies Convention was held in February 1938, charges that the convention was unnecessary and its leadership was disingenuous had been leveled. One fiery opinion piece, by a disgruntled white, Jorge Adams, criticized black clubmen for their allegations of Cuban racism. Adams suggested that since 1901, by constitutional decree, all blacks had enjoyed equal rights. They had no need to form their own organizations, he complained, and their charges of white racism and white privilege were false. Further, he insisted, blacks, unlike whites, had not acted patriotically in the recent revolutionary crisis that had toppled Machado because they had not participated in the bloody opposition to the *machadato*. In essence, he made it clear that for him blacks had no moral capital with which to advance social and economic claims on postrevolutionary society.[115]

In response to this antiblack climate, black civic activists defended their right to political participation. At least two groups of outraged prominent black leaders published responses to Adams's ranting piece, with both refuting his claim that blacks had not participated in Machado's overthrow.[116] They also insisted there was ongoing and widespread segregation of public space as well as differences in employment opportunities. Such circumstances, they assured Adams, had guaranteed ongoing racial disparities, first in colonial and then in republican socioeconomic structures. This defense of black civic activism had been preceded by the defense of a national black civic federation two years earlier, in February 1936, in the central city of Cienfuegos. After police there had detained blacks for ostensibly fomenting a race war, prominent local black societies, including Minerva and the Albores Sport Club, met with officials to challenge the accusations and free the detainees. Minerva and Albores members issued statements to the city's newspaper, *La Correspondencia*, denying any involvement in a race war. They also clarified their purpose as black society members, declaring that they sought only to struggle for blacks' cultural advancement and the reaffirmation of patriotic values.[117]

Yet neither the wave of antiblack repression following the Revolution nor the biting response by black political elites swayed black activists and intellectuals outside of the club movement to support the National Federation project. In part, many blacks did not believe antiblack repression could be redressed by the federation movement or even that black civic activism had, historically, been a representative voice for the masses of African-descended Cubans. Within weeks of the Organizing Committee's initial meeting in September 1936, for instance, the Havana-based black society Asociación Adelante (which supported both class and race consciousness and was among the most class conscious of the black clubs) questioned the federation's philosophical alignment with the black masses. The club's official publication, *Revista Adelante*, questioned clubmen's sincerity. Editorialists declared in October 1936 that "the majority of [black Cuban] societies, have been created to worship Terpsicore [the goddess of dance]." "These societies," they charged, "have only ever been concerned with dancing, leisure, and politicking in their salons."[118] The black newspaper *Atómo* attacked black societies as well, charging them with a lack of class unity. An August 1936 editorial asserted that black clubmen used antidiscrimination discourse to benefit patronage politicking rather than address blacks' needs in earnest. *Atómo* editorialists, who blasted black civic activists and political elites, argued that in truth *Atómo* interests were more closely aligned with "working-class whites than black clubmen, who live separated from their own because they are poor. With aristocratic airs they impose social distinctions at the same time that they call out their antiracist rage when election time draws near."[119]

Enrique Andreu, himself a member of the Central Organizing Committee, echoed these sentiments in 1936 in *Revista Adelante*. Referencing certain unnamed black societies in the federation movement, Andreu called attention to the differing interests among Organizing Committee affiliates. He suggested that although the federation movement had an activist structure, neither its ideological thrust nor its political tenor were a fait accompli. In fact, they were contested. In the December 1936 edition of *Adelante* he wrote, "We are open to the needles of criticism . . . of those rare, black Jesuses . . . that believe themselves the bellybutton of the world, the center of universal balance, and who spend their lifetimes postulating because they have the false belief that the only good is what they do and they know the right road to follow."[120] Thus, many black intellectuals, some even with ties to the black club movement, called attention to its internal disagreements and ideological tensions as well as its disconnect from the needs of most blacks. Later that year, however, black club organizers responded to the broader context of socioeconomic repression and blacks' ongoing marginalization. They would have had to risk being judged utter failures as advocates for the race as well as thoroughly irrelevant to Cuba's "black problem." In fact, placing the National Federation's first (1936) and final (1938) draft programs side by side reveals a philosophical shift from greater to less radicalization between 1936 and 1938.

The program that the Organizing Committee created in 1936 echoed several of the sweeping policy changes enacted by Cuba's interim head of state, Ramón Grau San Martín, during his brief time in office.[121] The 1936 draft focused on the dire social and economic straits faced by the overwhelming majority of black Cubans. As outlined in the introductory section of the 1936 organizational platform, 76 percent of blacks were unemployed and 86 percent of unemployed Cubans were black. Blacks inhabited 97.5 percent of neighborhoods that lacked adequate sanitation, which, according to program drafters, had given rise to disproportionately high rates of disease, specifically cases of intestinal parasites and tuberculosis. Further, the Organizing Committee's 1936 program was unique in its detail and specificity, especially when compared to amorphous demands traditionally made by black clubmen. The fifteen-page program emphasized many social issues that affected blacks; at the same time, it adopted reformist challenges to the social, political, and economic systems that oppressed Cubans of all colors. Following in the vein of the reformist measures enacted by Ramón Grau during his "100 days" in office (from September 1933 to January 1934), the program also anticipated some of the proposals on agrarian reform, education and literacy, health insurance, and culture that were called for (but that remained largely unfulfilled) by Fulgencio Batista's 1937 populist-leaning Plan Trienal (Three-Year Plan).[122] The committee's program stipulated changes in political, agrarian, public health, education, and labor structures and policies. Among many demands for agrarian reform, the committee called for concessions to the poor and to rural workers, calling on government to distribute lands among native-born farmers and to regulate production. Specifically, the program outlined how seeds and farm equipment should be distributed to peasants and provided guidelines to assess land values and budget resources toward agrarian reform. To boost the political participation of civic institutions and strengthen the checks and balances on Congress and the national government, the program called for a National Assembly of Social Corporations, to be made up of legally constituted corporations and associations that could exercise the right of "recall." To end widespread corruption and autocratic rule, the program called for an end to the presidential system of government in favor of a parliamentary one. This constitutional provision would do away with the old political elite and its two-party political system, which had controlled formal politics for decades, in favor of representative political participation.

The committee also issued a call for constitutional sanctions against acts of racial or gender discrimination. It demanded a state-sponsored literacy program, as well as significant public health planning. Owing to the public health connection between illness (such as tuberculosis and parasites) and black poverty and socioeconomic disparities, committee members demanded an increase in the number of trained medical professionals in the country's high-need areas. This could stamp out tuberculosis and intestinal parasites among rural and urban blacks, they reasoned, as well as combat widespread ignorance regarding public health measures, what the committee called "scientific illiteracy." Finally, they seconded the "50 Percent" nationalization of work decree, a long-standing reformist initiative finally implemented by Ramón Grau, which was meant to protect the jobs of native Cubans. It required Cuban nationality for 50 percent of jobs in industry, commerce, and agriculture and cancelled labor contracts for Jamaican and Haitian workers.[123] Addressing these problems, the committee believed, would assist the disaffected black population while also promoting the well-being of the entire Cuban social collective, irrespective of race.[124]

Yet not until two years later, in 1938, did the Organizing Committee's efforts bear fruit. It developed a final program, to be ready for presentation at the National Federation of Black Societies inaugural convention in Havana that year. More conventions were held in 1945, 1949, and 1952.[125] Yet each time the convention met, the federation's program became increasingly vague in its wording and corporatist rather than mass-based in its ideological scope. The 1938 platform, for example, differed significantly from the one drafted two years earlier in 1936. Unlike the 1936 draft, the 1938 program had no introductory remarks to summarize socioeconomic conditions faced by whites or blacks regarding health, hygiene, unemployment, and racial violence. By 1938, gone were demands for a state-sponsored literacy campaign as well as for compulsory education through the sixth grade. Gone was the call for the abolition of the presidential system in favor of a parliamentary one in order to improve political participation and restrict monopolization of public offices. Most significant, the 1938 program used ambiguous language, editing out the concrete solutions of the 1936 program that had mirrored Grau's populist reformism and Batista's early administration. The black societies that united in 1938, it seems, were purposefully vague on black issues, as an earlier black societies' mobilization effort in Havana in 1928 had been. At the time the Machado administration was becoming increasingly repressive and authoritarian, Havana-based societies convened for three days; they drafted a program that focused on cross-class black alliance, economic parity, and gender equity. By the end of the three-day meeting, however, they dropped their initial demands for structural reforms (such as the construction of medical facilities and workplace protections for male and female workers), instead calling for cultural activism and uplift. Historian Alejandra Bronfman has suggested that in the end the conveners of the 1928 meeting had "retreated from the most risky demands."[126]

Arguably, the postrevolutionary political context contributed to the shift in the federation's 1936 program. Historians such as Louis A. Pérez and Samuel Farber have argued that the defeat of the 1935 general strike (the "last revolutionary surge," when an estimated 500,000 students and teachers as well as postal, transportation, oil-industry, railway, cigar, and government employees, among others, defied military orders and stopped work) left Cuban radicals disillusioned and significantly altered their faith in radical politics.[127] Farber also suggests that popular-frontism and liberal antifascism were contributing elements to the cooled revolutionary passions in Cuba after 1933. Further, after Fulgencio Batista assumed national leadership, he began to conciliate politically, socially, and economically to popular demands and opposition groups on several counts (such as legalizing the Communist Party in 1937 and drafting the populist Three-Year Plan) in order to make his postrevolutionary administration appear viable and representative as well as to quell popular mobilization.[128] In 1936, Ramón Grau had spoken of "socialism, nationalism, and anti-imperialism," but by 1937 he recanted that statement, suggesting that his 1936 political position had been "extremist."[129] Following Farber's argument, this contraction of political militancy by 1938 likely directly impacted how black club activists crafted their 1938 program for socioeconomic change. To fulfill the requirements of antiracist, antidiscrimination advocacy, they would have been unwilling to stray too far from the national climate of revolutionary radicalism. Yet, dependent on government officials at the highest echelons, they would have also been unable to advance a sharply militant, radical platform of change for Cuban socioeconomic national structures. Nor is it clear that they would have been fully able to cast aside their elitist pretensions to advocate for mass black political and socioeconomic participation.

Another factor contributing to the 1938 program change might have been regional disparities, since both regionalism and patronage were highly influential factors in republican political life. Regional socioeconomic discrepancies (in employment, public health, and public works conditions, for example), though often glossed over in republican historical narratives, were obvious. Compared to other provinces and cities, Havana's disproportionately dense and powerful political networks, characterized as the island's *pulpo* (octopus), exercised tremendous authority in the distribution of national treasury funds at the regional level.[130] It seems logical that in the nation's capital, where a greater number of government posts made for denser and more lucrative patronage networks than in the interior provinces, black leaders likely exercised inordinate influence in the organizational proceedings of the national black federation. Likewise, local circumstances plaguing blacks in Oriente province would have informed the agendas of clubmen from that province.

In early 1936, when the provincial federation in Oriente met to draft its suggestions for the National Federation platform, the tenor of that meeting suggested a clear class and racial consciousness among participants.[131] Club members discussed issues pertinent to immigration, workers' rights, education, culture, and agriculture and socioeconomic problems. Santiago-based youth at the meeting denounced "strongman politics" and "false apostles" among black leadership. Further, activists demanded that government take action to humanize life and guarantee justice and equality in the full exercise of the citizens' rights. Focusing on the upcoming reforms to the Cuban constitution and with hope that changes in the structure of jurisprudence would help all Cubans exercise full citizenship rights, they made recommendations to elevate the standard of living for the popular classes on all fronts.[132] Their political position, as already discussed, related to their need for political legitimacy. After the 1933 Revolution, for instance, popular concerns and needs gained in importance, consonant with the political authority from having toppled the *machadato* in the first place. In fact, to win political support, activists and politicians had to reflect populist and radical tenets, if only in rhetoric.[133] Although this tone among clubmen from Oriente province is visible in the initial National Federation platform of 1936, as other provincial black societies' federations integrated into the national organization the national platform shifted.

Black federationists from Oriente province, seconded by convention delegates in Las Villas and Matanzas provinces, infused the National Federation program with progressive political goals. As early as 1935, black clubmen in Santiago de Cuba organized Plenum Social, a plenary of prominent societies in Oriente province that hoped to build its own provincial federation. Black societies from Matanzas also organized their own federation that year. In turn, Oriente and Matanzas targeted Las Villas province, specifically the town of Santo Domingo, as the 1936 site of the Central Organizing Committee's National Federation of Black Societies.[134] Havana and Camagüey provinces, the island's wealthiest, with the largest share of gross domestic income, did not form provincial federations until eighteen months after most other provinces had black federations. Further, the inaugural meeting of the National Federation was held up until clubmen from Havana and Camagüey provinces had founded their own provincial federations. Most important, soon after Havana and Camagüey provinces joined the National Federation, a decidedly different and more conservative platform was drafted.

Comparing the island's first and second cities (Havana and Santiago), regional discrepancies are suggestive of why there was ongoing frustration in less-resourced provinces such as Oriente. After the fall of Machado in 1933, for example, the national government's neglect of Oriente province was an important point of ideological mobilization for the citizens of the province, particularly in the provincial capital of Santiago. On several occasions, for example, Santiago's mulatto mayor, Justo Salas (1940–44), was forced to travel to Havana to press national administrators for public works funds, due to the province's inadequate budget for public works and social services.[135]

Meeting of the Matanzas Provincial Federation of Black Societies, 1944.
(Courtesy of the Archivo Nacional de Cuba, Havana)

Provincial mayors often traveled to the national capital to secure funds, a practice that emerged after the very first municipal budgets and projects were initiated in 1902—funds for the installation of streetlights and pavements and the building of hospitals and schools and an aqueduct system.

Despite the fact that Oriente was bigger than the other provinces in both land mass and population, it lagged far behind in resources (public works contracts as well as kickbacks, sinecures, and public administration appointments) allocated to the province by national administrators.[136] In 1930, for example, the total funds allotted to the province of Havana totaled $1,087,580; the capital city of Havana was given $7,367,868. In contrast, the province of Oriente was budgeted a mere $503,933 in government funds; and the capital city of Santiago was allotted $839,721.[137] Given that the 1931 census lists Oriente province as the country's largest in population size, these figures reveal regional economic discrepancies as well as differences in patronage power. Regional favoritism disadvantaged the citizens of Oriente province by drastically reducing their standard of living. Press reports on the conditions of Oriente in the 1930s, for example, paint a portrait of administrative neglect that affected the health and well-being of the residents. Despite numerous trips by provincial and municipal authorities to the capital in a quest for public works funds, many basic projects were never completed. In 1938, the Communist Party newspaper *Noticias de Hoy* called Oriente province a "limbless Moroccan" due to "lack of water and sanitation, hunger, and other miseries." *Noticias de Hoy* also pointed out that in 1938 there was not one working ambulance in the city of Santiago.[138] A 1944 visit to Santiago by President Batista raised hope that the lack of such basic services as "paving the streets" would be addressed.[139] The province's needs were, in truth, well known by national officials; numerous requests were made by Santiago's mayor, Justo Salas (1940–44), to Batista for public works funding.[140] That elected officials were forced to request monies from national administrators due to their own provincial budget shortfalls enhanced both the stature and the control of national politicians. In exchange for helping interior provinces with funds for basic public works projects and social services, politicians could expect political support. This was a strategy expertly implemented by Batista, who greatly increased the number of local and regional politicians who appealed directly to him and who, in turn, were politically indebted to him.[141]

Oriente's heavily agricultural economy further destabilized the region. The depression of the 1920s and early 1930s hit agriculture hard, especially in the sugar industry.[142] Cuba's per capita income from sugar, for example, fell at an astounding rate: from $107 in 1924 to $53 in 1929. Thus, economic dependence on agriculture, especially sugar production, did not bode well for Oriente province. Between 1931 and 1946, the area of cultivated farmland increased to just over 70 percent of total landmass, up from about 58 percent before 1931. In 1935, Oriente produced 85 percent of domestically consumed coffee; by 1946 almost half of the provincial landmass was dedicated to sugar production. About half of the province's labor force, largely comprised of native black and Antillean immigrants, worked in agriculture and were employed seasonally, on average working only about four months per year.[143] During the annual "dead time" between sugar harvests, unemployed sugar workers desperately searched for work. This period could last as long as ten months—during the economic crises of the early 1930s, one harvest season was just sixty-two days.[144] This improved during the wartime sugar boom of the early 1940s, but the dead time was always a period of precarious living for cane workers. As mulatto economist Alberto Arredondo suggested in 1944, during the annual dead time, "five hundred thousand men roam the countryside and cities in caravans, hungry and miserable without a place to find sustenance." They also went to the capital to beg, "becoming hobos and even stealing, inevitably promoting social ills such as epidemics, overcrowding, and delinquency."[145]

This context of crisis for black rural laborers, and the economy of the province, generally, was the socioeconomic backdrop informing the National Federation of Black Societies organizers in 1936 as they crafted their land reform platform. As already discussed, the initial program was authored by members of Oriente's provincial federation of black societies. Agricultural reform was central to strengthening the region's economy and in turn to improving the lives of the people in the province; in order to retain the credibility of black clubmen in Oriente as the voice of black Cubans, it received lengthy treatment in the 1936 black federation platform. This was in part a function of client-patron relations, in which clubs often brokered votes between politicians and local black constituencies during elections. Despite the fact that clubmen distinguished themselves from the majority of black Cubans, it was imperative for their own survival as black leaders to address the agrarian crisis of blacks in Oriente province.

One source of relief for such dire circumstances was to appeal directly to officials at all levels for financial support in exchange for giving political support. Officials used the public treasury for this purpose, such as the National Lottery (established in 1909), as part of their coffers to distribute financial resources to clients. As early as 1936, for instance, under the brief presidency of José Barnet (December 1935 to May 1936), a National Lottery commission for *sorteos* (monetary grants) for civic organizations was formed to manage "daily *sorteo* awards."[146] Batista relied on this and earlier political uses of National Lottery funds throughout his first term by cultivating relationships with political interest groups and funding them with lottery *sorteos*.[147] Among many groups, he awarded funds to the Catholic Church, labor unions, mainstream presses, social welfare projects, and civic institutions.[148]

As his first presidential term (1940–44) came to a close, Batista traveled to Oriente province to win political support before the presidential elections. He visited several towns and met with politicians and civic organizations, including black clubs such as Club Aponte and Luz de Oriente. Local presses recounted his trip in rich detail: walking tours with local elites; motor vehicle caravans; sumptuous civil society receptions in his honor; and numerous political meetings. Batista hoped to solidify his reputation as a dependable political figure in order to shore up political control of Oriente and boost his chances of defeating Ramón Grau in the upcoming presidential election.[149] The trip was meant to facilitate direct appeals to him in order to exchange public treasury resources for political support. After returning to Havana, Batista pledged financial assistance for numerous public works projects in municipalities in Oriente province, to be funded with an 11.3 million-dollar loan from the U.S. Export-Import Bank.[150] His promises to

Oriente administrators were extensive: 10,000 pesos to the town of Baracoa to augment a recent 40,000-peso grant for a rural children's home, of which 6,500 pesos were allocated to the minister of education himself; 34,000 pesos to fix the streets of Holguín; 15,000 pesos for Velasco Highway repairs leading to a sugar mill and for Velasco municipal streets; 26,072 pesos for street repairs in Banes, Batista's hometown; 25,000 pesos to fix Mayarí Highway; 25,000 pesos for public works and highway repairs in Sagua de Tánamo; and 5,000 pesos to repair roads from San José de los Naranjos to La Gran Piedra, located outside of the provincial capital, Santiago de Cuba. Santiago proper would receive additional funds: an immediate credit of 30,000 pesos (for a total of 300,000 pesos recently granted) to renovate the city jail; 50,000 pesos for street repairs; 10,000 pesos for construction of a highway from the city to Siboney beach; 17,000 pesos to help repair Santiago's Reporters' Association building; 20,000 pesos for Oriente's Normal School; 5,000 pesos for the Palace of Justice; 10,000 pesos to complete and beautify the new vault of the Veterans' Pantheon at the municipal cemetery; and 10,000 pesos (of a total 100,000 pesos promised) to a boarding school.[151]

Black civic organizations received their share of rewards in Batista's corporatist structure as well, including a bold move by the president to distribute *sorteos* directly to black clubs. When in late 1943, at Camagüey's black Victory Society, he announced his intention to fund black societies, he also proclaimed his intention to support the passage of complementary legislation to sanction violators of article 20 (equal rights) and article 74 (equal employment rights) of the 1940 constitution.[152] His announcement was at once an appeal for political support from black civic leaders and a gesture suggestive of the president's racial sympathies. By using lottery funds to promote black advancement and level Cuba's socioeconomic playing field, Batista helped black clubmen but avoided full engagement with republican racial disparities. And, although his plan to distribute *sorteos* to black clubs secured his standing among black civic leaders, it also severely undermined these leaders' position as independent black leadership, by calling attention to their ties to the Batista administration. Joining the state payroll placed in grave doubt the clubmen's objectivity and commitment to agitate for black socioeconomic opportunities as free agents. Batista's funds for black clubs were, of course, welcomed, and, following the Camagüey speech, societies across the island—including the organizing committee for the second National Federation of Black Societies' convention—sent congratulatory telegrams and letters to the president.[153] The Communist Party newspaper, *Noticias de Hoy*, in its bid to be a public advocate for racial equality and to cast black clubmen as part of a populist initiative, described its response to Batista's subsidies as a "popular" outpouring of support.[154]

If Batista the politician cultivated ties with black clubs according to the same political strategy as his predecessors, he was also feted by Santiago's most prominent black clubs (Club Aponte, Luz de Oriente, and Casino Cubano) during the February 1944 visit.[155] Longtime national politician Américo Portuondo Hardy hosted the event, along with José Cleger, Ulises Baquero, and Rafael Caraballo, presidents, respectively, of Club Aponte, Luz de Oriente, and Casino Cubano.[156] After the 1943 announcement at Camagüey's Victory Society, forty-four clubs received funds in 1943; more than eighty clubs requested *sorteos* from Batista in 1944.[157]

Between 1953 and 1959, *sorteos* continued to find their way into black club coffers, including the national black societies' federation, now named the National Federation of Societies of the Colored Race. Batista's relationship to the clubs remained intimate during his second administration, from 1952 to 1959. The *sorteo* gift monies were often sufficient to construct and repair clubs' headquarters as well as organize social, cultural, and political programming. *Sorteos*, in fact, kept many black societies afloat financially, such as the Sociedad Antonio Maceo de Nueva Paz, near Havana. Average monthly credits amounted to a mere 100 pesos for this club in the early 1950s, but the club was awarded 4,800 pesos in 1954 and 1,250 pesos in 1958 by Batista.[158] As long as Batista distributed resources to corporate interest groups according to their direct appeals to his administration, corporatist resource allocation (such as *sorteos*) would remain an important way to maintain groups' stake in his economic and political order.[159] Arguably, without having formed an interest group to appeal to Batista and other administrators, blacks would have experienced even greater social, economic, and political marginalization. Further, Cuba's myth of national racelessness and racial transcendence threatened to publicly erase black experiences, including their marginalization in public discourse. In this sense, despite clubmen's insistence on social, cultural, and political differences between them and the majority of Cuba's African-descended population, they consistently deplored Cuban race relations in the public sphere. Although Batista's racial policies deserve greater study, his belief that the clubs were an important constituency is evidenced by his pledge to support the clubs financially after 1943. In fact, although the impact of race on the relationship between Batista (who was rumored to be of African descent) and the clubs is still unclear, these civic organizations helped to support his public bid for civilian legitimacy, following years of military leadership in the 1930s.

Even before his presidential election in 1940, Batista effectively controlled national government as commander of the armed forces. Yet he also needed civilian legitimacy, which he tried to achieve by courting political constituencies among Communists, labor activists, and civic organizations. Batista hoped to exploit these groups according to the tradition of republican patronage relations. His support of them might translate into reciprocal support—garnering votes in formal political elections. By the time he won the presidential office in 1940 he had honed his strategy of actively and openly seeking relationships with groups such as black civic organizations.

Several years earlier, in 1938, he used a similar tactic by legalizing the Cuban Communist Party, which served to curb political opposition and build a base of political support as he moved from military to civilian leadership.[160] Given the radical optimism of the postrevolutionary period, he actively cultivated his image as a populist leader, and part of his populist image depended on an amicable relationship with organized labor. In 1939, Batista allowed the newly organized Confederation of Cuban Workers to hold its first meeting.[161] And he twice gave lottery monies to the organization for the construction of the Workers' Palace—its headquarters.[162] During a trip to Mexico in January 1939, at the invitation of the Mexican government under the leadership of popular nationalist Lázaro Cárdenas, Batista spoke before the Mexican Workers Confederation, proclaiming his abiding identification with Cuba's "popular" sectors.[163]

Batista's tribute to the popular classes was, of course, motivated by their growing political significance. Since the 1920s, the labor movement—an important sector of the popular classes—had increasingly organized, both nationally and according to trades, forming trade unions such as the National Maritime and Cuban Ports Federation and the Cuban Railway Brotherhood, both of which had, by 1925, founded trade union organizations.[164] Organized labor and leftist activists increasingly overlapped during the *machadato*, especially after 1929, when the Communist Party successfully controlled a large portion of organized labor. Communists, for example, established their leadership over the CNOC after its founding in 1925 and organized the SNOIA in 1932. Haitian and Jamaican workers constituted an important but hard-to-mobilize segment of the sugar industry. Nonetheless, the Communist Party made inroads among sugar workers, since both Communist and labor activists believed blacks were an important constituency.[165] As Alejandro de la Fuente argues, given their prominence in many labor unions, by the early 1930s Communists believed that unless they confronted racial discrimination in the workplace and in labor organizations, they could not achieve workers' unity.[166]

Even unorganized blacks were an important political constituency for organized labor because their support might translate to broad black voter support. Though the extent of their collaboration is unclear, unions and black civic organizations enjoyed an ongoing relationship, given that black club meetings were often held at local unions' headquarters. And after Batista announced that *sorteos* were available for black societies, many of those that petitioned his administration for black clubs were leaders of local trade organizations. This suggests that organized labor enjoyed an increasingly intimate relationship with the administration as well as with black civic organizations. It is also possible that black club and trade union memberships overlapped. Between December 1943 and February 1944, labor organizations, primarily from Las Villas province, requested funds from Batista on behalf of black societies. A women's tobacco workers' organization in the town of Baez (Asociación de Despalilladoras de Baez), for example, requested funds on behalf of the local Maceo Society. Unionized seamstresses, musicians, leatherworkers, construction workers, and workers of the "María Antonia" sugar mill all petitioned for *sorteos* for the Provincial Federation of Black Societies of Las Villas.[167]

Between the 1930s and the 1940s, in fact, the proportion of black leftists who were union organizers and/or in the leadership of Communist Party organizations (under their various shifting titles) and who ran as Communists in several elections surged in response to the postrevolutionary prominence of the popular classes and to Communists' emphasis on the issue of racial justice.[168] Black leftists such as Jesús Menéndez, Salvador García Agüero, Francisco Calderío (known as "Blas Roca"), and Lázaro Peña were important to both the Communist Party and organized labor. Jesús Menéndez, for instance, was a sugar worker as a youth. He later organized among tobacco and sugar workers and joined the Communist Party in 1931. As part of the party's focus on organized labor, he mobilized hunger marches and built workers' organizations, such as the Proletariat United Front, the Confederation of Cuban Workers, and the National Sugar Workers' Federation.[169] Menéndez was killed in 1948, allegedly on orders from President Ramón Grau. Black leftist Salvador García Agüero was an educator who continued to work as an activist-intellectual. He also had ties to the black club movement, serving in 1938 as a member of the executive committee of the National Federation of Black Societies convention and in the late 1930s as vice president of the Provincial Federation of Black Societies of Havana. In 1938, he joined the Union Revolutionary Party (the newly reorganized Communist Party) and was elected president.

As black radicals and leftists, both men focused primarily on building class consciousness and strengthening the labor movement. Yet they also brought racial concerns to republican politics, such as in 1939, when, as constitutional convention delegates for the Communist Party, Salvador García Agüero and Blas Roca insisted on the need for specific, tough penalties in the constitution for acts of racial discrimination. Roca, a Communist party member since 1929, in 1931 joined the Central Committee in charge of party organization in Oriente province.[170] Both men introduced a proposal for so-called complementary laws to the constitutional convention floor, in order to strengthen the antidiscrimination articles of the 1940 constitution, and Roca outlined the Communists' complementary laws in his speech to a black Club Atenas conference in 1939.[171] Representing the Communist Party at the Atenas conference, Roca stated that his party's struggle was against all forms of discrimination. These, he averred, exploited the working class and were an obstacle to its liberation. Further, he insisted, the party had worked hard to raise public consciousness about this issue and in doing so had distinguished itself from other political parties that put up candidates for the upcoming general elections.[172] Roca had taken this opportunity at the invitation of Club Atenas, which had invited all political parties to define their political platforms and achievements in a public conference series called Citizens' Orientation. Each party participating in national elections in 1940 was invited by Atenas to clarify its position regarding immigration, the economy, employment, education, and racial discrimination.[173] In his opening remarks, Atenas president Dr. Benjamín Muñoz Ginarte defined the club's relationship to society and national politics. As a "democratic" organization, he stated, Atenas members supported politics that were "humane, moral, and dignifying for man." On the one hand, Muñoz explained, for their values and pursuits Atenas members belonged to the "enlightened, cultured, and representative classes." Yet they were also tied by race to the "popular masses." In many ways, Muñoz defined their complex social position in politically expedient terms: they belonged to a class of people of historic political authority, yet they maintained ties to the popular classes whose political authority had been suppressed until the 1930s, when they began to enjoy greater political prominence.[174]

Club Atenas members likely organized the conference to shore up their declining political appeal. The club leadership in 1939 contained several traditional black political elites, such as Benjamín Muñoz Ginarte, Miguel Ángel Céspedes, Conrado Thorndike, Manuel Capestany, and Ángel Suárez Rocabruna, who had run previously for Congress.[175] And whereas in previous years many Club Atenas members had been elected to Congress, very few ran for and won seats in the 1940 elections. In fact, Atenas's public conference series coincided with national political processes following the 1933 Revolution: the 1939 constitutional delegate elections, the 1939–40 constitutional convention, and the 1940 general elections, when Batista ran for and won the presidency. When the traditional political elite was forced into retreat by the 1933 Revolution, black political elites ceded their historic leadership to those blacks running on labor and leftist tickets, such as Blas Roca, Lázaro Peña, and Jesús Menéndez. In fact, few blacks ran to be delegates to the 1939–40 constitutional convention, but among those blacks who did (such as César Vilar Aguilar, José Maceo González, Blas Roca, and Salvador García Agüero), the overwhelming majority ran on Communist coalition tickets.[176] Similarly, during the general elections of 1940, Communists, under the joint Revolutionary Union–Communist ticket, ran several black party members, including Blas Roca, Jesús Menéndez, Salvador García Agüero, and Lázaro Peña. José Maceo González (son of General José Maceo) ran under the National Revolutionary Party banner, outside of traditional black political networks, as did Justo Salas, who won the mayoralty of the city of Santiago de Cuba as a member of the Socialist-Popular Coalition.[177] Holding political office continued to be important for accessing public resources, and black clubmen faced political extinction if they relied solely on racial discourse to claim political relevancy while also failing to capture public offices. Given the political significance of workers, poor agrarian reformers, women, and anti-imperialists, black leftists emerged from the turbulent 1930s with greater ideological resonance than did traditional black political elites.

Yet black leftists and other political newcomers, though distinguishable from elite black society leaders, nonetheless cooperated with the societies' movement during Batista's black civic rapprochement. Following Batista's 1943 visit to the Victory Society in Camagüey, black attorney Francisco Guillén, a Partido Socialista Popular member from Camagüey province and president of the Provincial Federation of Black Societies of Camagüey, expressed his public support for Batista and the antidiscrimination legislation.[178] Further, extensive collaboration between black societies and labor unions resulted in a February 1944 publicity event and celebration of President Batista's plan to grant *sorteos* to black clubs and to work for the passage of antidiscrimination legislation. The Communist press, *Noticias de Hoy*, called the event, organized by Havana black societies, labor organizations, and cultural, artistic, and sports institutions, a push for the passage of the Law against Racial Discrimination.[179] The Confederation of Cuban Workers reiterated its commitment to ending the rising tide of discrimination against black workers, as did the Havana Workers' Federation, which called attention to a recent example of employment discrimination by the owners of a canning plant who had refused to hire black women as tomato canners. Eduardo Canas then spoke in his dual role as representative of the Association of Public Employees and of the San Carlos Society, announcing that the San Carlos Society publicly challenged recent acts of discrimination against black athletes by the local Committee of Amateur Athletes. Having introduced antidiscrimination legislation in Congress as a congressional representative of the Partido Socialista Popular, Salvador García Agüero closed the event by urging mass mobilization in order to guarantee the passage of the complementary laws.[180]

These ties, however, were fleeting, a result of the intimacy that both black clubs and Communists enjoyed with President Batista in the late 1930s and during his first term in office (1940-44). That racial politics, antidiscrimination legislation, and labor activism seems to have provided common ground upon which these disparate groups worked, collaborated, and publicly supported each others' initiatives did not preclude them from expressing significantly different philosophies on the need for corporatist institutions or mass-based labor organization, immigrant workers' rights, and working-class solidarity. Black clubmen maintained a corporatist structure and insisted that their chief political role was as social, political, and cultural cadre to the island's black masses, but black Communists charged ahead in defense of blacks and the Cuban worker. The gulf between these types of political organizations was too great to transcend. Arguably, neither sector hoped to transcend the divide in order to create a unified black movement.

Irreconcilable Differences

The National Federation succeeded in submitting its own manifesto for antidiscrimination complementary laws to the floor of the 1939-40 constitutional convention. Though constitutionalists voted "to study" the manifesto, it was rendered a dead letter. Only vague language regarding discrimination made its way into the new constitution of 1940. Article 20 and article 74 addressed discrimination and equal access to employment, respectively, stating in essence that all Cubans were equal and without special privilege before the law. After 1940, these complementary laws became the banner of black federation activism, a sufficiently public gesture of black leaders' commitment to the legalization and enforcement of racial equality.[181] Yet the complementary laws were never passed. Further, the extent to which clubs were united in earnest behind their passage is debatable, given the clubs' accommodationist relationship with government officials and the lack of commitment with which they promised to fight for the laws' passage. Further, Batista's decision to bankroll black societies, coupled with the National Federation's legislative focus to impose sanctions on discriminatory acts rather than advocate for improvement of the socioeconomic conditions under which the majority of blacks suffered, did not bode well for the National Federation's public image. Scandal rocked the organization. In 1952, its president, Prisciliano Becquer Piedra, and its treasurer, Mario Lamagne Romero, stood accused by federation members of altering bylaws so that the signature of the secretary of records was no longer necessary for withdrawing funds from the organization's bank account. Becquer was removed from office.[182] They were alleged to have absconded with a *sorteo* of 30,000 pesos, which was slotted for the National Federation of Black Societies. The Committee for the Defense and Rescue of the National Federation of Cuban Societies, founded in 1953, could not improve its public image. The following year, the federation's new president, Reinaldo Tamayo, and others on the executive board—those who had accused Becquer and Lamagne the year before—themselves stood accused of credentials tampering. Society affiliates charged that Tamayo had tried to prevent them from being able to vote in federation elections. Efforts to launch a fifth convention were futile.

Black societies' unwillingness to disassociate from state ties and their passivity in the face of the social and economic circumstances of the masses of blacks placed in doubt their agendas regarding racial justice. This was compounded by charges of misappropriation of funds at the local and national levels, which placed the leaders and even some lay members of the federation movement in direct conflict with the needs of the majority of Cuba's African-descended population. The effort to create a National Federation, which took flight in 1936, had gone down in flames by the early 1950s. Although populist sentiments and progressive activism in 1936 had generated a federation platform that was responsive to the black masses, by the 1940s this reformist, even radical, initiative waned.

The 1950s proved devastating to the black club movement. Hundreds strong at the beginning of the decade, there were just sixty-eight registered with the National Federation of Black Societies in 1956, and by 1960 a mere seventeen were listed as active.[183] As in the revolutionary 1930s, political and economic turmoil after the 1952 coup forced several societies to close and ruined the solvency of others, especially in that decade's later years. Although black societies had enjoyed an intimate relationship and significant support from the state during four consecutive administrations (Batista, Grau, Prío, and Batista again), the popular siege that overtook the Batista administration in 1958 proved too tumultuous for black societies. State subsidies dwindled then, and many societies found it difficult to exist without state support.[184]

It is not clear whether the National Federation of Black Societies turned away in 1938 from the initial race and class activism expressed in 1936 because of internal divisions, regional loyalties, or the self-interested machinations of its leadership. In fact, all of these factors seem to have affected the institutional stability and the political agendas of clubs overall. But certainly the contentiousness of the federation movement and of black societies in republican racial politics brings up questions about their political affinities. Further, the extent to which the National Federation of Black Societies, the most prominent mobilization of black public voices in the republican period, represented the true interests of black Cubans demands a more thorough examination. Despite the visible role of black societies as activist organizations and as the presidios of black political elites, their strategies for black socioeconomic advancement (such as corporate organizing, cultural improvement, shows of refinement, and political loyalty) cannot be viewed solely through the lens of racial consciousness or according to a presumption of universal black political unity. Other factors, including patronage politics, cultural and class differences among blacks, and regional loyalties, affected the politics of black societies and encouraged the growth of persistent factions among the black societies of Cuba's republican era. Importantly, the divide between "new" and "old" political ideologies among black leaders correlates to shifts in gender politics. Although black youth organizations and even relatively privileged black women did not clamor for full social justice (or absolute gender equality), they did challenge the patriarchal moorings and domesticity that permeated black political discourse and was practiced by privileged black clubmen and politicians. They questioned blatant male supremacy in black civic activism, as well as long-standing undemocratic strategies for building and retaining political authority.

Republican Politics and the Exigencies of Blackness

Because neither the formal birth of the Cuban republic nor the promulgation of the 1901 democratic constitution were defining moments in the black Cuban battle for resources, a narrative of republican black activism must draw on alternative watersheds. Arguably, a black activist atlas would include, among many other salient actions, the 1902 Veterans and Societies of Color mobilization for greater black representation in the civil service sector; the 1906 August Revolution, which confirmed the decisive importance of black participation in national political conflicts; the 1912 Race War, which violently demonstrated just how little tolerance dominant political parties had for challenges to their supremacy; the 1917 founding of the elite black Club Atenas, the result of increasingly intimate ties between black politicians and dominant political parties; the 1933 Revolution, which undermined the authority of traditional political elites, reconfigured the profile of national political activism, and introduced alternative black political voices to the public sphere; and Batista's 1943 declaration that he would subsidize black civic groups, a strategy that institutionalized formal patronage relations between black clubs and the national administration. In fact, the egalitarianism that fueled the wars of independence from 1868 to 1898 and that Cubans had hoped to inherit in 1902 had only a limited impact on equitable resource distribution in the republic—the issue that anchored most early twentieth-century black political activism. Moreover, although the 1901 constitution granted universal male suffrage to men of all colors and prohibited "special rights and privileges"[1] for any individual or group, other factors, chief among them vertical (rather than horizontal) relationships to the centers of political and economic power, allowed de facto resource inequalities to continue.[2]

Having obtained the vote in 1902, however, a small corps of black politicians and civic activists put it to good use. They negotiated patronage relationships with elected officials and pledged their support (often in the form of promised votes) in exchange for political favors. More important, they acted as intermediaries between the black publics and municipal, provincial, and national officials. The black publics that they serviced often took shape as locally constituted social organizations. In part, local and regional politics were critical to national elections because provincial electors, and not the popular vote, determined who won the presidency. That is, similar to the Electoral College system of the United States, electoral votes were aggregated at the provincial level in Cuba, which strengthened the political hand of local and regional politicians.[3] The local presence of black political activists, who worked to "deliver" votes (especially black votes) to their candidates and parties of choice, bound local and national processes in a pas de deux that antedated the republic's formal emergence in 1902, underscoring the importance of local processes to national politics. Historians surmise, for example, that a strong and, ultimately, decisive black and mulatto showing among Liberation Army leaders from Oriente province stemmed from local personal relationships. Prominent local blacks who took up arms for independence between 1868 and 1898 and who later became Liberation Army officers ascended in rank because of their talent for swaying large numbers of blacks and mulattos.[4] After independence, in 1912, local ties continued to be important, even shaping the mobilizing strategy of the Independent Party of Color. Party leaders, for example, decided to move their base of operations from the nation's capital in Havana to Santiago de Cuba in Oriente province, where blacks held a voting majority in several districts and where the Haitian-descended, mulatto party leader Pedro Ivonet lived, owned a farm, and likely was well known.[5] In fact, black social and political identities were concocted largely in the cauldron of the everyday, in local black coalitions and operations.

Blacks' local experiences constituted the basis of patriotic mobilizations, such as the group of black women from Santiago de Cuba who were moved in the early 1920s to declare publicly their "admiration" for Guillermo (the "Ebony Titan") Moncada, the martyred Liberation Army general, founding an organization later called Asociación Patriótica de Damas Admiradoras de Moncada in Santiago's poor black *barrio* of Los Hoyos. Among the group's stated goals was the following: "To love the patria and propagate the doctrines of its great heroes as well as respect fervently *all* [emphasis mine] Cuban liberators," with the implication that their nationalist allegiances were filtered through a connection to several high-ranking black and mulatto veteran officers of the Liberation Army, including Agustín Cebreco, Guillermo Moncada, José and Antonio Maceo, and Flor Crombet, all from in and around Santiago. In exalting black patriots, these women celebrated "local blackness" and emphasized the black presence in what was otherwise a predominantly white Cuban nationalist pantheon.[6] The black Legión Maceísta de Oriente (Maceo Legion of Oriente) worked similarly in Santiago's school district to teach area schoolchildren about black patriots. Their activities suggest that their identities were at least partially derived from specific experiences rather than from universal racial claims.[7] Black social clubs offered opportunities, activities, and entertainments for members and nonmembers in their towns and cities, thereby encouraging local black experiences. Although by the beginning of the republic they were scattered across the island as a loose conglomerate of institutions, and although they often lauded and chronicled each others' activities and efforts in black periodicals, they, in fact, created local relationships. Not until the 1930s, after nearly four decades had passed, did the clubs consolidate their provincial and national clubs, federating at the provincial level by 1936 and creating the National Federation of Black Societies, whose first convention was held in Havana in 1938. Though human motive is always difficult to ascertain, this study has suggested that the absence of a national, mass-based black civil rights movement in twentieth-century Cuba may be attributable to the importance of the local experience, which ultimately trumped black engagement with universal racial consciousness.

On the other hand, despite the pervasiveness of their local commitments, black politicians and club activists advocated on behalf of "the race of color," an imagined, homogeneous black Cuban "community." Although this community was invented and their relationship to it changeable, it served their political purpose. At times, they proclaimed their critical role as leaders of the "class of color." At other moments, a black imagined community was for them less politically significant, and they instead heralded the need for racial harmony, even Cuban racelessness, and championed what they called the truth (or, depending on one's perspective, a despicable myth) of Cuban racial democracy. In both instances, their assertions were pragmatic and rested on a monolithic conceptualization of republican racial order, in which the national community, if ostensibly unified, was also divided according to its discrete racial parts. Black participation in the electoral process helped to perpetuate a myth of a democratic union and enabled politicians to claim an authenticity where Cuban egalitarianism was concerned. Black leaders' struggle for resources, then, relied on a homogeneous construction of blackness that helped them to shore up their role as the cadre of the community and necessitated that they publicly refrain from discussing the implications of regional, gendered, class, and cultural diversity among the African-descended. Thus, while participating in local blackness, black political activists also peddled the universalizing idea that they presided over a unified black Cuban community. Their end goal, then, can more readily be linked to a desire to access republican resources than to blacks' need for socioeconomic restructuring to address their generally higher rates of disease, underemployment, unemployment, and unsanitary living conditions when compared to whites. Their activism related to advancing their individual and corporate interests (and, to a degree, those of their black followers), rather than those of an imagined racial collective united across social and economic divides.

Compared to all Cubans of African descent, prominent black activists enjoyed a degree of social and/or economic privilege. In fact, the historic divisions and motivations between black activists and the masses of black Cubans help to dispel both ahistorical conceptualizations about a monolithic "black community" in Cuba and the notion of a homogeneous black subject. Even as a strategy of racial unity, broadly conceived, for most of the republican period Cuban political activism was highly fractious, making it difficult to sustain a unified political community of any sort, much less a cross-class racial community mobilized against racial injustice. Although racial difference contributed to stratification, even among the African-descended, Cubans of all colors were ranked according to factors such as occupation, education, professional pedigree, nepotism, regional location, party affiliation, and patronage networks. During colonialism, slaves and free people of color were alternately divided and united by phenotype, slave status, occupation, education, ethnicity, place of birth, and organizational affiliation; these divisions generally obviated mass black racial mobilization while also facilitating the development among them of multiple experiences of blackness.

Privileged blacks (who amounted to no more than 3 percent of the black population at any time of republican history yet who dominated public sphere debates about blacks' circumstances and the nature of the black subject), in fact, worked very hard to distance themselves from the masses of black Cubans. Even among blacks, difference was consistently articulated as a matter of culture. Black club members and politicians publicly embraced patriarchy, refinements, self-denial, thrift, physical fitness, order, and ostentation, as a strategy to prove their fitness for leadership and in order to distinguish themselves from the masses of black Cubans. Black clubs held balls, conferences, sports competitions, and patriotic commemorations, thereby constituting a nodal site where blacks' excellence in cultural norms and civic responsibility were publicly confirmed.

Simultaneously, black civic organizations were formed to strengthen the black scramble for public resources. Scholars have noted that corporatism was encouraged during the Machado administration (1925–33) and during the first Batista administration (1940–44). Gerardo Machado publicly expressed his desire to negotiate policy and benefits with individual organizations rather than with mass organizations.[8] Batista cultivated a similar social, economic, and political culture. He encouraged the distribution of resources to corporatist interest groups, based on their policy negotiations with specific sectors of government bureaucracy. According to political scientist Jorge Domínguez, Cubans who mobilized benefited most from this system by receiving resources from government officials. In turn, this "prevented the development of nationwide political cooperation. . . . Cuban politics was organized by groups, but not by class."[9] Domínguez also argues that republican political parties did not emerge from social and economic cleavages but instead from personalistic ties and patronage mobilization. This sheds light on why black civic organizations and politicians generally did not advocate for the masses of marginalized blacks. They were strategic rather than ideological groupings—interest groups that appealed to political patrons and that, ideally, returned black votes to political parties.

Paradoxically, black politicians and civic activists needed the support of the masses of black Cubans in order to compete with other groups for resources. To bolster their claims—that they represented the black population vis-à-vis national government and enjoyed significant political authority (they were ostensibly able to "deliver" black votes to politicians as well as resources to blacks)—black political activists had to appear to be in control of black public opinion and resources and to be able to control black political behavior. Arguably, the ties between privileged blacks and the black masses may have been advantageous for a few among the masses. Requests for job placement, matriculation to professional school, letters of recommendation, and *botella* sinecures arrived in the hands of black brokers in the patronage system, and they distributed these favors to clients, if only for the purpose of "practicing politics." It is debatable whether blacks would have fared better under patronage or under representative democracy. The fact is that they and all Cubans navigated both. Given republican economic and social welfare scarcities, Cuba's electoral democracy and party activism were most often at the service of resource acquisition.

Most blacks did not benefit from patronage politics, which can be seen from race-based occupational disparities throughout the republic. And the lofty promises of the anticolonial insurgency—that Cubans of all colors were equal citizens—may have silenced many black activists, especially in the first years of the republic, when the clang of long-term republican resource disparities was more muffled than audible. Then, too, only after the rise of a discernible black professional class in the 1920s did the black public sphere reach its apex. By then, a new generation of black civic activists began to call for a change, based less on fundamental structural changes to socioeconomic hierarchy than on a demand for greater democracy and less autocracy in black civic institutions and republican politics. Further, the revolutionary political synergy that brought together proponents of anti-imperialism, radical nationalism, working-class consciousness, feminism, antidiscriminationism, and black consciousness took root and influenced black women (who often rejected limits historically imposed on their role in black activism and instead carved new roles for themselves) as well as black journalists, artists, civic activists, and labor organizers to challenge republican structures of black unemployment and underemployment. Many believed that Cuba's old guard, constituted by varied genealogies and colors, upheld the state's neglect of social and public services and attacks against the island's domestic workforce, by acquiescing to the demands of both patronage political culture and foreign domination.

Thus, black club leadership and politicians, having long sworn an ultimate allegiance to advancing the socioeconomic condition of "the class of color," found their backs to the wall by the 1930s. Even as state agents brought black clubs into the very bosom of the state's machinations and as those clubs expanded their networks across the island, black activists exposed the flimsiness of their plans for parity and the emptiness of their racial fraternity. Arguably, their participation in national politics, access to patronage systems, and insistence on keeping race debates alive in the public sphere were important to black mobilizations of all kinds, if only as agents of polemical debate and political organizing. Their societies and presence in political office, in fact, challenged what many racialist whites argued in the media, that despite, or perhaps because of, a myth of the "raceless" Cuban nation, blacks were unfit for participation in modern Cuban society and unfit to lead as elected officials. Rather, they were better regulated and their Africanist practices were better repressed if they were subordinated to white Cubans, to whom they owed their emancipation and cultural enlightenment.

Black activists rejected the limits placed on their full participation in the body politic and were vigilant in looking for opportunities to enter patronage networks. In this regard, the arc of history bent their way. By the 1940s, they enjoyed continuing formal subsidies from the national government. At the same time, however, their links to government officials, such as President Gerardo Machado and to Fulgencio Batista, eventually discredited them as agents of change. Further, the ripostes delivered to the black old guard by black youth and by class-conscious organizations show that by the 1933 Revolution, socially and economically marginalized blacks had begun to look to a different class of leader for ideological inspiration and practical reward. Others then arrived on the scene, such as black labor leaders Lázaro Peña (tobacco workers), Aracelio Iglesias (dockworkers), and Jesús Menéndez (sugar workers), who challenged foreign and domestic corporations and industries. That these men were influential is clear: in 1948, both Menéndez (a member of the Communist Party and secretary general of the national sugar workers' union) and Iglesias (a Communist and black dockworkers' labor leader) were assassinated. Intellectuals and artists of the 1930s, too, sought to bring into public view new strategies for black advancement, all of which challenged club leaders and politicians and threatened their ability to claim the privilege of being the race's "point persons."

In looking back through the history of black civic and political activists in republican Cuba, two issues are clear. First, black political ideals were differentiated and black leaders generally acted on behalf of their own, individual interests, even as they cleverly espoused black advancement and an end to racial barriers. In fact, black civic activists (as did all activists) sought patronage relationships with elected officials based on their presumed ability to sway voters; they were believed to be critical for the electoral success of politicians of all colors. Second, black Cubans were not completely marginalized in republican politics, as some historians have argued, nor did they fail to provide leadership on behalf of racial justice issues. That there was no continuing, racially conscious, mass black rights movement in republican Cuba was much less a failure of politicized black experience or leadership than it was a sign of the context within which they were activists—a fractious political culture in which actors primarily sought resources. That is, they swam with, rather than against, the republican political current.[10] In fact, wherever possible, they placed themselves at the very heart of its social and political operations. Their history destabilizes the categories and identities of Cuban racial politics.

This study has retrieved the often-silenced yet central role of African-descended Cubans in the nation's political structures and has examined the relationship of liberal democratic elections to patronage networks. I have argued that these are as much related to daily and local circumstances of history as to the ways that people embrace broad national and regional ideologies, set social and political agendas, and marshal their resources. The story of black Cuban activists, represented here only partially, reveals patterns of sociability and political engagement and brings clarity to the definition of political participation by placing civic organizations at the center of political struggle.

This study also challenges static historical narratives of blackness in republican Cuba, including those that presume a black/white binary, overarching racial consciousness, and utter black subordination. I argue that although black Cubans engaged with nationalist ideologies, black experiences and activism cannot be subsumed by a nationalist paradigm. This book recovers part of the history of a black Cuban struggle for resources, whether during the segregationist period of the U.S. occupation government or decades later when Cubans forged intimate ties with national administrations. To benefit from patronage reciprocity, black activists walked a fine line between negotiating with government officials and acknowledging widespread racial discontent. As the ostensible advocates for marginalized blacks, they both collaborated with politicians and reiterated dominant racial discourses. Their position then, as interlocutors between black public opinion on the one hand, and republican political hopefuls and elected officials on the other, was unstable and highly contradictory. This book argues that black leaders negotiated for power in the interstices of republican racial politics, between the slats of dominant racial discourse and mass black experience. In fact, as activists they refused to be limited by nationalist discourses and even moved beyond the powerful frame of national racelessness. Racelessness subsumed black political participation under the national project of egalitarianism and racial inclusion while also declining to induct blacks fully into the national community or provide them with access to public resources on par with whites. Even as they adopted nationalist ideologies in their own public debates, they also consistently rejected delimiting boundaries of national ideologies and myths of Cuban racial harmony and unity. In doing so, they asserted their desire to access resources alongside other Cubans similarly engaged in the supranational project of resource acquisition. Finally, as people of African descent, they did not wholly embrace community constituted by strict racial consciousness nor did they limit themselves to Cuban patriotic nationalism. For blacks in republican Cuba, acquiring power required far-more-nuanced negotiations.

Notes

Abbreviations

AHPSC   Archivo Histórico Provincial de Santiago de Cuba, Santiago de Cuba
ANC   Archivo Nacional de Cuba, Havana
exp.   expediente
leg.   legajo

Introduction

1. Though the men who authored this text called themselves Nationals, their party name was in transition and was sometimes given as Moderate Party. This was a transition begun by August 1904, when their party, the National Party of Oriente, fused with the Union Democratic Party and the Republican Conservative Party to form the national Moderate Party, led by Liberation Army general Domingo Méndez Capote. Moderates won the presidency in the 1905 general elections. Thus, these black men represented a party that would a year later dominate national government. The men were involved in both national and local politics, however, due to their activism in local civic organizations. And although the specific author of the article from which this text is taken is unknown, blacks in the National Party of Oriente (later the Moderate Party) were also political activists in several majority or all-black civic-political organizations. Men such as Virgilio Medina, Antonio R. Danger, Gregorio Galán, and Mónico Echevarría, for example, were in black civic clubs as well as the National Party of Oriente. "Todos con los Nacionales de Oriente o Moderados," *El Nuevo Criollo*, October 22, 1904. Unless otherwise noted, translations from Spanish to English are mine.

2. Prominent conference organizers and participants included Pan-Africanists Henry Sylvester Williams of Trinidad and W. E. B. Du Bois of the United States, as well as Liberia's onetime attorney general Frederick Johnson and Benito Sylvain, an aide-de-camp to Emperor Menelik II, among others. See J. R. Hooker, "The Pan-African Conference 1900," in *Transition* 46 (1974) (Indiana University Press on behalf of the W. E. B. Du Bois Institute): 20. In his memoir, the Reverend Alexander Walters relates the following list of attendees: "The meetings were held in Westmin-

ster Town Hall [London], which is near the House of Parliament. There were present the following representatives: Rt. Rev. A. Walters, D.D., New Jersey; M. Benito Sylvain, Aide-de-Camp to Emperor Menelik, Abyssinia; Hon. F. S. R. Johnson, ex-Attorney-General, Republic of Liberia; C. W. French, Esq., St. Kitts, B.W.I.; Prof. W. E. B. Du Bois, Georgia; G. W. Dove, Esq., Councilor, Freetown, Sierra Leone, W.A.; A. F. Ribero, Esq., Barrister-at-Law, Gold Coast, W.A.; Dr. R. A. K. Savage, M.B., Ch.B., Delegate from Afro–West Indian Literary Society, Edinburgh, Scotland; Mr. S. Coleridge Taylor, A.R.C.M., London, Eng.; A. Pulcherie Pierre, Esq., Trinidad, B.W.I.; H. Sylvester Williams, Esq., Barrister-at-Law, London, Eng.; Chaplain B. W. Arnett, Illinois; John E. Quinlan, Esq., Land Surveyor, St. Lucia, B.W.I.; R. E. Phipps, Esq., Barrister-at-Law, Trinidad, B.W.I.; Mr. Meyer, Delegate Afro–West Indian Literary Society, Edinburgh, Scotland; Rev. Henry Smith, London, Eng.; Prof. J. L. Love, Washington, D.C.; G. L. Christian, Esq., Dominica, B.W.I.; J. Buckle, Esq., F.R.G.S., F.C.I.E., London, Eng.; Hon. Henry F. Downing, U.S.A.[,] ex-Consul, Loando, W.A.; T. J. Calloway, Washington, D.C.; Rev. Henry B. Brown, Lower Canada; Dr. John Alcinder, M.B., L.R.C.P.; Counsellor Chas. P. Lee, New York; Mr. J. F. Loudin, Director Fisk Jubilee Singers, London, Eng.; A. R. Hamilton, Esq., Jamaica, B.W.I.; Rev. H. Mason Joseph, M.A., Antigua, B.W.I.; Miss Anna H. Jones, M.A., Missouri; Miss Barrier, Washington, D.C.; Mrs. J. F. Loudin, London, Eng.; Mrs. Annie J. Cooper, Washington D.C.; Miss Ada Harris, Indiana." See Walters, *My Life and Work*, 253–54.

3. W. E. B. Du Bois, "To the Nations of the World," in Walters, *My Life and Work*, 257–60.

4. See Loughridge, "'My Race': A Translation."

5. Limited suffrage rights were in force for the nation's first municipal elections and constitutional convention (both held in 1900), based on criteria such as age, literacy, assets of at least 250 dollars, and honorable service in the Liberation Army. The U.S. intervention government determined in 1899 that the total population was 1,572,577 and that, according to Louis Pérez, the electorate constituted just 5 percent (approximately 105,000) of the total population. See Louis A. Pérez, *Cuba*, 182. Political chronicler and historian Mario Riera argues for a greater number of electors. Of 185,501 Cubans eligible to vote, 131,627 voted to elect the delegates of the constitutional convention. See Riera, *Cuba política*, 24.

6. The Platt Amendment's infamous article 3, for example, states: "The government of Cuba consents that the United States may exercise the right to intervene for the preservation of Cuban independence, the maintenance of a government adequate for the protection of life, property, and individual liberty, and for discharging the obligations with respect to Cuba imposed by the treaty of Paris on the United States, now to be assumed and undertaken by the government of Cuba." *Statutes at Large of the United States* 31:895–98.

7. Bacon and Scott, *Military and Colonial Policy of the United States: Addresses and Reports*, 191.

8. Ibid., 189–203.

9. For discussion of North American efforts to shape and control the ideologi-

cal moorings and socioeconomic interests of new republican leadership, beginning with the election of "safe leaders" as delegates to the constitutional convention, see Louis A. Pérez, *Cuba under the Platt Amendment*, 39–55.

10. Cuba, *Constitución de la República de Cuba* (1902), 20. Title 4, article 11, reads: "All Cubans are equal before the law. The republic does not recognize special rights or privileges."

11. The 1907 Cuban census lists the African-descended population at just below 33 percent. Cuba, *Censo de la República de Cuba, 1907*, 206.

12. For a detailed discussion of early black efforts to penetrate the emergent political structure, see Fernández Robaina, *El negro en Cuba*, 36–45.

13. See Helg, *Our Rightful Share*, 165.

14. "Todos con los nacionales de Oriente o moderados," *El Nuevo Criollo*, October 22, 1904.

15. See 1907 census figures for rates of incarceration, literacy, and professional as well as academic titles conferred, organized by racial category. To provide one example, the rate of incarceration among whites in 1907 was .13 percent (1,934) of the total white population. For *negros* (blacks) and *mestizos* (mixed-race people), the incarceration rate was approximately 2.5 times greater. The percentage of jailed Cubans of African descent, in relationship to their total population, was .32 percent (1,937). Cuba, *Censo de la República de Cuba, 1907*, 135, 206, 233.

16. Examples of black political mobilization in the early republic are the Committee of Veterans and Societies of Color (1902); the emergence of a short-lived black civil rights directorate in Camagüey province in 1907; the rise of the Independent Party of Color between 1907 and 1912; and the short-lived Friends of the People Party in 1915. For more discussion, see Fernández Robaina, *El negro en Cuba*, especially chap. 3; Helg, *Our Rightful Share*, 126–27; Orum, "Politics of Color," 96; and de la Fuente, *A Nation for All*, 66–82. The 1907 Directorate argued against challenging mainstream political parties, while the integrants of the Independent Party of Color sought to join, not dismantle, the reigning party structure.

17. Early twentieth-century Cuban scientists, for example, who reified and then dismembered the national body in order to examine what they believed were its disparate, constituent segments (women, blacks, immigrants, peasants, urban, wealthy, impoverished, etc.) created studies on black pathology and Africanist cultural production. Their scholarship presumed that blacks were socially and culturally homogeneous and the source of Cuban social pathology. Work by Israel Castellanos and the early scholarship of Fernando Ortiz are exemplary. See Castellanos, *Medicina legal y criminología afro-cubanas*; Ortiz, *Hampa afrocubana*; Ortiz and Iznaga, *Los negros curros*; and Castellanos and Castellanos, *Cultura afrocubana*.

18. See Deschamps Chapeaux, *El negro en la economía habanera del siglo XIX*; Deschamps Chapeaux, *Contribución a la historía de la gente sin historía*; Deschamps Chapeaux, *El negro en el periodismo cubano en el siglo XIX*; Deschamps Chapeaux, *Los batallones de morenos y pardos libres*; Hevia Lanier, *El directorio central de las sociedades negras de Cuba*; Montejo Arrechea, *Sociedades negras en Cuba*; Carbonell, *Crítica*; Orum, "Politics of Color"; and Fernández Robaina, *El negro en Cuba*.

19. Herman Bennett argues that in recounting the process of Africans' transformation as slaves, scholars have subsumed their experiences within discussion of the slave trade, slave labor, and social mobility narratives, without adequately considering social and cultural dynamics for the process. Thus, historiographical emphases are on oppression and race relations and not on black experience. See Bennett, *Colonial Blackness*, 104. Michael Gómez argues similarly for the historiography of North American slavery. See Gómez, *Exchanging Our Country Marks*, especially chaps. 8 and 9.

20. See, for example, Fernández Robaina, *El negro en Cuba*; Helg, *Our Rightful Share*; Brock and Castañeda Fuertes, *Between Race and Empire*; de la Fuente, *A Nation for All*; Bronfman, *Measures of Equality*; Guridy, "From Solidarity to Cross-Fertilization"; Childs, *Aponte Rebellion in Cuba*; Orum, "Politics of Color"; and Mena, "Stretching the Limits of Gendered Spaces."

21. Here I concur with Herman Bennett's assessment that black experience is dynamic, historical, and largely self- and community-centric, rather than static and universalist. He argues for this in the case of colonial Mexico, suggesting that among Africans and their descendants a politics of daily life experiences can be at least partially mapped by using their patterns of marriage, family, and kinship ties—all of which were constituted at the local level rather than according to a universalist racial consciousness: "As a profoundly localized expression of subjectivity, blackness was manifest in community formation. . . . As the embodiment of a localized subjectivity, blackness was the antithesis of racial consciousness with its emphasis on some transcendent identity that purportedly linked all persons of African descent." In republican Cuba, social life and formal politics were shaped by local relations, which also constituted the basis of black Cuban experience. Bennett, *Colonial Blackness*, 21.

22. Gobierno Provincial, leg. 2624, exp. 6, AHPSC.

23. Ibid., exp. 6–8.

24. Scott Mainwaring argues that clientelism provides tangible benefits for "the poor" in a system that generally favors wealth. He suggests that "resources extracted through clientelistic relations are appropriated directly by the individuals or groups for their own benefit." For discussion of how economically vulnerable groups ("the poor") might benefit from clientelism, see Mainwaring, *Rethinking Party Systems*, 181.

25. Helg argues that blacks posed a "third-party threat" to the dominant two-party system when they mobilized autonomously (such as in the Independent Party of Color) for a greater share of resources. In fact, she suggests that their significant numbers of votes could tip the balance of traditional power and patterns of wealth distribution. See Helg, *Our Rightful Share*, 158.

Chapter 1

1. "Changüí Político," *La Lucha*, January 14, 1901. The article appeared just two weeks before constitutional convention delegates voted in favor of universal suffrage, on January 30, 1901.

2. Three political parties entered the island-wide municipal contests in 1901. The

Republican Federal Party was led by Liberation Army general, and later president of Cuba, José Miguel Gómez (1909-12), while long-standing politicians such as Domingo Méndez Capote and Carlos Fonts, as well as black military leaders such as Martín Morúa Delgado and Juan Felipe Risquet led the Havana-based Republican Party. Two other early political front-runner organizations were the National Party and the Union Democratic Party. Nationalists were generally Liberation Army leaders and from the popular classes; many of them were black. The Union Democrats were predominantly white and elite.

3. Other Republican parties were the Republican Federal Party of Las Villas province under the leadership of José Miguel Gómez, the Castillista Republican Party in Oriente province backed by army veteran generals Demetrio Castillo Duany and Rafael Manduley, and a Republican Party based in Matanzas province, to the north of Havana, led by Pedro E. Betancourt and Alfredo Betancourt. The Independent Republican Party, which existed in several provinces, supported Bartolomé Masó for the presidency. There were also two National parties (one in Havana and the other in Oriente province) and the socialist-leaning Working Peoples' Party led by poet Diego Vicente Tejera. See Riera, *Cuba política*, 44-46.

The term *cacique* is somewhat mutable as a political expression and refers to local-level political bosses or strongmen. Here "local" might be region, province, municipality, or town, and in this sense influence is limited, as well as challenged, by other *caciques. Caciques* generally function as political brokers or intermediaries in a vertical system of patron-client relations, and they generally influenced masses of people as well as answered to more powerful patrons. For a useful discussion of this type of operative and the structure within which it operated, see Knight and Pansters, *Caciquismo in Twentieth-Century Mexico*, 1-48.

4. Cuba's corporatist political legacy, which derived from a proliferation during colonialism of economic, mutual aid and cultural societies, as well as locally powerful officials and political bosses, shaped postindependence politics and contributed to early republican factionalism. For discussion of localized political mobilization during the colonial period, see Roldán de Montaúd, "Cuba," 515, 519. Although Crown corporate structures were constructed to facilitate administrative stability and control, they were also breeding grounds of anticolonial dissent. Many *cabildos* (town councils), *cofradías* (religious brotherhoods), associations, and societies, established as part of the Crown's own cultural and political foundation, supported conspiratorial networks. These forms of sociability were woven into the island's structures and proliferated throughout the colonial period. In fact, state administrators often depended on them. Cases in point are *cabildos de nación* (African ethnic councils), which were initiated as tools of political control over masses of African laborers, yet quickly became important to Africans and their descendants as a refuge for specific cultural practices, a political stronghold, and a source of economic self-aid. Other organizations of African-descended Cubans encouraged specific spiritualities and cultural practices, which also threatened the Crown's hegemony. By the nineteenth century, the island's myriad associations, clubs, and societies served as some of its most vibrant sites of political mobilization, which corporate members tried to con-

ceal from authorities. For discussion of the multiple forms of corruption prevalent in the Spanish colonial administration in Cuba and of how corrupt administrators gave preference to their local, individual interests rather than to elite business and economic expansion interests, see Quiroz, "Implicit Costs of Empire." Quiroz defines corruption as "the unlawful rent-extraction by those with privileged access to public office for personal or group gain inimical to public interest." Ibid., 474. Díaz-Briquets and Pérez-López, *Corruption in Cuba*, 85, argue that the republic struggled with its colonial past and, when founded in 1902, was already "burdened with a deeply-ingrained tradition of corruption that rested on governance practices instituted by colonial administrations that placed a premium on the extraction of rents from public office, a management approach that encouraged the sale of official positions, nepotism, and poorly compensated officials."

5. Cuban elections were bitter contests, due to elected officials' access to government budgets, and they were fragmented. A sample of the 1901 municipal elections results suggests that a party's electoral support was highly localized. For example, in the capital city area, the Republican Federal Party took the Regla mayoralty (later in that same year the interventionist governor Leonard Wood assigned Regla to the jurisdiction of Havana, making it a barrio of the capital city), and the Cuban National Party won Havana City. Republican Federalist Gonzalo García Vieta was elected in Cuba's central city of Cienfuegos. In eastern Cuba, in Santiago de Cuba, the National Party candidate, Emilio Barcardí, won. In Sancti-Spíritus, Indalecio Salas, who ran on both the Republican Federal and the Union Democratic tickets, beat the local National Party candidate. Electoral sweeps across jurisdictions were less likely because candidates organized to win support in neighborhood-by-neighborhood and city-by-city campaigns. For example, several early political parties (such as Republican Federal regional parties in Oriente province and Cienfuegos in Santa Clara province) competed only at the municipal or regional levels and were not necessarily affiliated with Republican Federal parties in other provinces. See Riera, *Cuba política*, 32–35. For discussion of Cuban political culture relating to ideology, practice, and party organization and competition during the anticolonial movement, see Roldán de Montaúd, "Cuba," 515–30.

6. Census recorders estimated that Pilar barrio, a subsection of Havana City, had a population of 6,747. See Cuba, *Censo de la República de Cuba, 1907*, 304.

7. *La Lucha*'s director, Antonio de San Miguel, was a conservative annexationist, famous for running sarcastic prognostications regarding Cubans' capacity for autonomous rule. See Ibarra, *Cuba, 1898–1921*, 223.

8. "Changüí político," *La Lucha*, January 14, 1901.

9. Peter Wade argues that Latin American elites desired to emulate Western nationalisms and their modernist, progressivist tenets but were confronted with a different social landscape. They contended with large, racially diverse (black and Indian) populations, as well as the idea of racial mixture, in a way that was much more forthright and politicized than in Western nationalist discourses. See Wade, *Race and Ethnicity in Latin America*, 31–32. The primacy of racial hierarchies in Latin American and Caribbean national communities led in many instances to the

creation of culturally hostile members of society, similar to Orlando Patterson's concept of "domestic enemies." See Patterson, *Slavery and Social Death*, 39.

10. Here, rather than argue that the cultural attacks against the men were in essence racial ones (where cultural practice is interchangeable with racial identity), I suggest that although the racial connotations are clear, also discernible are critiques about the modern nation and the political and economic status of all Cubans in post-independence society. Peter Wade, for example, argues that economics, politics, and social life are lived "through the medium of culture." Further, he posits that it is most useful to understand these not as separate entities of uneven significance but, rather, as interdependent categories, "mutually influencing each other, rather than one or two of these as determinative." Wade, *Race and Ethnicity in Latin America*, 112. For the relationship between cultural attributes and racial identities at the end of the Cuban War of Independence (1895–98), as well as the racialization of cultural practices in politics, see Ferrer, *Insurgent Cuba*, 178.

11. The exact origin of *changüí*, a style of Cuban music that is closely related to earlier music forms indigenous to Cuba's eastern, Oriente province—such as the *tumba francesa* and *nengón*—is still debated. *Tumba francesa* emerged in the early nineteenth century among rural slave communities populated by Haitian slaves and their masters fleeing the Haitian Revolution. Early forms combined Spanish guitar and song with African rhythms and percussion instruments of the Arará in central west Africa. Ethnomusicologist Benjamin Lapidus argues that from its first appearance in the mid-nineteenth century, a *changüí* was synonymous with a rural party, "at which participants consumed large quantities of rum, ate roasted pigs, danced, and engaged in musical duels (*controversias*) among *treseros* (*tres* players) and *trovadores* (improvisational singers)." He suggests that *changüí* is associated with rural culture and with blackness. See Lapidus, *Origins of Cuban Music and Dance*, xvi, 123–47.

12. See Horrego Estuch, *Juan Gualberto Gómez*, 180; Fernández Robaina, *El negro en Cuba*, 51–52; de la Fuente, *A Nation for All*, 62–63; and Helg, *Our Rightful Share*, 99.

13. Adjutant General T. Bently Mott ridiculed black political participation; Governor General Leonard Wood expressed anxiety to Secretary of War Elihu Root over black activists. See Orum, "Politics of Color," 66, 69.

14. See A. M. Beaupré to Philander C. Knox, February 27, 1912, U.S. Department of State, Division of Information, *Negro Uprising in Cuba*.

15. On the Territorial Council of the Veterans of Independence of Matanzas, see Orum, "Politics of Color," 69. On Alemán, see de la Fuente, *A Nation for All*, 57.

16. José Enrique Varona was a politician; independent Cuba's first secretary of education; and, among other high-profile, public offices, chair of Logic, Ethics, Psychology, and Sociology at the University of Havana (1898–1917).

17. See Helg, *Our Rightful Share*, 98–99.

18. Orum, "Politics of Color," 65.

19. See Ferrer, *Insurgent Cuba*, chap. 7.

20. Ibid., 171–72.

21. Calixto García and Máximo Gómez corresponded in January 1898 about restricting promotions. According to García, there was a need to "refrain from promoting so many rough and ignorant [and, coincidentally, black] men." See ibid., 178.

22. For a full discussion of the importance of race and cultural norms to definitions of leadership, as debated by the insurgency's leadership on the eve of Cuban independence, see ibid., chap. 7. After 1898, a common, though much less often articulated, government policy was biased appointments and hiring—often but not exclusively perpetuated by U.S. occupation officials. When Cuban protest in 1901 forced the U.S. military government to relax "white-only" hiring policies for the Cuban Artillery Corps, officials nonetheless upheld their policy that all officers be white. See Orum, "Politics of Color," 62, 93–108.

23. The Platt Amendment, presented by Senator Orville Platt of Connecticut to the U.S. Congress, was a rider to the new Cuban constitution of 1901. It signaled North American encroachment on Cuban political and economic autonomy.

24. Among the most well-known biographies of Juan Gualberto Gómez is Horrego Estuch's *Juan Gualberto Gómez*. See also Pappademos, "Juan Gualberto Gómez."

25. Risquet, *Rectificaciones*.

26. Correspondence to Juan Gualberto Gómez from civic organizations and political activists, in which they request various favors, counsel, and connections, is found in Adquisiciones, ANC. See, for example, a letter written in 1899 from black revolutionary activist, politician, and journalist Rafael Serra, asking Juan Gualberto Gómez if he might spare time to meet (and help) Serra's acquaintance. Rafael Serra to Juan Gualberto Gómez, March 7, 1899, Adquisiciones, leg. 45, exp. 3579, ANC. See also the letter written in November 1903 by Silvestre Enice, president of the Society San Lázaro y Santa Rita, asking Gómez to publish a statement in his newspaper, *La República Cubana*, that would clarify publicly the Africanist organization's legitimacy as a society "authorized by the Civil Laws" of Havana province. Silvestre Enice to Juan Gualberto Gómez, November 3, 1903, Adquisiciones, leg. 54, exp. 4089, ANC. See also the letter written in December 1903 to Juan Gualberto Gómez by Liborio Vega, secretary of the Camagüey Workers' Club in central eastern Camagüey province. Vega asks Gómez to assist Miguel Ángel Céspedes, a young *camagueyano* law student, and promises in return his organization's "gratitude" (presumably electoral support): "Any assistance you can provide Miguel Ángel will be new motivation for us to show you our gratitude." Vega to Juan Gualberto Gómez, December 17, 1903, Adquisiciones, leg. 54, exp. 4090, ANC.

27. See de la Fuente and Casey, "Race and the Suffrage Controversy," 222–23.

28. Spain and Cuba, *New Constitution Establishing Self-Government in the Islands of Cuba and Porto Rico*, 7.

29. De la Fuente and Casey, "Race and the Suffrage Controversy," 224.

30. Regarding communication between Root and Wood, see ibid.; and Orum, "Politics of Color," 65–70.

31. Orum, "Politics of Color," 69.

32. The African-descended predominated in low-skill jobs, such as agricultural laborers in rural areas, domestic workers, street vendors, and factory and other

workers in urban settings. They also faced greater job competition from immigrant (Spanish and Antillean) laborers. De la Fuente argues that even with blacks' access to professional degree programs and the growth of a small but prominent black professional class by the 1920s, the circumstances of black professional labor—most conspicuously remuneration—lagged egregiously behind that of white professionals. For highly coveted public sector jobs, despite ongoing complaints throughout the republican period, blacks constituted a much smaller percentage of the government bureaucracy than whites. When they were present, their greatest concentration was at the lowest rungs of public service employment, for example, as mailmen. See de la Fuente, *A Nation for All*, 137.

33. Ibid., 54.

34. For example, in 1900, one political leader of the Union Democratic Party, Eliseo Giberga, based in Mantazas province, warned against black political control of areas where they dominated numerically, such as in the island's eastern provinces. See also Orum, "Politics of Color," 73–74.

35. Riera, *Cuba política*, 53; Orum, "Politics of Color," 85–86.

36. U.S. occupation officials repeatedly articulated their doubts about Cubans' ability to self-govern and their need to "prove" cultural qualities that in practice were highly ambiguous and arbitrary. Cuban elites often succumbed to the pressure of delivering on such proof, however impossible the task, in light of U.S. capriciousness. Ada Ferrer suggests that Cuban national leaders used various discourses and practices to demonstrate to North American officials "their civility, their modernity, and their closeness to Americans." Ferrer, *Insurgent Cuba*, 191.

37. Carrera y Jústiz, *El municipio y la cuestión de razas*, 20.

38. Letter from Tomás Estrada Palma to Mayor General Juan Ríus Rivera, September 7, 1901, in Pichardo, *Documentos para la historia de Cuba*, 2:204.

39. Carrera y Jústiz, *El municipio y la cuestión de razas*, 6–7. Carrera y Jústiz argued the broad question of political ideology and government structure in a series of public lectures delivered in his capacity as professor at the Free Institute of Good Government, at Havana's Centro Gallego (Galician Social Center). The Free Institute was a subsidiary of the Association of Good Government in Havana— presumably its scholarly arm. The urbanization assertion is not born out by the censuses of 1899 or 1907, which show slight reductions overall in the urban population and an increase in the island's rural population. Enumerators suggested that likely this was due to an increase in the rural population without a corresponding increase in the number of persons residing in urban zones, rather than population outflows from urban to rural areas. Cuba, *Censo de la República de Cuba, 1907*, 195–97.

40. Carrera y Jústiz wrote numerous pamphlets and books on theories of municipal government, especially from a sociological perspective, examining Cuba as well as the broader, Latin American context: *La constitución de Cuba y el problema municipal* (1903); *Las ciudades del siglo xx y los monopolios de servicios públicos* (1904); *La ciencia cívica en su relación con la mujer y con la democracia: Tres conferencias pronunciadas en la escuela normal de maestras de La Habana* (1905); *Introducción á la historia de las instuituciones locales de Cuba* (1905); *Estudios político-sociales,*

orientaciones necesarias: Cuba y Panamá (1911); *El panamericanismo: La independencia de las colonias de Europa en América* (1917); and *El regimen de las grandes
ciudades con especial referencia á la Habana* (1930).

41. Carrera y Jústiz, *Las ciudades del siglo xx y los monopolios de servicios públicos.*

42. Carrera y Jústiz, *El municipio y la cuestión de razas*, 9–10.

43. Secretaría de Gobernación, leg. 94, exp. 578, ANC. These labels included
mulatto (mixed-race), *pardo* (some presumed degree of "European" and "African"
biological "mixing"), and *negro* and *moreno* (Africans and descendants with little or
no presumed "racial mixture").

44. Guerra, *Myth of José Martí*, 128–29.

45. The Morúa Amendment, passed in May 1910, was drafted and introduced to
Congress by mulatto senator Martín Morúa Delgado. It prohibited race-based political organizing. Morúa Delgado argued that black Cubans were citizens and that
since racial privileges had been eliminated by the constitution, a race-based party
was unconstitutional and unpatriotic.

46. Ibarra, *Cuba, 1898–1921*, 207.

47. The term "Complementary Laws" refers to legislation that clarifies specific details and enhances the enforceability of writs or other formal government documents
(such as the constitution).

48. Other black newspapers published by black civic organizations or by free-
standing black editors included *Labor Nueva* (1915–16), *La Estrella Refulgente*
(1906), *Previsión* (1908–10), *El Nuevo Criollo* (1904–6), and *Adelante* (Havana)
(1935–38), as well as columns, such as "Palpitaciones de la raza de color" (1915–16),
edited by "Tristán" (an alias for journalist Ramón Vasconcelos), in the newspaper
La Prensa, and "Ideales de una raza" and "Armonías," both edited by Gustavo E.
Urrutia and published by the conservative Havana daily *Diario de la Marina* from
1928 to 1931.

49. The exact figure is 32.1 percent, or 505,443 persons of the "element of color,"
out of 1,572,797 for the total population. Cuba, *Censo de la República de Cuba, 1907*,
206.

50. The figures for percentages of voting-age males by province are Camagüey
province, 21 percent; Havana province, 25 percent (Havana City, 28 percent);
Matanzas province, 40 percent; Oriente province, 44 percent; Pinar del Río province, 26 percent; and Santa Clara province, 31 percent. Cuba, *Censo de la República
de Cuba, 1907*, 233–39.

51. Ibid., 214.

52. In descending order, the percentages were Havana province (26 percent),
Santa Clara province (23 percent), Oriente province (20 percent), and Matanzas
province (13 percent). Ibid., 233–39.

53. De la Fuente, *A Nation for All*, 55.

54. Orum, "Politics of Color," 83.

55. De la Fuente, *A Nation for All*, 61.

56. Ibid.

57. Batrell, *Para la historia*, 170–71. The original text reads: "Se acabó la Guerra y

se derrocó el imperio ó reinado de España en Cuba: y con tristeza ví surgir un mono-polio con amaños é injusticia:—en la provincia de Matanzas, donde solo hicimos la guerra los hombres de color, tan pronto hubo el Armisticio empezaron á salir de sus escondites los pocos oficiales blanco que sin combatir y majasiando se mantuvieron en el campo de la revolución; los escalafones que nos correspondía, á los que com-batimos sin tregua, se les fueron dando, á esos (majases)."

58. Strikes and protests for jobs proliferated after 1898 among black and other tradesmen, and there were several public accusations of racism leveled by privileged blacks against the early government (especially the Estrada Palma administration). One of the most broadly based black protest mobilizations was launched in June 1902 by Havana's Committee of Veterans and Societies of Color. Many of the most prominent black leaders of the time spoke at the rally, demanding racial equality, the fulfillment of the democratic principles of the revolution, and a fair share of the racially designated public service jobs. Fernández Robaina, "El Comité de Vetera-nos y Sociedades de Color," in *El negro en Cuba*, 37–45; Helg, *Our Rightful Share*, 125–28.

59. Louis A. Pérez, *Cuba*, 219.

60. According to de la Fuente, during the decade of the 1920s alone the number of public employees doubled, from 26,000 in 1919 to 51,000 by the end of the decade. Additionally, he estimates that in 1921 *botellas* received a sum equal to 40 percent of the government payroll allocated to working or non-*botella* employees. Furthermore, he suggests that in 1899 only 1 percent of the population worked in government jobs. By the time of the 1959 revolution, the number of civil employees had increased by nine times. See de la Fuente, *A Nation for All*, 130. See also Ibarra, *Prologue to Revo-lution*, 54–56.

61. Barbarrosa, *El proceso de la república*, 107–8.

62. Ibid., 215–21, especially 220.

63. Personal correspondence of Silvestre Enice, president of the Society San Lázaro and Santa Rita, to Juan Gualberto Gómez, November 3, 1903, Adquisi-ciones, leg. 54, exp. 4089, ANC.

64. Scholars who take up study of this war and the PIC, particularly regarding the politics of race in the first decade of the republic, include Helg, *Our Rightful Share*; de la Fuente, *A Nation for All*, especially chap. 2; Fermoselle, *Política y color en Cuba*; Fernández Robaina, *El negro en Cuba*, especially 46–109; Orum, "Politics of Color"; Portuondo Linares, *Los independientes de color*; and Louis A. Pérez, "Politics, Peas-ants, and People of Color," 509–39.

65. *La guerrita del doce* (the Race War of 1912) began in May 1912, when several hundred, primarily black, disgruntled members of the Independent Party of Color occupied foreign property to protest the recent prohibition of their party. Govern-ment and U.S. armed forces, plus white, civilian brigades, repressed the *indepen-dentistas* as well as several thousand black civilians. The *independentista* dissension brought about mass hysteria among many sectors of the Cuban populace. By June, several thousand blacks are estimated to have been killed.

66. The Reciprocity Treaty reduced tariffs on Cuban exports to the United States

and duties on U.S. imports to Cuba. It led to Cuban economic dependency on the United States, particularly in regard to sugar, while also creating unfavorable conditions for the development of national industries. See Louis A. Pérez, *Cuba*, 186–88, 198–99.

67. The Platt Amendment, drafted by Secretary of War Elihu Root and presented to Congress by Connecticut senator Orville Platt, was proposed as an amendment to the first Cuban constitution (1901). It sanctioned special protections for U.S. economic interests in Cuba as well as U.S. political dominance of the island, until its abrogation in 1934, under the Ramón Grau administration.

68. Louis A. Pérez, *Cuba*, 196.

69. Ibid.

70. Ibid., 198.

71. Ibarra, *Cuba, 1898–1921*, 67–68.

72. De la Fuente, *A Nation for All*, 130.

73. This oft-quoted reference to the critical role that electoral politics played in republican social and economic development was first coined by social commentator Miguel de Carrión in 1921. See Louis A. Pérez, *Cuba*, 215, for discussion of the quote. For discussion on the social and economic landscape after the war, see ibid., especially chap. 4.

74. Here I emphasize the priority of financial exchange and political negotiation that undergirded social interactions in republican Cuban society. Richard Graham sees these as central to relationships of power and authority in Latin America and the Mediterranean world. He argues that patronage-client systems encouraged, among other things, a "'transactional' quality of personal relations within an ostensibly impersonal polity." See Graham, *Patronage Politics in Nineteenth-Century Brazil*, 1.

75. An example of the close relationship between social prestige and power are the black and mulatto colonial battalions of the late eighteenth and nineteenth centuries. As militia men ascended the ranks, they gained social prestige and power over other black or mulatto soldiers and officers, which helped to generate a hierarchy among black and mulatto officers. Ranking officers won pensions, professional opportunities for their children, and the prestige of intermarriage among ranking members of the colored militia. Creoles of all colors might intermarry, so long as social and economic positions (color caste, occupation, pedigree, economy, and so on) were similar, a criteria enforced by the Crown. See Deschamps Chapeaux, *Los batallones de pardos y morenos libres*. For race, caste, and marriage practices in colonial Cuba, see Martínez-Alier, *Marriage, Class, and Colour*.

76. See Louis A. Pérez, *Cuba between Empires*, 304. In Santiago, for example, ex-autonomists such as Prisciliano Espinosa Julivert, Eligio Bravo Correoso, and Manuel Yero Sagol were named councilmen of the municipal assembly, as were black politicians such as Rafael Serra y Montalvo and José Guadalupe Castellanos. See Meriño Fuentes, *Gobierno municipal y partidos políticos*, 32.

77. The electoral law passed by U.S. authorities in March 1900 stipulated that suffrage rights were limited to males who were at least twenty-one years of age; who were native-born Cubans or Spaniards who had not declared Crown allegiance; and

who had municipal residency for at least thirty days before an election. One additional requirement was to be met: either literacy or property ownership of at least 250 dollars (in U.S. gold) or service in the Liberation Army before July 18, 1898. See de la Fuente, *A Nation for All*, 57; and Orum, "Politics of Color," 68.

78. Meriño Fuentes, *Gobierno municipal y partidos políticos*, 43.

79. Among those named that, in fact, served were Emilio Bacardí y Moreau (first municipal mayor in the republic), Federico Pérez Carbó (secretary of the municipal council), and Demetrio Castillo Duany, named by occupation officials to provincial governorship after Wood's departure from that post. Riera, *Cuba política*, 16.

80. Ibid.

81. Ibid., 26.

82. Meriño Fuentes, *Gobierno municipal y partidos políticos*, 30.

83. Riera, *Cuba política*, 34.

84. Meriño Fuentes, *Gobierno municipal y partidos políticos*, 25.

85. For a discussion of the shift in the concept of leadership during the twilight of war, see Ferrer, "Rustic Men, Civilized Nation." Ferrer argues that the notion of leadership fitness and of who might lead in the postwar era was informed by notions of race, gender, and class and modernist and progressivist ideals about culture.

86. Louis A. Pérez, "Supervision of a Protectorate," 254.

87. Barnet, *Biography of a Runaway Slave*, 194.

88. Ada Ferrer suggests that during the War of Independence (1895–98) at least 40 percent of insurgent leadership was of African descent. Ferrer, *Insurgent Cuba*, 156.

89. "Manifestación," *Diario de la Marina*, September 4, 1899, 2.

90. Louis A. Pérez, "Supervision of a Protectorate," 258–59.

91. Officials named General Demetrio Castillo Duany in Santiago, General López Recio Loynaz in Camagüey, and General Pedro E. Betancourt Dávalos in Matanzas. The first governor of Havana, Federico Mora, was soon replaced by General Juan Ríus Rivera. General José Miguel Gómez became governor of Santa Clara, and Guillermo Dolz y Arango was made governor of Pinar del Río. See Riera, *Cuba política*, 8–9.

92. González cited in Orum, "Politics of Color," 55.

93. In response to domestic political unrest and, allegedly, to local appeals for U.S. assistance in domestic conflicts, the United States occupied Cuba four times in two decades: 1899–1902, 1906–9, 1912, and 1917–22.

94. See Riera, *Cuba política*, for detailed discussion of political party trajectories in the republican period. For discussion of political coalitions and their socioeconomic antecedents in the early republican period to 1921, see Ibarra, *Cuba, 1898–1921*.

95. The term *caudillo* refers, generally, to a political, sometimes military, leader operating at the regional and often national levels who enjoys massive public influence and loyalty through some combination of favors, coercion, and charismatic rule. See Knight and Pansters, *Caciquismo in Twentieth-Century Mexico*, 1–48.

96. Riera, *Cincuenta y dos años de política*, 47.

97. For discussions on the role of patronage in republican Cuba, see Joel James,

Cuba, 1900–1928; Meriño Fuentes, *Gobierno municipal y partidos políticos*; and Orum, "Politics of Color."

98. See Riera, *Cuba política*, for an in-depth discussion of changes to the electoral system in the republic as well as the dissolution and creation of political party coalitions.

99. See Domínguez, *Cuba*, 39.

100. Meriño Fuentes, *Gobierno municipal y partidos políticos*, 30–31.

101. "El Partido Nacional," *Diario de la Marina*, October 6, 1901.

102. "Por Masó," ibid., October 5, 1901.

103. "Mitín," ibid.

104. Domínguez argues that ideological difference, though not completely absent from the political arena, was not its driving force. Rather, aligning oneself with the winning candidate in order to receive benefits from the candidate once in office most often determined political allegiances. Further, he posits that in republican Cuba, party politics were only "weakly rooted" in the social cleavages and parties did not reflect the interests of differentiated and competing socioeconomic groups. See Domínguez, *Cuba*, 40.

105. See Graham, *Patronage Politics in Nineteenth-Century Brazil*, 155.

106. "Presidency of Cuba; Señor Palma Says He Does Not Wish to Be Candidate, Because of the Disjointed State of Opinion," *New York Times*, August 9, 1901.

107. Ibarra, *Cuba, 1898–1921*, 207.

108. For a discussion of patron-client relations in early republican politics, see ibid., 207–8; Louis A. Pérez, *Cuba*, 214–20; de la Fuente, *A Nation for All*, especially 128–37; Orum, "Politics of Color," especially 87–92; and Fermoselle, *Política y color en Cuba*, 40–53.

109. The *tumba francesa*, still practiced today by folklore artists in the central and southeastern sections of the island, refers to dance and music forms derived from the experiences of Cuban creoles of Haitian descent who came to Cuba, particularly after the Haitian Revolution, which ended in 1804.

110. "Fiestas en San Lázaro," *Diario de la Marina*, October 8, 1901.

111. *Círculos* were local organizations with simultaneous political and social ends. At organizational meetings and rallies, members expressed political support for their candidates or party of choice. Often *círculos* provided licit entertainment and social activities (such as games, music concerts, and dances) for their members and the general public, in order to build a political constituency. Although they were patriotic and fostered intellectual development, their primary function was to build political constituencies and strengthen their candidate's or party's position in elections.

112. Reglamento (Bylaws) of the Círculo Autonomista de Baracoa, Gobierno Provincial, leg. 2625, exp. 1, AHPSC.

113. Ibid.

114. Riera, *Cincuenta y dos años de política*, 50.

115. Other examples are the Círculo Conservador de Mayarí, the Círculo Político y de Recreo de Barrio de Dolores Juan Gualberto Gómez, of Santiago, in Oriente province (Constitutionalists for Oriente province in 1900), and the Centro Nacio-

nalista Bravo Correoso (whose senatorial candidate was elected in 1901 for Oriente province).

116. Gobierno Provincial, leg. 2625, exp. 17, AHPSC.

117. Gobierno Provincial, leg. 2384, exp. 3, leg. 2660, exp. 1, and leg. 2383, exp. 4, AHPSC.

118. Bronfman, *Measures of Equality*, 135–36.

119. Gobierno Provincial, leg. 2660, exp. 1, AHPSC.

120. Gobierno Provincial, leg. 2718, exp. 2, AHPSC.

121. Interview with Efraín Romero.

122. Gobierno Provincial, leg. 2697, exp. 3, AHPSC.

123. Gobierno Provincial, leg. 2384, exps. 1 and 3, AHPSC.

124. Riera, *Cincuenta y dos años de política*, 433.

125. Gobierno Provincial, leg. 2659, exp. 2, AHPSC. For information on elected officials, see Riera, *Cincuenta y dos años de política*, 214, 253, 266, 315, 444, 509.

126. Vantour to Gómez, October 28, 1906, Adquisiciones, leg. 48, exp. 3830, ANC.

127. Juan Gualberto Gómez did not compete in the 1908 senatorial race (the first elections after the 1906 August Revolution, which were also held under U.S. supervision) because he withdrew. He and others in the Liberal Party who supported Alfredo Zayas battled over the nomination process with yet another, more powerful, pro–José Miguel Gómez faction of the Liberal Party, which forced Zayas to concede the top spot and run as vice president alongside José Miguel Gómez. The Gómez-Zayas ticket won its electoral bid. See Riera, *Cuba política*, 135–49.

128. See Riera, *Cincuenta y dos años de política*, 94.

129. Helg, *Our Rightful Share*, 185.

130. For discussion of political violence meted out by Moderate Party leaders and adherents, see Orum, "Politics of Color," 109–13; Guerra, *Myth of José Martí*, 170–77; and Riera, *Cuba política*, 90–102.

131. Riera, *Cuba política*, 92.

132. Ibid., 92–93.

133. Ibid., 102–8.

134. See Helg, *Our Rightful Share*, 146.

135. Historians suggest that blacks represented a majority of Constitutional Army insurgents in the Liberal Revolt, some estimating that they constituted as much as 80 percent of total antigovernment forces. See Orum, "Politics of Color," 115; de la Fuente, *A Nation for All*, 65; Helg, *Our Rightful Share*, 138; Fernández Robaina, *El negro en Cuba*, 53; and Guerra, *Myth of José Martí*, 184.

136. Helg, *Our Rightful Share*, 158.

137. There were at least fourteen blacks elected to Congress, giving them 16 to 18 percent of all congressional seats (twenty-four Senate and sixty-three House seats in Congress). De la Fuente posits that fourteen black congressmen won seats in 1908. De la Fuente, *A Nation for All*, 64.

138. Orum, "Politics of Color," 127. See de la Fuente, *A Nation for All*, 65. Historians suggest that the Liberal Revolt was overwhelmingly made up of black insur-

gents, though none offer concrete statistics. For the use of racial ideas and images to heighten fear about the 1906 insurgents, see Guerra, *Myth of José Marti*, 182–84. For discussion of black participation in the Liberal Revolt, see Orum, "Politics of Color," 115–18.

139. See Helg, *Our Rightful Share*, 145.

140. "Manifiesto al pueblo cubano y a los ciudadanos de color," August 1907, Fondo Especial, leg. F.C., ANC. The Manifiesto is signed by several men: Emilio Céspedes, C. Federico Montané, Eduardo Rodríguez A., Miguel A. Sabatela, Juan Valdés Aguirés, Uldarico Varona, Aurelio Arteaga R., Ygnacio Rodríguez, Lorenzo Torres, Pablo Lombida, Manuel Coslo, Juan Varona, Rosendo Martínez, Alberto Morales V., Alberto Céspedes, Juan Jiménez, Alberto Morales Casalis, José E. Montejo, José Chaves, José Arias, Domingo Chacón, Salvador Chaves, Pascual Betancourt, José Álvarez, Eladio Zayas, Armondo Pérez Céspedes, Alfredo González, Eleodoro Pichardo, Francisco M. Piquero, and Rafael A. Céspedes.

141. José de la Guadalupe Pérez, Valeriano Hernández, Alberto Armstrong, and Camilo Quintada Vega to Juan Gualberto Gómez, August 12, 1907, Adquisiciones, leg. 52, exp. 4068, ANC.

142. Orum, "Politics of Color," 127–28.

143. Ibid.

144. Quoted in Portuondo Linares, *Los independientes de color*, 24.

145. Helg, *Our Rightful Share*, 165.

146. For an excellent discussion of the relationship between the Race War of 1912 and electoral politics, see Rebecca J. Scott, *Degrees of Freedom*, 235–52.

147. See ibid.; and Helg, *Our Rightful Share*, 189–91.

148. See Helg, *Our Rightful Share*, 207–24.

149. Louis A. Pérez, "Politics, Peasants, and People of Color, 531.

150. Ibid., 536.

151. José Miguel Gómez, open letter to the "People of Cuba," June 6, 1912, published in the *Gaceta Oficial*, June 7, 1912.

152. Ibid.

153. Suárez Findlay, *Imposing Decency*, 59–60. For discussion of the rural "folk" in early twentieth-century Jamaica, see Philogene, "National Narratives, Caribbean Memories, and Diasporic Identities." Derby and Turits have richly recounted how rural Dominicans and Haitians were racialized according to cultural economic practices, especially those outside the purview of state agents and white urban elites. See Turits, "A World Destroyed, a Nation Imposed," 590–632 and Derby, "Haitians, Magic, and Money." For discussion of early twentieth-century racial characterizations of rural residents of Oriente province versus rural whites in central Cuba, see Swanger, "Lands of Rebellion," 145–66.

154. For discussion on elite discourse and racialization of white colonists in frontier zones, see Stoler, "Sexual Affronts and Racial Frontiers," 198–237.

155. Suárez Findlay, *Imposing Decency*, 60.

156. Rebecca J. Scott, *Degrees of Freedom*, 239.

157. "En Luz de Oriente," *La Independencia*, May 27, 1912; "Club Aponte," ibid.

158. "En la Unión Fraternal," *La Independencia*, June 14, 1912; "Un Manifiesto," *La Independencia*, May 29, 1912.

159. *La Independencia*, May 31, 1912.

160. Meriño Fuentes, *Gobierno municipal y partidos políticos*, 29.

161. Ibid., 30.

162. Gobicrno Provincial, leg. 2625, exp. 3, AHPSC. Club Antonio Maceo, founded in 1899, was led by prominent black *santiagueros*, including Luis Mancebo, the ex-captain of the Liberation Army, Saturnino Cos y Riera, Manuel Mena Hechavarría, Pablo Sánchez Gastón, and Alberto Castellanos.

163. Prominent black revolutionaries such as Juan Gualberto Gómez, Quintín Bandera, Silverio Sánchez Figueras, and Generoso Campos Marquetti supported Masó and his platform; Gómez and Sánchez Figueras visited several black societies on Masó's behalf.

164. Orum, "Politics of Color," 99.

165. Societies visited included Club Aponte, Luz de Oriente, Casino Cubano, El Tivolí, Club Juan de Góngora, La Unión, La Estrella de Oriente, and Altopino. See "Seminaro Político Moderado," *El Nuevo Criollo*, October 15, 1904. See also Orum, "Politics of Color," 102.

166. *El Nuevo Criollo*, October 15, 1904.

167. Riera, *Cuba política*, 81.

168. Orum, "Politics of Color," 82.

169. Helg, *Our Rightful Share*, 124.

Chapter 2

1. See Horrego Estuch, *Juan Gualberto Gómez*, 176–77.

2. Ibid. According to Estuch, eighty of the one hundred jobs were allotted to the police force and twenty jobs were allotted to the postal service. Louis A. Pérez holds that in 1903, 20,000 people were employed in government jobs, a figure he suggests jumped to 35,000 in 1911, as the republican government bureaucracy expanded. He also suggests that a total of 8,000 of these jobs were located in Havana City, where most of Estrada Palma's set-asides for "deserving" blacks were eventually distributed. Based on these figures, one hundred set-aside appointments represented only about 1.3 percent of total government jobs in Havana and a paltry .5 percent of the total government jobs across the island for the year 1903. See Louis A. Pérez, *Cuba*, 219–20.

3. For a detailed discussion of the multiple forms of corruption prevalent in Cuba's Spanish colonial administration, see Quiroz, "Implicit Costs of Empire."

4. For a brief discussion of the use of patronage appointments in the first years of independence, see de la Fuente, *A Nation for All*, 128–31.

5. Census figures show that despite constituting one-third of the population in 1899 and slightly less (29.2 percent) in 1907, the African-descended were woefully underrepresented in civil service jobs. In 1899, 13 percent of blacks were "government employees," a dismal 3 percent worked as "government officials," and only 14 percent were employed in the police and army. Eight years later, in 1907, just 5 per-

cent worked as "government functionaries," 7 percent worked as teachers, and 20 percent were employed by the police and army forces. See Cuba, *Censo de la República de Cuba, 1907*, 545–46. See also de la Fuente, *A Nation for All*, 116.

6. For extended discussions on the role of patronage in republican Cuba, see Joel James, *Cuba, 1900–1928*; Meriño Fuentes, *Gobierno municipal y partidos políticos*; Louis A. Pérez, *Cuba*, especially chap. 4; and Orum, "Politics of Color." De la Fuente provides useful budgetary information on the expansion of state bureaucracy, in *A Nation for All*, 130.

7. The National Lottery, created in 1909, is but one example of the enormous control that officials wielded over public funds. The lottery's principal way to generate funds was collectorships, which were rights, purchased from the government, to sell lottery tickets at a profit. Each collectorship represented sixteen lottery tickets, to be sold for profit. Several hundred collectorships were reserved for sale by the office of the National Lottery, while many more collectorships were allocated by the lottery to senators and congressional representatives. This meant that, as a perk of office, public servants sold (or had someone else sell for them) the lottery tickets allotted to their particular elected post. Senators averaged ten collectorships; about five went to each congressman. For a discussion of the National Lottery, see Louis A. Pérez, *Cuba*, 218. Elected officials also controlled jobs in education, sanitation, public works, health care, police, customs, and so on, which were often sinecures used to attract political support.

8. Louis A. Pérez estimates that following the War of Independence (1895–98), about 30,000 veterans were set to enter the labor market, causing U.S. occupation officials grave concern. See Louis A. Pérez, *Army Politics in Cuba*, 8.

9. Helg, *Our Rightful Share*, 129.

10. Ibid., 136.

11. Ibid., 125. See also ibid., 124–28, for discussion of the Action Committee and Veterans and Societies of Color mobilization and early attempts to gain socioeconomic opportunities.

12. See Orum, "Politics of Color," 115.

13. Here I assert that contrary to the historiography, which suggests that blacks' efforts toward political mobilization were stymied (particularly after the brutal repression of the 1912 "Race War") during the republican period, blacks integrated republican political structures and wielded a measure of political authority. See Helg, *Our Rightful Share*, 19, 21, 123; and Gott, *Cuba: A New History*, 125. Further, electoral seasons often set the stage for violent political protest in the republic, including, for example, the Liberal Party August Revolution of 1906, the Race War of 1912, and the *Guerra de la Chambelona* (the Lollipop War) of 1917. Black activists launched significant initiatives for access to public employment and other socioeconomic opportunities and against racial exclusions in almost every year of the republic's first decade: 1902, 1903, 1904, 1905, 1906, 1907, 1908, 1910, and 1912. They often called on the black population generally for support, as well as on elected officials of all colors.

14. See Helg, *Our Rightful Share*, 146.

15. Ibid.

16. De la Fuente, *A Nation for All*, 64.

17. De la Fuente argues a similar point about black, racially conscious militancy when he states that "political competition for the black vote also opened opportunities for black candidates to exercise pressure with the parties." De la Fuente, *A Nation for All*, 63. I build on this argument by suggesting that black activists participated in political processes of one form or another from several vantage points and with various sets of interests. Racial justice was not the sole or even always the primary motivation for their political participation.

18. For discussion of these protests regarding public employment, including a call to members of the House of Representatives to protest race-based exclusions, in addition to meetings with President Estrada Palma and the mayor of Havana, see Orum, "Politics of Color, 93–98.

19. Ibid., 96.

20. Louis A. Pérez, "Politics, Peasants, and People of Color," 528.

21. See Orum, "Politics of Color," 96; and Helg, *Our Rightful Share*, 126–27.

22. For a detailed discussion of the rally, see Fernández Robaina, *El negro en Cuba*, 36–45. For discussion of Juan Gualberto Gómez's role in the early push for civil employment, including the militancy to repeal antiblack, U.S. military legislation promulgated during the occupation (1899–1902), see Horrego Estuch, *Juan Gualberto Gómez*, 176.

23. Fernández Robaina, *El negro en Cuba*, 41.

24. Ibarra, *Cuba, 1898–1921*, 239–40.

25. Ibid.

26. Veterans and Societies of Color met on May 25, 1902, at the prominent black society La Divina Caridad in Havana and elected the Veterans and Societies of Color Action Committee, which later presented a list of grievances to Estrada Palma and demanded from his administration the opening up of civil service jobs. By the end of June in that same year, the Action Committee's demands were debated by the House of Representatives. See Helg, *Our Rightful Share*, 125–26; Horrego Estuch, *Juan Gualberto Gómez*, 176; and Orum, "Politics of Color, 96–99.

27. Fondo Estrada Palma, Personal Communication between Tomás Estrada Palma and Francisco Sánchez Hechavarría, August 15, 1902, ANC.

28. Horrego Estuch, *Juan Gualberto Gómez*, 177.

29. Helg, *Our Rightful Share*, 126.

30. De la Fuente quotes black journalist Pedro Portuondo Calás, who in 1932 summed up a pattern of election-time negotiations consistent throughout the republican period. Pedro Portuondo Calas, "Palabras," *Renovación*, March 20, 1932. See de la Fuente, *A Nation for All*, 59n19.

31. De la Fuente, *A Nation for All*, 59.

32. De la Fuente states that four out of sixty-three representatives to the House were black in 1905; in 1908 he suggests that these numbers increased to fourteen blacks or mulattos elected to Congress—about 15 percent of the total number elected to Congress that term. See de la Fuente, *A Nation for All*, 64.

33. For this quote, see Orum, "Politics of Color," 96. For more detailed examples of patronage favors and Juan Gualberto Gómez's range of influence, see Adquisiciones, ANC, a rich repository of Gómez's personal papers, which contains, among other documents, hundreds of requests for patronage favors in the form of letters of recommendation, job appointments, legal assistance to intervene in local matters of the court, and political maneuvering, written by private citizens, politicians, friends, civic leaders, and club activists.

34. *El Nuevo País*, September 7, 1899. See also Orum, "Politics of Color," 75.

35. Club Atenas, "AL PAÍS," Secretaría de la Presidencia, leg. 89, exp. 66, ANC. Of particular significance in the text is the following: "We reject without rage and even without bitterness but with firmness, all types of denigrating insinuations, all depressive suspicions, all hurtful doubt about our stance regarding the acts of savagery that could have been committed by anyone, irrespective of the color of he who commits them. We understand that we have the right to be considered civilized men and not barbarians. We demand the right to not be questioned, where no cultured man of the white race is questioned. As we feel, we act and work just as do other good people to reject energetically all purposeful clouding of the issue that seeks to construe us as bad people." Other authors of the manifesto were Lino D'ou, Gustavo Urrutia, Juan Felipe Risquet, Dr. Ramiro N. Cuesta, and Saturnino Escoto Carrión. See also Bronfman, *Measures of Equality*, 99–103.

36. Gómez spent several years in Paris, traveling there in 1869 at age fifteen in the company of a wealthy Cuban landowner in order to learn carriage making. His obvious scholarly aptitude, however, quickly led to his enrollment at Paris's Munge School of Engineering and the Central School of Arts and Manufacture. Gómez studied in Paris for years, witnessing French revolutionary fervor as well as the devastation caused by the Franco-Prussian War (1870–71). Evenings he mixed with tradesmen at workers' clubs and attended parliamentary and public debates about citizens' rights. Gómez returned to Cuba after ten years had passed, in 1879, to lend his journalist's pen, considerable talent for popular organizing, and intellectual prowess to the anticolonial movement. For book-length biographies on Gómez, see Horrego Estuch, *Juan Gualberto Gómez*; and Edreira de Caballero, *Vida y obra de Juan Gualberto Gómez*.

37. The Central Directorate of Societies of the Colored Race's founding societies were Centro de Cocineros (Cook's Social Center), Centro de Cocheros (Driver's Social Center), La Bella Unión Habanera (The Beautiful Union of Havana), La Divina Caridad (The Divine Charity), Nuestra Señora de Mercedes (Our Lady of Mercy), Amigos del Progreso (Friends of Progress), Nuestra Señora de Guadalupe (Our Lady of Guadalupe), Nuestra Señora de Regla (Our Lady of the Order), Nuestra Señora de La Cinta (Our Lady of Cinta), Purísima Concepción (Our Lady of the Immaculate Conception), Artesanos de La Habana (Artisans of Havana), Ramón Nonato, San Benito de Palermo, and Nuestra Señora de Monserrate (Our Lady of Monserrate). For this list and for more information generally regarding the Central Directorate, see Hevia Lanier, *El directorio central de las sociedades negras de Cuba*, 20n26.

38. Horrego Estuch, *Juan Gualberto Gómez*, 221.

39. Gómez was the only black leader named to the Advisory Law Commission. Other prominent commission members were Alfredo Zayas, Manuel M. Coronado, Francisco Carrera Jústiz, Marío García Kohly, Felipe González Sarraín, Rafael Montoro, Erasmo Regüeiferos Boudet, and Miguel F. Viondi. U.S. officials serving on the commission were Major Blanton Winship, Judge Otto Schoenrich, and U.S. Army colonel Enoch H. Crowder, who served as commission president. For a full discussion of the commission, see Lockmiller, "Advisory Law Commission of Cuba."

40. Orum, "Politics of Color," 113.

41. Correspondence between the Centro de Recreo Juan Gualberto Gómez and Juan Gualberto Gómez, August 21, 1900, Adquisiciones, leg. 53, exp. 4076, ANC.

42. Rebecca Scott writes that although blacks were legally granted the right to use the appellation "Don" in 1893, this title of distinction was seen as part of white social privilege and some whites balked at its use by blacks. See Rebecca J. Scott, *Slave Emancipation in Cuba*, 274. Hevia Lanier documented that at an island-wide meeting of black civic organizations (societies) in Havana in 1893, activists there used as evidence of social inequality the fact that whites were able to assume hierarchical titles such as *Don* and *Doña*, whereas blacks were always categorized according to racial labels such as *pardos* (mixed bloods) or *morenos* (blacks). See Hevia Lanier, *El directorio central de las sociedades negras de Cuba*, 43.

43. *Caudillo* refers, generally, to a political, sometimes military, leader operating at the regional level, and often the national level, who enjoys massive public influence and loyalty through some combination of favors, coercion, and charismatic rule. Juan Gualberto Gómez almost always functioned as a powerful "broker" in a system of political patronage in which brokers were highly placed operatives who exchanged favors for political support of various types and magnitudes. Brokers competed for client-supporters and answered to more powerful patrons in the patronage hierarchy. Although in some instances Gómez functioned as a *cacique*, at other times his politics and influence were significant at the national level. Thus, he might, arguably, be considered a *caudillo* as well. For a useful discussion of this type of operative and the structure within which a *caudillo* operated, see Knight and Pansters, *Caciquismo in Twentieth-Century Mexico*, 1–48.

44. Orum, "Politics of Color," 77.

45. Dawson argues that race is the most important factor in defining socioeconomic status among African Americans. He writes: "The social category 'black' in American society cuts across multiple boundaries. African Americans and whites pray, play, and get paid differently." See Dawson, *Behind the Mule*, 76 and especially chap. 4.

46. See Serra, *Para blancos y negros*.

47. Liberal leader Fernando Ciria Vinent wrote to Gómez to let him know he had been accepted as a delegate. The full roster elected to represent Liberalists from Oriente province at the 1904 national convention included Alfredo Zayas, Fidel G. Pierra, Rafael Manduley, Filiberto Zayas Barzan, General Demetrio Castillo y Duany, Erasmo Regüeiferos, and Alberto Castellanos. Castellanos was elected

as representative to the House for Oriente province in 1908. See Adquisiciones, leg. 52, exp. 4068, ANC.

48. Riera, *Cuba política*, 72.

49. For discussions of the 1906 August Revolution, see Collazo, *La Revolución de Agosto de 1906*; Varela Zequeira, *La política en 1905*; Guerra, *Myth of José Martí*, chap. 5; and Orum, "Politics of Color," chap. 4.

50. Orum, "Politics of Color," 114-15.

51. See Ferrer, *Insurgent Cuba*, 3. Ferrer cites Louis Pérez for the figure on commissioned officers and Jorge Ibarra for a general discussion on the racial composition of the "Mambí Army," where "Mambí" refers to the Cuban anticolonial insurgents who fought from 1868 to 1898. See Louis A. Pérez, *Cuba between Empires*, 106; and Ibarra, *Cuba, 1898-1921*, 187. Ibarra writes on the exclusions of blacks from the national army, despite their significant presence in the Liberation Army over the course of thirty years: "If it is taken into account that 60 percent of the soldiers of the Mambí Army were black, we can see even more clearly what it meant to close off the entry of blacks into the republic's new [socioeconomic and political] institutions."

52. Meriño Fuentes, *Gobierno municipal y partidos políticos*, 29-30.

53. Asociación Patriótica de Damas Admiradoras de Moncada, Registro de Asociaciones, leg. 2624, exp. 7, ANC.

54. Bylaws of the Asociación Patriótica de Damas Admiradoras de Moncada, ibid.

55. "Postumo Homenaje a la Memoria del Mayor General Guillermo Moncada," *Luz de Oriente* 2, nos. 15, 16, and 17 (June, July, and August 1923), 55, 59.

56. Ibid.

57. Ibid.

58. Riera, *Cincuenta y dos años de política*, 214-509.

59. Vantour, for example, was put up for councilman under the Liberal banner for the 1908 general elections.

60. Vantour writes: "No hay esa actividad de propaganda que tanta falta hace para lo futuro, y es necesario que ingresen en nuestro Partido algunas personalidades muy caracterizadas que viven aqui y que estan alejadas de la política. [There is no real propagandizing here, which is so necessary for the future, and we need people who live here, of great reputation but not known as politicians, to join our party and bring a following to it.]" Vantour to Gómez, Adquisiciones, leg. 48, exp. 3830, ANC.

61. Adquisiciones, leg. 53, exp. 4071, ANC.

62. Ibid.

63. Adquisiciones, leg. 54, exp. 4091, ANC.

64. Personal correspondence to Juan Gualberto Gómez from members of La Sociedad Unión, December 9, 1898, Adquisiciones, leg. 53, exp. 4074, ANC.

65. Ibid.

66. See de la Fuente, *A Nation for All*, 130.

67. *Annual Reports of the Secretary of War, Report of the Military Governor of Cuba on Civil Affairs*, 40.

68. Instituto de Historia de Cuba, *Historia de Cuba*, 17.

69. Estrada Portuondo to Juan Gualberto Gómez, Adquisiciones, leg. 40, exp. 3059, ANC.

70. Ibid.

71. Adquisiciones, leg. 15, exp. 832, ANC.

72. Ambrosio Grillo Portuondo was elected councilman with a majority of votes (16,265) in his district (*primera circunscripción*), ranking the highest of six elected councilmen. In contrast, Manuel Yero Sagol, who won a total of 2,544 votes, was only the third-most-popular candidate in his political district (*tercera circunscripción*), ranking next to last of four councilmen elected in his district. See Riera, *Cincuenta y dos años de política*, 44–45.

73. Riera, *Cuba Republicana*, 147.

74. Helg suggests that blacks supported Liberals, except in Oriente province, where Moderates enjoyed a large black following due to the Moderate Party position on veterans' paid benefits. Helg, *Our Rightful Share*, 128.

75. Personal correspondence between José Vantour and Juan Gualberto Gómez, July 20, 1904, Adquisiciones, leg. 48, exp. 3830, ANC.

76. Ibid.

77. Orum, "Politics of Color," 105.

78. Lorenzo Castellanos to Juan Gualberto Gómez, December 14, 1910, Adquisiciones, leg. 15, exp. 833, ANC.

79. Martín Morúa Delgado to Juan Gualberto Gómez, May 15, 1906, Adquisiciones, leg. 34, exp. 2613, ANC. Morúa highlighted the most important elements of his proposal: 1) Recognition of the right of political parties to designate members of electoral boards and other electoral organisms; 2) representation of political minorities, not only in the electoral bodies but in all representative bodies, including the senatorial and presidential races; and 3) guarantee of economy of time, budgets, and popular energy in all electoral proceedings.

80. Martín Morúa Delgado to Juan Gualberto Gómez, November 6, 1906, Adquisiciones, leg. 34, exp. 2613, ANC.

81. Rafael Serra to Juan Gualberto Gómez, March 7, 1899, Adquisiciones, leg. 45, exp. 3579, ANC.

82. Adquisiciones, leg. 42, exp. 3244, ANC.

83. Riera, *Cuba política*, 145, 160.

84. Adquisiciones, leg. 42, exp. 3244, ANC.

85. The literal meaning of *relaciones* is "relations" or "relationships." But as used here, *relaciones* refers to strategic political relationships.

86. Risquet writes: "Quiero, ante todo, como disciplinado que soy, tener su ascentimiento convenciar hasta lo sumo que Ud. aprovara [*sic*] tal proyecto." Risquet to Juan Gualberto Gómez, January 26, 1899, Adquisiciones, leg. 42, exp. 3244, ANC.

87. Ibid.

88. Liborio Vega, Secretario del Círculo de Trabajadores de Camagüey, to Juan Gualberto Gómez, December 17, 1903, Adquisiciones, leg. 54, exp. 4090, ANC. The original text reads: "Junta General celebrada en esta Asociación en la noche del 15 del actual, se accordó dar á Ud las mas expresivas gracias, y manifestarle que cual-

quier beneficio que tenga Ud. la bondad de hacerle al expresado estudiante, será un nuevo motivo de agradecimiento de este Círculo para Ud. Lo que tengo el honor de comunicar á Ud. por este medio en cumplimiento de lo acordado."

89. Registro de Asociaciones, leg. 53, exp. 4075, ANC.

90. Céspedes served as president of Havana's Club Atenas (1925), the island's most prestigious black club, which counted over the years numerous doctors, attorneys, and statesmen among its members. Céspedes also sat on the boards of the National Permanent Committee against Racial Discrimination and the Society of AfroCuban Studies in the 1930s and 1940s. Adquisiciones, leg. 53, exp. 4075, ANC.

91. Adquisiciones, leg. 54, exp. 4089, ANC.

92. Cuba, *Censo de la República de Cuba, 1907*, 314-15.

93. Adquisiciones, leg. 54, exp. 4089, ANC.

94. See Orum, "Politics of Color," chaps. 3 and 4. See also de la Fuente, *A Nation for All*, especially chap. 2.

95. Bettelheim, *Cuban Festivals*.

Chapter 3

1. Governor of Santa Clara (José Miguel Gómez) to the Secretary of the Interior (Diego Tamayo), August 18, 1902, Secretaría de Gobernación, leg. 97, exp. 870, ANC.

2. Article 13 of the Moret Law reads: "Los que prefieran volver al África serán conducidos a ella. [Those who want to return to Africa will be transported there.]"

3. For discussion of the Moret Law, see Rebecca J. Scott, *Slave Emancipation in Cuba*, 63-83.

4. Governor of Santa Clara (José Miguel Gómez) to the Secretary of the Interior (Diego Tamayo), August 18, 1902, Secretaría de Gobernación, leg. 97, exp. 870, ANC.

5. According to archival records, no proof of African birth was attached to their petition, nor do records indicate that such proof was requested by provincial authorities. See Secretaría de Gobernación, leg. 97, exp. 870, ANC. Overseas birth records would have been difficult to produce two or three decades after emancipation and large-scale warfare. Yet census records suggest that these men were likely African-born. In 1899, when the island population was approximately 1.5 million people, Julia and Escobar's home province of Santa Clara had the highest number of Africans, about 2,920 persons (just under 1 percent of the total provincial population), followed by Matanzas province with 2,486 people (slightly more than 1 percent of its total population) of African birth. By comparison, the island's largest province, Havana, had 1,010 persons of African birth (.2 percent of the total population), with the remaining provinces counting 730 or fewer Africans. For 1899, the census lists the total populations of Santa Clara province at 356,536, Matanzas province at 202,444, and Havana province at 427,514. Moreover, Matanzas and Santa Clara provinces produced the majority of Cuban sugar, and by 1899 not only were most Africans concentrated in these provinces, but the vast majority labored in agriculture, especially as sugar workers. Finally, the census data of 1899 records 171 resi-

dents of African birth in Remedios, about 70 more persons than are purported to have petitioned authorities for state repatriation assistance. See Cuba, *Censo de la República de Cuba, 1907*, 190, 338–40, 576–78. See also Ibarra, *Cuba, 1898–1921*, 67.

6. For a rich discussion of black left internationalism, the formation of political community, and "translation," as evoked in the work of Brent Edwards's *The Practice of Diaspora*, see Hanchard, "Translation, Political Community, and Black Internationalism."

7. At the Cuban National Archive, the Registro de Asociaciones is a list of hundreds of civic organizations extant during the colonial and republican periods. Here legs. 100, 160, 384, 421, and 1246 are important sources of information about Havana-based Africanist clubs. The Archivo Provincial de Santiago de Cuba has a rich repository of archival documents on Africanist societies. Particularly useful are legs. 2383, 2384, and 2750.

8. Hanchard, "Translation, Political Community, and Black Internationalism," 116.

9. See Mudimbe, *The Idea of Africa*, xiii.

10. For a book-length discussion of the political and economic relationship between European imperialists and Africa, see Rodney, *How Europe Underdeveloped Africa*.

11. For a general discussion of European colonialism and social and political conflict with indigenous populations in the twentieth century, see Davidson, *Modern Africa*.

12. Speech delivered by Kaiser Wilhelm II of Germany to the North German Regatta Association, Hamburg, June 18, 1901. Gaus, *German Emperor*, 181.

13. Sarracino Magriñat, *Los que volvieron a África*, 234–35.

14. Helg, *Our Rightful Share*, 123–24.

15. Published letter from the Remedios Chief of Police R. Rebollar to Fernando Ortiz, June 1903. See Ortiz, *Hampa afrocubana*, 297–98.

16. This figure is from Ibarra, *Cuba, 1898–1921*, 187. Ada Ferrer posits that this figure and all figures regarding the insurgency's racial demography are estimates because army rosters for the wars of independence did not use racial identifications for soldiers. See Ferrer, *Insurgent Cuba*, 204n4.

17. Cuba, *Constitución de le República de Cuba* (1902), title 4, section 1, article 27.

18. Manifiesto Culto religioso Africano Lucumí, "Santa Bárbara," Sociedad "Santa Rita de Casia, y San Lázaro": "Al honorable Presidente, Secretario de Gobernación, Secretario de Justicia, al Sr. Alcalde Municipal de la cuidad de La Habana y al pueblo en general: LA VERDAD CON CARA AL SOL!," July 19, 1913, cited in Bronfman, *Measures of Equality*, 94.

19. Secretaría de Gobernación, leg. 97, exp. 870, ANC. The precise reason for the denial was that the men could be naturalized as Cuban citizens, according to article 6 of the constitution. This suggests that their access to political status made repatriation unnecessary and their request unconstitutional. Article 6, clause 5, reads: "The Republic's constitution declares naturalized those Africans who were once slaves or, who were emancipated according to article thirteen of the treaty of June 28, 1835, celebrated between Spain and England."

20. José Miguel Gómez, "Open Letter to the People of Cuba," June 6, 1912, published in the *Gaceta Oficial*, June 7, 1912. Scholars who take up study of this war and the Independent Party of Color, particularly regarding the politics of race in the first decade of the republic, include Helg, *Our Rightful Share*; de la Fuente, *A Nation for All*, especially chap. 2; Fermoselle, *Política y color en Cuba*; Fernández Robaina, *El negro en Cuba*, especially 46–109; Orum, "Politics of Color"; Portuondo Linares, *Los independientes de color*; and Louis A. Pérez, "Politics, Peasants, and People of Color," 509–39.

21. Meriño Fuentes, *Gobierno municipal y partidos políticos*, 53–54.

22. Jenks, *Our Cuban Colony*, 165. Here Jenks lists American property holdings as analyzed by Consul-General J. L. Rodgers for 1911.

23. For the impact of the U.S. presence in Cuba on Cuban culture and national identity, see Louis A. Pérez, *On Becoming Cuban*.

24. For a succinct discussion of republican constitutionalism, see Sánchez-Roig, "Cuban Constitutionalism and Rights."

25. Cuba, *Constitución de le República de Cuba* (1902), title 2, article 5, clauses 1, 2, and 3.

26. The Spanish text for the constitution of 1901, article 6 (regarding those eligible for naturalization), clauses 1, 2, and 5, reads, respectively: "Los extranjeros que habiendo pertenecido al Ejército Libertador reclamen la nacionalidad cubana dentro de los seis meses siguientes á la promulgación de esta Constitución;" "Los extranjeros que establecidos en Cuba antes del 1ro de Enero de 1899 hayan conservado su domicilio después de dicha fecha, siempre que reclamen la nacionalidad cubana dentro de los seis meses siguientes á la promulgación de esta Constitutción, o, si fueren menores, dentro de un plazo igual desde que alcanzaren la mayoría de edad;" and "Los africanos que hayan sido esclavos en Cuba, y los emancipados comprendidos en el Art. 13 del Tratado de 28 de Junio de 1835, celebrado entre España é Inglaterra." Cuba, *Constitución de la República de Cuba* (1902).

27. Louis Pérez estimates that during the final War of Independence (1895-98), up to 40 percent of the senior commissioned officers for the Liberation Army were of African descent. Louis A. Pérez, *Cuba between Empires*, 106. Scott suggests that even Spaniards confidentially reported that Africans and their descendants were "numerous" among the insurgent ranks during the Ten Years' War. Rebecca J. Scott, *Slave Emancipation in Cuba*, 58. Ada Ferrer has suggested that during the remaining decades of the insurgent movement, the numbers of African and African-descended in the insurgency swelled. Ferrer, *Insurgent Cuba*, 148 and chap. 6.

28. Bergad, Iglesias, and Barcia, *Cuban Slave Market*, 27, 31.

29. Ibid., 31.

30. Ibid., 206.

31. Cuba, *Censo de la República de Cuba, 1907*, 206.

32. Ibid., 211.

33. Quoted in Portuondo Linares, *Los independientes de color*, 24.

34. "Manejos Misteriosos de los Racistas," *La Prensa*, September 29, 1915.

35. The original Spanish text reads: "Ningún problema sustancial dividía intensa-

mente la opinión; todos estaban resueltos de antemano. La esclavitud se había abolido desde hacía ya varios años. Vivía aún la generación que la conoció; pero las dos razas principales pobladoras del país y de las cuales había sido una la dominadora y otra la dominada, coexistían en paz sobre bases de mutual tolerancia y hasta de confraternidad. Juntas habían hecho la independencia y borraron así las naturales antinomias surgidas del character mismo de la institución bajo cuyo régimen se habían desarrollado. Los antagonismos tan hondos entre las dos razas y que alcanzan hasta declarer ilegítimos los matrimonies entre blancos y negros o descendientes de negros, como sucede en algunos estados de la Unión Americana, eran desconocidos, por lo menos en gran parte en Cuba. El tiempo acabaría por borrar las fronteras y por asentar sobre bases inconmovibles la igualdad y la fraternidad cubanas." See Martínez Ortiz, *Cuba, los primeros anos de independencia*, 87–88.

36. Serra, "Solos," printed in *La Discusión*, April 25, 1904. The original text reads: "Para crear una nación progresista y robusta, de existencia segura y libertades amplias; para crear una nación feliz, donde propios y extraños vivamos confundidos en el pleno disfrute de los beneficios del derecho; para crear una nación en fin, donde todos podamos satisfechos mantener un hogar venturoso y tranquilo, para eso, y no para otra cosa, hemos llevado nuestra parte de concurso, y ya que con lujo de afortunada suerte, gracias á los esfuerzos indescritibles y á tiempo reforzados por la valiosa protección de un pueblo amigo; gracias á todo esto, hemos podido constituir sobre bases de respeto la República, y no hemos de caer cobardes y rendidos á las flaquezas de espíritu, alentado por la pecadora tentación de convertir la patria en fatídicas estátuas."

37. Letter from Tomás Estrada Palma to Mayor General Juan Ríus Rivera, September 7, 1901, in Pichardo, *Documentos para la historia de Cuba*, 2:204.

38. Ibid.

39. Sanguily, "José de la Luz Caballero," 85.

40. See Guerra, "From Revolution to Involution in the Early Cuban Republic," 139n14.

41. Iglesias, *Las metáforas del cambio en la vida cotidiana*, 84.

42. Ibid., 81–82.

43. Louis A. Pérez, *On Becoming Cuban*, 322.

44. "Manifiesto de Masó," *Diario de la Marina*, October 31, 1901, 1.

45. Helg, *Our Rightful Share*, 98. "Legally established families" was in fact a racial concept, given that it was widely believed that black couples and their children were joined in common law, not civil, unions at much higher percentages than white Cubans.

46. N. Estrada Mora, mayor of Havana, "Ordinance, 'Ayuntamiento de la Habana,'" *Gaceta de la Habana: Periódico oficial del gobierno* 1, no. 82 (April 6, 1900): 655.

47. *El Diario Cubano*, March 1905.

48. "A 'Papá Silvestre' ha sucedido 'Papá Colás,'" *El Día*, October 1, 1915, 1.

49. Ortiz, *Hampa Afrocubana*, 186.

50. Brackette Williams, "Impact of the Precepts of Nationalism," 153.

51. Letter from the Governor of Santa Clara province (José Miguel Gómez) to the Secretary of State and the Interior (Diego Tamayo) under Leonard Wood, as General Governor of Cuba during the United States occupation, April 17, 1900, Secretaría de Gobernación, leg. 94, exp. 578, ANC.

52. Antonio Póveda de Ferrer to Estrada Palma, May 29, 1903, Correspondencia, Serie Felicitaciones y Muestras de Apoyo, Secretaría de la Presidencia, ANC.

53. Ortiz's first book, *Hampa afrocubana: Los negros brujos*, was published in 1906; it judged Africanist practices and the African-descended generally as inherently criminal.

54. Silvestre Enice to Juan Gualberto Gómez, November 3, 1903, Adquisiciones, leg. 54, exp. 4089, ANC.

55. Palmié, *Wizards and Scientists*, 220.

56. Louis A. Pérez, *On Becoming Cuban*, 322.

57. For discussion of *cabildos de nación* and *cofradías*, see Montejo Arrechea, *Sociedades de instrucción y recreo de pardos y morenos*, chap. 1.

58. Ibid., 15.

59. For discussion of the role of *cabildos* in building social and political consensus among African-born slaves and their descendants, both slave and free, see Childs, *Aponte Rebellion in Cuba*, 97–118.

60. Ortiz, "Los cabildos afrocubanos," 10.

61. Mendoza Lorenzo, "Estudio sobre el cabildo de Congos Reales 'San Antonio' de Trinidad," 53–54.

62. See Montejo Arrechea, *Sociedades de instrucción y recreo de pardos y morenos*, 43–45; and Howard, *Changing History*, 177–78.

63. Due to Cuba's importation of African laborers until quite late in the nineteenth century and its relatively late abolition of slavery (1886), sizable numbers of country-born Africans existed in Cuba until the early decades of the republic. In fact, some societies list their members as being mostly, though not exclusively, African-born.

64. Sociedad Religiosa Africana y Sus Hijos de Instrucción y Recreo y Socorro Mutuo "San Benito de Palermo," Gobierno Provincial, leg. 2750, exp. 7, AHPSC.

65. Ibid.

66. Ortiz, *Hampa afrocubana*, 386–88.

67. José Vantour to Juan Gualberto Gómez, October 28, 1906, Adquisiciones, leg. 48, exp. 3830, ANC.

68. Bylaws of the Sociedad de Instrucción, Recreo, y Socorro Mutuo "San Emilio" Continuadora del Cabildo "Lucumí" de Santiago de Cuba, Gobierno Provincial, leg. 2677, exp. 3, AHPSC.

69. Bylaws of the Sociedad de Instrucción y Recreo "El Cocoyé," Gobierno Provincial, leg. 2383, exp. 2, AHPSC.

70. Bylaws of the Sociedad de Instrucción, Recreo, y Socorros Mutuos "El Tiberé," Gobierno Provincial, leg. 2383, exp. 5, AHPSC.

71. Sociedad de Beneficencia y Recreo, Club Juan de Góngora was one society that listed its members' birthplaces. According to the society's 1912 membership roster,

eighteen of twenty-six men were "Natural de África." Gobierno Provincial, leg. 2383, exp. 4, AHPSC.

72. Nancy Pérez et al., *El Cabildo Carabalí Isuama*, 41.

73. Bylaws for the Sociedad de Socorros Mutuos del Antiguo Cabildo Carabalí Agro, Gobierno General, leg. 432, exp. 13579, ANC.

74. Bylaws for the Sociedad de Recreo y Beneficia de los Congos, Club Juan de Góngora, Gobierno Provincial, leg. 2383, exp. 4, AHPSC.

75. Bylaws for the Sociedad de Socorro Mutuo Club Nuestra Señora del Carmen antes Cabildo de Carabalí Olugo, Gobierno Provincial, leg. 2383, exp. 7, AHPSC.

76. Bylaws of the Club San Salvador de Horta antes Cabildo de Viví, Gobierno Provincial, leg. 2384, exp. 2, AHPSC.

77. Bylaws of the Sociedad Admiradores de San Miguel Arcangel, Gobierno Provincial, leg. 2750, exp. 1, AHPSC.

78. Club San Juan de Góngora, Gobierno Provincial, March 19, 1910, Juez de Instrucción, AHPSC.

79. Sociedad Cabildo "Santa Bárbara," Gobierno Provincial, leg. 2383, exp. 6, and Club San Salvador de Horta antes Cabildo de Viví, Gobierno Provincial, leg. 2384, exp. 2, AHPSC.

80. Sociedad de Recreo y Beneficia de los Congos, Club Juan de Góngora, Gobierno Provincial, leg. 2383, exp. 4, AHPSC.

81. Prominent white journalist, war veteran, and Senate president Manuel Sanguily declared in 1907 that the preservation of the republic was above all a question of morality. In 1913, black statesmen Juan Gualberto Gómez suggested to Havana's prestigious Society of Conferences that the path of nation building was also one of progress, cultural advancement, and liberty.

82. Sociedad de Recreo y Beneficia de los Congos, Club Juan de Góngora, Gobierno Provincial, leg. 2383, exp. 4, AHPSC.

83. See Hanchard, "Afro-Modernity," 274.

Chapter 4

1. El Negro Falucho, "Ser o no ser," *El Nuevo Criollo,*November 19, 1904. Also in Helg, *Our Rightful Share*, 135–36.

2. For a biography of Serra, see Deschamps Chapeaux, *Rafael Serra y Montalvo*.

3. For discussion of *El Nuevo Criollo*, see Helg, *Our Rightful Share*, 133–37.

4. Serra, "Solos," *La Discusión*, April 25, 1904. Reprinted in Serra, *Para blancos y negros*, 14.

5. Rafael Serra, "A la clase de color," *El Nuevo Criollo*, July 16, 1905.

6. El Negro Oriental, "Mi Hermano Falucho," *El Nuevo Criollo*, November 19, 1904.

7. "El Negro Oriental" means "Black Man of Eastern Cuba." *Falucho* can be translated in at least two ways, both of which evoke masculinist and nationalist images. A *falucho* is a schooner used for ocean transport for fishing or military ventures. "Falucho" is also the nickname of Antonio Ruíz, an Argentine nationalist hero and soldier

of African descent from Buenos Aires, Río de la Plata, who died in 1824 fighting against the Spanish on behalf of Argentine national independence. For more on Falucho the soldier, see Mitre, *Emancipation of South America*. Mitre was an Argentine statesmen; he immediately preceded the infamous Faustino Sarmiento as the Argentine head of state, from 1862 to 1868.

8. El Negro Oriental, "Ser o no ser," *El Nuevo Criollo*, November 5, 1904.

9. Ibid.

10. "El Negro Falucho," *El Nuevo Criollo*, November 12, 1904.

11. Ibid.

12. Miguel Gualba, "Tema Inagotable," *La Estrella Refulgente*, February 17, 1906.

13. Rebecca J. Scott's seminal text, *Slave Emancipation in Cuba*, offers a book-length discussion of freed and free black struggles for greater political, social, and economic participation in the late colonial period. See especially chap. 11.

14. For a lengthy discussion of multiple and contentious interpretations of the relationships among race, nation, and Cuba's anticolonial insurgencies, see Ferrer, *Insurgent Cuba*, especially chap. 5.

15. The original Spanish text reads: "Los africanos que en 1506 se trajeron a Santo Domingo, ya en 1522 no pudieron resistir el peso de la despótica servidumbre, y se sublevaron seriamente. . . . Y en ésto que no ven los españoles más que un acto indigno e insubordinado, se extiende nuestra mirada y vemos la dignidad intuitiva del hombre, pugnando siempre por romper el yugo del despotismo y la soberbia dominadora." Martín Morúa Delgado, "Ensayo político o Cuba y la raza de color," in Morúa Delgado, *Integración cubana y otros ensayos*, 67–68.

16. Ibid., 102. The original Spanish text reads: "Puede un pueblo anochecer bajo la opresión de un gobierno despótico, y amanecer abrazado estrechamente á la libertad, á la independencia, sin que el cambio le ocasione perjuicio alguno?"

17. Martín Morúa Delgado, "Ilustración," in *El Pueblo*, ca. 1879, cited in Morúa Delgado, *Integración cubana y otros ensayos*, 115. The original Spanish reads: "Un hombre instruido no puede ser un siervo que se subyuga; un hombre ilustrado es un hombre libre. Sólo esto queremos," and "nada se logrará si no se destruye la más terrible de las servidumbres, la servidumbre de la ignorancia."

18. See a biography of Gómez written by his daughter, Angelina Edreira de Caballero, *Vida y obra de Juan Gualberto Gómez*, 116.

19. Letter to Juan Gualberto Gómez from La Sociedad Instrucción y Recreo La Caridad, December 24, 1886, Adquisiciones, leg. 54, exp. 4089, ANC.

20. Societies that attended the meeting were Centro de Cocheros, Centro de Cocineros, Bella Unión Habanera, Amigos del Progreso, Nuestra Señora de las Mercedes, Purísima Concepción, Nuestra Señora de Guadalupe, Divina Caridad, Nuestra Señora de la Cinta, Nuestra Señora de Regla, Artesanos de La Habana, Ramón Nonato y San Benito de Palermo, and Nuestra Señora de Monserrate. See Hevia Lanier, *El directorio central de las sociedades negras de Cuba*, 20n26.

21. Ibid., 25.

22. Ibid., 26.

23. Ibid.

24. Colonial authorities believed that *ñáñigos* posed a political threat, particularly during the anticolonial insurgency. By 1876, they were outlawed and persecuted consistently by police. *Gaceta de la Habana*, Department of Public Order, decree 21-8-1876.

25. Juan Gualberto Gómez, Las Sociedades de Africanos, October 5, 1892, Donativos y Remisiones, leg. 144, exp. 24, ANC.

26. In the midst of the anticolonial insurgency, the colonial state instituted a number of late nineteenth-century decrees aimed at stemming antigovernment dissent and creating a more liberal state: Law of Access to Public Education for Children of Color (1878), the Press Law (1886), the Law of Public Assembly (1881), and the Law of Association (1886).

27. Gómez, "Las Sociedades de Africanos."

28. For the debate, see *Diario de la Marina*, May 19, 1893.

29. See Childs, "A Black French General Arrived to Conquer the Island," 140.

30. Juan Gualberto Gómez, *La Igualdad*, May 23, 1893.

31. Martí cited in Ortiz, *Martí y las razas*, 22.

32. Ibid., 121: "La libertad es accessible a todos los hombres. El que no nace en esa condición puede escalar a ella [Liberty is accessible to all men. He who is not born in this condition can ascend to it]."

33. Juan Gualberto Gómez, "Program of *La Fraternidad*," Havana, August 29, 1890.

34. Juan Gualberto Gómez, *La Igualdad*, April 7, 1892. The original Spanish text reads: "Novicia en las contiendas públicas, poco acostumbrada a las combinaciones de la política, nada tiene de sorprendente que, al entrar en la vida pública, aparezca en el scenario social sin cohesion y sin unidad."

35. See Rebecca J. Scott, *Slave Emancipation in Cuba*, 264–65.

36. Scott provides a book-length discussion of the transformation of plantation society to wage labor. See ibid., especially chap. 10.

37. Morúa Delgado suggested in *El Pueblo*: "No necesitamos mas que Instrucción e Ilustración; solo Instrucción e Ilustración." Cited in Morúa Delgado, *Integración cubana y otros ensayos*, 115.

38. Martín Morúa Delgado, "La Mujer—Sus Derechos," conference, January 17, 1887, "El Progreso" Society, Key West, Florida, reprinted in *Minerva: Revista Quincenal Dedicada a la Mujer de Color* 2, no. 9 (February 1889): 2–3.

39. Minerva was a Roman goddess of warriors, poetry, medicine, wisdom, commerce, crafts, and music and, as suggested here, represented one's self-cultivation in terms of intellect, refinement, and creativity through formal instruction. See Memorias de la Sociedad Económica de Amigos del País, 1823–26, quoted in Deschamps Chapeaux, *El negro en la economía habanera del siglo XIX*, 121.

40. Juan Gualberto Gómez, "Minerva," *Minerva: Revista Quincenal Dedicada a la Mujer de Color* 2, no. 9 (February 1889): 2–3.

41. Ibid.

42. Kop Y Torres, "La felicidad del hogar," *Minerva: Revista Quincenal Dedicada a la Mujer de Color* 2, no. 7 (1889): 8.

43. María Cleofa, "Á Onatina," *Minerva: Revista Quincenal Dedicada a la Mujer de Color* 2, no. 7 (January 1889): 6–7.

44. Rebecca J. Scott, *Slave Emancipation in Cuba*, 273.

45. Vásquez to Gualberto Gómez, June 11, 1892, Adquisiciones, leg. 74, exp. 4306, ANC.

46. Meeting minutes prepared by Pedro Rojas, secretary and president of Sociedad La Bella Unión, July 19, 1892, Adquisiciones, leg. 75, exp. 4310, ANC.

47. El Negro Oriental, "Al Negro Falucho," *El Nuevo Criollo*, November 5, 1904.

48. Du Bois, "The Talented Tenth," 41.

49. Serra, "Á la clase de color," in *Para blancos y negros*, 101.

50. Saturnino Escoto Carrión, "Educación y Economía," *Estrella Refulgente* 2, no. 9 (March 11, 1906): 7, 8.

51. See Mintz, "Enduring Substances, Trying Theory," especially 295; and África Céspedes, "Á Cuba," February 1880, printed in *Minerva: Revista Quincenal Dedicada a la Mujer de Color* 2, no. 11 (March 1889): 3–4.

52. Céspedes Casado, *La cuestión social cubana*, 3–4.

53. Ibid., 7.

54. See *Boletín Oficial del Club Atenas* 1, no. 9 (September 20, 1930): 15–28.

55. Céspedes Casado, *La cuestión social cubana*, 15.

56. Ibid., 4.

Chapter 5

1. Registro de Asociaciones, leg. 427, exp. 13449, ANC.

2. Roniger argues that "competition for positions of formal power becomes connected with the public projection in its various forms . . . and with symbolic struggles over the definition and enactment of evaluative criteria." See Roniger, "Comparative Study of Clientelism," 14.

3. See Helg, *Our Rightful Share*, 167–79.

4. Rama, *Lettered City*, 24.

5. Ibid., 53.

6. For a lengthy discussion of *Previsión*, the organ of the Agrupación Independiente de Color, later named the Partido Independiente de Color (the Independent Party of Color [PIC]), see Helg, *Our Rightful Share*, 146–55.

7. Fernández Robaina discusses Vasconcelos's column in *El negro en Cuba*, 113–15.

8. "El General Menocal y 'Labor Nueva,'" *Labor Nueva* 1, no. 1 (February 20, 1916).

9. "Nuestro Programa," ibid.

10. "Deberes y Derechos de la Raza de Color," ibid.

11. "Palabras del Doctor Varona," *Labor Nueva* 1, no. 3 (March 5, 1916).

12. Alfredo Martín Morales, "Claroscuro," *Labor Nueva* 1, no. 4 (March 12, 1916).

13. Riera, *Cuba política*, 237.

14. For discussion on Machado's *prórroga de poderes* (extension of powers), see Whitney, *State and Revolution in Cuba*, 55–58; and Riera, *Cuba política*, 349–54.

15. See Riera, *Cuba política*, 81; and Orum, "Politics of Color," 101–2.

16. For cabinet members newly appointed after Machado's "prolongation of powers," see Riera, *Cuba política*, 360. For the number of black politicians that won or were appointed to administrative posts during the *machadato*, see de la Fuente, *A Nation for All*, 91–92.

17. *Boletín Oficial del Club Atenas* 1, no. 9 (September 20, 1930).

18. "Charla Semanal," *Labor Nueva* 1, no. 33 (October 15, 1916).

19. "Charla Semanal," *Labor Nueva* 1, no. 35 (October 29, 1916).

20. Participating societies included Unión Fraternal, El Club Caridad, Club Benéfico, Sociedad de Estudios Científicos, y Literarios de la Habana, Jovenes del Progreso, Royal Cyclemen, Sport Habanero, Nueva Aurora, Maine Club, Centro de Cocineros, Juventud Progresista, Liceo Cultural, Bellman Club, Nuevo Pensamiento, Labores Culturales, Plácido, Helipolis, Los Jovenes de la Mariposa, and El Centro de Cocheros.

21. Key figures of the Comité Gestor included Generoso Campos Marquetti, Miguel Ángel Céspedes, Saturnino Escoto Carrión, Juan Gualberto Gómez, Juan Felipe Risquet, Primitivo Ramírez Ros, Lino D'ou, Venancio Milián, Juan Armenteros, and José Gálvez. See Tristán, "Á un señor de Melena," *La Prensa*, October 5, 1915.

22. Horrego Estuch, *Juan Gualberto Gómez*, 221.

23. Though few documents on the Directorate of Citizens of Color have been recovered by historians thus far, the Manifiesto is signed by several men, presumably in leadership: Emilio Céspedes, C. Federico Montané, Eduardo Rodríguez A., Miguel A. Sabatela, Juan Valdés Aguirés, Uldarico Varona, Aurelio Arteaga R, Ygnacio Rodríguez, Lorenzo Torres, Pablo Lombida, Manuel Coslo, Juan Varona, Rosendo Martínez, Alberto Morales V., Alberto Céspedes, Juan Jiménez, Alberto Morales Casalis, José E. Montejo, José Chaves, José Arias, Domingo Chacón, Salvador Chaves, Pascual Betancourt, José Álvarez, Eladio Zayas, Armondo Pérez Céspedes, Alfredo González, Eleodoro Pichardo, Francisco M. Piquero, and Rafael A. Céspedes. "Manifesto al pueblo cubano y a los ciudadanos de color," August 1907, Fondo Especial, leg. F.C., ANC.

24. Ibid.

25. For a discussion of land usurpation and peasants' title, deed, and property losses after the War of Independence (1895–98), see Louis A. Pérez, "Politics, Peasants, and People of Color, 509–39, especially 516–19; and Rebecca J. Scott, "Race, Labor, and Citizenship in Cuba," 687–728.

26. Quoted in Portuondo Linares, *Los independientes de color*, 24.

27. "Manejos Misteriosos de los Racistas," *La Prensa*, September 29, 1915.

28. For discussion of the Amigos del Pueblo Party, see Helg, *Our Rightful Share*, 240; Orum, "Politics and Color," 258; and de la Fuente, *A Nation for All*, 81–82.

29. "39 Racistas han sido procesados en Sagua," *La Prensa*, January 15, 1915. According to *La Prensa*, among those arrested were Ismael Recio, Antonio Echanbrán, Enrique René, Santiago Condique, Mamerto Stincer, Manuel Moré, Pedro Manzano, Luis Hernández, Silvestre Madám, Arturo Lara, Beigno Hernández, Antonio Acosta, Filiberto Fernández, Juan Aguila, Victor Peraza, Florencio Condique, and Alfredo Lara Blás Samat.

30. "No asistieron," *El Día*, October 4, 1915.

31. "La supuesta conspiración racista es sólo una anagaza de carácter político," *El Día*, October 2, 1915.

32. "Los Manejos Misteriosos de los Racistas," *La Prensa*, September 29, 1915.

33. Ibid.

34. De la Fuente, *A Nation for All*, 81–82.

35. *La Lucha*, September 12, 1915. See also Helg, *Our Rightful Share*, 240.

36. Riera, *Cuba política*, 431, 448.

37. "Al Olvidado Meleago," *La Prensa*, October 19, 1915.

38. Alejandro Sorís, "Mis Puntos de Vista," *La Prensa*, October 3, 1915.

39. For a detailed explanation of race, economy, and political mobilization between 1900 and 1912, see Louis A. Pérez, "Politics, Peasants, and People of Color," especially 530. See also Orum, "Politics of Color."

40. Jenks, *Our Cuban Colony*, 177–78.

41. Instituto de Historia de Cuba, *Historia de Cuba*, 117. See also Jenks, *Our Cuban Colony*, chap. 10.

42. "Asamblea de la unificación de las sociedades de color," *El Día*, May 16, 1915.

43. "Sotto Voce," *La Prensa*, October 24, 1915.

44. "Socio Fundadores," *Boletín Oficial del Club Atenas* 1, no. 9 (September 20, 1930).

45. "Cumplimos el deber," *Atenas: Revista Illustrada* 1, no. 1 (May 1917).

46. Pedro Calderón to Juan Gualberto Gómez, Adquisiciones, leg. 54, exp. 4088, ANC.

Chapter 6

1. Editorial, *Atómo* 1, no. 1 (May 3, 1936).

2. Ibid.

3. Here I use Robert Whitney's definition of the *clases populares*: "All social sectors outside the political elite and large sugar, commercial and industrial classes, such as the urban and rural wage labourers, peasants, the lower middle-class groups of students, low level government employees and those involved in petty commerce." See Whitney, "Architect of the Cuban State," 435.

4. The original Spanish text reads: "Nuestra política ha sido un truco igualmente. Partidos sin programa, sin principios, sin íntima vinculación con las apremiantes necesidades criollas, el campo de la política cubana ha visto transitar vehículos de toda índole." Arredondo, "El Truco de Nuestra Democracia."

5. Ibarra, *Prologue to Revolution*, 66. A significant amount of foreign investment in Cuba was related to sugar production, and by 1920 the island's hefty reliance on sugar had created a boom-and-bust economic cycle that eventually spiraled out of control. The sugar boom of 1920, for instance, which came on the heels of World War I, was known at its pinnacle as "The Dance of the Millions." In the first half of the year 1920, per-pound sugar prices soared. That same year, however, the over-expanded sugar market collapsed. From a dizzying record high of 22.5 cents per pound in May, prices plunged to just 3.8 cents per pound by December, sending

sugar industrialists and workers headlong into economic devastation. This unstable market, in fact, portended a cycle of severe economic crises that lasted throughout the 1933 Revolution. See Louis A. Pérez, *Cuba*, 224-25.

6. Louis A. Pérez, *Cuba*, 235.

7. Ibid., 234-35.

8. The 1903 Reciprocity Treaty set an important precedent for trade between re-publican Cuba and the United States. It reduced both tariffs on Cuban exports and duties on U.S. imports. Less beneficial for the fledgling republican economy than touted, its outcome was to encourage sugar dependency related to favorable export conditions to the United States as well as to flood the island with cheap U.S. manu-factures. See ibid., 198-99 and 232-34.

9. Ibid.

10. Stoner, *From the House to the Streets*, 59.

11. Louis A. Pérez, *Cuba*, 244, 246.

12. Moore discusses art and youth activism in *Nationalizing Blackness*, especially chap. 7.

13. Ibid.

14. Junta Cubana de Renovación Nacional-Cívico, Manifiesto of April 2, 1923, in *Heraldo de Cuba*, April 4, 1923. Cited in Chapman, "Cuban Constitution and Con-gress," 34.

15. See Stoner, *From the House to the Streets*, 88; Louis A. Pérez, *Cuba*, 237; and Ibarra, *Prologue to Revolution*, 66.

16. Wright, "Intellectuals of an Unheroic Period of Cuban History," 118.

17. President Alfredo Zayas's "Honest Cabinet" was a strategy to regain political legitimacy after fraud, graft, and corruption turned public opinion against Zayas. The cabinet was imposed on him by General Enoch H. Crowder, a U.S. State De-partment appointee in charge of Cuban affairs, in June 1922. Crowder determined that confidence in Cuban national leadership was dismal and could be remedied only by an overhaul of the national administration. He replaced many of Zayas's cabinet members with new government ministers. See Louis A. Pérez, *Cuba*, 227. For dis-cussion of the problem of legitimacy in the formal political arena in Cuba from the 1930s to 1959, see Domínguez, *Cuba*, 55-56, 110-12.

18. Whitney, "Architect of the Cuban State," 436.

19. Whitney, *State and Revolution in Cuba*, 182.

20. "Rumbos," *Renacimiento* 1, no. 3 (May 1933).

21. Ibid.

22. Pedro Portuondo Calás, "Palabras," *Renovación*, March 20, 1933.

23. Domínguez, *Cuba*, 55-56. Here Domínguez discusses government legitimacy using concepts similar to those articulated in Max Weber's theory "The Three Pure Types of Authority." Weber argues that three, rarely isolatable forms of political legitimacy exist, including "rational [legal]," traditional," and "charismatic." For a full elaboration of the theory, see Weber, *Economy and Society*, 215-51.

24. "Todos con los Nacionales de Oriente o Moderados," *El Nuevo Criollo*, Octo-ber 22, 1904. Aline Helg shows in her extensive research on the 1912 Race War that

contemporary sources document blacks' widely held belief in their equal capacity with whites as they argued for a "rightful share" of "power, wealth, services, and employment." So frequent did the term "rightful share" appear in her sources that she was inspired to use it for her book title. See Helg, *Our Rightful Share*, 10.

25. Louis A. Pérez, *Cuba*, 249. For general discussion of Machado, see Gott, *Cuba: A New History*, 129–31; Pérez-Stable, *The Cuban Revolution*, 39–40; and de la Fuente, *A Nation for All*, 91–94. For discussion of Machado's role in national politics and the factors leading to the Revolution of 1933, see Whitney, *State and Revolution in Cuba*, 55–80.

26. Machado used a combination of repressive tactics to secure the sole presidential nomination from all three contending (Popular, Liberal, and National) parties for the 1928 elections. For discussion of *cooperativismo*, see Whitney, *State and Revolution in Cuba*, 57–58; Pérez-Stable, *The Cuban Revolution*, 39; and Louis A. Pérez, *Cuba*, 252.

27. Louis A. Pérez, *Cuba*, 252–64. For in-depth treatment of the Revolution, see Aguilar, *Cuba 1933*.

28. See Domínguez, *Cuba*, 42–46; Pérez-Stable, *The Cuban Revolution*, 39; and de la Fuente, *A Nation for All*, 94.

29. Riera, *Cincuenta y dos años de política*, 199.

30. The *sargento* was a precinct captain who functioned as a political broker in charge of a certain number of voters with whom he or she had extensive contact in the exchange of votes and patronage favors.

31. Riera, *Cincuenta y dos años de política*, 199. The *piña* system helped to institutionalize patronage leadership, which had since the republic's inception depended on loyal followers and factions within political parties. *Piña* candidates could, and often did, sweep elections, ensuring their hold on particular political seats. If *piña* coalition candidates won their respective posts, regardless of whether their party as a whole had swept the election, they maintained control over the distribution of favors and, ultimately, secured political backing and their ongoing reign in office at the local, regional, or national levels. The *piña* system, which helped to entrench local *caciques* (though not necessarily political parties), was partly responsible for the political success of long-standing *piña caciques*, such as Anselmo Alliegro in Baracoa, Olimpo Fonseca in Bayamo, Sebastián Planas in Manzanillo, and Ramón de León in Guantánamo. See ibid. Outsider coalitions known as *piñas agrias* ("sour pineapples") also emerged as an attempt to disrupt *piña* insider monopolies. A split in the Liberal Party during the election of 1926 is a case in point. In that year, José R. Barceló Reyes, two-term governor of Oriente province as well as the Liberal Party's reigning political boss in Oriente province, created a *piña* that won the election yet excluded many members of the Liberal Party. Those Liberals outside of Barceló's *piña* electioneering created a *piña agria*, which had little success at the urns. Besides illustrating interparty coalition politics, the *piña* system also underscores that social relations were a necessity for political hopefuls. Given the amount of politicking that occurred outside of formal parameters and the coalitions that politicians used to acquire and manage their political territories, it is also clear that local processes were

fundamental to regional and even national political success. These self-interested alliances encouraged malfeasance, by facilitating politicians' access to economic and other resources. Such was the case in 1920 in Oriente province, when the provincial governor, Alfredo Lora, of the National League Party, and three councilmen, two from the Conservative Party and one from the Liberal Party, stood accused of joint misappropriation of public assets. See Riera, *Cuba política*, 298.

32. Riera, *Cuba política*, 332.

33. Urrutia, "Complejo de inferioridad."

34. Bronfman, *Measures of Equality*, 99. For discussion of the 1919 *brujo* scare, see ibid., 99-104. Bronfman recounts that *El Día* reported that black men were "nefarious *brujos* who dishonor an era and a nation with their ferocious insanity."

35. Club Atenas, "Asamblea de Elementos Representativos de la Raza de Color," July 2, 1919, Adquisiciones, leg. 53, exp. 4075, ANC. Club Atenas and other black societies in Havana (Unión Fraternal, Centro Maceo, and Casino Musical) decided to join black congressmen and local officials in their meeting with the president and other authorities in an energetic protest against the lynching. Further, they decided that prominent black activists Lino D'ou, Gustavo Urrutia, Juan Felipe Risquet, Dr. Ramiro N. Cuesta, Saturnino Escoto Carrión, Juan Gualberto Gómez, and Aquilino Lombard would draft a document titled "Manifesto to the Country," in protest of the events in Regla and Matanzas.

36. Club Atenas, "Manifesto Al País," Secretaría de la Presidencia, leg. 89, exp. 66, ANC.

37. Ibid.

38. Ibid.

39. See de la Fuente, *A Nation for All*, 190. De la Fuente points out that the Confederación Nacional de Obreros Cubanos (National Confederation of Cuban Workers) "Grievances Program" of 1929 argued for workers' rights irrespective of race or nationality, while the 1932 Cuban Communist Party platform denounced abuses of all workers, including West Indians, Jews, and Chinese.

40. Ibid., 191-92.

41. Registro de Asociaciones, leg. 262, exp. 7171, ANC.

42. Gobierno Provincial, leg. 2456, exp. 2, AHPSC.

43. Registro de Asociaciones, leg. 1132, exp. 23699, ANC.

44. Registro de Asociaciones, leg. 376, exp. 11382, ANC.

45. "Nuestra posición ante el problema inmigratorio," *Atenas: Revista Mensual* 2, no. 13 (January 1931): 1.

46. De la Fuente, *A Nation for All*, 195.

47. "No hay tal peligro negro," *Adelante: Revista Mensual* 1, no. 4 (September 1935): 1.

48. Ibid.

49. Guillén, *Sóngoro cosongo*.

50. Pedroso, *Poesías*.

51. The bongó is a percussive instrument widely used in Cuba and associated with the island's African legacy. See Pedroso, "Hermano Negro," in *Poesías*, 78-80.

52. María Luisa Vélez Betancourt, "Á Mi Raza," *Renacimiento* 1, no. 1 (March 1933).

53. De la Fuente, *A Nation for All*, 166–67.

54. Gobierno Provincial, leg. 2455, exp. 5, 6, AHPSC.

55. For club records, see Gobierno Provincial, leg. 2688, exp. 1, leg. 2452, exp. 7, leg. 2688, exp. 4, and leg. 2693, exp. 3, respectively, AHPSC.

56. Tomás Vélez Velázquez, "La Vida Nueva," *Renacimiento* 1, no. 1 (March 1933).

57. Aristides Llorente, "Nuestra Juventud y el Cultivo de las Letras," ibid.

58. Ibarra, *Prologue to Revolution*, 154–55.

59. Ibid., 159.

60. "Las Sociedades de Color Pedirán Reformas e Igualdad de Derechos Ciudadanos," *La Correspondencia*, February 1, 1936, 8.

61. See Stoner, *From the House to the Streets*, 125.

62. Stoner posits that "morality" was defined by some feminists as nuclear family and marriage. Other feminists argued that social, economic, and political freedom should be given to all people; that illegitimate children should be granted legal rights and familial recognition, such as, for instance, in the case of inheritance or if they needed shelter; that prostitutes should be provided with jobs and respectability; and that women should have authority in the republic's "moral life," which included "modern ideas" about family, society, and politics. See ibid., 67.

63. Ibid.

64. For discussion of race, gender, and class politics in multiple nationalisms, see McClintock, "No Longer in a Future Heaven."

65. Calixta Hernández de Cervantes, "Horizonte," *Atómo* (June 1936): 7.

66. María Luisa Vélez Betancourt, "Á Mi Raza," *Renacimiento* 1, no. 1 (March 1933).

67. De la Fuente, *A Nation for All*, 156.

68. Ramón Vasconcelos, *La Prensa*, 1916, in ibid., 155.

69. The 1907 census, for example, states that 25.4 percent of whites in Cuba were married, while only 9.6 percent of the "colored" population was legally married. See Cuba, *Censo de la República de Cuba bajo la administración provisional de los Estado Unidos, 1907*, 248. See also de la Fuente, *A Nation for All*, 155.

70. Tristán, "Dos Reflexiones," *La Prensa*, September 30, 1915.

71. *Boletín Oficial del Club Atenas* 1, no. 9 (September 1930): 27, 47.

72. Dr. Miguel Ángel Céspedes, "Orígen, tendencias y finalidad del Club Atenas," in *Atenas: Revista Mensual* 1, no. 1 (December 1920): 8.

73. Stoner, *From the House to the Streets*, 51–52.

74. María Luisa Vélez Betancourt, "Marcelina Adán Arencibia," *Renacimiento* 1, no. 1 (March 1933).

75. Interview with Daisy Heredia.

76. Fabio Luaces, *Renacimiento* 1, no. 2 (April 1933): 28–29.

77. Ibid. The original text reads: "Cuando a esta Directiva llegue el conocimiento de que una socia no se halle en condiciones de seguir figurando en el seno de la Sociedad, se le tachará el número de orden que le corresponda y no se le dará ninguna

explicación sobre la resolución tomada; pero si se persistiera en pedirlas se hará' uso de este artículo que supone un pacto inapelable entre partes."

78. Ibid. The original text reads: "Á la juventud que surge, menos prejuiciosa, mas emprendedora y reformista que la nuestra y que la que nos precedió, dedico la siguiente narración, para que al trazar los programas de las sociedades nuevas, no calquen ni los actuales ni lo anteriores."

79. For discussion of modernist discourse among black public intellectuals in the early decades of the republic, see de la Fuente, *A Nation for All*, 155-56.

80. For a book-length discussion of the Cuban women's movement in the republican period, see Stoner, *From the House to the Streets*.

81. María Teresa Ramírez, "Mujeres de ayer y de hoy," in *Boletín Oficial del Club Atenas* 1, no. 9 (September 1930): 26-27.

82. Directorio Social Revolucionario Renacimiento: Frente Único de Sociedades de Color de la República, "Manifiesto: Al Pueblo de Cuba," ca. 1934, Fondo Especial, leg. 10, exp. 26, ANC.

83. Ibid.

84. Ibid.

85. Del Valle, "Para concejal," in $\frac{4}{4}$ *Fambá y 19 cuentos mas*, 94-99.

86. De la Fuente, *A Nation for All*, 170; Bronfman, *Measures of Equality*, 136-37.

87. Letter to Juan Gualberto Gómez from Cornelio Elizalde, June 30, 1929, Adquisiciones, leg. 53, exp. 4075, ANC.

88. See Bronfman, *Measures of Equality*, 138.

89. Aguilar, *Cuba 1933*, 113.

90. See de la Fuente, *A Nation for All*, 92-93; and Bronfman, *Measures of Equality*, 136.

91. "Benjamín Muñoz Ginarte" and "El Secretario de Comunicaciones," *Renovación* (March 20, 1932). For the list of newly appointed cabinet members after Machado's "extension of powers," see Riera, *Cuba política*, 360. For the number of black politicians who won or were appointed to government administration before and during the *machadato*, see de la Fuente, *A Nation for All*, 91-92.

92. Bylaws of the Plenum Social, Gobierno Provincial, leg. 2456, exp. 7, AHPSC.

93. For discussion of Cubans' use of the North American occupation to settle domestic political crises, see Helg, *Our Rightful Share*, 189-90; Domínguez, *Cuba*, 44-45; Guerra, *Myth of José Martí*, 189-90; and Whitney, *State and Revolution in Cuba*, 91.

94. Other African-descended politicians who held leadership positions in societies were Francisco Pérez Acosta of Luz de Oriente in Santiago, who was also elected to the constitutional convention of 1939-40 under the Democratic Republican Party. For the constitutional convention of 1939-40, for which the one-time mulatto governor of Oriente, José Maceo, was the official delegate, Mario Lacret Paisán was elected as deputy delegate under the National Revolutionary Party banner, along with the mulatto José Guadalupe Castellanos, a politician since the birth of the republic. (In August 1898, North American occupation authorities named him one of twenty-nine councilmen for Santiago.) See Riera, *Cincuenta y dos años de política*,

414. To give a sense of his political trajectory and political networks, Lacret Paisán also served on the boards of Havana's highly prestigious Club Atenas, the Club Aponte (Santiago), the Provincial Federation of Black Societies in Oriente, the Provincial Federation of Black Societies of Havana, and the Cuban Civic Front against Discrimination. See Gobierno Provincial, leg. 2718, exp. 2, and leg. 2660, exp. 1, AHPSC; and Registro de Asociaciones, leg. 181, exp. 3736, leg. 1112, exp. 23267, and leg. 1067, exp. 22464, ANC. Castellanos's own networks included service on the boards of Santiago de Cuba's Luz de Oriente Political, Instruction, and Recreation Association, the Casino Cubano Club of Santiago, the Provincial Federation of Cuban Societies of Oriente, the National Federation of Black Societies, the Society for Afro-Cuban Studies, and the Martín Morúa Delgado Patriotic Cultural Center. Gobierno Provincial, leg. 2659, exp. 2, leg. 2718, exp. 2, leg. 2455, exp. 10, and leg. 2661, exp. 2, AHPSC; Registro de Asociaciones, leg. 1104, exp. 23114, and leg. 213, exp. 5167, ANC.

95. Gobierno Provincial, leg. 2718, exp. 2, and leg. 2697, exp. 3, AHPSC; Registro de Asociaciones, leg. 1104, exp. 23114, ANC.

96. See Riera, *Cincuenta y dos años de política*, 456–86.

97. Riera, *Cuba política*, 520.

98. Ortiz Domínguez, *Memorias: 3 años de Gobierno*; Gobierno Provincial, leg. 2698, exp. 3, AHPSC.

99. Ortiz Domínguez, *Memorias: 3 años de Gobierno*.

100. Ibid.

101. Bronfman, *Measures of Equality*, 141.

102. Montejo Arrechea, *Sociedades negras en Cuba*, 221.

103. Pérez-Stable, *The Cuban Revolution*, 42.

104. For discussion of race, nation, and the Afrocubanidad cultural movement in the early republic, see Moore, *Nationalizing Blackness*.

105. The Tribunal de Urgencia, for instance, a special unit of the judiciary, was created in 1934 to enhance state powers of prosecution against primarily political activism, such as crimes "against national stability," as well as sedition, theft, subversive activity or activity counter to public security, resistance, Communist meetings and rallies, theft for political purposes, and prostitution. See Tribunal de Urgencia, 1934–58, ANC; and Pérez and Scott, *The Archives of Cuba*, 175.

106. José Miguel Gómez, "Open Letter to the People of Cuba," June 6, 1912, published in the *Gaceta Oficial*, June 7, 1912.

107. Helg, *Our Rightful Share*, 240.

108. "El Ku Klux Klan Kubano," *Diario de la Marina*, October 30, 1933. Quoted in de la Fuente, *A Nation for All*, 204. See also Fernández Robaina, *El negro en Cuba*, 135.

109. De la Fuente, *A Nation for All*, 199.

110. Ibid.

111. "Changó Sonriente," Secretaría de la Presidencia, leg. 108, exp. 46, ANC. See also *Time*, April 10, 1933. *Changó* is an *orisha*, or religious icon consecrated with the Catholic Saint Barbara, in the Yoruba-derived *regla de Ocha* religious pan-

theon. Often representative of virility as well as thunder, *Changó* is venerated in the Africanist religious practice *Santería*. For discussion of this religion, particularly its movement from African origins to various parts of the Americas, see Brandon, *Santería from Africa to the New World*; and Brown, *Santería Enthroned*.

112. "¡Revolucionarios Alerta!" September 7, 1933, Fondo Especial, leg. 1, exp. 160, ANC.

113. Letter to the president of Club Atenas, dated January 18, 1931, and signed by Baltasar Mesa, José, Pilar Herrera, Santiago Herrera, Carmelo García, Pedro Ordone, José Leon, Román Brindis, Arturo D. Ramos, Ángel Tamayo E., and Virgilio Tamayo, Adquisiciones, leg. 75, exp. 4312, ANC.

114. "Detenidas 35 personas en un Templo Brujo," *La Correspondencia*, April 27, 1936; "Various Brujos Detenidos," *La Correspondencia*, May 4, 1936.

115. Jorge Adams, "¿Tienen razón los negros para quejarse de los blancos?," *Oriente*, February 21, 1938.

116. Lino D'ou, "Mi Contestación," *Oriente*, February 26, 1938; Mario Lacret Paisán, Dr. José Guadalupe Castellanos, José I. Rosell, and Dr. Rafael Caraballo, "Federación de Sociedades Cubanas á un artículo de Jorge Adams," *Oriente*, February 23, 1938.

117. Gregorio Calderón, "'Albores Club' ante la supuesta conspiración," *La Correspondencia*, February 15, 1936.

118. "Iniciativas Plausibles," *Revista Adelante* 2, no. 17 (October 1936).

119. "Sonriendo," *Atómo* (August 1936).

120. Enrique Andreu, "La Convención Nacional de Sociedades: Aclaración Necesaria," *Adelante*, December 1936.

121. During Grau's "100 days" in office, policy changes were made in many areas: in political and economic structures and in labor and employment. Traditional political parties were dissolved, utility rates were lowered by 40 percent, and labor arbitration and an eight-hour workday were installed, as was the nationalization of labor decree, which required 50 percent of all employees in industry, commerce, and agriculture to be Cubans. Grau also established the Labor Department and recognized labor's right to organize. In a move reflecting nationalist chauvinism, the Grau administration cancelled labor contracts with the Haitian and Jamaican governments and had Antillean workers deported. Significantly, Grau abrogated the Platt Amendment. See Louis A. Pérez, *Cuba*, 268; and Domínguez, *Cuba*, 77–79, 114-15.

122. For a brief discussion of the policies implemented by Grau, see Louis A. Pérez, *Cuba*, 268. After 1933, from 1934 until he was elected president in 1940, Batista promoted his image as a populist while also strengthening the military and its entanglement with national government. Among other provisions, Batista's Three-Year Plan proposed health and old-age insurance, a literacy campaign, attention to rural libraries, cultural centers, and sports' facilities, balancing the sugar economy with profit sharing via the Sugar Coordination Law, and distribution of state-held lands according to the Bill for the Colonization, Reclamation, and Distribution of State Lands (1937). The bill contained a provision for the distribution of livestock, seed, and agricultural implements, which was important to rural workers during

the annual "dead season," the annual sugar industry employment hiatus related to agricultural work cycles. During this time, many were left without work and wages or with greatly reduced wages, other than what they might plant and harvest individually. For discussion of Batista's Three-Year Plan, see Whitney, *State and Revolution in Cuba*, 157-61; de la Fuente, *A Nation for All*, 208; and Louis A. Pérez, *Cuba*, 278-79.

123. See Louis A. Pérez, *Cuba*, 268.

124. Convención Nacional de Sociedades de la Raza de Color, *Programa*.

125. Montejo Arrechea, *Sociedades negras en Cuba*, 228-42.

126. Bronfman, *Measures of Equality*, 141-43.

127. Farber, *Revolution and Reaction in Cuba*, 88. For details on the strike, see Whitney, *State and Revolution in Cuba*, 131-32; Farber, *Revolution and Reaction in Cuba*, 79, 84; and Louis A. Pérez, *Cuba*, 276.

128. Farber, *Revolution and Reaction in Cuba*, 88.

129. Ibid.

130. Luis Aguilar notes that the island's political power was concentrated in Havana to the exclusion of other regions. See Aguilar, *Cuba 1933*, 240.

131. "Las Sociedades de Color Pedirán Reformas e Igualdad de Derechos Ciudadanos," *La Correspondencia*, February 1, 1936.

132. Ibid.

133. Whitney, *State and Revolution in Cuba*, 181.

134. "Inauguran la Convención de las Sociedades de Color," *Oriente*, February 5, 1938, 1.

135. "Justo Salas," *El Diario de Cuba*, January 28, 1944, 1-2.

136. The 1931 census ranked the provinces according to population size as follows: Oriente, 1,072,757; Havana, 985,500; Las Villas, 815,412; Camagüey, 408,076; Pinar del Río, 343,480; and Matanzas, 337,119. For 1943, the figures read as follows: Oriente, 1,356,489; Havana, 1,235,939; Las Villas, 938,581; Camagüey, 487,701; Pinar del Río, 398,794; and Matanzas, 361,079. Cuba, Dirección General del Censo de 1943, *República de Cuba, censo de 1943*, 811.

137. Federación de la Prensa Latina de América, *Libro de Cuba*, 352, 371, 444-45.

138. "No Hay Ambulancia," *Noticias de Hoy*, June 17, 1938, 9.

139. "Recorrido por las calles" and "En la Sociedad Aponte," *El Diario de Cuba*, February 27, 1944.

140. "Ayer en Palacio Alcalde Salas," *El Diario de Cuba*, February 8, 1944; "Justo Salas," *El Diario de Cuba*, January 28, 1944. In November 1941, led by mayor Justo Salas, aldermen in Santiago requested funds from President Batista to construct an emergency room for the Civil Hospital. See Secretaría de la Presidencia, leg. 117, exp. 88, ANC.

141. Domínguez states that Batista was a "broker among the competing bureaucracies captured by organized interest groups. Because access to government was both essential and available to interest groups, they never openly opposed it." Domínguez, *Cuba*, 56.

142. For an informative discussion of social and economic change during the first

half of the twentieth century, see Hoernel, "Sugar and Social Change in Oriente, Cuba."

143. Ibid., 241–42.

144. Louis A. Pérez, *Cuba*, 252–53.

145. Arredondo, *Cuba: Tierra Indefensa*, 333–34.

146. The commission was made up of the treasury secretary as well as representatives from the National Council of Tuberculosis, the Civic-Military Institute, the National Corporation for Public Assistance, the Public Health Services, the National Tourism Corporation, the Bank of Welfare and Tourism, and the Maternity Hospital. "Sorteos de Beneficencia," *Gaceta Oficial*, extra edition 136, April 30, 1936.

147. Domínguez, *Cuba*, 94.

148. Ibid.

149. Figures listed in the 1943 census suggest that Oriente was undeniably a region important to electoral contests. After Havana province, according to the 1943 census, Oriente province had the second-largest population of eligible voters. In Havana, 804,568 (or 31 percent of the island's total voting-age population) people were of voting age, versus 628,360 (24 percent) in Oriente. See Cuba, *Informe general del censo de 1943*, 862.

150. Becker and McClenahan, *The Market, the State, and the Export-Import Bank of the United States*, 47.

151. "Situados los creditos para obras en Oriente," *El Diario de Cuba*, March 2, 1944.

152. Letter from Antonio Meléndez Lahera to Presidente Batista, dated February 8, 1944, states that the declaration was published in *Noticias de Hoy*, February 6, 1944. See Secretaría de la Presidencia, leg. 4, exp. 93, ANC.

153. "Felicitan al Presidente Batista por el Congreso de Sociedades Negras," *Noticias de Hoy*, January 11, 1944. Secretaría de la Presidencia, leg. 4, exp. 93, ANC, contains telegrams and other communication received by the president in early February from about forty black societies, all congratulating Batista on his plan to fund black societies using the National Lottery.

154. "Simpatía Popular por el Sorteo Para las Sociedades Negras," *Noticias de Hoy*, February 9, 1944.

155. "En la Sociedad Aponte," *El Diario de Cuba*, February 27, 1944.

156. "Recepción al Honorable Señor Presidente en Aponte," *El Diario de Cuba*, February 16, 1944.

157. De la Fuente, *A Nation for All*, 163.

158. Registro de Asociaciones, leg. 1206, exp. 25242, ANC.

159. Domínguez, *Cuba*, 56. Domínguez argues that interest groups accessed "power" through direct appeals to Batista; Roniger suggests that interest groups ("clients") do not access this potential ("power") because it is neutralized by patron and patron-broker avenues to resource conversion and access to political centers. See Roniger and Güneş-Ayata, *Democracy, Clientilism, and Civil Society*, 4.

160. Whitney, *State and Revolution in Cuba*, 165–75; de la Fuente, *A Nation for All*, 222–35.

161. Whitney, *State and Revolution in Cuba*, 170.

162. Farber, *Revolution and Reaction in Cuba*, 86.

163. Speaking before the Confederación de Trabajadores Mexicanos (Confederation of Mexican Workers), Batista spoke about his populist intentions: "La Revolución de setiembre es una revolución realizada por los de abajo, por el Ejercito del Pueblo, por y para el Pueblo. [The September (1933) Revolution is a Revolution of and for the people brought about by those from below and by the peoples' army.]" See Batista, *Estoy con el pueblo, cuatro discursos en Mexico y Cuba*, 9.

164. Louis A. Pérez, *Cuba*, 243.

165. Ibid., 244, 255. See also de la Fuente, *A Nation for All*, 190-91.

166. De la Fuente, *A Nation for All*, 190-91.

167. See, for example, "Brigida Sarduy to President of the Republic," December 23, 1943, and "Las costureras apoyamos petición de Unión Social Sorteo extraordinario ayuda Sociedades Negras de Las Villas," December 29, 1943, Secretaría de la Presidencia, leg. 4, exp. 93, ANC.

168. For lengthy discussion of the importance of race and a black constituency for the Communist Party, see de la Fuente, *A Nation for All*, 222-35.

169. García Galló, *General de las cañas*, 41, 50, 53, 58.

170. See "Blas Roca, Cuban Communist and Party Theoretician, Dies," *New York Times*, April 27, 1987; and "Blas Roca: Maestro de revolucionarios," *Granmá Diario*, April 24, 2002.

171. An excerpt of the text drafted by García Agüero reads: "Any discrimination because of sex, race, class or any other motive is illegal and punishable." Quoted in de la Fuente, *A Nation for All*, 218.

172. Ibid., 263.

173. Club Atenas, *Los partidos políticos y la asamblea constituyente*, 264-66.

174. Ibid., 12.

175. Ibid., 417. See also Riera, *Cuba política*, 394.

176. Riera, *Cuba política*, 478-82.

177. Club Atenas, *Los partidos políticos y la asamblea constituyente*, 496-512.

178. "Dr Francisco Guillén, Presidente de la Federación de Sociedades Negras de Camagüey," *Noticias de Hoy*, January 25, 1944.

179. "Gran asamblea contra la discriminación se efectuó anoche: Estuvieron representadas numerosas entidades," *Noticias de Hoy*, February 16, 1944. Participating groups and their representatives in attendance were Pedro Rojas Rodríguez, president of the Federation of Black Societies of Havana; José M. Espino and Buenaventura López, Confederación de Trabajadores de Cuba; Eduardo Canas Abril, Association of Public Employees; Juan Chapotten, Federation of Cuban Teachers; Segundo Quincosa, general secretary of the Havana Province Workers' Federation; Salvador García Agüero, parlimentary leader of the Peoples' Socialist Party; Serafín Portuondo and Francisco Goyri, National Committee in Favor of Congressional Black Societies; Elias Rescalla and Fajardo Escalona, Cuban Revolutionary Youth; Dr. Pablo F. Lavín, dean of the School of Public Law of the National University;

Beningno Ibáñez, Club Atenas; and Alberto Hernández, Sociedad Unión Fraternal, among other Black Society Federation members.

180. "Gran acto contra la discriminación," *Noticias de Hoy*, February 6, 1944.

181. To call public attention to the Complementary Laws, the Provincial Federation of Black Societies of Havana organized a rally with workers and other groups in 1944. "Gran Acto Contra la Discriminación Racial: Será el 15 en el Salón de Torcedores." *Noticias de Hoy*, February 3, 1944, 1, 7.

182. Gobierno General, leg. 1211, exp. 25389, ANC.

183. Editorial, *Orientación Social: Órgano Oficial de la Federación Provincial de Sociedades Cubanas de Oriente* 9, no. 12 (September 1960): 13.

184. A few examples: In February 1949, the Fraternal Union Club of Havana received 18,000 pesos; in July 1957, Club Aponte in Santiago de Cuba received a donation from national government in the amount of 12,000 pesos; in early 1958, the Antonio Maceo Society of Nueva Paz, just outside of Havana, received 1,200 pesos.

Conclusion

1. Title IV, section 1, article 11, of the 1901 constitution states, "Todos los cubanos son iguales ante la Ley. La República no reconoce fueros ni privilegios personales." Cuba, *Constitución de le República de Cuba* (1902), 6.

2. Scholars uniformly argue that due to foreign domination of the domestic economy throughout the republican period, local and national administration was an important and consistently expanding source of employment. Historians Jorge Ibarra and Alejandro de la Fuente argue specifically that the number of state employees increased dramatically between 1899 and the decade of the 1940s. See Ibarra, *Prologue to Revolution*, 54–56; and de la Fuente, *A Nation for All*, 130.

3. Domínguez, *Cuba*, 39.

4. See, for example, Helg, *Our Rightful Share*, 33.

5. Rebecca J. Scott, *Degrees of Freedom*, 239.

6. Gobierno Provincial, leg. 2624, exp. 7, AHPSC. For discussion of black family and community formation as a local phenomenon constituting "local blackness," see Bennett, *Colonial Blackness*, chapter 5.

7. Gobierno Provincial, leg. 2624, exp. 8, AHPSC.

8. Bronfman, *Measures of Equality*, 138.

9. Domínguez, *Cuba*, 57.

10. According to historian Richard Gott, after the Race War of 1912, blacks "almost never took part in politics again, devoting themselves to music and retreating into their own African religions, and participating in white Cuban society in the only institutions to which they had easy access—the lower ranks of the army and the police force." See Gott, *Cuba: A New History*, 125. Aline Helg has a far more nuanced assessment that nonetheless draws similar conclusions. She insightfully argues that even though racial identity was "imposed from above and outside, it was also used by black and mulatto leaders as a catalyst to mobilize Cubans of African descent," which my research confirms. Yet her conclusion that black leadership sought to mobilize for

collective black political action misses a critical point about the republican political landscape. Political mobilization for all Cubans was fractious, racial identities were often consolidated by local experiences more so than by universal racial consciousness, and among Cubans of all colors political unity was generally forged along the vertical lines of patronage relations rather than by creating horizontal activist networks based on a shared commitment to mass struggle, at least until the 1920s and the growth in political mobilization leading up to and following the 1933 Revolution, especially among trade unions and labor. Helg also argues that after the birth of the republic, although blacks "shared [a] consciousness of racial discrimination, many of them were immersed in the struggle to find solutions to urgent individual problems." This is a conclusion similar to my own, based on my research. Yet she goes on to argue that in the republic, "most sociedades [black clubs] now focused on black entertainment rather than on the defense of racial equality. Thus, Afro-Cuban protest lacked leadership and an organizational network." This conclusion is not born out by my research, and in fact, my study draws very different conclusions that reveal significant black involvement in republican politics. Finally, the notion that blacks lacked leadership rests on the presumption that they *should have* mobilized according to both universal racial consciousness and mass-based struggle, both of which run counter to the very structure of the republican political arena, and which obscure the history of republican black Cuban experience. See Helg, *Our Rightful Share*, 125.

Bibliography

Archives

Archivo Histórico Municipal de Trinidad, Trinidad
Archivo Histórico Provincial de Cienfuegos, Cienfuegos
Archivo Histórico Provincial de Santiago de Cuba, Santiago de Cuba
  Fondo Gobierno Provincial
  Fondo Partidos Políticos
Archivo Municipal de Santiago de Cuba (Vivac), Santiago de Cuba
Archivo Nacional de Cuba, Havana
  Fondo Adquisiciones
  Fondo Asuntos Políticos
  Fondo Convención Constituyente, 1928 and 1940
  Fondo Donativos y Remisiones
  Fondo Especial Legajo Fuera
  Fondo Estrada Palma
  Fondo Gobierno General
  Fondo Instrucción Pública
  Fondo Registro de Asociaciones
  Fondo Secretaría de Gobernación
  Fondo Secretaría de la Presidencia
  Fondo Tribunal de Urgencia

Libraries

Biblioteca del Archivo Nacional de Cuba, Havana
Biblioteca del Centro de Investigación y Desarrollo de la Cultura Cubana
  Juan Marinello, Havana
Biblioteca del Instituto de Historia de Cuba, Havana
Biblioteca de Literatura y Linguística, Havana
Biblioteca Municipal de Cienfuegos, Cienfuegos
Biblioteca Municipal de Guantánamo, Guantánamo

Biblioteca Nacional José Martí, Havana
Biblioteca Provincial de Oriente Elvira Cape, Santiago de Cuba
New York Public Library, New York, New York
Schomburg Center for Research in Black Culture, New York Public Library,
New York, New York

Periodicals

Adelante (Santiago)
Adelante: Revista Mensual, Órgano de la Asociación "Adelante" (Havana)
Amanecer
Archivo del Folklore Cubano
Atenas: Revista Illustrada
*Atenas: Revista Mensual Ilustrada de Afirmación Cubana, Órgano Oficial
del Club Atenas*
Atómo
Baraguá
Boletín Oficial del Club Atenas, Publicación Mensual
Cuba, Convención Constituyente, Diario de Sesiones
Cuba Contemporanea
Cuba Republicana
Destellos
Diario de la Marina
El Cometa
El Cubano Libre
El Día
El Diario de Cuba
El Nuevo Criollo
El Nuevo País
El Veterano
Estudios Afrocubanos
Fragua de la Libertad
Gaceta de la Habana: Periódico Oficial del Gobierno
Granmá Diario
Labor Nueva
La Correspondencia
La Discusión
La Estrella Refugente
La Fraternidad
La Igualdad
La Independencia
La Lucha
La Prensa
La Voz del Pueblo

Luz de Oriente
Minerva: Revista Quincenal Dedicada a la Mujer de Color
Minerva: Revista Universal Ilustrada
New York Times
Noticias de Hoy
Nuevos Rumbos
Orientación Social
Oriente
Renacimiento: Revista Mensual
Revista: Cuba
Revista Bimestre Cubana
Revista de Avance
Time
Unión Fraternal: Revista de Avance

Interviews Conducted by Author

Daisy Heredia, Santiago de Cuba, June 2000
Efraín Romero, Santiago de Cuba, December 2000

Government Documents

Annual Reports of the Secretary of War, Report of the Military Governor of Cuba on Civil Affairs, for the Fiscal Year Ended June 30, 1900. "Report of Señor Diego Tamayo, Secretary of State and Government for the Island of Cuba," vol. 1, part 2. Washington: Government Printing Office, 1901.

Cuba. *Censo de la República de Cuba bajo la administración provisional de los Estado Unidos, 1907.* Washington: Oficina del Censo de los Estados Unidos, 1908.

———. *Constitución de la República de Cuba.* Havana, 1902.

———. *Constitución de la República de Cuba.* Edited by Jesús Montero. Havana: Impresora Berea, 1940.

Cuba. Comisión de la Higiene Especial. *La prostitución en Cuba y especialmente en La Habana.* 2 vols. Havana: P. Fernández & Cia, 1902.

Cuba. Dirección General del Censo de 1943. *República de Cuba, censo de 1943.* Havana: P. Fernández y Cía, 1943.

Cuba. Oficina Nacional del Censo. *Censo de la República de Cuba, año de 1919.* Havana: Oficina Nacional del Censo, 1922.

Cuba Advisory Commission. *Project of Municipal Law Adopted by the Advisory Commission and Submitted to the Provisional Governor, January 24, 1908.* Havana: Rambla and Bouza, 1908.

United States. Department of State. Division of Information. *Negro Uprising in Cuba.* July 1912.

United States Statutes at Large 31.

Books

Aguilar, Luis E. *Cuba 1933: Prologue to Revolution*. Ithaca: Cornell University Press, 1972.

Alonso, Gladys, and Ernesto Chávez Álvarez. *Memorias inéditas del censo de 1931*. Havana: Editorial de Ciencias Sociales, 1978.

Álvarez Estévez, Rolando. *La "reeducación" de la mujer cubana en la colonia*. Havana: Editorial de Ciencias Sociales, 1976.

Ameringer, Charles D. *The Cuban Democratic Experience: The Auténtico Years, 1944-1952*. Gainesville: University Press of Florida, 2000.

Anderson, Benedict. *Imagined Communities: Reflections on the Origin and Spread of Nationalism*. 2d ed. New York: Verso, 1991.

Andrews, George Reid. *Blacks and Whites in São Paulo, Brazil, 1888-1988*. Madison: University of Wisconsin Press, 1991.

Arredondo, Alberto. *El negro en Cuba*. Havana: Editorial Alfa, 1939.

———. *Cuba: Tierra Indefensa*. Havana: Editorial Lex, 1945.

Bacon, Robert, and James Brown Scott, eds. *The Military and Colonial Policy of the United States: Addresses and Reports by Elihu Root*. Cambridge: Harvard University Press, 1916.

Barbarrosa, Enrique. *El proceso de la república: Análisis de la situación política y económica de Cuba bajo el gobierno presidencial de Tomás Estrada Palma y José Miguel Gómez*. Havana: Imprenta "Militar," 1911.

Barnet, Miguel. *Biography of a Runaway Slave*. Translated by Nick Hill. New York: Curbstone Press, 1994.

Barreda, Pedro. *The Black Protagonist in the Cuban Novel*. Amherst: University of Massachusetts Press, 1979.

Batista, Coronel F. *Estoy con el pueblo, cuatro discursos en Mexico y Cuba*. Havana: Ediciones Sociales, 1939.

Batrell, Ricardo. *Para la historia: Apuntes autobiográficos de la vida de Ricardo Batrell Oviedo*. Havana: Seoane y Álvarez Impresores, 1912.

Becker, William H., and William McClenahan Jr. *The Market, the State, and the Export-Import Bank of the United States, 1934-2000*. New York: Cambridge University Press, 2003.

Bederman, Gail. *Manliness and Civilization: A Cultural History of Gender and Race in the United States, 1880-1917*. Chicago: University of Chicago Press, 1995.

Bennett, Herman L. *Colonial Blackness: A History of Afro-Mexico*. Bloomington: Indiana University Press, 2009.

Bergad, Laird W., Fé Iglesias García, and María del Carmen Barcia. *The Cuban Slave Market, 1790-1880*. Cambridge: Cambridge University Press, 2003.

Betancourt, Juan René. *Doctrina negra: La única teoría certera contra la discriminación racial en Cuba*. Havana: P. Fernández y Cía, [1954].

Bettelheim, Judith. *Cuban Festivals: A Century of Afro-Cuban Culture*. Kingston: Ian Randle Publishers, 2001.

Black Public Sphere Collective. *Black Public Sphere: A Public Culture Book.* Chicago: University of Chicago Press, 1995.

Brandon, George. *Santería from Africa to the New World: The Dead Sell Memories.* Bloomington: Indiana University Press, 1993.

Brock, Lisa, and Digna Castañeda Fuertes, eds. *Between Race and Empire: African-Americans and Cubans before the Cuban Revolution.* Philadelphia: Temple University Press, 1998.

Broderick, Francis L., and August Meier. *Negro Protest Thought in the Twentieth Century.* New York: Bobbs-Merrill, 1965.

Bronfman, Alejandra. *Measures of Equality: Social Science, Citizenship, and Race in Cuba, 1901–1940.* Chapel Hill: University of North Carolina Press, 2004.

Brown, David H. *Santería Enthroned: Art, Ritual, and Innovation in an Afro-Cuban Religion.* Chicago: University of Chicago Press, 2003.

Butler, Kim D. *Freedoms Given, Freedoms Won: Afro-Brazilians in Post-Abolition São Paulo and Salvador.* New Brunswick: Rutgers University Press, 1998.

Cabrera, Lydia. *El monte.* Havana: Editorial Letras Cubanas, 1989.

Calhoun, Craig. *Habermas and the Public Sphere.* Cambridge: MIT Press, 1996.

Carbonell, Walterio. *Crítica: Cómo surgió la cultura nacional.* Havana: Ediciones Yaka, 1961.

Carpentier, Alejo. *Ecue-yambo-o!* Buenos Aires: Octavo Sello, 1977.

Carrera y Jústiz, F. *La constitución de Cuba y el problema municipal.* Havana: Librería é Imprenta "La Moderna Poesía," 1903.

———. *El derecho público y la autonomía municipal: El fraude de un régimen; conferencia pronunciada en el Ateneo de la Habana.* Havana: Librería é Imprenta "La Moderna Poesía," 1913.

———. *Introducción á la historia de las instituciones locales de Cuba.* Havana: Librería é Imprenta "La Moderna Poesía," 1905.

———. *El municipio y la cuestión de razas.* Havana: Librería é Imprenta "La Moderna Poesía," 1904.

Castellanos, Israel. *Medicina legal y criminología afro-cubanas.* Havana: Molina y Cía, 1937.

Castellanos, Jorge, and Isabella Castellanos. *Cultura afrocubana: El negro en Cuba.* Vols. 1 and 2. Miami: Ediciones Universal, 1990.

Castillo Bueno, María de los Reyes. *Reyita: The Life of a Black Cuban Woman in the Twentieth Century.* Durham: Duke University Press, 2000.

Caulfield, Sueann. *In Defense of Honor: Sexual Morality, Modernity, and Nation in Early-Twentieth-Century Brazil.* Durham: Duke University Press, 2000.

Céspedes Casado, Emilio. *La cuestión social cubana: Conferencia leída en el instituto, la noche del día 21 de abril de 1906.* Havana: La Propagandista, 1906.

Childs, Matt D. *The Aponte Rebellion in Cuba and the Struggle against Atlantic Slavery.* Chapel Hill: University of North Carolina Press, 2006.

Club Atenas. *Los partidos políticos y la asamblea constituyente: Inmigración, economía, trabajo, educación, discriminación.* Havana: Club Atenas, 1939.

Collazo, Enrique. *La Revolución de agosto de 1906*. Havana: Imprenta C. Martínez y Compañía, 1907.

Conte, Rafael, and José M. Capmany. *Guerra de Razas (negros contra los blancos en Cuba)*. Havana: Imprenta Militar de Antonio Pérez, 1912.

Convención Nacional de Sociedades de la Raza de Color. *Programa*. Havana: Imprenta Molina y Cía, 1936.

Córdova, Efrén/Center for Labor Research and Studies of Florida International University. *Clase Trabajadora y Movimiento Sindical en Cuba*. Vol. 1, *1819-1959*. Miami: Ediciones Universal, 1995.

Cunard, Nancy. *Negro Anthology, 1931-1933*. New York: Negro Universities Press, 1934.

Da Costa Viotti, Emilia. *The Brazilian Empire: Myths and Histories*. Chapel Hill: University of North Carolina Press, 2000.

Davidson, Basil. *Modern Africa: A Social and Political History*. London: Longman Group UK, 1983.

Dawson, Michael. *Behind the Mule: Race and Class in African-American Politics*. Princeton: Princeton University Press, 1994.

De Armas, Ramón. *Los partidos políticos burgueses en Cuba neocolonial, 1899-1952*. Havana: Editorial de Ciencias Sociales, 1985.

De Certeau, Michel. *The Practice of Everyday Life*. Translated by Steven Rendall. Berkeley: University of California Press, 1984.

De la Fuente, Alejandro. *A Nation for All: Race, Inequality, and Politics in Twentieth-Century Cuba*. Chapel Hill: University of North Carolina Press, 2001.

Del Valle, Gerardo. *¼ Fambá y 19 cuentos mas*. Havana: Ediciones Unión, 1967.

De Pereda, Diego. *El nuevo pensamiento político de Cuba*. Havana: Editorial Lex, 1943.

Deschamps Chapeaux, Pedro. *Los batallones de pardos y morenos libres: Apuntes para la historia de Cuba colonial*. Havana: Editorial Arte y Literatura, 1976.

———. *Contribución a la história de la gente sin história*. Havana: Editorial de Ciencias Sociales, 1963.

———. *El negro en el periodismo cubano en el siglo XIX*. Havana: Ediciones Revolución, 1963.

———. *El negro en la economía habanera del siglo XIX*. Havana: Unidad Productora, 1971.

———. *Rafael Serra y Montalvo: Obrero incansable de nuestra independencia*. Havana: Unión de Escritores y Artistas de Cuba, 1975.

Díaz-Briquets, Sergio, and Jorge F. Pérez-López. *Corruption in Cuba: Castro and Beyond*. Austin: University of Texas Press, 2006.

Directorio central de la raza de color. *Reglamento del directorio central de la raza de color*. Havana: Imprenta La Lucha, 1892.

Domínguez, Jorge. *Cuba: Order and Revolution*. Cambridge: Belknap Press of Harvard University Press, 1978.

Duharte Jiménez, Rafael. *Nacionalidad e história*. Santiago de Cuba: Editorial Oriente, 1989.

———. *El negro en la sociedad colonial*. Santiago de Cuba: Editorial Oriente, 1988.

Edreira de Caballero, Angelina. *Vida y obra de Juan Gualberto Gómez*. Havana: R. Méndez, 1973.

Entralgo, José E. *La liberación étnica cubana*. Havana, 1953.

Fanon, Frantz. *Black Skin, White Masks*. New York: Grove Press, 1967.

Farber, Samuel. *Revolution and Reaction in Cuba, 1933-1960*. Middletown, CT: Wesleyan University Press, 1976.

Federación de la Prensa Latina de América. *Libro de Cuba*. Havana: N.p., 1930.

Fermoselle, Rafael. *Política y color en Cuba: La guerrita de 1912*. Montevideo: Editorial Geminis, 1974.

Fernández, Damián J., and Madeline Cámara Betancourt. *Cuba, the Elusive Nation: Interpretations of National Identity*. Gainesville: University Press of Florida, 2000.

Fernández Robaina, Tomás. *El negro en Cuba, 1902-1958*. Havana: Editorial de Ciencias Sociales, 1990.

Ferrer, Ada. *Insurgent Cuba: Race, Nation, and Revolution, 1868-1898*. Chapel Hill: University of North Carolina Press, 1998.

Foner, Philip. *The Spanish-Cuban-American War and the Birth of American Imperialism, 1895-1902*. New York: Monthly Review Press, 1972.

Foreign Policy Association. *Problems of the New Cuba: Report of the Foreign Policy Association*. New York: Foreign Policy Association, 1935.

Forment, Carlos E. *Crónicas de Santiago de Cuba, continuación de la obra de Emilio Bacardí, era republicana*. Vol. 1. Santiago de Cuba: Editorial Arroyo, 1953.

Foucault, Michel. *The History of Sexuality: An Introduction*. Vol. 1. New York: Random House, 1990.

Franco, José Luciano. *La conspiración de Aponte*. Havana: Consejo Nacional de Cultura, 1963.

French, John D., and Daniel James, eds. *The Gendered Worlds of Latin American Women Workers: From Household and Factory to the Union Hall and Ballot Box*. Durham: Duke University Press, 1997.

Gaines, Kevin. *Uplifting the Race: Black Leadership, Politics, and Culture in the Twentieth Century*. Chapel Hill: University of North Carolina Press, 1996.

García, Gervasio L., and A. G. Quintero Rivera. *Desafío y solidaridad: Breve historia del movimiento obrero puertorriqueño*. Puerto Rico: Ediciones Huracán, 1982.

García Galló, Gaspar Jorge. *General de las cañas*. Havana: Editora Política, 1983.

García González, Armando, and Raquel Álvarez Peláez. *En busca de la raza perfecta: Eugenesia e higiene en Cuba (1898-1958)*. Madrid: Consejo Superior de Investigaciones Científicas, 1999.

García Moreira, Francisco. *Tiempo muerto: Memorias de un trabajador azucarero*. Havana: Ediciones Huracán, Instituto del Libro, 1969.

Gaus, Christian. *The German Emperor as Shown in His Public Utterances*. New York: Charles Scribner's, 1915.

Gilroy, Paul. *The Black Atlantic: Modernity and Double Consciousness*. Cambridge: Harvard University Press, 1993.

Gómez, Juan Gualberto. *Por Cuba Libre*. Havana: Editorial de Ciencias Sociales, 1974.

Gómez, Michael A. *Exchanging Our Country Marks: The Transformation of African Identities in the Colonial and Antebellum South*. Chapel Hill: University of North Carolina Press, 1998.

Gott, Richard. *Cuba: A New History*. New Haven: Yale University Press, 2004.

Graham, Richard. *The Idea of Race in Latin America*. Austin: University of Texas Press, 1990.

———. *Patronage Politics in Nineteenth-Century Brazil*. Stanford: Stanford University Press, 1990.

Grillo, David. *El problema del negro cubano*. 2d ed. Havana, 1953.

Guerra, Lillian. *The Myth of José Martí: Conflicting Nationalisms in Early Twentieth-Century Cuba*. Chapel Hill: University of North Carolina Press, 2005.

Guillén, Nicolas. *Sóngoro cosongo: Poemas mulatos*. Havana: Ucar, García y Cía, 1931.

Guirao, Ramón. *Orbita de la poesía afrocubana, 1928-1937: antología*. Havana: Ucar, García y Cía, 1938.

Habermas, Jürgen. *The Structural Transformation of the Public Sphere: An Inquiry into a Category of Bourgeois Society*. Cambridge: Cambridge University Press, 1992.

Hanchard, Michael. *Orpheus and Power*. Princeton: Princeton University Press, 1994.

———. *Party/Politics: Horizons in Black Political Thought*. New York: Oxford University Press, 2006.

Harris, Joseph. *Global Dimensions of the African Diaspora*. Washington, DC: Howard University Press, 1993.

Helg, Aline. *Our Rightful Share: The Afro-Cuban Struggle for Equality, 1886-1912*. Chapel Hill: University of North Carolina Press, 1995.

Hevia Lanier, Oilda. *El directorio central de las sociedades negras de Cuba, 1886-1894*. Havana: Editorial de Ciencias Sociales, 1996.

Horrego Estuch, Leopoldo. *Juan Gualberto Gómez: Un gran inconforme*. Havana: La Milagrosa, 1954.

———. *Martín Morúa Delgado: Vida y mensaje*. Havana: Editorial Sánchez, 1957.

Howard, Philip A. *Changing History: Afro-Cuban Cabildos and Societies of Color in the Nineteenth Century*. Baton Rouge: Louisiana State University Press, 1998.

Huggins, Nathan. *The Harlem Renaissance*. New York: Oxford University Press, 1971.

Ibarra, Jorge. *Cuba, 1898-1921: Partidos políticos y clases sociales*. Havana: Editorial de Ciencias Sociales, 1992.

———. *Prologue to Revolution: Cuba, 1898-1958*. Boulder, CO: Lynne Rienner, 1998.

Iglesias Utset, Marial. *Las metáforas del cambio en la vida cotidiana: Cuba, 1898–1902*. Havana: Ediciones Unión, 2003.

Instituto de Historia de Cuba. *Historia de Cuba: La neocolonial, organización y crisis desde 1899 hasta 1940*. Havana: Editora Política, 1998.

Instituto de Historia del Movimiento Comunista y de la Revolución Socialista de Cuba. *El movimiento obrero cubano*. Havana: Editorial Ciencias Sociales, 1985.

James, C. L. R. *A History of Pan-African Revolt*. 2d ed. rev. Washington, DC: Drum and Spear Press, 1969.

James, Joel. *Cuba, 1900–1928: La república dividida contra sí misma*. Havana: Editorial Arte y Literatura, 1974.

James, Winston. *Holding Aloft the Banner of Ethiopia: Caribbean Radicals in Early Twentieth-Century America*. New York: Verso, 1998.

Jenks, Leland. *Our Cuban Colony*. New York: Vanguard Press, 1928.

Jerez Villarreal, Juan. *Oriente (biografía de una provincia)*. Havana: Imprenta El Siglo XX, 1960.

Kelley, Robin D. G. *Race Rebels: Culture, Politics, and the Black Working Class*. New York: Free Press, 1994.

Kelley, Robin D. G., and Sidney Lemelle, eds. *Imagining Home: Class, Culture, and Nationalism in the African Diaspora*. London: Verso, 1994.

Knight, Alan, and William Pansters, eds. *Caciquismo in Twentieth-Century Mexico*. London: Institute for the Study of the Americas, 2005.

Knight, Franklin. *Slave Society in Cuba during the Nineteenth Century*. Madison: University of Wisconsin Press, 1970.

Kutzinski, Vera. *Sugar's Secrets: Race and the Erotics of Cuban Nationalism*. Charlottesville: University Press of Virginia, 1993.

Lachatañeré, Rómulo. *¡Oh, mío yemayá!* Manzanillo, Cuba: Editorial El Arte, 1938.

Lamar, Alberto Schweyer. *Como cayó el presidente Machado*. Havana: La Casa Montalvo Cárdenas, 1938.

Lapidus, Benjamin. *Origins of Cuban Music and Dance: Changüí*. Lanham, MD: Scarecrow Press, 2008.

Leuchsenring, Emilio Roig de. *Cuba no debe su independencia a los EEUU*. Havana: Ediciones la Tertulio, 1960.

Levine, Lawrence. *Black Culture and Black Consciousness: Afro-American Folk Thought from Slavery to Freedom*. New York: Oxford University Press, 1977.

Lumsden, Ian. *Machos, Maricones, and Gays: Cuba and Homosexuality*. Philadelphia: Temple University Press, 1996.

Magubane, Bernard. *The Ties That Bind: African-American Consciousness of Africa*. Trenton, NJ: Africa World Press, 1987.

Mainwaring, Scott. *Rethinking Party Systems in the Third Wave of Democratization: The Case of Brazil*. Stanford: Stanford University Press, 1999.

Mañach, Jorge Robato. *Indagación del choteo: La crisis de la alta cultura en Cuba*. Miami: Ediciones Universal, 1991.

Marcos Vegueri, Pascual B. *El negro en Cuba: Reflexiones sobre la república a que el Titán de Bronce se consagrara en Baraguá, en San Pedro y siempre*. Havana, 1955.

Marks, George P., III. *The Black Press Views American Imperialism (1898–1900)*. New York: Arno Press/New York Times, 1971.

Martínez-Alier, Verena. *Marriage, Class, and Colour in Nineteenth-Century Cuba: A Study of Racial Attitudes and Sexual Values in a Slave Society*. 2d ed. Ann Arbor: University of Michigan Press, 1989.

Martínez Furé, Rogelio. *Diálogos imaginarios*. Havana: Ediciones El Puente, 1963.

Martínez Ortiz, Rafael. *Cuba, los primeros anos de independencia: La intervencón y el establecimiento del gobierno de Tomás Estrada Palma*. Paris: Imprimerie Artistique "LUX," 1921.

McClintock, Anne. *Imperial Leather: Race, Gender, and Sexuality in the Colonial Contest*. New York: Routledge, 1995.

Meriño Fuentes, María de los Ángeles. *Gobierno municipal y partidos políticos en Santiago de Cuba (1898–1912)*. Santiago de Cuba: Ediciones Santiago, 2001.

Mintz, Sydney W., and Richard Price. *The Birth of African-American Culture: An Anthropological Perspective*. Boston: Beacon Press, 1992.

Mitre, Bartolomé. *The Emancipation of South America (Historia de San Martín)*. Whitefish, MT: Kessinger Publishing, 2009.

Montejo Arrechea, Carmen. *Sociedades de instrucción y recreo de pardos y morenos que existieron en Cuba colonial, período 1878–1898*. Veracruz: Instituto Veracruzano de Cultura, 1993.

——— . *Sociedades negras en Cuba, 1878–1960*. Havana: Editorial de Ciencias Sociales/Centro de Investigación y Desarrollo de la Cultura Cubana Juan Marinello, 2005.

Moore, Robin D. *Nationalizing Blackness: Afrocubanismo and Artistic Revolution in Havana, 1920–1940*. Pittsburgh: University of Pittsburgh Press, 1997.

Morúa Delgado, Martín. *Integración cubana y otros ensayos*. Vol. 3 of *Obras completas de Martín Morúa Delgado*. [1882.] Havana: Publicaciones de la Comisión Nacional del Centenario de Don Martín Morúa Delgado, 1957.

Mudimbe, V. Y. *The Idea of Africa*. Bloomington: Indiana University Press, 1994.

Oostindie, Gert. *Ethnicity in the Caribbean: Essays in Honor of Harry Hoetink*. London: Macmillan Education, 1996.

Ortiz, Fernando, and Diana Iznaga. *Los negros curros*. Havana: Editorial de Ciencias Sociales, 1986.

Ortíz Domínguez, Oscar. *Memorias: 3 años de gobierno, 1945–1948*. Holguín, Cuba: Editorial Eco, 1948.

Ortiz y Fernández, Fernando. *Los cabildos y el día de los reyes*. Havana: Editorial de Ciencias Sociales, 1992.

——— . *El engaño de las razas*. Havana: Editorial de Ciencias Sociales, 1975.

——— . *Hampa afrocubana: Los negros brujos (apuntes para un estudio de etnología criminal)*. Madrid: Librería de Fernando Fé, 1906.

——— . *Hampa afrocubana: Los negros esclavos*. 2d ed. Havana: Editorial de Ciencias Sociales, 1975.

————. *Martí y las razas*. Havana: Comisión Nacional Organizadora de los Actos y Ediciones del Centenarío y del Monumento de Martí, 1953.

Padrón, Carlos. *Franceses en el suroriente de Cuba*. Havana: Ediciones Unión, 1997.

Palmié, Stephan. *Wizards and Scientists: Explorations in Afro-Cuban Modernity and Tradition*. Durham: Duke University Press, 2002.

Paquette, Robert L. *Sugar Is Made with Blood: The Conspiracy of La Escalera and the Conflict between Empires over Slavery in Cuba*. Middletown, CT: Wesleyan University Press, 1988.

Patterson, Orlando. *Slavery and Social Death*. Cambridge: Harvard University Press, 1985.

Pedras Marcos, Azucena. *Quimeras de África: La Sociedad Española de Africanistas y Colonistas: El colonialismo español de finales del siglo XIX*. Madrid: Ediciones Polifemo, 2000.

Pedroso, Regino. *Poesías*. Havana: Editorial Letras Cubanas, 1984.

Pérez, Louis A. *Cuba: Between Reform and Revolution*. New York: Oxford University Press, 1988.

————. *Cuba between Empires, 1878–1902*. Pittsburgh: University of Pittsburgh Press, 1983.

————. *Cuba under the Platt Amendment, 1902–1934*. Pittsburgh: University of Pittsburgh Press, 1986.

————. *On Becoming Cuban: Identity, Nationality, and Culture*. Chapel Hill: University of North Carolina Press, 1999.

————. *Ties of Singular Intimacy*. Athens: University of Georgia Press, 1997.

Pérez, Louis A., and Rebecca Jarvis Scott. *The Archives of Cuba*. Pittsburgh: University of Pittsburgh Press, 2003.

Pérez, Nancy, Clara Domínguez, Rosa Rodríguez, Orlando Silva, and Danubia Terry. *El Cabildo Carabalí Isuama*. Santiago de Cuba: Editorial Oriente, 1982.

Pérez de la Riva, Juan. *El barracón y otros ensayos*. Havana: Editorial de Ciencias Sociales, 1975.

Pérez Sarduy, Pedro, and Jean Stubbs. *Afrocuba: An Anthology of Cuban Writing on Race, Politics, and Culture*. Melbourne: Ocean Press, 1993.

————. *Afro-Cuban Voices: On Race and Identity in Contemporary Cuba*. Gainesville: University of Florida Press, 2000.

Pérez-Stable, Marifeli. *The Cuban Revolution: Origins, Course, and Legacy*. New York: Oxford University Press, 1999.

Pichardo, Hortensia. *Documentos para la historia de Cuba*. Vols. 1–4. Havana: Editorial de Ciencias Sociales, 1976.

Plummer, Brenda Gayle. *Rising Wind: Black Americans and U.S. Foreign Affairs, 1935–1960*. Chapel Hill: University of North Carolina Press, 1996.

Portuondo Linares, Serafín. *Los independientes de color: Historia del partido independiente de color*. Havana: Editorial Librería Selecta, 1950.

Quintana, Julia Ulacía, and Froilán Francisco Cuéllar. *Las asociaciones y su legislación*. Edited by Centro Técnico de Corredores de Negocios. Havana: Talleres Tipográficos Maron, 1955.

Rama, Ángel. *The Lettered City*. Durham: Duke University Press, 1996.

Ravelo, Juan María Ravelo. *Páginas de Ayer*. Manzanillo: Editorial "El Arte," 1943.

Riera, Mario. *Cincuenta y dos años de política: Oriente, 1900-1952*. N.p., 1953.

———. *Cuba política, 1899-1955*. Havana: Impresora Modelo, 1955.

———. *Cuba Republicana, 1899-1958: Ocupación americana, república, elecciones desde el año 1900 a 1958*. Miami: Editorial AIP, 1974.

Risquet, Juan F. *Rectificaciones: La cuestión político-social en la isla de Cuba*. Havana: Tipografía "América," 1900.

Robinson, Cedric. *Black Marxism: The Making of the Black Radical Tradition*. London: Zed Press, 1983.

Rodney, Walter. *How Europe Underdeveloped Africa*. London: Bogle-L'Ouverture Publications, 1972.

Roig de Leuchsenring, Emilio. *Historia de la Enmienda Platt*. Havana: Ediciones de Ciencias Sociales, Instituto del Libro, 1973.

Ruiz Suárez, Bernardo. *The Color Question in Two Americas*. New York: Hunt Publishing, 1922.

Sarracino Magriñat, Rodolfo. *Los que volvieron a África*. Havana: Editorial de Ciencias Sociales, 1988.

Scott, James. *Domination and the Arts of Resistance: Hidden Transcripts*. New Haven: Yale University Press, 1990.

———. *Weapons of the Weak: Everyday Forms of Peasant Resistance*. New Haven: Yale University Press, 1989.

Scott, Rebecca J. *Degrees of Freedom: Louisiana and Cuba after Slavery*. Cambridge: Belknap Press of Harvard University Press, 2005.

———. *Slave Emancipation in Cuba: The Transition to Free Labor, 1860-1899*. Princeton: Princeton University Press, 1985.

Scraton, Sheila, and Anne Flintoff, eds. *Gender and Sport: A Reader*. London: Routledge, 2002.

Segrera, Francisco López. *Cuba: Cultura y sociedad (1510-1985)*. Havana: Editorial Letras Cubanas, 1989.

Serra, Rafael. *Para blancos y negros: Ensayos políticos, sociales y económicos*. Havana: Imprenta "El Score," 1907.

Serviat, Pedro. *El problema negro en Cuba y su solución definitiva*. Havana: Editorial Política, 1986.

Sewell, William H. *Work and Revolution in France: The Language of Labor from the Old Regime to 1848*. New York: Cambridge University Press, 1980.

Sheller, Mimi. *Democracy after Slavery: Black Publics and Peasant Radicalism in Haiti and Jamaica*. London: Macmillan Education, 2000.

Sims, Lowery Stokes. *Wilfredo Lam and the International Avant-Garde, 1923-1982*. Austin: University of Texas Press, 2002.

Sosa, Enrique. *Los Ñáñigos*. Havana: Casa de las Américas, 1982.

Stallybrass, Peter, and Allon White. *The Politics and Poetics of Transgression*. Ithaca: Cornell University Press, 1986.

Stepan, Nancy Leys. *"The Hour of Eugenics": Race, Gender, and Nation in Latin America*. Ithaca: Cornell University Press, 1991.

Stevenson, Nick. *Culture and Citizenship*. London: Sage, 2001.

Stocking, George W., Jr. *Race, Culture, and Evolution: Essays in the History of Anthropology*. New York: Free Press, 1968.

Stoler, Ann. *Race and the Education of Desire: Foucault's History of Sexuality and the Colonial Order of Things*. Durham: Duke University Press, 1995.

Stoler, Ann, and Frederick Cooper. *Tensions of Empire: Colonial Culture in a Bourgeois World*. Berkeley: University of California Press, 1997.

Stoner, Lynn K. *From the House to the Streets: The Cuban Women's Movement for Legal Reform, 1898-1940*. Durham: Duke University Press, 1991.

Suárez Findlay, Eileen J. *Imposing Decency: The Politics of Sexuality and Race in Puerto Rico, 1870-1920*. Durham: Duke University Press, 1999.

Trouillot, Michel-Rolph. *Haiti, State against Nation: The Origins and Legacy of Duvalierism*. New York: Monthly Review Press, 1990.

Varela, Padre Félix. *Memoria que demuestra la necesidad de extinguir la esclavitud en la Isla de Cuba, atendiendo a los intereses de sus propietarios*. Havana: Escritos Políticos Editorial de Ciencias Sociales, 1977.

Varela Zequeira, Eduardo. *La política en 1905, episodios de una lucha electoral*. Havana: Imprenta y Papelería de Rambla y Bouza, 1905.

Vignier E., and G. Alonso. *La corrupción política y administrativo en Cuba, 1944-1952*. Havana: Editorial de Ciencias Sociales/Instituto Cubano del Libro, 1973.

Wade, Peter. *Race and Ethnicity in Latin America*. Chicago: Pluto Press, 1997.

Walters, Bishop Alexander. *My Life and Work*. New York: Fleming H. Revell, 1917.

Watkins-Owens, Irma. *Blood Relations: Caribbean Immigrants and the Harlem Community, 1900-1930*. Indiana: Indiana University Press, 1996.

Weber, Max. *Economy and Society*. Edited by Guenther Roth and Claus Wittich. Berkeley: University of California Press, 1968.

Whitney, Robert. *State and Revolution in Cuba: Mass Mobilization and Political Change, 1920-1940*. Chapel Hill: University of North Carolina Press, 2001.

Williams, Raymond. *Keywords: A Vocabulary of Culture and Society*. New York: Oxford University Press, 1983.

Zanetti, Oscar, and Alejandro García. *Sugar and Railroads: A Cuban History, 1839-1959*. Translated by Franklin Knight and Mary Todd. Chapel Hill: University of North Carolina Press, 1998.

Articles, Essays, and Dissertations

Apter, Andrew. "Herskovits's Heritage: Re-thinking Syncretism in the African Diaspora." *Diaspora: A Journal of Transnational Studies* 1, no. 3 (1991): 235-60.

Arredondo, Alberto. "El Truco de Nuestra Democracia." *Oriente* (January 24, 1938).

Bair, Barbara. "True Women, Real Men: Gender, Ideology, and Social Roles in the Garvey Movement." In *Gendered Domains: Re-thinking Public and Private in Women's History*, edited by Dorothy O. Helly and Susan Reverby, 154-66. Ithaca: Cornell University Press, 1992.

Balibar, Etienne. "Is There a Neo-Racism?," "Racism and Nationalism," and "The Nation-Form: History and Ideology." In *Race, Nation, Class: Ambiguous Identities*, edited by Etienne Balibar and Immanuel Wallerstein, 17-28, 37-68, and 86-106. London: Verso, 1991.

Boose, Lynda. "Techno-Muscularity and the 'Boy Eternal': From the Quagmire to the Gulf." In *Cultures of United States Imperialism*, edited by Amy Kaplan and Donald E. Pease, 581-616. Durham: Duke University Press, 1993.

Carby, Hazel. "'On the Threshold of the Women's Era': Lynching, Empire, and Sexuality in Black Feminist Theory." In *Dangerous Liaisons: Gender, Nation, and Postcolonial Perspectives*, edited by Anne McClintock, Aamir Mufti, and Ella Shohat, 330-43. Minneapolis: University of Minnesota Press, 1997.

Carr, Barry. "Mill Occupations and Soviets: The Mobilisation of Sugar Workers in Cuba, 1917-1933." *Journal of Latin American Studies* 28, no. 1 (February 1996): 129-58.

Chapman, Charles E. "The Cuban Constitution and Congress." *California Law Review* 14, no. 1 (November 1925): 22-35.

Chasteen, John Charles. "Fighting Words: The Discourse of Insurgency in Latin American History." *Latin American Research Review* 28, no. 3 (1993): 83-111.

Childs, Matt D. "'A Black French General Arrived to Conquer the Island': Images of the Haitian Revolution in Cuba's 1812 Aponte Rebellion." In *The Impact of the Haitian Revolution in the Atlantic World*, edited by David P. Geggus, 135-56. Columbia: University of South Carolina Press, 2001.

Chomsky, Aviva. "The Aftermath of Repression: Race and Nation in Cuba after 1912." *Journal of Iberian and Latin American Studies* 4, no. 2 (1998): 1-40.

Cooper, Fred. "Race, Ideology, and the Perils of Comparative History." *American Historical Review* 101, no. 4 (1996): 1122-38.

De la Fuente, Alejandro. "Race, National Discourse, and Politics in Cuba: An Overview." *Latin American Perspectives* 25, no. 3 (1998): 43-69.

———. "Two Dangers, One Solution: Immigration, Race, and Labor in Cuba, 1900-1930." *International Labor and Working-Class History* 51 (Spring 1997): 30-49.

De la Fuente, Alejandro, and Matthew Casey. "Race and the Suffrage Controversy in Cuba, 1898-1901." In *Colonial Crucible: Empire in the Making of the Modern American State*, edited by Alfred W. McCoy and Francisco A. Scarano, 220-29. Madison: University of Wisconsin Press, 2009.

Derby, Lauren. "Haitians, Magic, and Money: *Raza* and Society in the Haitian-Dominican Borderlands, 1900-1937." *Comparative Studies in Society and History* 36, no. 3 (1994): 488-526.

De Velasco, Carlos. "El problema negro." *Cuba Contemporanea* 1 (February 1913): 73–79.

D'ou, Lino. "La evolución de la raza de color en Cuba." In *Libro de Cuba*, 333–37. Havana, 1930.

Du Bois, W. E. B. "The Talented Tenth." In Booker T. Washington et al., *The Negro Problem: A Series of Articles by Representative Negroes of To-Day*, 31–76. New York: James Pott, 1903.

Duke, Cathy. "The Idea of Race: The Cultural Impact of American Intervention in Cuba, 1898-1912." In *Politics, Society, and Culture in the Caribbean*, edited by Blanca Silvestrini, 87–109. San Juan: Universidad de Puerto Rico, 1983.

Ferrer, Ada. "Cuba, 1898: Rethinking Race, Nation, and Empire." *Radical History Review* 73 (Winter 1999): 22–46.

———. "Rustic Men, Civilized Nation: Race, Culture, and Contention on the Eve of Cuban Independence." *Hispanic American Historical Review* 78, no. 4 (1998): 663–86.

García Domínguez, Bernardo. "Garvey and Cuba." In *Garvey: His Work and Impact*, edited by Rupert Lewis and Patrick Bryan, 299–305. Trenton, NJ: Africa World Press, 1991.

Guerra, Lillian. "From Revolution to Involution in the Early Cuban Republic: Conflicts over Race, Class, and Nation, 1902-1906." In *Race and Nation in Modern Latin America*, edited by Nancy P. Appelbaum, Anne S. Macpherson, and Karin Alejandra Rosemblatt, 132–62. Chapel Hill: University of North Carolina Press, 2003.

Guiral Moreno, Mario. "Nuestros problemas políticos, económicos, y sociales." *Cuba Contemporanea* 5 (August 1914): 401–24.

Guridy, Frank A. "From Solidarity to Cross-Fertilization: Afro-Cuban/African American Interaction during the 1930s and 1940s." *Radical History Review* 87 (Fall 2003): 19–48.

Hall, Stuart. "The Formation of a Diasporic Intellectual: An Interview with Stuart Hall" and "Gramsci's Relevance for the Study of Race and Ethnicity." In *Stuart Hall: Critical Dialogues in Cultural Studies*, edited by Kuan-Hsing Chen and David Morley, 486–505, 411–41. London: Routledge Press, 1996.

Hanchard, Michael. "Afro-Modernity: Temporality, Politics, and the African Diaspora." In *Alternative Modernities*, edited by Dilip Parameshwar Gaonkar, 272–98. 2d ed. Durham: Duke University Press, 2001.

———. "Translation, Political Community, and Black Internationalism: Some Comments on Brent Hayes Edwards's *The Practice of Diaspora*." *Small Axe* 17 (March 2005): 112–19.

Higginbotham, Evelyn Brooks. "African American Women's History and the Metalanguage of Race." *Signs* 17, no. 2 (1992): 251–74.

Hoernel, Robert. "Sugar and Social Change in Oriente, Cuba, 1898-1946." *Journal of Latin American Studies* 8 (November 1976): 215–49.

Hoetink, Harry. "'Race' and Color in the Caribbean." In *Caribbean Contours*, edited by Sidney Mintz and Sally Price, 55–84. Baltimore: Johns Hopkins University Press, 1985.

Holt, Thomas C. "Marking: Race, Race-Making, and the Writing of History." *American Historical Review* 100, no. 1 (1995): 1–20.

Kaplan, Amy. "Black and Blue on San Juan Hill." In *Cultures of United States Imperialism*, edited by Amy Kaplan and Donald E. Pease, 219–36. Durham: Duke University Press, 1993.

———. "Homeland Insecurities: Reflections on Language and Space." *Radical History Review* 85 (Winter 2003): 82–93.

Klein, Herbert. "The Colored Militia of Cuba: 1568–1868." *Caribbean Studies* 6, no. 2 (1966): 17–27.

Lockmiller, David A. "The Advisory Law Commission of Cuba." *Hispanic American Historical Review* 17, no. 1 (February 1937): 2–29.

Loughridge, Rachel. "'My Race': A Translation." *Phylon (1940–1956)* 6, no. 2 (1945): 126–28.

Marques Dolz, María Antonia. "The Nonsugar Industrial Bourgeoisie and Industrialization in Cuba, 1920–1959." Translated by Luis Alberto Fierro. *Latin American Perspectives* 22, no. 4 (1995): 59–80.

Marx, Anthony W. "Contested Citizenship: The Dynamics of Racial Identity and Social Movements." *International Review of Social History* 40, Supplement 3 (December 1995): 159–83.

Masferrer, Marianne, and Carmelo Mesa-Lago. "The Gradual Integration of the Black in Cuba: Under the Colony, the Republic, and the Revolution." In *Slavery and Race Relations in Latin America*, edited by Robert B. Toplin, 348–84. Westport, CT: Greenwood Press, 1974.

McClintock, Anne. "'No Longer in a Future Heaven': Gender, Race and Nationalism." In *Dangerous Liaisons: Gender, Nation, and Postcolonial Perspectives*, edited by Anne McClintock, Aamir Mufti, and Ella Shohat, 89–112. Minneapolis: University of Minnesota Press, 1997.

McLeod, Marc Christian. "Undesirable Aliens: Haitian and British West Indian Immigrant Workers in Cuba, 1898 to 1940." Ph.D. diss., University of Texas at Austin, 2000.

Mena, Luz. "Stretching the Limits of Gendered Spaces: Black and Mulatto Women in 1830s Havana." *Cuban Studies/Estudios Cubanos* 36 (January 2006): 87–104.

Mendoza Lorenzo, Leidy. "Estudio sobre el cabildo de Congos Reales 'San Antonio' de Trinidad." *Islas* 85 (September–December 1986): 49–73.

Mintz, Sydney W. "Enduring Substances, Trying Theory: The Caribbean Region as Oikoumenê." *Journal of the Royal Anthropological Institute* 2, no. 2 (June 1996): 289–311.

———. "The Industrialization of Sugar Production and Its Relationship to Social and Economic Change." In *Background to Revolution: The Development of Modern Cuba*, edited by Robert Freeman Smith, 176–86. New York: Alfred A. Knopf, 1966.

Morrison, Karen Y. "Civilization and Citizenship through the Eyes of Afro-Cuban Intellectuals during the First Constitutional Era, 1902–1940." *Cuban Studies/Estudios Cubanos* 30 (1999): 76–99.

Ortiz, Fernando y Fernández. "Los cabildos afrocubanos." *Revista Bimestre Cubana* 16 (January–February 1921): 5–39.

———. "Origen de los afrocubanos." *Cuba Contemporanea* 11 (1916): 213–39.

Orum, Thomas. "The Politics of Color: The Racial Dimension of Cuban Politics during the Early Republican Years, 1900–1912." Ph.D. diss., New York University, 1975.

Pappademos, Melina. "Juan Gualberto Gómez." *Encyclopedia of African-American Culture and History: The Black Experience in the Americas*, edited by Colin Palmer et al., 924–25. Farmington Hills, MI: Macmillan Reference USA, 2006.

Pérez, Louis A. "Insurrection, Intervention, and the Transformation of Land Tenure Systems in Cuba, 1895–1902." *Hispanic American Historical Review* 65, no. 2 (May 1985): 229–54.

———. "Politics, Peasants, and People of Color: The 1912 'Race War' in Cuba Reconsidered." *Hispanic American Historical Review* 66 (August 1986): 509–39.

———. "Supervision of a Protectorate: The United States and the Cuban Army, 1898–1908." *Hispanic American Historical Review* 52, no. 2 (May 1972): 250–71.

Pérez, Luis Marino. "La aclimatación del cubano." *Cuba Contemporanea* 4, no. 3 (1914): 288–94.

Pérez-Stable, Marifeli. "Estrada Palma's Civic March: From Oriente to Havana, April 20–May 11, 1902." *Cuban Studies/Estudios Cubanos* 30 (1999): 113–21.

Philogene, Jerry. "National Narratives, Caribbean Memories, and Diasporic Identities: Haitian and Jamaican Modern Art, 1920–1960." Ph.D. diss., New York University, 2008.

Quintero Rivera, Ángel. "The Somatology of Manners: Class, Race, and Gender in the History of Dance Etiquette in the Hispanic Caribbean." In *Ethnicity in the Caribbean: Essays in Honor of Harry Hoetink*, edited by Gert Oostindie, 152–81. London: Macmillan Education, 1996.

Quiroz, Alfonso. "Implicit Costs of Empire: Bureaucratic Corruption in Nineteenth-Century Cuba." *Journal of Latin American Studies* 35, no. 3 (August 2003): 473–511.

Roldán de Montaúd, Inés. "Cuba." In *El poder de la influencia: Geografía del caciquismo en España (1875–1923)*, edited by José Varela Ortega et al., 515–40. Madrid: Marcial Pons, Ediciones de Historia, 2001.

Roniger, Luis. "The Comparative Study of Clientelism and the Changing Nature of Civil Society in the Contemporary World." In *Democracy, Clientelism, and Civil Society*, edited by Luis Roniger and Ayşe Güneş-Ayata, 1–18. Boulder, CO: Lynne Rienner, 1994.

Rushing, Fannie. "Cabildos de nación and Sociedades de la Raza de Color: Afro-

Cuban Participation in Slave Emancipation and Cuban Independence, 1865–
1895." Ph.D. diss., University of Chicago, 1992.

Sánchez-Roig, Rebeca. "Cuban Constitutionalism and Rights: An Overview of the
Constitutions of 1901 and 1940." "Cuba in Transition," vol. 6, Proceedings of the
Fifth Annual Meeting of the Association for the Study of the Cuban Economy
(ASCE), University of Miami, Miami, FL, August 8-10, 1996.

Sanguily, Manuel. "José de la Luz Caballero." In *Defensa de Cuba: vida y obra de
Manuel Sanguily*, edited by Emilio Roig de Leuchsenring. Havana: Oficina del
Historiador de la Ciudad, 1948.

Sarabasa, Ricardo. "Alrededor del divorcio." *Cuba Contemporanea* 5, no. 1 (1914):
6-13.

Schwartz, Rosalie. "The Displaced and the Disappointed: Cultural Nationalists
and Black Activists in Cuba in the 1920s." Ph.D. diss., University of California,
San Diego, 1977.

Scott, Rebecca J. " 'The Lower Class of Whites' and 'the Negro Element':
Race, Social Identity, and Politics in Central Cuba, 1899–1909." In *La nación
soñada: Cuba, Puerto Rico y filipinas ante el 98*, edited by Consuelo Naranjo
Orovio, Miguel A. Angel Puig-Samper, and Luis Miguel García Mora, 179-91.
Aranjuez: Doce Calles, 1996.

———. "Race, Labor, and Citizenship in Cuba: A View from the Sugar District of
Cienfuegos, 1886–1909." *Hispanic American Historical Review* 78, no. 4 (1998):
687-728.

Stoler, Ann. "Sexual Affronts and Racial Frontiers." In *Tensions of Empire:
Colonial Culture in a Bourgeois World*, edited by Ann Stoler and Frederick
Cooper, 198-237. Berkeley: University of California Press, 1997.

Stubbs, Jean. "Social and Political Motherhood in Cuba: Mariana Grajales
Cuello." In *Engendering History: Caribbean Women in Historical Perspective*,
edited by Verene Shepherd, Bridget Brereton, and Barbara Bailey, 296-315.
Kingston: Ian Randle Publishers, 1995.

Swanger, Joanna Beth. "Lands of Rebellion: Oriente and Escambray
Encountering Cuban State Formation, 1934-1974." Ph.D. diss., University of
Texas, Austin, 1999.

Tilly, Charles. "Citizenship, Identity, and Social History." *International Review
of Social History* 40, Supplement 3 (December 1995): 1-17.

Trelles, Carlos M. "Bibliografía de autores de la raza de color." *Cuba
Contemporanea* 43, no. 169 (January–April, 1927): 30-78.

Turits, Richard. "A World Destroyed, a Nation Imposed: The 1937 Haitian
Massacre in the Dominican Republic." *Hispanic American Historical Review* 82,
no. 3 (2002): 590-632.

Urrutia, Gustavo E. "Complejo de inferioridad" (December 18, 1935). In *Cuatro
charlas radiofónicas*. Havana, 1935.

———. "Racial Prejudice in Cuba: How It Compares with That of the North
Americans." In *Negro Anthology*, edited by Nancy Cunard. New York:
Continuum, 1934.

Whitney, Robert. "The Architect of the Cuban State: Fulgencio Batista and Populism in Cuba, 1937–1940." *Journal of Latin American Studies* 32 (2000): 435–59.

Williams, Brackette. "The Impact of the Precepts of Nationalism on the Concept of Culture: Making Grasshoppers of Naked Apes." *Cultural Critique* no. 24 (Spring 1993): 143–91.

Wright, Ann. "Intellectuals of an Unheroic Period of Cuban History, 1913–1923: The 'Cuba Contemporanea' Group." *Bulletin of Latin American Research* 7, no. 1 (1988): 109–22.

Index

Note: Page numbers in italics refer to illustrations.

and patronage politics, 90–91; police harassment of, 117, 118; and politics, 112–15, 122–24; purposes of, 94–95, 111, 114, 116, 118, 122–23; and regional and national values, 122–24; and *rezo* (collective song or prayer), 119. *See also* Africanisms and African legacy

African Lucumí "Santa Bárbara" Mutual Aid and Recreation Society, 98

Afro-Antillean workers, 180–81, 212, 239 (n. 32)

Afro-Cuban: as term, 15. *See also* Black Cubans

Afrocubanidad and *Afrocubanismo*, 178, 181–82, 183

Afro-Modernity, 123

"Afro" prefix, 15

Agrarian League, 34

Agrarian reform, 170, 202, 207, 213, 219

Agriculture: and agricultural workers, 160, 176, 180, 181, 207–8, 212–13, 238 (n. 32), 254 (n. 5), 271 (n. 121); in colonial period, 144; destruction of, by War of Independence, 103; and economic crises of 1920s–1930s, 176, 180, 212–13; and foreign/immigrant workers, 180–81, 239 (n. 32); legislation on, 181, 207–8, 271–72 (n. 122); National Federation of Black Societies on, 207, 209; North American investment in, 100; in Oriente, 209, 212–13; and slaves, 102. *See also* Sugar industry; Tobacco industry and tobacco workers

Agrupación de Color (Group of Color). *See* Independent Party of Color

Albores Sport Club, 205

Alemán, José B., 19

Alliegro, Anselmo, 266 (n. 31)

Amigos del Pueblo (Friends of the People), 159, 160–61, 203

Andreu, Enrique, 206

Antidiscrimination legislation, 9, 214, 218, 219–21, 228, 274–75 (n. 179)

Arango Mantilla, Miguel, 155

Argentina, 259–60 (n. 7)

Arredondo, Alberto, 170–71, 212

Asbert, Ernesto, 164

Asociación Adelante, 179, 180, 205

Asociación de Veteranos (Veterans' Association), 49, 171

Asociación Patriótica de Damas Admiradoras de Moncada (Patriotic Ladies' Association of Admirers of Moncada), 9, 80–81, 196, 224–25

Association of Good Government (Havana), 25, 239 (n. 39)

Association of Public Employees, 220

Atómo (The Atom), 170, 173, 177, 205–6

August Revolution (1906): blacks in Constitutional Army during, 53–54, 145; casualties of, 78; cause and purpose of, 40–41, 65, 74, 78–79, 172, 248 (n. 13); elections following, 245 (n. 127); and Estrada Palma, 65, 144; and José Miguel Gómez, 74; and Juan Gualberto Gómez, 74, 79, 86; and Morúa Delgado, 79, 86; and racial politics, 54–55, 79, 160, 164, 223; removal of Moderates from office following, 53; U.S. intervention following, 53, 56, 245 (n. 127)

Ayón, Felix, 156

Ayuntamiento (town council), 35, 37

Bacardí y Moreau, Emilio, 36, 39, 40, 99, 236 (n. 5), 243 (n. 79)

Baliño, Carlos, 171

Bandera, Quintín: and black civic clubs, 89–90; command stripped from, 21; death of, during August Revolution, 78; Estrada Palma refuses to meet with, 18; in Liberation Army, 38, 79; manifesto of, against U.S. military occupa-

Black brokers. *See* Brokers

Black civic clubs: and antidiscrimination legislation, 220–21; and Batista, 51, 162, 168, 214–15, 217, 219–21, 228, 273 (n. 153); and black activists, 9, 11–12, 75; and black brokers, 42, 52, 75; and black elites, 114, 173; and black politicians, 89–90, 156, 269–70 (n. 94); and black press, 150–51, 156; bylaws of, 186–87; Castellanos's participation in, 42; and Céspedes, 88–89, 152; class critiques by, in 1930s, 179; compared with Africanist societies, 114–15; criticisms of, by black activists and intellectuals outside of club movement, 196–97, 205–6, 228–29; decline of, 221–22; distancing of, from African legacy, 13, 14, 125–26, 187, 189; family departments of, 193; and family networks, 81–82; and Juan Gualberto Gómez, 73, 75, 82–83, 88, 89, 134, 136, 152, 157, 165; and high-level officeholders, 168–69; importance of, to officeholders, 58–60, 247 (n. 165); and labor movement, 217, 219–20; and Machado, 90, 155, 168, 197, 198, 203, 204, 228; membership of black women in, 194–96; membership requirements for, 186–87; and Menocal administration, 90, 168; and National Party of Oriente, 231 (n. 1); in 1950s, 221–22; and patronage politics, 12, 48–61, 89–91, 168, 194, 196–202, 206, 222, 223, 227, 228; police harassment of, 51–52, 117–18; and political sociability, 12, 58–60; and politics of race, 12–13, 156, 221; purposes of, 12–14, 58, 59, 112, 148, 166, 168, 276 (n. 10); and Race War, 58, 166; respectability and "modern" values of members of, 13, 148, 151, 166, 186–87, 190, 194, 202, 226; state subsidies for, 197, 200, 214,
215, 217, 219, 221–22, 275 (n. 184); strategies of, for black socioeconomic advancement, 222; unification movement of, 152, 157–69, 201; and women, 145, 185–87, 189–96, *191*. *See also* Africanist societies; Black activists and politicians; Directorate of Societies of the Colored Race; National Federation of Black Societies; *and specific clubs*

Black Cubans: in Constitutional Army, 53; "Don" title for, 75, 251 (n. 42); doubts about abilities of, 19, 22, 24, 155, 228, 239 (n. 36); historical narratives and scholarship on, 6–11, 233 (n. 17); incarceration rate of, 233 (n. 15); in Liberation Army, 2, 9, 21, 29, 38, *39*, 79–80, 97–98, 224–25, 238 (n. 21), 243 (n. 88), 252 (n. 51), 256 (n. 27); living conditions of, 103, 206–7, 226; and patronage networks, 48–60, 81–82; as political candidates, 4, 54, 66, 71–72, 89, 156, 163, 164–65, 249 (n. 17); political strength of, 28–29, 54, 71–72, 107–8, 156, 217, 227, 234 (n. 25), 248 (n. 13); population of, 27, 28, 71, 89, 92, 102–3, 138, 233 (n. 11), 240 (n. 49), 254–55 (n. 5); scientific research on, 109, 111, 116–17; segregation of, 12, 27, 141, 205; stereotypes of, 19, 57, 99, 109, 117, 125, 158–59, 203; stratification of, 226; as third-party threat, 234 (n. 25). *See also* Cultural improvement and racial uplift; Discrimination; Education; Employment of blacks; Families; Government employment; Race; Slavery

Black elites: on Africa, 125–47; and black press, 27–28, 150–51, 156–57; criticisms of, 173–74, 196–97, 205–6, 228–29; and cultural improvement and racial uplift, 69, 71, 73, 74, 83,

126–29, 132–47, 158, 160, 165, 166, 168, 178, 192; definition of, 14; distancing of, from African legacy, 13, 14, 125–26, 174, 178, 187, 189; Du Bois on "Talented Tenth," 143, 146; and education as avenue for advancement, 142–45; employment of, 14; Eurocentrism of, 174, 178; leadership capability of, 144, 146–48, 150–51; "modern" values and tactics of, 71, 146–48, 178; motives for speaking for majority of blacks, 173–74, 178–79, 196–97; and nationalist heroes, 114; photographs of, 151, 156; privileged status of, compared with culturally "backward" black Cubans, 138–39, 142, 145–47, 166, 178, 226; professional class of, 228; rejection of PIC by, 57–58; statistics on, 27, 226; wealth of, 14, 114. *See also* Black civic clubs; Patronage politics

Black intellectuals-activists and radicals: compared with traditional black leaders, 173–74, 178–79, 222, 228; cooperation with black civic clubs by, 219–20; criticisms of traditional black leaders and black civic clubs by, 178, 185, 196–97, 205–6, 228–29; influences on, 228; and National Federation of Black Societies, 205–6; and patronage politics, 173–74, 196–201; and postrevolution black politics, 177–83, 196–201; protests against government corruption and political mismanagement by, 170–73; on racial uplift approach, 173–74; and youth civic organizations, 170, 173, 174, 183–86. *See also* Communist Party, Cuban; Labor movement

Black newspapers and periodicals: audience of, 150–51; and black elites, 27–28, 150–51, 156–57; contents of, 150–51; editorial boards of, 151; examples of, 240 (n. 48); and Juan

Gualberto Gómez, 73, 74, 86, 136–37, 151; and mainstream politicians, 155–56; and Menocal, 150, 153–55, 199; photographs in, 151, 156; and politics of black public sphere, 151–57; purposes of, 150; on racial inequality, 155; and Risquet, 87–88, 151; and Serra, 127; and white elites, 150, 153, 155; for women, 139–41, 148–49. *See also specific newspapers*

Black politicians. *See* Black activists and politicians

Black women: and black civic clubs, 145, 185–87, 189–96, *191*; black clubs' power over, 193–96; and black patriots, 9, 80–81, 196, 224–25; and cultural improvement of blacks, 139–41, 145, 149, 189–90, 192; employment discrimination against, 220; and female-only civic organizations, 80, 196; feminist ideology of, 185–89, 195, 202–3, 228, 268 (n. 62); and labor movement, 217; as members of black civic clubs, 194–96; *Minerva* magazine for, 139–41, 148–49; patriarchal gender roles of, 139, 185–90, 192–93, 195–96; political participation by, 174, 177, 186–89, 192–93; as prostitutes, 268 (n. 62), 270 (n. 105); sexuality of, 190, 192; slavery of, 190; stereotypes of, 181; suffrage for, 177, 185, 186; Vasconcelos on, 189–90, 195; violence by, 204

Black youth civic organizations, 170, 173, 174, 183–86, 222, 229

Blanco (white), 110

Blanco, Ramón, 114–15

Bongó, 267 (n. 51)

Booker T. Washington Institute of Popular Education, 144–45

Booker T. Washington Society, 183

"Borracha, La" (The Female Drunk; Luaces), 193–94

Botellas (government sinecures), 31, 44,

164, 227, 241 (n. 60). *See also* Government employment

Boudet, Felipe, 121–22

Bravo Correoso, Antonio, 46–47, 78, 85, 198

Bravo Correoso, Eligio, 242 (n. 76)

Brazil, 43

Brokers: and black civic clubs, 42, 52, 75; Juan Gualberto Gómez as broker, 75–79, 165, 251 (n. 43); increased number of, 61; and increase in state revenues and state bureaucracy, 163–64; and political system, 70; Risquet as broker, 87; role of, in patronage system, 87, 173, 224, 227, 251 (n. 43); and Spanish merchants versus black laborers, 60. *See also* Patronage politics

Bronfman, Alejandra, 208

Brooke, John R., 38

Brujos (witch doctors), 73, 97, 108–9, 117, 159, 161, 178–79, 204, 250 (n. 35)

Budou, Serafín, *50*

Buena Vista Social Club, 180

Bueno, José, 82

Cabildos (town councils), 235 (n. 4)

Cabildos de nación (African ethnic societies), 94, 112–13, 115, 136, 235 (n. 4)

Caciques (political bosses): and black leaders, 60, 86–87; black youths' criticism of, 185; definition of, 36, 235 (n. 3); function of, 235 (n. 3); Juan Gualberto Gómez as, 75–79, 82–89, 251 (n. 43); and political parties, 41; and Republican Party, 17. *See also* Patronage politics

Calderío, Francisco, 217

Calderón, Pedro, 168

Callejas, Antonlín, 80

Callis, José B., *39*

Campos Marquetti, Generoso, *68*;

and cultural improvement of blacks, 142–43; disrespect toward, 19; and government employment of blacks, 63–64, 67, 72, 142–43; as Liberation Army general, 38, 70, 79; as Masó's supporter, 28–29, 247 (n. 163); on patronage politics by Juan Gualberto Gómez, 72; political career of, 67, 164; and Unification of Black Societies movement, 164

Canales Carazo, Juan, 151

Canas, Eduardo, 220

Canas Abril, Eduardo, 274 (n. 179)

Capestany, Manuel, 156, 198

Capestany, Miguel A., 49

Caraballo, Rafael, 215

Cárdenas, Lázaro, 216

Caridad de Oriente, La, 45

Carillo Morales, Francisco, 40

Carrera y Jústiz, Francisco, 25, 239–40 (nn. 39–40), 251 (n. 39)

Carrión, Miguel, 35, 242 (n. 73)

Carvajal, Odiociato, *39*

Casey, Matthew, 22

Casino Cubano, 215, 247 (n. 165), 270 (n. 94)

Castellanos, Alberto, 77, 166, 247 (n. 162), 251–52 (n. 47)

Castellanos, Israel, 117, 233 (n. 17)

Castellanos, José Guadalupe, 42, 70–71, 82, 84–85, 242 (n. 76), 269–70 (n. 94)

Castellanos, José Lorenzo, 86

Castillo Duany, Demetrio, 74, 77, 235 (n. 3), 243 (nn. 79, 91), 251 (n. 47)

Catholic Church, 98, 113, 115, 150, 213

Caudillos (political strongmen): and black club leaders, 194; definition of, 243 (n. 95), 251 (n. 43); Juan Gualberto Gómez as, 75–79, 82–89, 251 (n. 43); and political coalitions, 41

Cebreco, Agustín, 9, *39*, 79, 82, 224

Centro de Cocheros (Drivers' Club), 136

79, 267 (n. 35); and women, 190–92, *191*, 195

Club "Bartolomé Masó," 47

Club Femenino, 172

Club Juan de Góngora, 48, 121, 123, 258–59 (n. 71)

Club "Los XXI" de Santiago, 184

Club Moncada, 35–36, 45

Club Político y Recreativo "Antonio Maceo," 42, 59, 247 (n. 162)

Clubs. *See* Africanist societies; Black civic clubs; Youth civic organizations; *and specific clubs*

Club San Carlos, 45

CNOC. *See* National Confederation of Cuban Workers

Cofradías (Catholic brotherhoods), 112–13, 235 (n. 4)

Colás, Papá, 109

Colonial period of Cuba: Africanist societies during, 94, 112–15; associations, clubs, and societies during, 37, 94, 112–15, 235–36 (n. 4); black and mulatto battalions during, 242 (n. 75); and constitution (1897), 22; corruption during, 63, 236 (n. 4); education during, 44, 141–42, 261 (n. 26); laws during 1870s–1880s, 51, 137, 138, 261 (n. 26); legacy of, 20, 23–24, 33; *letrados* (learned class) in, 149–50; local governments during, 35; political administrators during, 15; political parties during, 37, 44–45; repatriation of ex-slaves to Africa during, 92–93

Colonization, Reclamation, and Distribution of State Lands Law (1937), 271–72 (n. 122)

Comité Gestor, 157, 162, 163, 164, 263 (n. 21)

Committee of One Hundred, 171

Communist Party, Cuban: and Batista, 209, 216, 220; and black leftists, 217–19; founding of, 171, 179; and labor movement, 179, 216, 218, 220, 229, 267 (n. 39); legalization of, by Batista, 209, 216; newspaper of, 212, 214–15, 219; on race, 179–80, 214, 218; and Tribunal de Urgencia, 270 (n. 105)

Comparsas, 108

Complementary Laws, 27, 214, 218, 220, 240 (n. 47), 275 (n. 181)

Confederación de Trabajadores Cubanos (Confederation of Cuban Workers, CTC), 216, 217, 219–20

Confederación de Trabajadores Mexicanos (Confederation of Mexican Workers), 274 (n. 163)

Confederación Nacional de Obreros Cubanos, 267 (n. 39)

Congress, Cuban: black and mulatto members of, 21, 54, 87, 156, 162, 164, 165–66, 200, 218, 245 (n. 137), 249 (n. 32); corruption in, 172; on divorce, 192; on immigrant workers, 180–81; influence of Carrera y Jústiz on, 25; and "white-only" hiring policy for government jobs, 67

Conjunción Party, 164

Conservative Party, 54, 56, 155, 159–61, 163, 165, 176, 267 (n. 31)

Constitution, Cuban (1897), 22

Constitution, Cuban (1901): on citizenship requirements, 101, 102; on naturalization rights, 101, 102; on presidential powers, 155; provisions of, 4, 100, 101, 223, 233 (n. 10); on right to petition, 98; on sovereign authority of Cuba, 100; U.S. as model for, 100. *See also* Platt Amendment

Constitution, Cuban (1934), 186

Constitution, Cuban (1940), 27, 214, 218, 220

Constitutional Army, 53, 55, 65

Constitutional convention (1900–1901): delegates to, 2, 21, 36, 72–73, 74, 75, 84, 198; number of voters electing delegates of, 2, 232 (n. 5); and Platt Amendment, 2, 21, 73, 75; political compromise in, 2–3; and social egalitarianism and race-transcendent relations, 3; and suffrage, 3, 17, 22, 108, 234 (n. 1)

Constitutional convention (1939–40), 198, 214, 218, 219, 220, 269 (n. 94)

Cooperativismo, 176

Corona, Enrique, 80

Coronado, Manuel M., 251 (n. 39)

Corporatism, 227

Correspondencia, La, 205

Corruption: and black leaders, 152; during colonial period, 63, 236 (n. 4); electoral fraud, 24, 78, 165, 172, 183; graft charges in Africanist societies, 121; Machado's promise to end, 173; and political parties, 267 (n. 31); protests against, 170–73; during Zayas's presidency, 265 (n. 17)

Cos y Riera, Saturnino, 247 (n. 162)

Criollos (those of African descent born in Cuba), 97, 121–22

Crombet, Flor, 9, 224

Crowder, Enoch H., 251 (n. 39)

Cuba: African-born population of, 102–3; black population of, 27, 28, 71, 89, 92, 102–3, 138, 233 (n. 11), 240 (n. 49), 254–55 (n. 5); economic crises in, during 1920s and 1930s, 171, 176, 180, 181, 204, 212–13; foreign investments in, 33–34, 64, 65, 100, 264 (n. 5); foreign population of, 103; founding of republic in, 33, 132–33, 170, 236 (n. 4); Havana's political authority in, 209, 211; national budget of, 31, 211; population of, 27, 28, 71, 89, 102–3, 138, 232 (n. 5), 233 (n. 11), 236 (n. 6), 240 (nn. 49–50, 52), 254–55 (n. 5), 272 (n. 136); population of provinces of, 272 (n. 136); trade between

U.S. and, 33, 99, 241–42 (n. 6); U.S. interventions in, 54, 56, 65, 78, 176, 198, 243 (n. 93); urban versus rural population of, 239 (n. 39). *See also* Black Cubans; Colonial period of Cuba; Constitution, Cuban; Republican political structures; U.S. occupation government of Cuba

Cuba Company, 33

"Cuba Is Not Haiti" (Gómez), 137

Cubanidad (Cubanness), 24

Cuban Liberation Army. *See* Liberation Army

Cuban militia, 42

Cuban National Party, 36, 40, 45, 235 (n. 3)

Cuban Popular Party, 77

Cuban Railway Brotherhood, 216

Cuesta, Ramiro N., 28, 67, 166, 250 (n. 35), 267 (n. 35)

Cultural improvement and racial uplift: and black civic clubs, 158, 168; and black intellectuals-activists and radicals, 173–74; black leaders as model for, 166; black leaders' support for, 71, 158, 160, 168, 174, 178, 192; black women's role in, 139–41, 145, 149, 189–90, 192; and black youth civic organizations, 184; and Campos Marquetti, 142–43; Céspedes Casado on, 144–45; Juan Gualberto Gómez on, 73, 74, 138–40, 165; Gualba on, 132; Morúa Delgado on, 134, 138, 139; and racial politics, 142–47; self-blaming premise of racial uplift, 174, 177; and Serra, 126–27, 129, 143; and slave emancipation, 132–33. *See also* Education

Curanderos (religious quacks), 204

Danger, Antonio R., 231 (n. 1)

Dantín, Clemente, 38

Dawson, Michael, 77, 168, 251 (n. 45)

Décimas music, 20

De la Fuente, Alejandro, 9, 22, 23, 28, 64, 70, 216, 239 (n. 32), 241 (n. 60), 245 (n. 135), 249 (nn. 17, 30, 32), 267 (n. 39), 275 (n. 2)

De León, Ramón, 266 (n. 31)

Delgado, Manuel J., 156, 166, 198

Del Rosal, Luis, 80

Del Valle, Gerardo, 197

Democratic Republican Party, 269 (n. 94)

Derby, Lauren, 246 (n. 153)

De San Miguel, Antonio, 236 (n. 7)

Día, El, 109, 159–60

Diario Cubano, El, 108–9

Diario de la Marina, El, 137, 181

Díaz, Jeronimo, 121

Díaz-Briquets, Sergio, 236 (n. 4)

Directorate of Citizens of Color (1907), 54, 65, 157–58, 163, 168, 175, 263 (n. 23)

Directorate of Citizens of Color (1915), 157, 163, 263 (n. 20)

Directorate of Societies of the Colored Race, 73, 134, 136, 138–42, 157, 250 (n. 37)

Discrimination: black activists on, 64–65; blacks' consciousness of, 276 (n. 10); in employment of blacks, 14, 27, 29, 54–55, 63–64, 66–67, 70, 205, 220, 241 (n. 58); in government employment, 29, 54–55, 63–64, 66–67, 70; National Federation of Black Societies on, 207; and racial marginalization, 4–6, 8, 14, 23, 27–30, 61–65, 111, 126, 174, 179, 183, 204, 206, 215, 229; and resource disparities for black Cubans, 5, 29, 64–65, 146, 156, 205, 207. *See also* Antidiscrimination legislation; Racism; Segregation

Divina Caridad, La, 134

Divorce, 192

Dolz y Arango, Guillermo, 243 (n. 91)

Domestic enemies, 237 (n. 9)

Domínguez, Jorge, 41, 227, 244 (n. 104), 265 (n. 23), 273 (n. 159)

Dominicans, 246 (n. 153)

"Don" title, 75, 251 (n. 42)

D'ou, Lino: and *Afrocubanidad* (Afro-Cuban culture), 178; and Club Atenas, 166; and government jobs for blacks, 67; as Liberation Army officer, 79; and manifesto against "witchcraft scare," 250 (n. 35); as Masó supporter, 107; and *Minerva* magazine, 151; and protest against lynching, 178–79, 267 (n. 35)

Du Bois, W. E. B., 1, 2, 143, 146, 231 (n. 2)

Dupin, Prudencio, 39

Echevarría, Mónico, 50, 231 (n. 1)

Edreira, Oscar G., 166

Education: Africanist societies' support of, 122–23; as avenue for advancement, 142–45; and black civic clubs, 12, 83, 148, 168; of black Cubans, 27, 65, 125, 140–45, 157–58; about black patriots, 225; of black women, 140; and black youth civic organizations, 183; during colonial period, 44, 141–42, 261 (n. 26); and literacy, 120, 149, 183, 207, 208, 271 (n. 122); and modernity, 120; Morúa Delgado on, 134, 139; and National Federation of Black Societies, 207, 208; after 1933 Revolution, 27; in Oriente, 209, 214; Popular University of Unión Fraternal, 168; scholarships for black students, 158; school closings in Liberal Party areas, 52–53; segregation of schools, 141; and Serra, 125, 126–27; and teaching jobs, 14, 52, 80, 84, 87, 139, 208, 248 (n. 5); during U.S. occupation, 2, 84, 100; as voting requirement, 108; women of color as teachers, 139. *See also* Cultural improvement and racial uplift

(nn. 18, 26); on harmony and political stability, 105–6; and Moderate Party, 52; on patronage politics, 43; presidency of, 4, 18–19, 24, 52, 53, 63, 65, 106, 241 (n. 58); presidential campaign of, 40, 65, 107; public disrespect and humiliation of black leaders by, 18–19; and racial categories in government documentation, 26, 110; resignation of, from presidency, 65, 144; Serra's support of, 77, 127, 155–56, 166; in U.S., 127

Estrada Portuondo, Juan, 82, 84

Estrella Refulgente, La, 143–44, 240 (n. 48)

Estuch, Horrego, 238 (n. 24), 247 (n. 2)

Ethiopia, 180

European descent. *See* Whites

Fajardo Ortiz, Daniel, 80

Falange de Acción Cubana, 172

Falucho, 259–60 (n. 7)

Families: black civic clubs' monitoring of members' families, 193; and divorce, 192; feminists on, 268 (n. 62); and illegitimate children, 189, 268 (n. 62); legal marriage by blacks, 114, 125, 126, 151, 189, 190, 257 (n. 45); marriage of black club members, 114, 187, 189, 190; and patronage networks, 48–60, 81–82

Farber, Samuel, 208–9

Female roles. *See* Black women; Gender

Feminism, 185–89, 195, 202–3, 228, 268 (n. 62). *See also* Black women; Gender; Women's suffrage

Fernández Robaina, Tomás, 241 (n. 58)

Ferrara, Mario, 150

Ferrara Marino, Orestes, 153

Ferrer, Ada, 20, 239 (n. 36), 243 (nn. 85, 88), 252 (n. 51), 255 (n. 16), 256 (n. 27)

Ferrer, Justiana, 120

50 Percent Law, 181, 207–8

Figarola, Manuel, *50*

Fonseca, Olimpo, 266 (n. 31)

Fonts, Carlos, 235 (n. 2)

Foreign investments in Cuba, 33–34, 64, 65, 100, 264 (n. 5)

Foreign workers. *See* Employment; Immigration

Franchise. *See* Suffrage

Franco-Prussian War (1870–71), 250 (n. 36)

Fraternal, El, 74

Fraternidad, La, 74, 136

Fraud. *See* Corruption

Free Institute of Good Government, 239 (n. 39)

French Revolution, 73, 250 (n. 36)

Frías, Pío Arturo, 156, 166, *167*

Friends of the People Party, 66, 233 (n. 16)

Frye, Alexis E., 84

Galán, Gregorio, *39, 50*, 231 (n. 1)

Gálvez, José, 166

Gálvez, Zoila, 49, 198

García, Calixto, 238 (n. 21)

García Agüero, Salvador, 217–20, 274 (nn. 171, 179)

García Kohly, Marió, 251 (n. 39)

García Vélez, Carlos, 172

García Vieta, Gonzalo, 236 (n. 5)

Garriga, Marcelino, 156

Gastón, Tomás, *50*

Gelis, Ramón, *50*

Gender: black civic clubs and women, 145, 185, 186, 189–96; and black modernity, 189–96; and black youth civic organizations, 185; female-only civic organizations, 80, 196; and feminism, 185–89, 195, 202–3, 228, 268 (n. 62); masculinist ideals, 188, 190, 192, 202, 226; and old guard politicians and activists, 186–89; and

79, 142–43, 238 (n. 32), 239 (n. 32), 247 (n. 2), 247–48 (n. 5); discrimination in, 29, 54–55, 63–64, 66–67, 70; elected officials' control of, 248 (n. 7); and Estrada Palma, 4, 63, 65, 67, 69, 72, 142–43, 247 (n. 2), 249 (nn. 18, 26); and patronage politics, 64; statistics on, 31, 34–35, 84, 241 (n. 60), 247 (n. 2), 247–48 (n. 5), 275 (n. 2); and unemployment during 1920s and 1930s, 180; of veterans, 38; of whites, 54, 55, 67, 69. *See also* Police; Postal services

Government officials: and access to economic resources, 3–4, 5, 23, 24, 31–32; black activists as, 71; black candidates for office, 4, 54, 66, 71–72, 89, 156, 163, 164–65, 249 (n. 17); black claims-making on, 160; and black press, 151–52; control of jobs by, 248 (n. 7); Machado's appointment of black officials, 156; as white Cuban elites, 4. *See also* Congress, Cuban; Elections; Patronage politics

Goyri, Francisco, 274 (n. 179)

Graham, Richard, 43, 242 (n. 74)

Grajales, Mariana, 81

Grau San Martín, Ramón: and Batista, 213; and black civic clubs, 221; and 50 Percent Law, 181, 207–8, 271 (n. 121); and murder of Menéndez, 217; and Platt Amendment, 242 (n. 67), 271 (n. 121); reformist measures of, during "100 days" administration, 180–81, 206–9, 271 (n. 121); youth support of, 184–85

Grillo Portuondo, Ambrosio, 85, 253 (n. 72)

Grupo Minorista, 171, 172

Gualba, Miguel, 125, 132

Guerra de la Chambelona. See Lollipop War

Guerrita del doce, La. *See* Race War

Guillén, Francisco, 219

Guillén, Nicolás, 82, 178, 181–82, 183

Guirao, Ramón, 178

Haciendo política (practicing politics), 35, 48

Haiti and Haitians, 137, 181, 203, 208, 246 (n. 153), 271 (n. 121)

Haitian Revolution, 19, 22, 45, 237 (n. 11), 244 (n. 109)

Hampa Afrocubana (Ortiz), 111, 117

Hanchard, Michael, 94, 123

Havana Workers' Federation, 219–20

Health. *See* Public health

Helg, Aline, 9, 54, 56, 64, 201, 234 (n. 25), 253 (n. 74), 265–66 (n. 24), 275–76 (n. 10)

Heraldo de Cuba, El, 153

Hermandad de Jóvenes Cubanos, 183

"Hermano Negro" (Pedroso), 181–82

Hernández, Alberto, 275 (n. 179)

Hernández, Serafín, 121–22

Hernández de Cervantes, Calixta, 186

Herrera y Herrera, Pablo, *167*

Hevia, Aurelio, 104

Hevia Lanier, Oilda, 73

Ibáñez, Beningno, 275 (n. 179)

Ibarra, Jorge, 26–27, 64, 97–98, 184, 252 (n. 51), 275 (n. 2)

Iglesias, Aracelio, 229

Iglesias, Marial, 106–7

Igualdad, La, 74, 136, 137

Illegitimacy, 189, 268 (n. 62)

Immigration, 101–3, 180–81, 203, 209, 218, 220, 239 (n. 32)

Independence wars (1868–98), 38, 45, 54, 64, 95–98, 102, 104, 223. *See also* War of Independence

Independent Party of Color (PIC): base of operations of, 224; black elites' rejection of, 57–58, 156; founding of, 6, 53, 55, 66, 86; government opposition to, 55; leadership of, 54; local-level mobilizing strategy of, 224; and

Morúa Amendment, 55, 56; and 1908 elections, 55; and 1912 elections, 66; purpose of, 4–5, 149, 158, 175; rise of, 233 (n. 16); as third-party threat, 54, 234 (n. 25). *See also* Race War

Independent Republican Party, 77

Infanzón, Matías, 40

International Society for Black Defense, 180

Italy, 180

Ivonet, Pedro, *39*, 59–60, 224

Jamaica and Jamaicans, 181, 203, 208, 246 (n. 153), 271 (n. 121)

Johnson, Frederick, 231 (n. 2)

Joint Commission of Revolutionary Administration, 198–99

Joubert, Celso, 49

Joubert, Germán, 49

Joubert, Rádames, 49

Jóvenes de L'Printemps (Youth of Springtime), 183

Julia, Domingo, 92–98, 110

Junta Cubana de Renovación Nacional-Cívico (Cuban Committee for National and Civic Renovation), 172

Juventud Apontista, 185

Juventud Minerva (Youth of Minerva), 183, 184

KKKK. *See* Ku Klux Klan Kubano

Knox, Philander, 19

Ku Klux Klan Kubano (KKKK), 203

Labor movement: and antidiscrimination legislation, 219–20; assassination of leaders of, 229; and Batista, 213, 216, 274 (n. 163); and black activists, 174; and black civic clubs, 217, 219–20; black voter support for, 217; and Communist Party, 179, 216, 218, 220, 267 (n. 39); in different industries, 60, 176, 216; and global black consciousness, 180; and Grau

presidency, 271 (n. 121); leaders of, 200, 229; political mobilization in, 276 (n. 10); and Serra's campaign, 60; and strikes, 176, 208, 241 (n. 58); and women, 217; and workers' rights, 267 (n. 39)

Labor Nueva, 152, 153–57, *154*, 165, 240 (n. 48)

Lachatañeré, Rómulo, 178

Lacoste, Eugenio, 159, 161

Lacret Paisán, Mario, 198, 269–70 (n. 94)

Lamagne Romero, Mario, 221

Landa, Evaristo, 89

Lanier, Hevia, 251 (n. 42)

Lapidus, Benjamin, 237 (n. 11)

Larrosa, Marcelino, *50*

Lavín, Pablo F., 274 (n. 179)

Law against Racial Discrimination, 219–21, 274–75 (n. 179)

Legión Maceista de Oriente (Santiago de Cuba), 9, 196, 225

Leopold II, 96

Letrados (learned class), 149–50

Lettered City, The (Rama), 149–50

Liberal National Party, 77

Liberal Party: on Amigos del Pueblo, 159; and black candidates, 163, 164–65; black supporters of, 253 (n. 74); and *círculos* (centers), 46; and corruption, 267 (n. 31); formation of, 77, 78; and Genova de Zayas, 87; and Juan Gualberto Gómez, 18, 74, 77, 78, 82, 85–86, 245 (n. 127), 251 (n. 47); localized mobilization by, 82; and Lollipop War, 165; and Machado presidency, 176; members of, 51; and 1912 elections, 159; and 1926 election, 266 (n. 31); and Race War, 159; and Salas Arzuaga brothers, 82; split of, in 1908 elections, 53–54; and Unification of Black Societies organizers, 164; and Vasconcelos, 162; violence and fraud in rivalry between Moder-

for blacks, 79; and Liberal Party, 79; political career of, 47, 133–34; and prohibition against race-based political organizing (Morúa Amendment), 55, 240 (n. 45); on racelessness, 174; relationship between Juan Gualberto Gómez and, 86, 134; and Republican Party, 26, 235 (n. 2); on slavery, 133

Mott, T. Bently, 237 (n. 13)

Movimiento de Veteranos y Patriotas, 172

Mudimbe, V. Y., 95

Mulattos, 14, 102, 240 (n. 43)

Muñíz, Nicolás, 87

Muñoz Ginarte, Benjamín, 156, 198, 218

Music and musicians, 18, 20, 45, 50, 117, 119, 237 (n. 11), 244 (n. 109), 267 (n. 51)

Ñáñigos (Abakúa secret society members), 117, 136, 197, 261 (n. 24)

Nápoles, Alberto, 50

Nápoles, Felix, 50

Nápoles, Guillermo, 50

Nápoles, José de los Santos, 50

Nápoles, Pedro, 50

Nápoles, Tomás, 50

Nation, 22

National Association of Cuban Industrialists, 171

National Confederation of Cuban Workers (CNOC), 176, 179, 267 (n. 39)

National Congress of Women, 171

National Federation of Black Societies: Adams's criticisms of, 204–5; and antiblack climate after Revolution of 1933, 203–5; and antidiscrimination legislation, 220–21, 274–75 (n. 179); and Batista, 214; decline of, 221; factors leading up to founding of, 201–6; first convention of, 204; founding of, 201–2, 225; lack of support for, by

black intellectuals-activists, 205–6; 1936 draft program of, 206–8; officers of, 49, 200, 217; Organizing Committee of, 201, 205–8; and Oriente, 209–14; and Ortiz, 200; scandal within, 221; shift from 1936 to 1938 draft programs of, 206–10, 222

National Federation of Cigar Workers, 176

National Federation of Economic Corporations, 171

National Federation of Societies of the Colored Race. *See* National Federation of Black Societies

Nationalism: and Africa, 119; and Africanist societies, 113, 125; and "Afro" prefix, 15; and black Cubans, 230; and black patriots, 9, 80–81, 196, 224–25; and egalitarianism, 103; global dimensions of, 99; Juan Gualberto Gómez on, 134; and Grau, 180–81, 209; and intellectuals, 172; and modernity, 95; El Negro Oriental on, 131; and patriarchy, 195; populist nationalism, 194; radical nationalism, 170, 228; and republican political culture, 32–33; scholarship on, 7, 9–10; and white supremacy, 95

Nationalization of Labor decree (50 Percent Law), 181, 207–8

National League of Oriente, 36, 42, 79–80

National League Party, 267 (n. 31)

National Liberal Party of Oriente, 77, 78

National Lottery, 164, 213–15, 248 (n. 7), 273 (nn. 146, 153)

National Maritime and Cuban Ports Federation, 216

National Party: black members of, 175, 235 (n. 2); and Bravo Correoso, 78, 85; and *círculos*, 46–47; founding of, 36; local-level organizing by, 82; and Masó, 107; in 1901 elections, 107, 236 (n. 5); platform of, 46–47; rift

networks of, 48–60, 81–82; and black voters, 32; and *botellas*, 31, 241 (n. 60); brokers' role in, 87, 173, 224, 227, 251 (n. 43); club radicals and postrevolutionary patronage, 196–201; and disparities regarding blacks' access to resources, 29; Estrada Palma on, 43; functions of, 30–31; and Juan Gualberto Gómez, 32, 51–52, 54–55, 62–64, 72–79, 82–89, 117–18, 238 (n. 26), 250 (n. 33); and government jobs, 63–67, 69–70; Graham on, 242 (n. 74); and increase in state revenues and state bureaucracy, 163–64; and Machado, 49, 50, 197–98; and Moderate Party, 5–6; and *piña* system, 266–67 (n. 31); and political parties, 43–46, 227; and reciprocity, 83, 86, 197; and republican political structures, 5, 24, 26–27, 43–44, 48–62, 197, 223–24; and social services and personal favors, 27, 32, 43–44, 227; and socioeconomic benefits, 6, 12

Patterson, Orlando, 237 (n. 9)

Pedroso, Regino, 181–82

Peña, Lázaro, 174, 217, 219, 229

Pérez, Louis A., 64, 100, 107, 112, 208, 232 (n. 5), 247 (n. 2), 252 (n. 51), 256 (n. 27)

Pérez, Pedro A., 38

Pérez Acosta, Francisco, 269 (n. 94)

Pérez Carbó, Federico, 51

Pérez-López, Jorge F., 236 (n. 4)

PIC (Partido Independiente de Color). *See* Independent Party of Color

Piedra, Prisciliano, 156

Pierra, Fidel G., 251 (n. 47)

Piñas agrias (outsider coalitions), 266 (n. 31)

Piña system, 177, 266–67 (n. 31)

Pita, Valdés, 28

Planas, Gonzalo, 121

Planas, Sebastián, 266 (n. 31)

Platt, Orville, 100, 238 (n. 23), 242 (n. 67)

Platt Amendment: abrogation of, 242 (n. 67), 271 (n. 121); and constitutional convention (1900–1901), 2, 21, 73, 75; as infringement on Cuban constitution, 100–101; opposition to, by Cubans, 21, 37, 73, 75, 100–101; passage of, by U.S. Congress, 100; purpose and provisions of, 6, 33, 232 (n. 6), 238 (n. 23), 242 (n. 67); and sanitation, 99; support for, by Cubans, 33, 40

Plenum Social (Santiago de Cuba), 198, 210

Police: and Africanist societies, 136; blacks employed as, 69, 247 (n. 2), 248 (n. 5), 275 (n. 10); harassment of blacks and violence by, 27, 51–53, 117–18, 205; Salas Arzuaga as chief of police, 82; "white-only" hiring policy of, 67

Political parties: avoidance of talk of race and racial injustice by, 72; and black Cubans, 23; black leadership positions within, 71–72; and *círculos*, 46–48; during colonial period, 37, 44–45; and cross-party/extraparty political coalitions after Machado's presidency, 176–77; fragmentation of, 17, 41, 235 (n. 3); and Grau administration, 271 (n. 121); and ideology, 26, 176–77, 244 (n. 104); instability of, 41; local-level organizing by, 41–43, 45–46, 224–25; and loyalty to localized political communities, 79–82, 224; in municipal elections of 1901, 234–35 (n. 2); national-level parties in 1900, 36–37; number of, during republican era (1902–59), 41; and patronage politics, 43–46, 227; regionalism among, 79–82; and republican political structures, 41–46. *See also* Patronage politics; *and specific political parties*

Political sociability, 12, 46–48, 174

Politics: black political candidates, 4, 54, 66, 71–72, 89, 156, 163, 164–65, 249 (n. 17); and black press, 151–57; blacks' political strength, 28–29, 54, 71–72, 156, 217, 234 (n. 25); and black women, 174, 186–89, 192–93; black youth groups' attack on "traditional" politics, 184; and exigencies of blackness, 223–30; and *piña* system, 177, 266–67 (n. 31); postrevolution black politics, 177–83, 196–201; women's participation in, 174, 177, 186–89. *See also* Black activists and politicians; Corruption; Elections; Patronage politics; Political parties; Republican political structures

Ponvert, Hermengildo, 166

Popular classes. See *Clases populares*

Popular Party, 176

Populism, 175–76, 197, 202, 214–15, 216, 221, 274 (n. 163)

Porristas (hired thugs), 204

Portuondo, Arnaldo, 49

Portuondo, Efraín Romero, 49

Portuondo, Fausto, 49

Portuondo, Nacarina, 80

Portuondo, Nelsa, 80

Portuondo, Serafín, 274 (n. 179)

Portuondo Calás, Pedro, 174, 249 (n. 30)

Portuondo Hardy, Américo, 48–49, 70–71, 80, 215

Portuondo Hardy, José Guadalupe, 49

Postal services, 63, 69, 156, 247 (n. 2)

Póveda Ferrer, Antonio, 19, 25–26, 110

Prensa, La, 152, 159, 161, 162, 189–90, 240 (n. 48), 263 (n. 29)

Previsión, 152, 240 (n. 48)

Prío Socarrás, Carlos (president of Cuba, 1948–52), 221

Prisons, 2–3, 6, 233 (n. 15)

Privileged blacks. *See* Black elites

Proletariat United Front, 217

Prostitution, 268 (n. 62), 270 (n. 105)

Protest of the Thirteen, 172

Provincial Federation of Black Societies of Camagüey, 219

Provincial Federation of Black Societies of Havana, 210, 217, 275 (n. 181)

Provincial Federation of Black Societies of Oriente, 49, 200, 209–10

Public health, 27, 99, 170, 206, 207, 209

Public service employment. *See* Government employment

Public works projects: and Batista administration, 212–14; in colonial period, 63; and José Miguel Gómez administration, 43; housing project, 43; and Machado administration, 175; and Menocal administration, 164; in Oriente, 210–14; and patronage politics, 12, 29, 34, 44, 63, 209–14, 248 (n. 7); in Santiago, 37; and U.S. occupation government, 37, 38, 63; veterans employed in, 38

Puerto Rico, 22

Pupo family, 49

Quincosa, Segundo, 274 (n. 179)

Quiroz, Alfonso, 236 (n. 4)

Rabí, Jesús, 38, 59, 64

Race: and Africanity, 13, 125–26; black activists' "modern" values versus race consciousness, 13, 21–23, 71, 74, 225–26; black charges of white racism, 204–5; black civic clubs and politics of, 12–13; black newspapers on racial inequality, 155; categories of, 14–15, 25–26, 96, 102, 110, 240 (n. 43), 251 (n. 42); and "class of color," 1, 9, 14, 142, 173, 180, 186, 225, 228, 230; Communist Party on, 179–80, 214, 218; and cultural improvement and racial uplift, 69, 71, 73, 74, 83, 126–29, 132–47, 158, 160, 166, 168; Dawson's "linked fate" theory of race consciousness, 77, 168; deep cultural "blackness," 13, 126; Du Bois on, 1, 2; global black consciousness in 1930s, 180; historical narratives and scholarship on black Cubans, 6–11; Martínez Ortiz on, 104–5; Masó on, 107–8; in Mexico, 104; Ortiz on, 111; prohibition against race-based political organizing, 4–5, 26, 55, 240 (n. 45); race relations histories, 7, 10; and racial affinity among Cuban blacks, 75, 77; and racial unity, 225–26; and republican political structures, 28–33, 104–12, 223; rhetoric of egalitarianism versus racial inequality, 2, 29–30, 32, 61–62, 64, 65, 175, 223, 227–28; scientific racism, 109, 111, 116–17; in U.S., 7, 10, 251 (n. 45); Vasconcelos's newspaper column on, 152, 161–62, 189–90. See also Africanisms and African legacy; Africanist societies; Racelessness ideal; Slavery

Racelessness ideal: disappointments with, 6, 175, 179; and egalitarianism, 104, 230; implications and limitations of, 4, 7, 28, 29, 30, 110, 117, 123–24, 179, 215, 225, 228; Labor Nueva on, 153; Martí on, 2, 69, 174; and repression of non-normative cultural modes, 110; and republican political culture, 32; scholarship on, 8, 9; and stereotype of forward-looking European and backward-facing African, 123–24. See also Egalitarianism

Race War (1912): beginning of, 56, 158, 241 (n. 65); and black activists, 58–61, 74, 99; and black civic clubs, 58, 166; casualty statistics of, 158, 241 (n. 65); José Miguel Gómez on, 57, 58, 99, 203; Helg on, 9, 201, 265–66 (n. 24); leadership of, 60–61; media coverage of, 158–59; Menocal on, 153; purpose of, 26, 32, 56, 69, 172, 265–66 (n. 24); Varona on, 153;

vicious depiction of blacks during, 99, 109, 158–59, 203; violent opposition to and repression following, 5, 32, 56, 57, 66, 99, 158, 159, 160, 201, 203, 223, 241 (n. 65), 248 (n. 13). See also Independent Party of Color

Racial discrimination and marginalization. See Discrimination

Racial uplift. See Cultural improvement and racial uplift

Racism, 109, 111, 116–17, 204–5, 228, 241 (n. 58). See also Discrimination; Race; Segregation

Radicals. See Black intellectuals-activists and radicals

Railroads, 33, 34, 100, 216

Rama, Ángel, 149–50

Ramírez, María Teresa, 195

Ramírez Ros, Primitivo, 70–71, 152, 153, 155, 165–66

Raza cósmica (cosmic race), 104

Recio Loynaz, López, 243 (n. 91)

Reciprocity Treaty (1903), 33, 171, 241–42 (n. 6), 265 (n. 8)

Rectificaciones (Risquet), 21

Regionalism, 79–82, 209–14, 222

Regüeiferos Boudet, Erasmo, 77, 172, 251 (nn. 39, 47)

Relaciones (strategic political relationships), 87, 253 (n. 85)

Renacimiento, 173, 183, 184, 192–94

Renovación, 174, 187–88

Repatriation to Africa, 92–98, 110, 254–55 (n. 5), 255 (n. 19)

República Cubana, La, 73, 74, 238 (n. 26)

Republican Conservative Party, 231 (n. 1)

Republican Democratic Federal Party of Santiago de Cuba, 36

Republican Federal Party, 36

Republican Independent Party, 43

Republican Party: black activists in, 26, 235 (n. 2); formation of, 77;

fragmentation of, 17, 235 (n. 3), 236 (n. 5); and Juan Gualberto Gómez, 26, 77, 87–88; *La Lucha* editorial on, 17–18; in municipal elections of 1901, 234–35 (n. 2), 236 (n. 5); and Risquet, 87–88

Republican political structures: and black activists, 61–62, 229; and black voters, 28–29, 156, 160, 227; "Changüí Político" (*La Lucha*) on, 17–18, 23, 61, 62; and *círculos* (centers), 46–48, 61, 244 (n. 111), 244–45 (n. 115); corruption in, 170–73; and *Cubanidad* (Cubanness), 24–28; and exigencies of blackness, 223–30; and formal politics in New Cuba, 20, 33–52; influences on, 20, 23–24, 33; and Liberation Army veterans, 38–41; and patronage politics, 5, 24, 26–27, 43–44, 48–62, 197, 223–24; and political modernity, 21–25, 93, 95; and political party organizing, 41–46; and political sociability, 46–48, 174; and racial inequality, 28–33, 223; and racial labels, 25–26; and racial relations, 104–12; and regionalism, 79–82, 209–14; and social and cultural organizations, 44–46; U.S. as model for Cuba, 100, 107; and universal male suffrage, 3–4, 19, 22–23, 28, 35, 47, 108, 149, 223, 234 (n. 1); and white supremacy, 104, 107. *See also* Constitution, Cuban; Patronage politics; Politics

Rescalla, Elias, 274 (n. 179)

Residents' Assembly (Santiago), 36

Revista Adelante, 206

Revolucionarios Auténticos (Authentic Revolutionaries), 204

Revolutionary Communist Union Party, 51, 82

Revolutionary Social Directorate–Only Front of the Republic's Societies of Color, 196–97

Revolutionary Union Party, 217, 219

Revolution of 1933: Batista on, 274 (n. 163); black civic clubs after, 168, 175; and blacks, 203–4, 229; and economic crises, 265 (n. 5); and labor movement, 276 (n. 10); national political processes after, 219; results of, 27, 185, 202–3, 210, 223; and traditional political elite, 219; youth after, 173

Rezo (collective song or prayer), 119

Riera, Mario, 232 (n. 5)

Risquet, Juan Felipe: as black activist, 71; criticisms of, 17–18; and manifesto against "witchcraft scare," 250 (n. 35); *Minerva* on, 151; and patronage politics, 22, 87–88; political career of, 21, 26; and protest against lynching, 178–79, 267 (n. 35); and Republican Federal Party, 235 (n. 2); and Republican Party, 87–88; and republican political newspaper, 87–88; as writer, 21, 71

Ríus Rivera, Juan, 106, 243 (n. 91)

Roca, Blas, 218, 219

Rodríguez, Alejandro, 37

Rojas Rodríguez, Pedro, 274 (n. 179)

Roniger, Luis, 148, 262 (n. 2), 273 (n. 159)

Roosevelt, Theodore, 75

Root, Elihu, 2, 22, 237 (n. 13), 242 (n. 67)

Ruíz, Antonio, 259–60 (n. 7)

Saco, José Antonio, 106

Salas, Indalecio, 236 (n. 5)

Salas Arzuaga, Justo, 51, 80, 82, 210, 219, 272 (n. 140)

Salas Arzuaga, Pedro, 51, 82

Salcedo, Rafael, 37

"San Benito de Palermo" Society, 115–16, 122, 123

San Carlos Society, 220

Sánchez, José, 50

Traditional black political elites. *See* Black elites

Tribunal de Urgencia, 270 (n. 105)

Tumba francesa music, 45, 237 (n. 11), 244 (n. 109)

Turits, Richard, 246 (n. 153)

Unemployment. *See* Employment

Unification of Black Societies movement, 152, 159, 161–68, 201

Union Democratic Party, 36, 41, 43, 231 (n. 1), 235 (n. 2), 236 (n. 5), 239 (n. 34)

Unión Fraternal (Fraternal Union), 58, 88, 148, 165, 168, 267 (n. 35), 275 (n. 184)

Unión Lajera, 89, 90

Union of Workers and Staff of Electrical Plants, 176

Unión Revolucionaria Cubana Party, 200

Union Revolutionary Party, 217, 219

Unions. *See* Labor movement

Unión Social of Santo Domingo, 201

United Fruit Company, 33

United States: Electoral College system of, 224; interventions in Cuba by, 54, 56, 65, 78, 176, 198, 243 (n. 93); race in, 7, 10, 251 (n. 45); and Reciprocity Treaty with Cuba, 33, 171, 241–42 (n. 6); Serra in, 127; trade between Cuba and, 33, 99, 171, 241–42 (n. 6), 265 (n. 8). *See also* Platt Amendment; U.S. occupation government of Cuba

U.S. Export-Import Bank, 213

U.S. occupation government of Cuba (1899–1902): Advisory Law Commission of, 74, 251 (n. 39); appointment of civilian administrators during, 4, 24, 35–38, 40; Bandera's manifesto against, 59; as "civilizing invasion," 24; and constitutional convention, 17; and *Cubanidad* (Cuban-

ness), 24–28; and doubts about Cubans' ability to self-govern, 22, 24, 239 (n. 36); and Juan Gualberto Gómez, 75; infrastructure improvements by, 2–3, 24, 100; and municipal governments, 35–38, 40; North American–style governance system during, 63; segregationist propensity of, 4; and suffrage, 2, 19, 22, 35, 242–43 (n. 77); and veterans of War of Independence, 38–40; and white-only hiring policies for government jobs, 67, 238 (n. 22)

University of Havana, 88, 153, 171

Uplift ideology. *See* Cultural improvement and racial uplift

Urrutia, Gustavo E., 174, 178, 181, 240 (n. 48), 250 (n. 35), 267 (n. 35)

Valdés Ariza, Pantaleón, *167*

Valverde, Nicolás, 25, 110

Vanguardia, La, 137

Vantour, José, 51–52, 82, 85, 117–18, 252 (nn. 59–60)

Varela, Padre Félix, 106

Varona, Enrique José, 19, 36, 40, 84, 108, 153, 237 (n. 16)

Vasconcelos, José, 104

Vasconcelos, Ramón ("Tristán"), 152, 161–63, 165, 189–90, 195, 240 (n. 48)

Vázquez, Victor, 141

Vega, Emilio, 55

Vega, Liborio, 88, 238 (n. 26)

Vélez, María Luisa, 192–93

Veterans and Societies of Color Action Committee (Havana), 65–67, 70, 72, 168, 175, 223, 233 (n. 16), 241 (n. 58), 249 (n. 26)

Veterans' Association, 49, 171

Victory Society (Sociedad Victoria), 45, 214, 215, 219

Vilar Aguilar, César, 200, 219

Villuendas, Enrique, 53

Violence: black violence against whites,

203–4; by black women, 204; lynchings of blacks during "witchcraft scare," 178–79, 267 (n. 35); and political parties and elections, 52–53. *See also* Police; Race War

Vioni, Miguel F., 251 (n. 39)

Voting. *See* Elections; Suffrage

Wade, Peter, 236 (n. 9), 237 (n. 10)

War of Independence (1895–98), 22, 28, 29, 37, 103, 243 (n. 88), 256 (n. 27). *See also* Liberation Army

Weber, Max, 265 (n. 23)

White elites: and Africanist societies, 91; on African legacy as antithetical to nation building and modernity, 95–96, 98–99, 111–12, 123; and black press, 150, 153, 155; as civilian administrators and elected officials, 4; and legislation of social behavior and public order, 108–9; as national heroes, 106–7; and universal male suffrage, 19, 108; wealth of, 14. *See also* Whites

Whites: *afrocubanista* literature by, 181; in Constitutional Army, 55; definition of, 15; employment of, 6, 14, 54, 55, 67, 69; government jobs for, 54, 55, 67, 69; incarceration rate of, 6, 233 (n. 15); marriage of, 189; patriarchal authority of, 57, 131; as police officers, 67; promotion of white officers in Liberation Army, 21, 238 (n. 21); sexual propriety of white women, 57; in Union Democratic Party, 235 (n. 2); violence against, by blacks, 203–4; and white supremacy, 104, 107, 228; women's movement among, 195; and women's suffrage, 186; youth groups of, 171, 172. *See also* White elites

Whitney, Robert, 173, 264 (n. 3)

Wilhelm, Kaiser, II, 96

Williams, Brackette, 110

Williams, Henry Sylvester, 231 (n. 2)

Wilson, James H., 19

Winship, Blanton, 251 (n. 39)

Witchcraft, 73, 97, 108–9, 117, 159, 161, 178–79, 204, 250 (n. 35)

Women. *See* Black women; Feminism; Gender

Women-only civic organizations, 80, 196

Women's suffrage, 177, 185, 186

Wood, Leonard, 19, 22, 35–37, 75, 84, 236 (n. 5), 237 (n. 13)

Working class. See *Clases populares*; Labor movement

Working Peoples' Party, 235 (n. 3)

World Pro-Ethiopia Federation, 180

World War I, 163

Yero Buduén, Eduardo, 84

Yero Sagol, Manuel, 85, 242 (n. 76), 253 (n. 72)

Youth civic organizations, 170–74, 183–86, 222, 229

Zayas, Alfredo: and Advisory Law Commission, 251 (n. 39); fraud, graft, and corruption in administration of, 172, 265 (n. 17); and Juan Gualberto Gómez, 89; and "Honest Cabinet," 265 (n. 17); and Liberal Party, 78, 251 (n. 47); and National Liberal Party of Oriente, 77; in 1908 election, 52, 53, 245 (n. 127); presidency of, 40, 77, 89, 265 (n. 17); Protest of the Thirteen against, 172; and U.S. occupation officials, 37; as vice-presidential candidate, 52, 245 (n. 127)

Zayas Barzan, Filiberto, 251 (n. 47)

Envisioning Cuba

Melina Pappademos, *Black Political Activism and the Cuban Republic* (2011).

Frank Andre Guridy, *Forging Diaspora: Afro-Cubans and African Americans in a World of Empire and Jim Crow* (2010).

Ann Marie Stock, *On Location in Cuba: Street Filmmaking during Times of Transition* (2009).

Alejandro de la Fuente, *Havana and the Atlantic in the Sixteenth Century* (2008).

Reinaldo Funes Monzote, *From Rainforest to Cane Field in Cuba: An Environmental History since 1492* (2008).

Matt D. Childs, *The 1812 Aponte Rebellion in Cuba and the Struggle against Atlantic Slavery* (2006).

Eduardo González, *Cuba and the Tempest: Literature and Cinema in the Time of Diaspora* (2006).

John Lawrence Tone, *War and Genocide in Cuba, 1895–1898* (2006).

Samuel Farber, *The Origins of the Cuban Revolution Reconsidered* (2006).

Lillian Guerra, *The Myth of José Martí: Conflicting Nationalisms in Early Twentieth-Century Cuba* (2005).

Rodrigo Lazo, *Writing to Cuba: Filibustering and Cuban Exiles in the United States* (2005).

Alejandra Bronfman, *Measures of Equality: Social Science, Citizenship, and Race in Cuba, 1902–1940* (2004).

Edna M. Rodríguez-Mangual, *Lydia Cabrera and the Construction of an Afro-Cuban Cultural Identity* (2004).

Gabino La Rosa Corzo, *Runaway Slave Settlements in Cuba: Resistance and Repression* (2003).

Piero Gleijeses, *Conflicting Missions: Havana, Washington, and Africa, 1959–1976* (2002).

Robert Whitney, *State and Revolution in Cuba: Mass Mobilization and Political Change, 1920–1940* (2001).

Alejandro de la Fuente, *A Nation for All: Race, Inequality, and Politics in Twentieth-Century Cuba* (2001).

CPSIA information can be obtained
at www.ICGtesting.com
Printed in the USA
LVHW040036120123
736860LV00004B/410